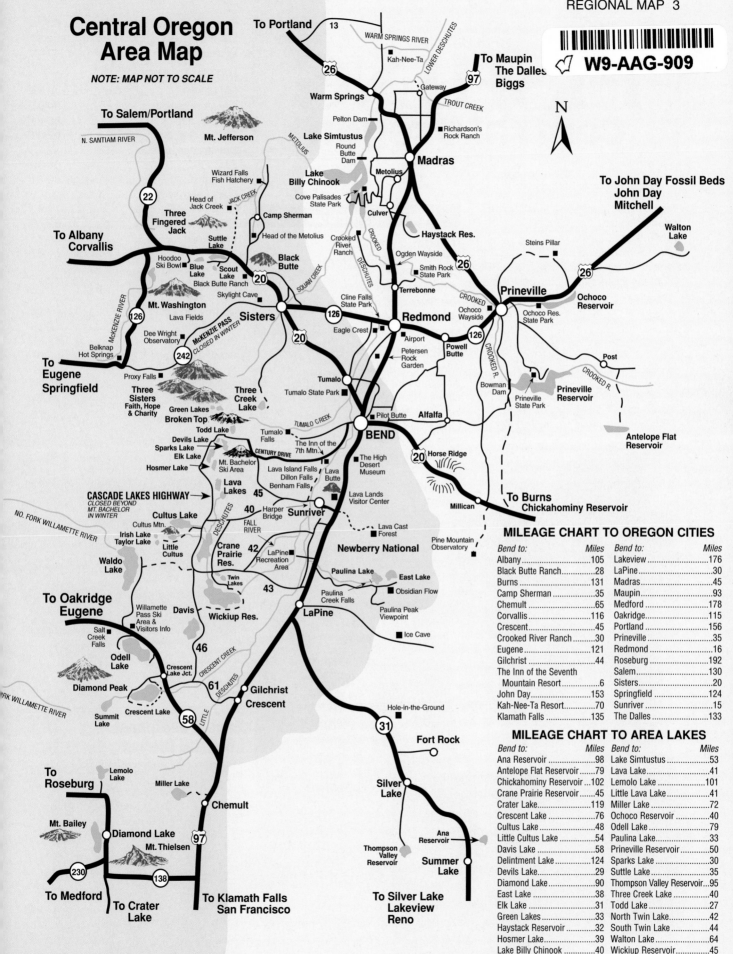

FIFTH EDITION

FISHING
Central Oregon
and Beyond

CENTRAL OREGON ... 3

RIVERS

RESERVOIRS

NATURAL LAKES

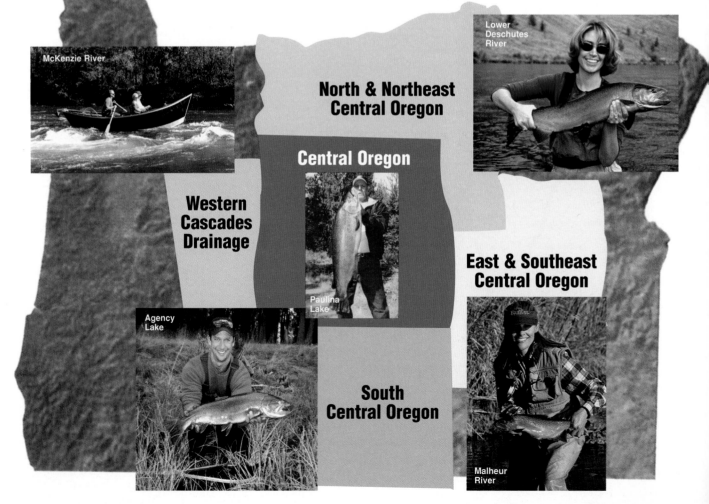

McKenzie River

North & Northeast Central Oregon

Lower Deschutes River

Central Oregon

Western Cascades Drainage

Paulina Lake

East & Southeast Central Oregon

Agency Lake

South Central Oregon

Malheur River

FIFTH EDITION

FISHING
Central Oregon
and Beyond

PERSONNEL

GEOFF HILL
Publisher/Editor/Advertising

VICKI HILL
Financial Manager

JAN SIEGRIST
Art Director/Production

STARR HUME
Production

GARY LEWIS
Advertising

CONTRIBUTING WRITERS

GEOFF HILL, GARY LEWIS,
BROOKE SNAVELY, RAVEN WING

PRINCIPAL PHOTOGRAPHERS

GEOFF HILL, GARY LEWIS,
BRIAN O'KEEFE, BROOKE SNAVELY

Produced by

Sun Publishing

716 NE 4th Street
Bend, Oregon 97701

(541) 382-0127

www.sun-pub.com
sunpub@sun-pub.com

© Copyright 2005

ON THE COVER

CENTER: Judith O'Keefe holds a Sycan
River rainbow. Photo by Brian O'Keefe.

LEFT: Lucky angler with Crane Prairie
rainbow. Photo courtesy Garrison's Guide Service

RIGHT: Brett Dennis prepares to release
near record bull trout at Lake Billy Chinook.
Photo courtesy cofishing.com

W̲e thank you for making the purchase of this book and feel confident you'll be happy with your investment. We have gone to great lengths to provide readers with upgraded quality and additional information. Previous additions have received *"Best Seller"* recognition, and 40,000 copies sold supports that claim.

Geoff says "Let's go fishin'!"
Photo by Vicki Hill

The book has proven very popular with local anglers as well as vacationers.

The emphasis has always been on quality, in the book's content as well as its presentation. Quality publications have been the standard at Bend's Sun Publishing for the past 33 years.

This, the fifth edition of **FISHING Central Oregon (and beyond)**, has been updated and expanded by 64 pages, includes over 500 color photos, many new waters, detailed maps, and illustrations that help to complete the overall picture of Central Oregon's renowned waters.

It seems every edition we hear from readers about waters that we didn't include that they would like to see included. As usual, we listened and did the research so we could fulfill one more request. This edition we got a little carried away. We heard that we needed to add some places to take the kids fishing, so we included three pages of waters for kids, like Shevlin Pond, Fireman's Pond, and Mirror Pond to name a few. Some thought we should cover more private waters such as Antone Ranch Lakes, Alder Creek Ranch, Buckhorn, Bear Creek Reservoir and Grindstone lakes … so we did.

We also stretched our coverage to the north, east, and south to please even more readers. Six pages now describe how to fish for a wide variety of fish in the Columbia River. Other waters in the Umatilla area are covered. Folks in Burns informed us we were missing a lot of good fishing opportunities in their region … we discovered they were right.

I've recently explored Oregon's "outback" a little with trips to the Ana and Chewaucan rivers. These small streams hold some pleasant surprises. The Sycan and Sprague rivers can also be rewarding … *see the front cover*. And yes, female fishers are becoming a common sight on Central Oregon waters. In fact, a woman's fly fishing club, *Wild Women of the Water,* has been growing by leaps and bounds … *see page 225 for information on joining*. Many such clubs are popping up all around the Northwest. A fair number of our photos in the book include women fishers. Of course, men still dominate the sport and several organizations and fishing clubs are there for them as well. Locally, the *Central Oregon Flyfishers* is a popular club accepting both men and women.

Gary Lewis

We feel fortunate to have local outdoor writer, **Gary Lewis**, as our contributing author in this fifth edition. Gary devoted a lot of his time traveling to many new waters a little beyond what most consider Central Oregon. His writing and photos speak for his knowledge and expertise. *See Gary's biography on the back cover.*

Although Brooke Snavely and Raven Wing were not involved in this edition, much of their work remains from the earlier editions.

See the *"How-To"* section to learn tips for all techniques of fishing, from trolling to jigging, from fly fishing to bait fishing, from spinners to crankbaits, and reading water and stalking.

Many fishermen and fisherwomen opt to hire a guide when fishing the lakes and rivers of Central Oregon. So, we included information on how to hire a guide and what to expect on a guided trip.

Oregon's tremendous growth continues and that means a lot more fishing pressure on our lakes and streams. Therefore, we ask that you do your part in preserving our fisheries. Please read the section on catch-and-release; it's the most important information in the book. We are not advocating that every fish caught be released, but

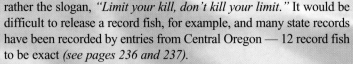

rather the slogan, *"Limit your kill, don't kill your limit."* It would be difficult to release a record fish, for example, and many state records have been recorded by entries from Central Oregon — 12 record fish to be exact *(see pages 236 and 237)*.

In 2005, the Oregon Sport Fishing Regulations booklet included changes in our coverage areas. We make many references to this booklet in our text, using "OSFR" as the identifying abbreviation.

Since this book will have a long life and fishing regulations are always subject to change, we strongly recommend that anglers carry the current OSFR with them and always check it before fishing.

Again, we have provided advertisers with an opportunity to tell of their products or services, such as resort/lodging accommodations, guided fishing trips, fishing equipment, and more *(see the advertisers index, page 240)*. We feel this is valuable information that would not otherwise be included. Advertising revenue also allows us to keep this high-quality book priced competitively.

Based on comments I hear, there are a couple of misconceptions I feel I should address in this introduction. First, some folks think I have little involvement in the book other than take-on the financial risks and publish the book. That thinking is far from my actual involvement. While I do recruit contributing authors to do most of the leg-work and research on new waters and updates, I have always determined our coverage, format, and style; organized the layout; selected photos and edited and proofed every page. I've taken to the air in an open-sided plane a couple of times to shoot aerial photos of many of our waters, and put in my two-bits worth editorially. At times I believe the book is a labor of love, it has taken much of my time over the last three years, and I may be lucky to realize an hourly rate to equal the minimum wage. Oh, yes! I also was responsible for more than 90% of the advertising sales.

The second misconception is that people think I'm a *professional* fly fisherman. While I've always been an avid angler and enjoy all techniques employed to catch fish, I do not qualify myself as a pro … maybe to my grandkids.

Central Oregon, the Cascades, and beyond offer some of the best fishing in the country. Read this book thoroughly, and you'll be better prepared to be a successful angler and experience the thrill of catching fish!

Good Luck!

Geoff Hill
Editor/Publisher

1. Deschutes steelhead. Photo by Justin Karnopp
2. Rainbow. Photo courtesy Garrison's Guide Service
3. Atlantic salmon. Photo by Gary Weber
4. Largemouth bass. Gary Lewis photo
5. Ana Reservoir hybrid "wiper" bass. Photo by Geoff Hill
6. Crescent Lake brown trout. Photo by Rick Arnold
7. Lake in the Dunes rainbow. Photo courtesy The Patient Angler
8. Elk Lake brook trout. Photo by Brian O'Keefe
9. Columbia River sturgeon. Gary Lewis photo
10. Krumbo Reservoir catch. Photo by Brian O'Keefe
11. Mann Lake Lahontan cutthroat. Photo by Gary Weber

Donner und Blitzen River

Antone Ranch Lake

DESCHUTES RIVER

Size:	252 miles long
Depth:	flows vary with irrigation season & runoffs
Main Catch:	rainbow, brown & brook trout, kokanee, whitefish, steelhead
Best Methods:	depends on stretch of river
Season:	regulations complex; check OSFR

LITTLE LAVA LAKE TO WICKIUP RESERVOIR

From its origin as a murmuring brook exiting Little Lava Lake in the High Cascades, the Deschutes River flows 252 miles to its junction with the Columbia River and drops from an elevation of 4,739 feet above sea level to 186 feet. The uppermost 7 miles above Crane Prairie Reservoir is the only remaining free-flowing section of the river, offering outstanding spawning and rearing habitat for rainbow trout and kokanee. Excellent spawning gravel, healthy riparian zones, and natural flow and temperature regimes support stocked and wild rainbow trout, wild brook trout, native whitefish, spawning kokanee, and, below Crane Prairie Reservoir, brown trout.

In the 15-mile stretch from Little Lava Lake to Wickiup Reservoir, rainbow trout average 6 to 9 inches, with frequent catches of 12 to 18 inches in length. Brook trout average under 10 inches in length, even though the state record brook trout of 9 pounds, 6 ounces was caught in the headwaters in 1980. Brown trout, present between Crane Prairie and Wickiup Reservoirs, will average 12 to 14 inches, with some much larger. The native whitefish here are typically 6 to 8 inches and up to 15 inches. Packs of them can be seen resting on the bottom of deep holes.

From the headwaters down, the Deschutes River is a small stream meandering through mixed conifer and pine forest. More like a creek than a river, it can be waded across at many points. Many downed logs occupy the clear, cold water. The river has a large variety of water types including slow, deep slough-like pools near the headwaters and shallow, fast rocky riffles farther downstream. One of the prettiest stretches, full of meadows, flowers, pines, and views of Mt. Bachelor, is upstream from the Route 40 bridge above Crane Prairie. At Browns Creek, 4 miles below Crane Prairie, the Deschutes becomes considerably larger. Some spots along the river are marshy, and mosquitoes can be bad, but mountain views, flora, and fauna are also abundant. Flows are lowest in the spring and highest in the fall.

Angling from the bank is possible in a few spots, but the best fishing is had by bushwhacking and wading. Fly angling with dry flies is the most productive method in the shal-

Fly anglers try their luck in the headwaters of the Deschutes. Photo by Brian O'Keefe

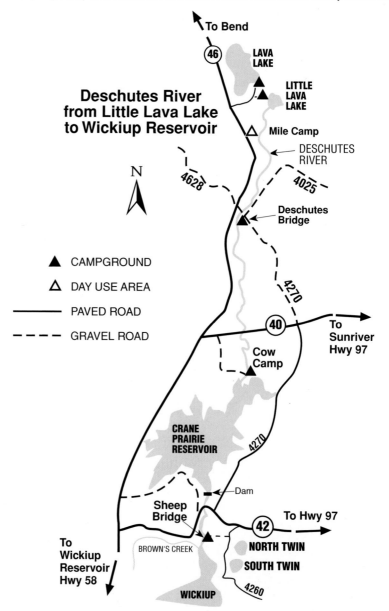

Deschutes River from Little Lava Lake to Wickiup Reservoir

lowest portions of the stream. Small Renegade, Adams, Elk Hair Caddis, ant imitations, and yellow Humpys are good choices for dries. Where conditions allow, fish nymphs, such as Pheasant Tail, Gold Ribbed Hare's Ear, and black APs. Close quarters with native vegetation doesn't leave a great deal of casting

| Elk Hair Caddis | Flying Ant |

Fly photos courtesy Umpqua.com

room, so bring extra flies. Along undercut banks and in deeper pools, some anglers work small spinners such as Colorados, Rooster Tails, or Panther Martins.

Anglers should be aware of varying seasons and catch limits for the upper Deschutes River, always check the current Oregon Sport Fishing Regulations (OSFR) pamphlet before fishing. From Little Lava to Crane Prairie, the river is open the last Saturday in May to September 30, flies and lures only. Catch and release for all rainbow trout, 2 brook trout per day, 8-inch minimum. From Wickiup to Crane Prairie, the river is open the last Saturday in May to August 31, flies and lures only, 2 trout per day, 8-inch minimum. Only one trout over 20 inches per day. No limit on brook trout in this section.

This is a popular area for big game and waterfowl hunting, wildlife viewing, and bird watching. A favorite place for family outings, the Deschutes has many camping areas. Many other excellent fishing spots are nearby as well as opportunities to watch spawning fish, to boat, and to participate in other water sports. In the winter, this is a popular snowmobile and cross-country ski area.

Forest Service campgrounds on the river are located at Little Lava Lake, Mile Camp, Deschutes Bridge, Cow Meadow, and Sheep Bridge. Little Lava, Deschutes Bridge, and Sheep Bridge have drinking water. Only Mile Camp is no fee camping. All have outhouses and river frontage. Many opportunities for primitive camping are also available.

There is easy access to about 3 miles of the

Megan Wiley is all smiles over her upper Deschutes "monster" brown trout.
Photo by Osprey Adventures

river along Route 46, beginning 2 miles south of Lava Lake and continuing downstream. Other road access is available at Mile Camp, Deschutes Bridge Campground, the Route 40 crossing, Cow Meadow, and below Crane Prairie at Brown's Crossing and Sheep Bridge Campground. These are the most heavily fished spots on the river. To observe the rest of the river requires a hike.

To reach this section of the Deschutes River follow directions to Lava Lake via Sunriver (page 85). Route 40 crosses the river 21 miles west of U.S. Highway 97 and meets Route 46 in another mile.

DESCHUTES RIVER: WICKIUP TO SUNRIVER

The best population of stream-inhabiting brown trout in the state lives in the Deschutes River below Wickiup Reservoir. Highly accessible and easy to drift, the river changes dramatically below Wickiup dam to become a slow, meandering, powerful body of water. This part of the river harbors brown and rainbow trout, the rare brook trout, whitefish, and transient fingerling coho and kokanee from Wickiup. Wild browns up to 15 pounds have been pulled out of this stretch, catches

between 12 and 16 inches are common, and good numbers are available in the 20- to 24-inch range. A genetic mix of wild and stocked rainbow trout average 6 to 10 inches, with an occasional fish in the 12- to 14-inch range. Native whitefish are abundant and average 6 to 14 inches in length.

The OSFR from Wickiup Reservoir to Benham Falls allows 5 trout per day, which may include 2 non fin-clipped rainbow. Bait is allowed in this section. The season opens the Saturday of Memorial Day weekend and runs to October 31. Always check current OSFR before fishing.

The river runs in mainly one channel throughout this stretch, undercut banks are common, and shorelines lined with pine, bitterbrush, and willow are often highly eroded. Flows vary drastically with the irrigation season. The riverbed of fine sediment becomes sticky mud when exposed during low water. Woody debris in the river is scarce but is being added through habitat improvement projects. The river here is basically unwadable, often with steep shorelines and deep, powerful water. Bank fishing or drift fishing from a boat is the norm. Bordered mainly by Forest Service land above the LaPine State Recreation Area, the stretch below, through Sunriver is lined with homes.

All fishing methods can produce large browns through this reach of the river, but most anglers use whole crayfish or nightcrawlers, particularly near Sun-

Continued on page 10

ABOVE: A scenic bend in the river below Wickiup Dam.

RIGHT: This view of the Deschutes is from McGregor Memorial Viewpoint in LaPine State Recreation Area. Paulina Peak in the distance.

Photos by Geoff Hill

BELOW: A Rooster Tail spinner fooled this beautiful Deschutes brown trout. Photo by Brian O'Keefe

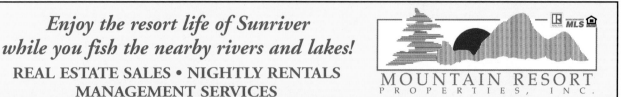

For obvious reasons, the stretch of water near Lava Island Falls is not recommended for canoe travel! Photo by Doug Emerson

Canoe Safety on the Deschutes

Floating the famed Deschutes River in a canoe or boat can be a delightful, never-to-be-forgotten experience. In most respects, the Deschutes is a perfect river for drifting. While most of the river is quiet, rather placid water, *a few stretches are very dangerous and should not, under any circumstances, be attempted. Lives have been lost because people ignored the warning signs or underestimated the cascades.*

"All along the river, the Forest Service has posted warning signs of upcoming falls or rapids. If a boater or canoeist heeds these warning signs, they should have no problem. The time to pull in to shore is when you first see the warning sign. Inexperienced boaters or canoeists often underestimate the power of the river at the head of falls or rapids. Once you are caught in the fast water, consider yourself lucky if you get out alive.

"Just remember that the relative ease of floating the Deschutes can be misleading. Remember, too, that the river doesn't care.

"If boaters and canoeists observed just these three rules, there would be no deaths on the Deschutes. *First, a life preserver is a must. Second, know the river and the limitations of your craft. And, third, observe all the boating safety rules."*

The Boating Safety Rules recommended by the U.S. Coast Guard and the State Marine Board are printed herein.

The Deschutes National Forest has published a pamphlet on floating the Deschutes River. We recommend that you pick up a copy before you try the river. It could save your life.

Boating & Canoeing Safety Rules
(Recommended by the U.S. Coast Guard & State Marine Board)

1. Do not go out in rough water or threatening weather.

2. Never leave shore in a leaky or poorly constructed boat.

3. Equip boat properly with anchor, life preservers, oars or spare paddle, flashlight, and fire extinguisher (if motor boat).

4. Tell someone when and where you are going and when you plan to return (your chances of rescue are better).

5. Do not overload the boat (have plenty of freeboard).

6. Wear your life preserver. Have one for each person on board.

7. Instruct at least one of the passengers on how to operate the boat.

8. Keep clear of swimmers.

9. Familiarize yourself with the area.

10. Know how to swim.

11. Avoid excessive or sudden bursts of speed (you may be thrown overboard).

12. Reduce speed in narrow passages and congested areas.

13. Take the river brochure or a map in a sealed plastic bag.

14. Take drinking water and some extra food in case you have to stay out longer than expected.

15. Sheriff Search & Rescue – (541) 388-6502.

DESCHUTES

Continued from page 8

river. One should fish close to the banks where the browns lurk. An especially effective technique is casting from a boat toward shore with spinning gear and a plug or lure such as a Rapala that imitates a baitfish. The best times of day are early and late when the sun is off the water. Fly fishers going for brown trout use streamers, such as brown Woolly Buggers, brown Matukas, and red and white bucktails. Good caddis and mayfly hatches make fly fishing for small rainbow and whitefish particularly productive, using dry flies such as Adams, Elk Hair Caddis, Comparaduns, and even Royal Wulffs. One may also want to try nymphing with orange Tied-down Caddis.

Often the mouths of the Little Deschutes and Fall River can be profitable areas to fish. Fall River joins the Deschutes just below the LaPine Recreation Area, and the Little Deschutes enters a mile above Sunriver.

There is a boat speed limit of 5 mph.

Just lazily drifting the river is a very popular pastime. However, the float from Wyeth Campground to Tetherow Log Jam should not be attempted in order to avoid Pringle Falls, a dangerous obstacle. A few miles below Sunriver, another stretch of life-threatening water begins at Benham Falls. Warning signs and take-outs keep boaters safe. *(See information on pages 9 through 11 for safe passage around these sections.)* The most popular drifts are the 7 miles from just below Wickiup Dam to above Pringle Falls, a 13.5-mile drift from Tetherow to Big River Campground, and the 7 miles from Big River to Sunriver. Five good boat ramps are available between Wickiup and Sunriver. Other amusements in the area include camping, hunting, bird watching, horseback riding, hiking, and wildlife viewing.

The guide paddles while his client tries his luck on the Deschutes above Sunriver.
Photo courtesy Cascade Guides & Outfitters

Beginning just below Wickiup Dam, Forest Service facilities include Bull Bend Campground and raft launch; Wyeth

Deschutes River Canoe Trip Guide: Wickiup Dam to Meadow Picnic Area

	Hours	Accumulative Elapsed Time	Approximate River Mileage
Wickiup Dam* to Wampus Butte Campground*	2:45	2:45	2.5
Wampus Butte Campground* to Bull Bend*	2:20	5:05	3.0
Bull Bend* to Wyeth Campground*	0:45	5:50	1.0
Wyeth Campground* to Pringle Falls*	0:30	6:20	0.5
PRINGLE FALLS – CANOE TRAVEL NOT RECOMMENDED – PORTAGE TIME 0:45			
Pringle Falls* to Tetherow Log Jam*	2:45	9:05	2.5
TETHEROW LOG JAM – CANOE TRAVEL NOT RECOMMENDED – PORTAGE TIME 0:10			
Tetherow Log Jam* to LaPine State Park	1:55	11:00	5.5
LaPine State Park to mouth of Fall River	2:20	13:20	3.0
Mouth of Fall River to Big River Campground*	2:40	16:00	5.0
Big River Campground* to Harper Bridge	4:10	20:10	7.0
Harper Bridge to Besson Camp*	1:00	21:10	1.5
Besson Camp* to Benham Falls*	5:10	26.20	8.5
BENHAM FALLS TO JUST SOUTH OF SLOUGH CAMP – TRAVEL NOT RECOMMENDED – ROUGH WATER			
Just south of Slough Camp* to Dillon Falls*	1:15	–	2.0
Dillon Falls* to Aspen Camp	1:00	–	1.5
ASPEN CAMP TO BIG EDDY – CANOE TRAVEL NOT RECOMMENDED – ROUGH WATER			
BIG EDDY TO LAVA ISLAND – CANOE TRAVEL NOT RECOMMENDED – ROUGH WATER			
LAVA ISLAND TO SOUTH OF MEADOW CAMP – CANOE TRAVEL NOT RECOMMENDED			
South of Meadow Camp to Meadow Picnic Area	0:15	–	0.5
MEADOW PICNIC AREA TO NATIONAL FOREST BOUNDARY – CANOE TRAVEL NOT RECOMMENDED – ROUGH WATER			

*Boat Ramps to 18 feet

Campground and boat launch; Pringle Falls Campground and raft launch; Tetherow boat launch; and Big River Group Camp and boat launch. LaPine State Recreation Area, also with a crude boat launch, is situated between Tetherow and Big River. None of these sites has drinking water, except the state park. All charge a fee to camp. There are also many primitive sites available for camping, and there is a small boat ramp suitable for canoes at Harper Bridge on Route 40.

Several Forest Service roads parallel the river. The segment of the river from Wickiup Dam to Route 43 is paralleled by Forest Route 4370 on the west bank. Route 4370 can be reached either from Wickiup Reservoir (see directions to Wickiup Reservoir on page 45) or from County Route 43 off U.S. Highway 97, 3 miles north of LaPine. Forest Route 4360 runs west of the river from Route 43 to County Route 42. Below Route 42 and Big River Campground the only public access is along the west bank across from Sunriver which can be reached by taking the Sunriver turn (Route 40) from U.S. Highway 97, 15 miles south of Bend. Stay on Route 40 crossing the river at Harper Bridge. Small-boat access is available at the bridge. Continue another 2 miles to Forest Route 41 and turn right. Many gravel and dirt spur roads lead down to the river from Route 41.

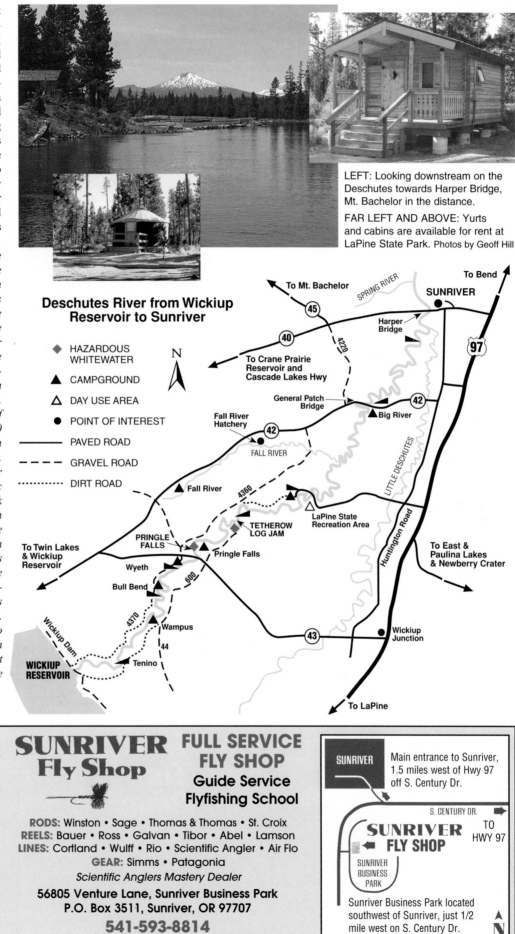

LEFT: Looking downstream on the Deschutes towards Harper Bridge, Mt. Bachelor in the distance.

FAR LEFT AND ABOVE: Yurts and cabins are available for rent at LaPine State Park. Photos by Geoff Hill

Deschutes River from Wickiup Reservoir to Sunriver

◆ HAZARDOUS WHITEWATER
▲ CAMPGROUND
△ DAY USE AREA
● POINT OF INTEREST
—— PAVED ROAD
– – – GRAVEL ROAD
········· DIRT ROAD

DESCHUTES RIVER: SUNRIVER TO BEND

The steepest gradient in the entire 252 miles of the Deschutes River begins 6 miles downstream from Sunriver at Benham Falls. From the falls to Bend, the river moves swiftly within a basalt channel, dodging a lava flow and breaking into a series of hurtling rapids and thundering falls. Upstream from Benham Falls, the river has the same placid character as between Wickiup and Sunriver. The brown trout fishing here is second only to the stretch above, with fish in the same size range. Some are monsters. Wild rainbow of 7 to 11 inches, occasionally to 14 inches in length, dominate the river from Benham Falls downstream. Whitefish are available all the way to Bend.

Below Sunriver, the vegetation changes to old growth ponderosa and aspen, and shorelines vary from marshy meadows to basalt bedrock. Flows fluctuate less because of tributaries, and the river features many deep pools, a more stable bank, and rocky instream structure. Spring River enters the Deschutes a mile downstream from Route 40. This mile-long "spring creek" holds few resident fish and is mainly spawning and rearing habitat for the rainbows, browns, and whitefish of the Deschutes. The lower half-mile of Spring River is accessible through Forest Service land.

Untamed whitewater and dangerous cataracts begin at Benham Falls and continue past Dillon Falls to Lava Island Falls 5 miles south of Bend. This section accurately reflects the river's name, Deschutes, "River of the Falls." The safest stretch for boaters is calm water between Benham and Dillon Falls. Popular whitewater run frequently by professional guides lies between Dillon and Lava Island Falls. Rafting trips can be booked with experienced companies in Bend and Sunriver.

Though much of the water is fast and dangerous between Sunriver and Bend there are still many good fishing spots along the banks. As with all of the upper Deschutes, the river travels mostly within one channel and water levels vary with the irrigation season. Few areas are wadable and most would be hazardous to attempt. From 1 mile below Meadow Picnic Area to Bend, the river is entirely flanked by private land. A short distance upstream from Bend, much of

BELOW: The wild whitewater of Dillon Falls on the upper Deschutes near Bend. Photo by Geoff Hill
RIGHT: Fall color along the Deschutes can be spectacular. Photo by Bob Woodward.

the river is siphoned off for irrigation from April to October, and, again, the character of the river changes as its volume drops.

Upstream of the falls, anglers should try bait or Rapalas early and late in the day for brown trout. From Benham Falls down, it is primarily a bank fishery and, at times, provides great fly fishing, although small lures are also used successfully. Small, flashy lures such as Thomas and Rooster Tails are productive. A fly box containing Adams, Elk Hair Caddis, Comparadun, and salmonfly patterns plus stonefly nymph imitations, Hare's Ears, and Pheasant Tails should be adequate. Whitefish are often caught while fly fishing for rainbow. Many anglers fish the tailouts of falls in October. Bait is no longer allowed from Benham Falls to Lake Billy Chinook, with the exception of Mirror Pond in Bend ... especially for kids.

Below Benham Falls to Lake Billy Chinook, the river is open to angling year-round. The trout catch limit below Benham Falls is 2 per day, 8-inch minimum length, and no more than 1 over 20 inches. There is no limit on whitefish.

Boat launching is available at Harper Bridge, Besson Camp, Slough Camp, Dillon Falls Camp, Aspen Camp, and Lava Island Camp recreation sites. There is a boat speed limit of 5 mph.

Forest Service day use areas exist at Besson Camp, Slough Camp, and Dillon Falls Camp. None of them have drinking water. Benham Falls, Besson Camp, Slough Camp, Dillon Falls Camp, and Meadow Camp also have picnic areas.

In addition to fishing, boating, and whitewater rafting, other options for entertainment include waterfowl hunting, photography, horseback riding, mountain biking, and hiking. Forest Service trails for mountain bikes, horses, and hikers begin at Meadow Camp and continue to Benham Falls.

For access from Sunriver, follow directions in the Wickiup to Sunriver section (see page 11) to Route 41. To reach Besson Camp take spur road 200 off of Route 41 downstream from Sunriver. Back on 41 continue north, downstream, about 8 miles and turn on marked spur roads to Slough Camp. Dillon Falls Camp is 2 miles north of Slough Camp, Aspen Camp another 2 miles, Lava Island Camp another 2 miles. All are reached by dirt spur roads from Route 41. About a mile north of Lava Island Camp Route 41 inter-sects with Century Drive, Route 46. A right turn here will take you back to Bend in 7 miles. These directions can also be followed in reverse by taking Century Drive out of Bend toward Mt. Bachelor and turning left in 7 miles onto Route 41 toward Deschutes River Recreation Sites. To reach the Benham Falls area from Highway 97, turn at the Lava Lands Visitor Center and follow signs.

Deschutes River from Sunriver to Bend

Jill Ryder electrified the Sunriver angling community by catching this 15-pound rainbow trout from the Deschutes River near Harper Bridge in the summer of 2004. A few years back, a 16-pound brown was caught near the same area ... it was mounted and is on display at the Sunriver Country Store. Photo courtesy Sunriver Scene

DESCHUTES RIVER:
BEND TO LAKE BILLY CHINOOK

The Deschutes River flows smack through the center of downtown Bend, attracting many visitors at Drake, Sawyer, Harmon, Pioneer, Farewell Bend, and McKay parks. At Drake Park, Mirror Pond offers a wonderful atmosphere for walks, relaxation, picnics, bird watching, floating, and fishing, especially for the kids. A little farther downstream, below the North Canal Dam all the way to Lake Billy Chinook, the river offers excellent winter fishing. In some spots, the river is wadable, in other areas, bank fishing is the rule. A preferred area for fly fishing, this section is not open to bait fishing; however, lures are popular. All fish in the river are wild, including rainbow trout up to 18 inches, averaging 7 to 14 inches. Brown trout can be found in all sizes, including a few monsters pushing 8 pounds. Bull trout are present below Steelhead Falls, and profuse numbers of whitefish are available throughout the river. Crayfish are common. Boating is not possible due to low flows and, because of frequent waterfalls farther downstream, is unsafe to attempt. The only navigable expanse is in the Deschutes Arm of Lake Billy Chinook.

From the north end of 1st Street in Bend down to the North Canal Dam, the river is accessible along the west bank, and fishing can be decent, especially when water levels are low in the summer. Deep pools and slow runs between rock-strewn stretches produce mostly small fish. In the winter, the river rushes over big boulders; during summer low flows, it swirls slowly past the same rocks. Water levels fluctuate greatly with the irrigation season. Fishing is best in between and around the boulders.

As the river leaves Bend, it passes the last man-made obstruction for 40 miles and becomes a wild, canyon river. More of the river banks are public land. Shorelines vary from flooded, marshy ground to blocky talus with some heavy vegetation of willow and alder. Around Lower Bridge, 25 miles below Bend, cattails and sedges dominate. Springs below Lower Bridge help to stabilize water levels, as does inflow from Squaw Creek. The uplands are covered with juniper trees and bitterbrush, and the basalt canyon is of varying depth. Outstanding wild rainbow and brown trout habitat exist from Lower Bridge downstream 10 miles to Lake Billy Chinook. The deepest part of the canyon, below Lower Bridge, has excellent slots and pools and the best potential for fishery on the river if flows could be stabilized. In-stream structure in the form of rocks, some woody debris, and occasional weedbeds is plentiful throughout the canyon. The area is rich in wildlife.

Access is limited by private land and steep canyon walls. The largest concentration of wild fish is from Big Falls about a mile below Lower Bridge to Lake Billy Chinook. Steelhead Falls is about 5 miles below Lower Bridge. At Lake Billy Chinook, the Deschutes joins the Crooked and Metolius rivers.

When fishing these rocky reaches, make sure your lure is near the bottom. Small, flashy lures, such as Thomas and Rooster Tails, are productive. For fly fishers, a fly box containing winter stone fly, March brown, and salmonfly dry flies is a must when these hatches are in progress. Brown Woolly Buggers and beadhead nymphs are standard. Other productive patterns are Elk Hair Caddis, Comparadun, stonefly nymph imitations, Hare's Ear, and Pheasant Tail. Whitefish are often caught while fly fishing for rainbow.

Developed campgrounds are located at Tumalo State Park, Cline Falls State Park, and Lake Billy Chinook. No other official campgrounds are located on the river between Bend and Lake Billy Chinook, but, legally, you can camp anywhere on BLM land or the

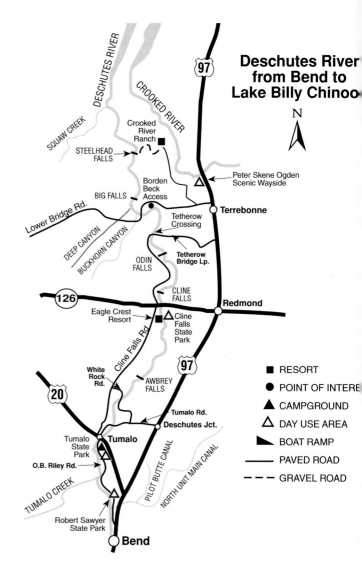

Deschutes River from Bend to Lake Billy Chinook

N

■ RESORT
● POINT OF INTERE[ST]
▲ CAMPGROUND
△ DAY USE AREA
◣ BOAT RAMP
— PAVED ROAD
- - - GRAVEL ROAD

ABOVE: Perched upon a large boulder in the Deschutes River, this great blue heron is either resting one leg or showing off. Photo by Bob Woodward

RIGHT: Steelhead Falls, on the Deschutes, can be accessed through the Crooked River Ranch development. Photo by Geoff Hill

Crooked River National Grasslands not otherwise posted. Recreation options other than hiking and fishing are limited because of private land. Some hunting is possible. An abundance of raptors, fur-bearing mammals, and waterfowl make wildlife viewing rewarding.

Roads reach the river at Sawyer Park in Bend, Tumalo State Park north of Bend, Cline Falls State Park west of Redmond, Tetherow Crossing north of Cline Falls, and at Lower Bridge west of Terrebonne. Between Lower Bridge and Lake Billy Chinook, all access is by foot; nowhere can you drive right to the water. In only a few places can you get down to the river without ropes and pitons, and hiking within much of this steep canyon is strenuous.

Sawyer Park in Bend is reached by turning west onto O.B. Riley Road from U.S. Highway 97 across from Bend River Mall. The park is .5 mile down O.B. Riley. Continuing north on O.B. Riley Road will bring you to Tumalo State Park in another 4 miles. To reach Cline Falls State Park from Bend, take Highway 97 north then U.S. Highway 20 west toward Sisters. In 4 miles turn right toward the town of Tumalo and stay on this road (Cline Falls Road) for about 10 miles until it reaches the junction with State Highway 126. Cline Falls is just a stone's throw east on 126 and can also be reached from downtown Redmond, 4.5 miles farther east on 126. A primitive road follows the west bank of the river downstream from Highway 126 just west of Cline Falls through mostly private land. The BLM is currently negotiating a land exchange to add public land north of Highway 126 along the river. At Tetherow Crossing about 1.5 miles downstream from Cline Falls, there is a .75-mile stretch of BLM land. Another mile downstream is a brief .25-mile segment of public land above Odin Falls. The next chunk of BLM land is above Lower Bridge and can be reached by numerous spur roads heading upstream off of Lower Bridge Market County Road. The Lower Bridge road heads west off Highway 97 just north of Terrebonne.

The most remote section of the river from Lower Bridge to Lake Billy Chinook has very limited access. Steelhead Falls and a primitive BLM road heading upstream from it offer the few access points reached through the Crooked River Ranch (CRR) development northwest of Terrebonne. *From Terrebonne, take the Lower Bridge road turning right into CRR in 2 miles. Stay on this main road (NW Chinook Drive) for 1.5 miles then turn left on Badger Road. Badger becomes Blacktail Drive and T's with Quail Road in about 1.5 miles. Turn right on Quail and in about a mile turn left on River Road which reaches the parking area for the trail to Steelhead Falls in about .75 mile.*

Steelhead Falls is about a half-mile hike downstream. From this point, the BLM road heads upstream with a few more trails down to the river coming off it before the road turns back toward the east, away from the river. From Steelhead Falls to Lake Billy Chinook, access is difficult to impossible except by hiking downstream from Steelhead Falls or upstream from Lake Billy Chinook.

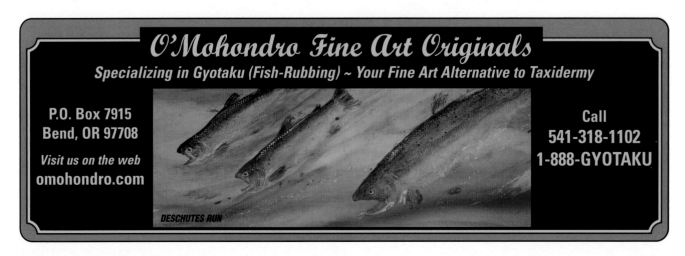

Fly fishing is the most popular technique for fishing on the Deschutes. Photo by Gary Weber

DESCHUTES RIVER: PELTON DAM TO COLUMBIA RIVER

In the 100 miles of water from Pelton Dam to the Columbia River, the Deschutes River reveals itself as a big, broad-shouldered and powerful, desert-canyon river, decisively carving its course. Remarkable for its excellent flows year-round, world-class fishing for wild trout, a strong summer steelhead run, and spring and fall runs of chinook salmon, the lower Deschutes is nationally recognized and passionately appreciated. Add an atmosphere of cultural diversity created by the involvement of the Warm Springs Tribes in use and management and the river's designation as a National Wild and Scenic River, as well as a State Scenic Waterway, and you start to get the picture. Even though the Deschutes feeds into the Columbia only a 2-hour drive east of Portland, the majority of the river, accessible only by boat or long hikes, still maintains a feeling of wildness.

Rich in insect numbers and diversity, the Deschutes supports up to 1,500 wild rainbow trout over 8 inches per mile. Trout numbers gradually decrease downstream to the mouth. Fishing is great year-round. Lined with alder groves along some of its shorelines, talus slopes, and grass-covered banks scattered in between, the riverbed often has steep drop-offs or may grade into mucky eddies. Mainly, the river has a gradual slope covered with gravel and cobble. In places, weedbeds thrive in the river, and islands frequently split the river, but primarily it flows in one big channel. This is big water that cannot be waded across. Stream flow averages over a 69-year period show a range from 3,380 cubic feet per second (cfs) in July to 5,489 cfs in March. Thirteen major rapids and an impassible falls punctuate the waters between Pelton Dam and the Columbia. Main tributaries are the Warm Springs River and the White River.

One of the most important recreational areas in the state, the river attracts diverse users: anglers for trout, steelhead, salmon, and whitefish, whitewater enthusiasts, splash-and-giggle rafters, jet boaters, commercial guides, hunters, campers, and wildlife watchers. Land ownership is shared by the Bureau of Land Management (BLM), the Confederated Tribes of Warm Springs (CTWS), Oregon State Parks and Recreation Department, numerous private parties, and two railroads. Rules and regulations are continually changing. The lower Deschutes River Management Plan Record of Decision II, and addenda are available from BLM, describes current and future management plans for the river. The river corridor has special regulations for boating, camping, firearms, fishing, and fires. As use continues to increase, it becomes more and more important to know the regulations and to be considerate of other users in order to maintain the rare quality of the Deschutes experience.

It is normal for a river to change from year to year. Before running the river, talk to local river guides to find out if anything has changed since you last drifted that section. Since 1996 there have been major changes in

Camping on the Deschutes. Photo by Brian O'Keefe

changes in the Deschutes from Pelton Dam to the Columbia River. One Class 4 rapids in particular, Whitehorse Rapids, has seen significant changes. Many other less dangerous alterations also occurred in the river channel.

RULES AND REGULATIONS

Fishing Regulations: An Oregon Angling License is required and all rules as described in "Oregon Sport Fishing Regulations" must be followed. Special "tags" are required for salmon and steelhead. Special permits are also required to fish the CTWS side of the river. The regulations are complicated; check the rules before fishing.

Boating Regulations: In an effort to reduce river use conflicts, measures have been applied by the BLM to reduce river access by commercial users. New regulations are being phased in each year. Various restrictions concerning the use of motors are in effect. A Boater's Pass is required of everyone in a floating device on the river and may be purchased for the day. Visit www.boaterspass.com to read the current regulations and print out a Boater's Pass. Several car shuttle services are available.

Disabled Angler Regulations: For disabled anglers, it is legal to fish from a parked boat on the lower Deschutes River. See the OSFR for details on applying for a Permanent Disabilities Permit.

BLM Camping Regulations: For all drive-in campgrounds and for BLM land between the locked gate upstream from Maupin to Macks Canyon, the stay limit is no more than 14 days out of any 28 days. At boat-in (undeveloped) sites, campers may stay no more than 4 days and must vacate a site for 3 days before reoccupying. The new site must not be less than .25 mile away. No more than 16 people are allowed in a group at boat-in sites, except between the locked gate and Sherars Falls where the limit is 24 people.

BLM charges $8.00 per night Sun.–Thurs. and $12.00 Fri.– Sat. for overnight use of drive-in campgrounds and a charge for each additional vehicle at that site. The maximum number of people per single site is 8. Some larger group sites are available for a charge of $25.00 per night Sun.–Thurs. and $35.00 Fri.– Sat. No fees are charged at undeveloped sites. Drinking water is available only at Maupin City Park and Macks Canyon BLM Recreation Site, and at Deschutes River State Park.

BLM recreation sites change periodically. Facilities may be different from those outlined in the following descriptions.

Private Property: Permission is required to camp on or use private property. The railroad tracks are private property. Walking along the tracks is technically trespassing and potentially dangerous, although warnings are rarely heeded, and laws are seldom enforced.

Warm Springs Reservation: Only 6 miles of river on the reservation side between Dry Creek and Trout Creek are open to the public for fishing, and a CTWS fishing permit ("Indian permit") is required. Along all other reservation land, you may not land a boat, fish, walk, or camp, including all islands and gravel bars west of mid-river.

Dangers: Be aware of the potential for incidents involving heat exhaustion, sunstroke, dehydration, sunburn, rattlesnakes, poison ivy, drowning, high winds, temperature extremes, fire, scorpions, and black widow spiders. Wading is dangerous; use a wading staff, studded felt soles, or cleats, if necessary.

Fire Regulations: From June 1 to October 15, rules are as follows:

No open fires, wood fires, or smoking outside of buildings, closed vehicles, or boats on the river.

During the remainder of the year, fires may be built only in fire pans (stoves are preferred). All ashes and charcoal must be packed out.

It is illegal to cut any firewood, dead or alive, in the river corridor.

Considerate use of the river includes disposing of cigarette butts in an ash tray or garbage can — not in the water or on the banks.

Litter: If you pack it in, pack it out! Never use toilets for garbage disposal. BLM is proposing that all human waste be packed out in the near future.

Firearms: No shooting from the third Saturday in May to August 31. No discharging of firearms in developed recreation sites.

Fish Species: All trout in the lower Deschutes are wild fish and native to the river. Stocking of trout was ended in 1979, whereas hatchery steelhead and spring chinook salmon are still stocked. Fall chinook are a wild run, but numbers are extremely low. Rainbow trout in the lower Deschutes are a unique group called "redsides" because of their broad, deep red stripes. The average catch is between 10 and 15 inches; 16- to 18-inch

A typical lower Deschutes native "redside" rainbow.
Photo by Osprey Adventures

trout are not uncommon, and a few are even larger. These fish are strong and feisty and put up a great fight.

The stretch from Pelton Dam to Maupin holds the most trout, with numbers gradually decreasing downstream to the mouth. During spawning season from April through mid-June, trout are especially

vulnerable to exhaustion. Play the big ones gently at this time of year, revive carefully, and stay off the spawning beds.

Deschutes steelhead are a summer run of both wild and hatchery fish averaging 4 to 6 pounds, 24 to 26 inches in length. They usually show up at the mouth in July and are available near Pelton Dam through December. Steelhead "strays" from other rivers sometimes enter the Deschutes and stay for variable lengths of time. Some of these fish are as large as 20 pounds.

Two runs of chinook salmon enter the Deschutes: the spring run in April and fall chinook in June. The average spring chinook is 8 to 12 pounds with a few between 12 and 18 pounds. Fall chinook average 20 pounds. Some individuals may be as large as 40 pounds. Special regulations apply to the salmon seasons, so check before fishing.

Whitefish are native to the Deschutes and an indicator of excellent water quality. They are a member of the salmonid family along with trout, steelhead, and salmon. Usually easier to catch than the other species, they can be a lot of fun on light gear. They are good eating if cleaned "while still twitching" and kept cool, and they are superb smoked. Whitefish angling is especially good during the winter with small nymphs. Sometimes you'll catch them on big stonefly nymphs while trout fishing.

Bull trout are present mainly above Sherars Falls. These native fish are now on the threatened and endangered species list. While releasing them as the law requires, do so very carefully.

Coarse-scale suckers are often found in fast water where they hug the bottom, scraping algae off rocks. They will sometimes take a fly off the bottom and are also foul-hooked occasionally. A big sucker on the end of a line can give the angler the thrill of the day, at least until seeing what it is.

Northern pikeminnow are a native predator and are not very numerous in the cold water of the Deschutes, but become more common as the water warms downstream. They are part of the natural balance, feeding on juvenile salmonids. They will take dry flies, unfortunately.

Many other non-game species are present in the river, but they are seldom seen or caught.

FISHING TECHNIQUES

Trout and Whitefish: Ninety percent of anglers on the lower Deschutes are fly fishers. Catching trout on the Deschutes follows the usual scenario of attempting to find where the fish are and what they are eating. Whitefish are often caught while fishing for trout. The four most important groups of insects on the Deschutes are mayflies, caddisflies, stoneflies, and midges. Choose your fly patterns accordingly. Trout are most likely to be found near seams, drop-offs, small troughs, depressions in the bottom, back eddies, banks, in rock gardens and foam lines, and in the flats during a hatch.

Fly fishing techniques most often used are dry flies cast upstream, deep nymphing, emergers cast upstream, and the wet fly swing. Popular dry fly patterns are Blue Wing Olive, Pale Morning Dun, Sparkle Dun, Humpys, salmonfly patterns, Golden Stone, Griffiths

Gnat, and Elk Hair Caddis. Emerger patterns should include a floating mayfly nymph, hatching midge, soft hackles, and caddis emerger. For wet flies, one should have soft hackles in all colors,

Sparkle Pupa, Hare's Ear, Pheasant Tail, beadhead nymphs, flashback nymphs, Prince Nymph or Zug Bug, Serendipity, October Caddis, and stonefly nymphs (Rubber Legs, Kaufmann's). Terrestrials such as hoppers and ant patterns should also be included in one's fly selection.

Spin fishers are successful during non-hatch times using small trout lures, such as Mepps, Rooster Tail, Panther Martin, and FlatFish, or flies with a casting bubble.

A "real" salmonfly checks out an imitation. The native redside rainbow went for the fake! Photos by Gary Weber

Bright-colored lures can be used throughout the day since the Deschutes is always slightly off-color. Retrieve as slowly as possible, casting near rocks and into the flats.

Steelhead: Recognizing good steelhead water is even more difficult than finding trout lies. Usually the speed of the current, depth of the water, and bottom structure are the most important factors to consider. Prime lies are 2 to 6 feet deep and moving at the speed of a slow walk. The more difficult a run is to wade because of an assortment of boulder sizes, the more steelhead like it. Ledges and other drop-offs can be good, too. Fly fishers need heavier gear than for trout and at times sink tip lines. Fly patterns are much less important than finding the right water, but popular patterns are Green Butt Skunk,

Lisa Vlessis caught her first steelhead ten minutes into her first steelhead trip.
Photo courtesy The Patient Angler

Articulated Leech, Macks Canyon, Purple Peril, Brad's Brat, Thor, Coal Car, Freight Train, and Silver Hilton. Some skaters or steelhead

dries are used, too. All are presented with a 45 degree down and across technique. Deep nymphing with stonefly patterns will also catch steelhead. Persistence and being in the right place at the right time are the keys to catching steelhead.

Many anglers on the Deschutes fish successfully for steelhead with hardware and drift rods or heavier spinning rods. Spinners, spoons, and plugs can all be used effectively. Spinner and spoon selections can be bigger and brighter than knowledge would usually indicate because of the off-color water. Size 3, 4, or even 5 spinners in silver, nickel, brass, or black are popular choices. Mepps Aglia, Blue Fox Vibrax, Metric and Rapalas are all good choices. Stee-lee spoons are good producers as are plugs in silver, gold, purple, green, or blue. Some anglers use side-planers. Lures can be fished in the same areas as flies just as effectively and can be better than flies

in deeper and rougher water. Spoons are usually better in deeper water than spinners, and plugs are definitely suited for deeper water. Retrieve lures as slowly as possible for best results.

Salmon: Open only occasionally, the Deschutes has been closed for salmon fishing in most years. However, the 2005 spring chinook run is strong, and the season is from April 7 to July 31. Fall chinook have a much longer run from mid-June to late October. The fish pool up below Sherars Falls, and most are caught within a mile (downstream) of the falls. Drift fishing tackle is used, usually with salmon eggs or commercially canned fish, a little yarn, a Spin n' Glo or Corkie in peach or green, and lead sinkers. Most anglers fish from the top of basalt cliffs below the falls by casting upstream and bouncing the bait along the bottom. Things can get crowded, often shoulder to shoulder. Bait can be used from the falls downstream 3 miles. Those shaky wood platforms at Sherars Falls are for Indian use only.

Deschutes River from Pelton Dam to Whitehorse Rapids

PELTON TO WHITEHORSE RAPIDS

Warm Springs to Trout Creek

The most heavily fished stretch of the whole river for trout, Warm Springs to Trout Creek is used by drift, walk-in, and bike-in anglers. The most intense fishing use is during the salmonfly hatch in late May. Excellent trout and steelhead fishing and non-technical boating along 9 miles of river give good reason for the popularity of this stretch. Warm Springs lies at river mile 97 (97 miles to the Columbia), 14 miles north of Madras, and about 3 miles below Pelton Dam. U.S. Highway 97 crosses the Deschutes River at Warm Springs. The boat ramp and parking area

RIGHT: Poplars bring fall color along the river near Mecca. Photo by Geoff Hill

BOTTOM: A bicycle is a great way to get to isolated spots on the Deschutes. Photo courtesy Osprey Adventures

.25 mile south of the bridge has a double outhouse, garbage cans, lots of room to set up rafts and driftboats, and a gravel ramp. Camping is not allowed. Warm Springs has services and Indian permits, and Madras offers services, shuttles, and permits.

From the Warm Springs boat ramp, there is public access along the east bank about a mile upstream to private property. *To reach Mecca Flat, the next drive-in access, turn north onto a dirt road at the east end of the Warm Springs Bridge between the market and Deschutes Trailer Park. The road forks almost immediately; the first fork leads to the trailer park, the second is a private driveway, and the third is the road to Mecca Flat. It's about 2 miles to the parking area on a road which has deep holes, big rocks, and slides. High clearance vehicles will usually have no problem, but, after a hard rain, much of it turns to slime.*

The camping/parking area at Mecca has one outhouse only. Heavy use is obvious. About a mile of river can be fished upstream, but passing through the stile at the north end of the parking area leads to many miles of trail along the river that are suitable for hiking or mountain bikes. The trail runs all the way to Trout Creek Recreation Site 7.5 miles downstream.

A half-dozen latrines and boat-in campsites are situated along the trail between Mecca and Trout Creek. About a mile down from Mecca Flat, the property owners have kindly granted access to the river along their property. Across the river on the CTWS side lies Dry Creek Campground.

To drive to Dry Creek, take U.S. Highway 26 east from Portland or west from Madras. Just north of the bridge over the Deschutes at Warm Springs, turn onto a paved road toward Kah-Nee-Ta Resort. Stay on this road (Warm Springs Route 3) for 3 miles to the sign to Dry Creek. Turn right onto the gravel road and at the fork go right another .5 mile to the next fork. Take the left fork, and in .2 mile you will reach Dry Creek Campground. A Warm Springs permit is required to camp and fish here. There is an outhouse and garbage cans but no drinking water or boat launch. Camping is not allowed anywhere else along the river on the reservation side. There is a maximum stay of 10 consecutive days at Dry Creek. At the gate on the north end of the campground, a dirt road leads to the only stretch of river along the reservation from which the public is allowed to fish, with a permit. This 6-mile stretch ends across from Trout Creek Campground. You may walk or take a mountain bike on the road.

Trout Creek Campground is one of the more developed campgrounds and has the next boat ramp downstream from Warm Springs. This can be a very busy place during prime fishing season since it is the last boat ramp before Class 4 Whitehorse Rapids and for the next 30 miles. Trout Creek Campground has a good gravel boat ramp, level sites suitable for trailers and RVs, outhouses, garbage cans, a campground host, and no drinking water. Camping is $8.00 per night Sun.–Thurs. and $12.00 Fri.– Sat. nights.

To drive to Trout Creek, stay on U.S. Highway 97 north of its junction with Highway 26 at Madras. In 2.5 miles, turn left at the sign to Gateway and Trout Creek BLM. At the fork in 4 miles continue on straight to Gateway in another 4 miles. Turn right just after crossing the railroad tracks at the sign to Deschutes River and Trout Creek. The road down to Trout Creek can be extremely rough and slow-going. It's about 3 miles to the campground.

Access downstream of the campground is cut off by private property, but the east bank can be fished for the entire 7.5 miles back upstream to Mecca Flat. It's a good trail, suitable for mountain bikes and hikers. The trail begins at the far south end of Trout Creek Campground. Horse access is allowed for the first 5.5 miles upstream.

Trout Creek to Whitehorse Rapids

Once below Trout Creek Campground, boaters are committed to running Whitehorse Rapids, a dangerous, lengthy Class 4 rapid, capable of capsizing any craft. Whitehorse Rapids is 12 miles downstream from Trout Creek Campground. The next boat ramp below Trout Creek is 30 miles downstream. The only drive-in site between Trout Creek and Whitehorse is at South Junction, but several boat-in campsites lie along the river between Trout Creek and South Junction.

To drive to South Junction, take the gravel road west, just north of the junction of U.S. Highway 97 with U.S. Highway 197, 33 miles north of Madras. There is a small sign to "South Junction" at the turn. The road is about 10 miles long, cut precariously into a steep sidehill for the last few miles. At the bottom of the hill take the right fork to reach the campground in another .5 mile. The road dead-ends at private property. The campground has two outhouses, picnic tables, a few juniper trees, and charges $8.00 per night Sun.–Thurs. and $12.00 Fri.– Sat. Campsites are quite a distance above the river and on the "wrong" side of the tracks. There is about 1.5 miles of river access blocked above and below by private property. Some anglers walk the railroad tracks to reach more public land, technically trespassing but seldom enforced. At South Junction, poison ivy grows profusely and persists all the way to the Columbia. The next drive-in recreation site is 25 miles downstream from South Junction at Nena day-use area.

LEFT: The start of Whitehorse Rapids, a challenging two-mile section that is a workout for the oarsman. Photo courtesy Osprey Adventures

WHITEHORSE RAPIDS TO LOCKED GATE

From Whitehorse Rapids at river mile 76 to the locked gate at river mile 59, all sites are boat-in or hike-in only. At river mile 69, the Warm Springs Reservation ends, and fishing and camping are again allowed on BLM land along the west bank. This point is also the powerboat deadline and a boundary for changes in fishing regulations. Regulations upstream from the boundary are regular season with an extended steelhead season along the east bank only. Below the boundary the river is open year-round on both banks.

Many anglers walk up from the locked gate to fish. The road goes in 13 miles all the way to North Junction (Davidson) at river mile 73 but passes through mostly private land. Access to the river is limited from these points. Bicycles are not allowed on the road. In the first 9 miles, private and BLM land alternate with "Deschutes Club" property, so be careful to stay on the road when it is paralleled by private land. The 4 miles farthest upstream is all private property. The gate-keepers house, a few miles above the locked gate, has a register outside near the front door where one must sign in and out.

LOCKED GATE TO SHERARS FALLS

Locked Gate to Maupin

From the locked gate, the river is accessible by road all the way downstream to Macks Canyon, a total of 35 river miles. Eight miles of rough road parallel the river between the locked gate and Maupin. Whitewater between the locked gate and Maupin includes one Class 3 and one Class 4 rapids plus many other minor chutes.

Numerous BLM campgrounds lie along this part of the river, but none has drinking water. All charge $8.00 per night Sun.–Thurs. and $12.00 Fri.– Sat. to camp and have at least one outhouse, garbage cans, and a few tables. There is no campground at the locked gate. Nena Recreation Site is .8 mile below the gate, Devil's Canyon 2 miles below the gate, Long Bend 2.5 miles, Harpham Flat (CTWS) 3.5 miles, and Wapinitia is 4 miles from the gate and 3 miles from Highway 197. Most have launching areas. Harpham Flat is popular with rafters putting in for the drift to Maupin or Sherars Falls. Harpham Flat is the major take-out point for commercial drifters coming from

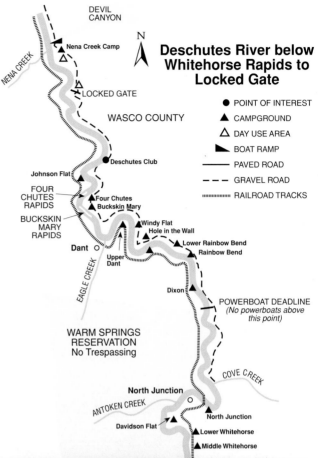

Deschutes River below
Whitehorse Rapids to
Locked Gate

● POINT OF INTEREST
▲ CAMPGROUND
△ DAY USE AREA
◣ BOAT RAMP
— PAVED ROAD
--- GRAVEL ROAD
.... RAILROAD TRACKS

DEVIL CANYON
NENA CREEK
Nena Creek Camp
LOCKED GATE
WASCO COUNTY
Deschutes Club
Johnson Flat
FOUR CHUTES RAPIDS
Four Chutes
Buckskin Mary
BUCKSKIN MARY RAPIDS
Windy Flat
Hole in the Wall
Dant
Lower Rainbow Bend
Rainbow Bend
Upper Dant
EAGLE CREEK
Dixon
POWERBOAT DEADLINE
(No powerboats above this point)
WARM SPRINGS RESERVATION
No Trespassing
COVE CREEK
North Junction
ANTOKEN CREEK
North Junction
Davidson Flat
Lower Whitehorse
Middle Whitehorse

LEFT TO RIGHT:
Penny Tolva, the publisher's sister, shows off her catch.
Indian Head rock formation on the lower Deschutes.
Scott Hughes, the publisher's nephew,
removes a rattlesnake from camp.
Photos by Geoff Hill

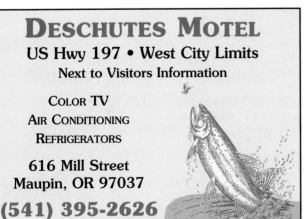

Warm Springs or Trout Creek and has five group sites.

Maupin is located on U.S. Highway 197 at its crossing of the Deschutes. From Portland, take U.S. Highway 26 and turn east on State Highway 216 between mileposts 71 and 72. Travel east 27 miles to the junction with Highway 197, turn right, and Maupin is 3 miles south. To get to the locked gate, continue through Maupin to the southern edge of town just south of The Oasis Resort and take a paved road to the right before going up the hill to leave town.

From Madras, take U.S. Highway 97 for 33 miles to the junction with Highway 197, continuing on Highway 197 another 22 miles to Maupin.

To get to Maupin from I-84 east of The Dalles, take U.S. Highway 197 south through Dufur (small community, some services) past the turn to Tygh Valley, reaching Maupin in 40 miles.

Maupin to Sherars Falls

The most popular whitewater section on the river is between Long Bend Recreation Site, 2.5 miles below the locked gate, to Sandy Beach (CTWS) above Sherars Falls. Trout and steelhead fishing is good between Maupin and Sherars Falls. The Falls is the best place to fish for chinook salmon. Maupin is a small town of 400 souls who cater to fishing and whitewater enthusiasts. Activity revolves around river recreation, and the town really hops during summer vacation. Maupin has gas, lodging, restaurants, guide services, groceries, taverns, a fly shop, shuttle service, and boat rentals. The only RV hookups on the entire lower river are at Maupin City Park for a cost of $16.00 a night on weekends, $14.00 weekdays. Tent camping is $10.00 a night for up to two tents and two vehicles, with additional charges for extra vehicles and people. The Park also has group sites for $50.00 a night, drinking water, and a

TOP: Boxcar Rapids on the lower Deschutes near Maupin.
BOTTOM: Sherars Falls. Photos by Geoff Hill

new dock available from April 1-October 31.

Downstream from Maupin, a paved road follows the river for 8 miles to Sherars Falls. From the south end of the bridge over the Deschutes in Maupin, take a paved road (Bakeoven Road) that runs along the east bank of the river to "Deschutes River Rec Area." In about .5 mile, past Maupin City Park, there is a left turn onto the Deschutes River Access Road which continues along the east bank to Sherars Falls. Sherars Falls and Bridge may also be reached from Grass Valley on Highway 97 by taking State Route 216 for 21 miles to the west, or from Tygh Valley on Highway 197 by driving State Route 216 east for 8 miles.

Oak Springs Hatchery, an access point on the west river bank, is reached by turning off Highway 197 about 3 miles north of the junction of 197 with State Route 216 west. It's about 3 miles to the hatchery, of which the first 2 miles are paved. Continue past the hatchery and park near the railroad tracks. Footpaths run both up and downstream.

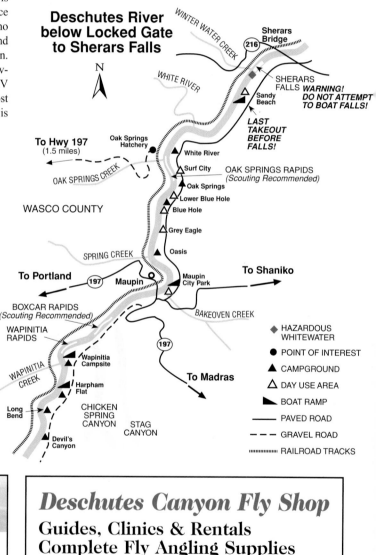

Deschutes River below Locked Gate to Sherars Falls

Among the many campgrounds and day-use sites between Maupin and Sherars Falls, Maupin City Park is the only site with full facilities. One mile downstream from the beginning of the access road, Oasis Recreation Site offers camping, outhouses, and garbage cans and charges a fee. There is no drinking water.

Grey Eagle, at 1.5 miles from the access road, is a small area for day-use only. Blue Hole, 3 miles below the beginning of the access road, provides camping and is set up specifically for handicapped access, with a ramp and platform from which the wheelchair-bound can fish. The outhouse and picnic areas are wheelchair accessible, as well. Handicapped anglers have priority.

Oak Springs Recreation Site and Oak Springs Rapid, a Class 4, is next at 3.5 miles. Some rafts take-out at Oak Springs Campground above the rapids.

CTWS-owned White River, at 5 miles, has a toilet, no water, tables, shade, or boat launch but has campsites. CTWS-owned Sandy Beach, at 6 miles, is a heavily used take-out point above Sherars Falls and has no overnight camping. There is a nice beach here and lots of room for rafts. Sherars Falls take-out (CTWS-owned), located .5 mile above Sherars Falls on the west bank, is now closed to the public.

Overnight parking for RVs and trailers is available at Sherars Bridge, but it's too rocky for tent camping. This site is also owned by CTWS. There are no tables or drinking water. Below Sherars Falls, the access road continues down the east bank to Macks Canyon, but it is a rough gravel road.

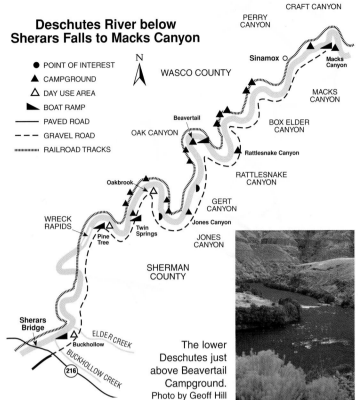

Deschutes River below Sherars Falls to Macks Canyon

- ● POINT OF INTEREST
- ▲ CAMPGROUND
- △ DAY USE AREA
- ◤ BOAT RAMP
- —— PAVED ROAD
- - - - GRAVEL ROAD
- ▪▪▪▪▪ RAILROAD TRACKS

The lower Deschutes just above Beavertail Campground. Photo by Geoff Hill

SHERARS FALLS TO MACKS CANYON

The primary use of the Sherars Falls area and the heaviest fishing pressure anywhere on the lower Deschutes occur during the chinook salmon runs. Some folks walk the railroad tracks to reach more river for other types of fishing. Otherwise, there is little use by anglers in this area. Less than a mile east of the falls on State Highway 216, a very rough gravel road, the Deschutes River Access Road, parallels the river for 18 miles to dead-end at Macks Canyon Recreation Site. From Sherars to the mouth, most anglers are after steelhead. Trout fishing is only fair. Prime time for steelhead is August to mid-October. At other times of the year, this stretch enjoys peace and quiet with anglers few and far between. The access road is notorious for eating tires; be prepared! Macks Canyon is a major destination for driftboats coming from Twin Springs and for jet boats coming upstream from the mouth.

There are two developed campgrounds in the 18 miles along the access road: Beavertail and Macks Canyon, but there are many other primitive campgrounds available. Buckhollow is located .5 mile from the junction with State Route 216 and this is the first boat put-in below

Sherars Falls. There are not any signs, no camping, and no facilities except a rough boat launch.

Pine Tree is next, 3 miles below the junction, and is a popular boat launch before the 1996 flood. Twin Springs, 4 miles from the junction, is the first campground and was developed in 1997 as a boat launch. Oakbrook, 6.5 miles down, has camping and no ramp. Jones Canyon, at 8 miles, has camping but no boat ramp, although some rafters use the bank at the far north end. Gert Canyon is at 8.5 miles, has camping and no ramp. Beavertail Recreation Site, 9.5 miles down the road, is a large campground with hand pumps for drinking water, a good gravel boat launch, and a sandy area for rafts. Rattlesnake Recreation Site has two sections separated by a gulch, 10.5 miles down the access road. Both parts offer camping but no boat ramp. Macks Canyon is at the end of the 18 miles of motor vehicle torture. It is the largest of the campgrounds, has a pressurized water system, wheelchair-accessible toilets, a day-use area, good gravel boat ramp, and lots of parking. All of the campgrounds mentioned previously have outhouses, garbage cans, and tables. The BLM has plans for many changes in these sites in the near future.

MACKS CANYON TO KLOAN

Macks Canyon to the Columbia has the lowest concentration of trout but is a very popular steelhead fishing area, especially for jet boaters. The heaviest fishing pressure is from July through October during the steelhead run. All boaters in this section, drifters and motorized, alike, need to be experienced. The next take-out is at the mouth 24 miles downstream from Macks Canyon, and several nasty rapids are in between. The only drive-in access is at Macks Canyon and 16 miles below at Kloan.

It is possible to continue below Macks along an abandoned railroad grade on foot or mountain bike all the way to the Columbia, but rockslides and gullies in the first 4 miles make the going tough. After 4 miles, the going is easy all the way to the mouth.

To get down to the river at Kloan, for the last 1.5 miles, it is recommended that you have a high-clearance vehicle with 4-wheel low and a surplus of intestinal fortitude. Don't even think about attempt-

A jet-boat charges upstream through Washout Rapids taking steelheaders to prime waters. Photo by Osprey Adventures

ing it after a good rain; it turns to slime. The simplest way in to Kloan is off Highway 197, east of The Dalles (services available at The Dalles). Get onto Fifteenmile Road heading east and paralleling I-84, following a sign for "Petersburg School" and passing The Inn at The Dalles. Three miles from the Highway 197 junction, the road forks; bear left. In 3.5 miles you pass through the town of Petersburg School, after nearly 9 miles, Fairbanks. At 12.5 miles, turn left onto graveled Fulton Road which forks in 1.5 miles, take the right fork. In another 2 miles, you arrive at the canyon rim. You may want to stop here and contemplate an imminent demise as you squint at the river nearly 1,000 feet below. The road reaches the river in a little over 1 mile, and at that point you may drive either upstream or down and park near the railroad tracks. Then it's a short hike to the river. Several footpaths head upstream and downstream. You can camp here, but there are no facilities.

KLOAN TO COLUMBIA RIVER

It is 7 river miles from Kloan to the mouth of the Deschutes. The only drive in access points are at Kloan, Heritage Landing, and Deschutes River State Park at the mouth. All other campsites are

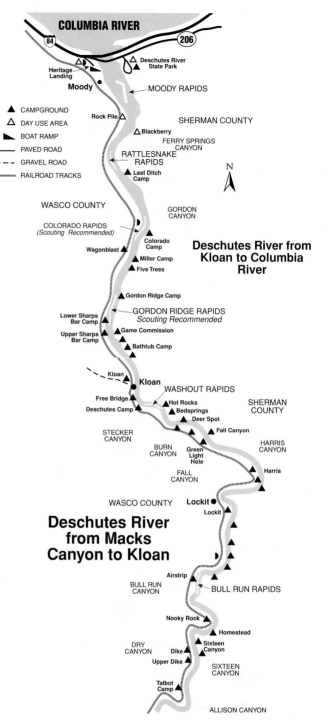

Deschutes River from Kloan to Columbia River

Deschutes River from Macks Canyon to Kloan

boat-, hike-, or bike-in from either the mouth or Macks Canyon. Trout fishing is only fair due to a smaller population, but the fish are more willing since they have much less pressure from anglers. From just above Kloan down to the Columbia River, the Deschutes falls through a series of serious rapids beginning with Class 4 Washout Rapids just above Kloan and continuing 2 miles below Kloan with Class 2+ Gordon Ridge Rapids. Colorado Rapids, a Class 3, is a mile below Gordon; Class 4 Rattlesnake Rapids comes up in another mile; and 2 miles farther is Moody Rapids, a Class 2. Then you're in The Dalles Pool.

At the mouth of the river there are two developed sites, one on each bank of the river. Both are managed by the Oregon State Parks and Recreation Department. The State Park is on the east bank, Heritage Landing, on the west bank. To reach these locations, drive to Biggs either from I-84 exit 97, or from Highway 97, following signs to Deschutes State Park. Biggs is a small town with some services. It can be very busy at the mouth during steelhead and salmon season.

The state park is a verdant campground with drinking water, toilets, garbage cans, grass and shade trees, and picnic areas. There is no boat ramp here; one should use Heritage Landing. The state park can accommodate motor homes up to 30 feet in length with electric hookups. Deschutes River State Park is open from mid-March to early November and can be continually full from July through October, depending on fishing success. The park is open for day use the rest of the year. There are 35 primitive campsites, stays are limited to 10 out of 14 days. The fee to camp is $12.00 a night for hookup, $5.00 for primitive. From May through October fees are: $16.00 for hookup, $8.00 for primitive. Access to the river upstream from the State Park is excellent for 20 miles. Access via hiking, mountain biking, and limited horseback riding is allowed.

ABOVE: The Deschutes changes faces around every bend. Photo by Brian O'Keefe

Heritage Landing is the take-out for drifters and the put-in for jet boats. There is a 5 mph boat speed limit in this area. The ramp can be extremely busy, so courtesy is a must. Rafters should use the adjacent beach and not the concrete ramp. There is a 15-minute maximum allowed for loading and unloading. The Landing has coin-op scat disposal machine ($1.00 fee), flush toilets, and parking for trailers and day-use. Camping is not allowed. There is a poorly maintained trail upstream from the day-use parking lot. Many anglers walk up the railroad tracks to their favorite spots.

RIGHT: Scott Hughes, the publisher's nephew, proudly displays his dandy, "contest winning," Deschutes steelhead! Photo by Geoff Hill

ABOVE: The publisher, Geoff Hill, displays his "runner-up" steelie. Photo by Scott Hughes

METOLIUS RIVER

Size:	23 miles in length
Depth:	varies; maintains constant flow
Main Catch:	rainbow & bull trout, kokanee, whitefish
Best Methods:	fly fishing
Season:	entire year; check OSFR
Best Time:	late April through early July
Tips:	catch-and-release of all fish

The Metolius River basin is an exceptional collection of lush meadows, gushing springs, robust riparian zones, giant ponderosa pines, raging rapids, basalt canyons, transparent, turquoise-colored water, and huge, native bull trout. Spring-fed, the Metolius maintains constant temperatures, flow, and superb water quality in a stable channel. It supports a tremendous variety of insects. One of the most beautiful areas in Central Oregon, the Metolius is mainly a fly fisher's stream. Fishing is good year-round. This river takes time to learn but offers substantial rewards. Catch-and-release of all wild fish is required throughout the length of the river.

The Metolius supports wild rainbow trout, wild bull trout, a few brook and brown trout, whitefish, kokanee, and chinook salmon. All age classes of rainbow trout are present. Wild rainbow average 8 to 16 inches, with many as big as 3 to 5 pounds and a few even larger. Bull trout range up to 15 pounds, averaging 5 to 6 pounds. Brook trout are rare, very small, and mainly in the uppermost 5 miles of the river. Native whitefish are fairly abundant throughout the river. A spawning run of kokanee enters the river in September from Lake Billy Chinook. Since the mid-1990s, stocks of chinooks have been reestablished in the river. Currently, fish passage around Round Butte Dam is being examined. It is hoped that, someday, Metolius chinook will once again run to the ocean and return to spawn.

Heavy stocking of rainbow trout in the Metolius River ended in 1996. The river is now managed entirely for wild fish. Small native rainbow are common in the easily wadable section from Lake Creek to Camp Sherman. Elsewhere, look around bridges, under bank cover, and near in-stream structure. Some of the most productive patterns are Comparadun, Clarks Stone, Elk Hair Caddis, Green Drake, Flying Ant, Blue Dun, Renegade, beadhead nymphs, Olive Hare's Ear, Zug Bug, Golden Stone, October Caddis, Serendipity, Sparkle Pupa, and Woolly Bugger. Try streamers for the larger fish, quarter downstream and retrieve slowly with occasional twitches. Keep streamers on the bottom with a fast sink tip line. Zonkers, Matukas, Stovepipes, white or black Deceivers, and variations on Muddlers are all good streamer choices.

The larger, wild rainbow trout prefer the deeper spots in the river, like Popcorn Hole below the Camp Sherman bridge, the deep pool where Canyon Creek enters, and the Idiot Hole 150 yards upstream from Wizard Falls Bridge on the east bank. Bank cover and bank structure are very important habitat for all fish in the Metolius, particularly since there is little cover mid-stream. Bridges also offer an agreeable environment. No fishing is allowed within 100 feet of the Camp Sherman Bridge.

Bull trout are known to lurk beneath underwater ledges and logs and under heavy bank cover, waiting to ambush rainbow and whitefish. These piscivorous char will take a 10-inch streamer and the same size natural. The bull trout can be found throughout the river, and fishing for them is best at the Dolly Hole, Canyon Creek inflow, and Allingham Bridge. Articulated flies, sculpins, and big streamers of all kinds, size 2/0 to 6, are most commonly used.

Brown trout populations are low in the Metolius, and these trout are seldom fished for specifically. More and more brown trout are being caught in the upper river, between the Camp Sherman Campground and the Camp Sherman Bridge.

Brook trout numbers are very small as are the fish, most no larger than 8 inches in length. They can be caught on dries and nymphs.

Native whitefish are found throughout the river and are usually taken on small weighted nymphs. Winter angling for whitefish can be excellent.

Fishing for aggressive male kokanee in the

A nice Metolius rainbow.
Brian O'Keefe Photo

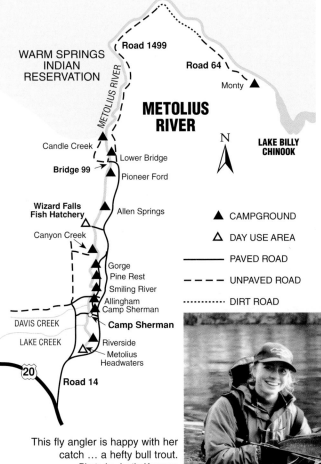

WARM SPRINGS
INDIAN
RESERVATION

Road 1499

Road 64

Monty

METOLIUS
RIVER

N

LAKE BILLY
CHINOOK

Candle Creek
Lower Bridge
Bridge 99
Pioneer Ford
**Wizard Falls
Fish Hatchery**
Allen Springs
Canyon Creek
Gorge
Pine Rest
Smiling River
Allingham
Camp Sherman
Camp Sherman
DAVIS CREEK
LAKE CREEK
Riverside
Metolius
Headwaters
20
Road 14

METOLIUS RIVER

▲ CAMPGROUND
△ DAY USE AREA
—— PAVED ROAD
- - - UNPAVED ROAD
······· DIRT ROAD

This fly angler is happy with her
catch ... a hefty bull trout.
Photo by Justin Karnopp

fall can be a lot of fun with bright flies
as the fly fisher's best bet.

The Metolius emerges as a small
wadable river from springs at the base of Black Butte and flows
about 23 miles to Lake Billy Chinook. Shorelines are primarily composed of brushy banks with forest behind. There are some weeds in
the river and a few small islands. The river follows mainly one channel. There are many good spots to fish from shore, and in many
stretches, bank-fishing is the only option. Where possible, wade into
the river to escape grabby vegetation and cast toward the opposite
shore.

Regulations require that all fish must be released unharmed. No
fishing is allowed from a floating device. Special seasons apply to
specific sections on the Metolius. The river above Allingham Bridge
is open the Saturday of Memorial Day weekend through October 31,
fly-angling-only with barbless hooks and catch-and-release for all
fish. Below Allingham Bridge the river is open the entire year. The
same fly-angling-only requirement to Bridge 99. Below Bridge 99,
flies and lures are allowed. This stretch is also catch-and-release for
all fish. Anglers should always check the current OSFR before fishing as there may be additional special regulations for the Metolius.

A wide variety of hatches occur on the Metolius. Midges hatch year-
round, and there are Blue-winged Olives and hatches of small caddis in
the middle of winter. Other mayfly and caddis species emerge in
warmer months, and stoneflies in late spring and early summer. Popular hatches include a size 14 to 16 March Brown from February through
April, and Green Drakes in sizes 6 to 10 from late May through early
July. Golden Stones and Salmonflies in sizes 6 and 8 produce explosive
surface takes mid-summer. Little Summer Stones and Yellow Sallys,
sizes 14 to 16, hatch from August to the first week in October. Don't forget ants and hoppers during the warm summer months. Up-to-date hatch
information is available from The Fly Fisher's Place in Sisters and the
Camp Sherman Store and Fly Shop in Camp Sherman.

For the sake of explanation, the river is often divided into three
sections, one from Lake Creek to Canyon Creek, the second from
Canyon Creek to Bridge 99, and the last from Bridge 99 to Lake
Billy Chinook, but even within these sections there is a great variety
of water types. The most popular section of
the river is the 10-mile stretch from Lake
Creek to Bridge 99.

Lake Creek to Canyon Creek: This stretch
is the easiest to wade. Some very large, wild
fish hang out between Lake Creek and Camp
Sherman. No angling is allowed within 100
feet of the Camp Sherman Bridge. There is
some private property along the west bank in
the Camp Sherman area. Camp Sherman to
Allingham is heavily fished, and,
downstream, Allingham Bridge is a popular
and very productive spot. Below Gorge
Campground, the river is bordered by private
land on both banks for .5 mile, but then
Forest Service land continues from Lower Canyon Creek
Campground on downstream. Allingham Bridge is mid-way
between Lake Creek and Canyon Creek.

Canyon Creek to Bridge 99: "The canyon" is the most isolated
area in this length of the river. Accessible only by trail, the canyon
starts at Lower Canyon Creek Campground and ends just above
Wizard Falls Hatchery. It is accessible from trails on both banks,
most easily from downstream. There is good fishing for 10- to 13-
inch wild fish in this stretch. The river gains size, depth, and
strength from Canyon Creek, and wading becomes difficult to
impossible. A .75-mile stretch above Pioneer Ford Campground is
bordered by private property.

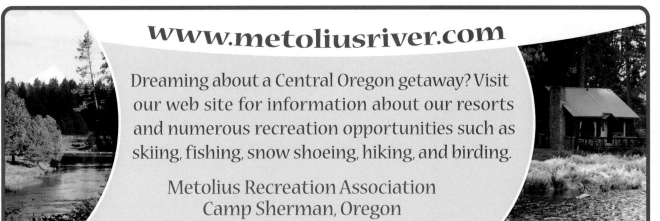

Bridge 99 to Lake Billy Chinook: Heavy water predominates from Bridge 99 to the mouth. Angling is difficult, but there are some nice fish. Good lies are few and far between, and 4-wheel drive and bushwhacking skills may be required. At Bridge 99, Forest Route 1499 (walk-in or bike-in only) begins where the pavement ends and runs downstream on the east side of the river for about 11 miles to its end at a trailhead. The trail continues for 2 miles along the river to connect with County Route 64, 6 miles from Monty Campground and Lake Billy Chinook. Candle Creek Campground is located on the west side of the river and is accessed by crossing Bridge 99 and following the unpaved road. Just north of the campground, the Warm Springs Indian Reservation occupies most of the west bank, and access is denied.

Artificial flies and lures are legal in this stretch, and, in this fast-moving section of the river, compact, heavy lures work best. Try FlatFish, Wobble Rites, Mepps, Super Dupers, and maybe even Rapalas.

Excellent camping facilities in old growth ponderosa pines exist along much of the river. Heading downstream from the headwaters, the Forest Service campgrounds are Riverside, Camp Sherman, Allingham, Smiling River, Pine Rest, Gorge, Canyon Creek, Allen Springs, Pioneer Ford, Lower Bridge, Candle Creek and finally, Monty Campground, about a mile upstream from Lake Billy Chinook. A store, gasoline, and fly shop are available in Camp Sherman; and several motels, resorts, and RV parks are situated in Camp Sherman.

The Metolius is an excellent family recreation area. Non-fishing options include visiting The Head of the Metolius, a gorgeous area, or the Wizard Falls Hatchery to view brook trout, brown trout, rainbow trout, cutthroat, kokanee, large Atlantic Salmon, and huge brood trout. The Metolius basin is also a beautiful area for camping, hiking, and mountain biking.

To reach the Metolius River from Bend take U.S. Highway 20 west through Sisters.

Ten miles west of Sisters turn right onto County Route 14 following signs to Camp Sherman and the Metolius River.

From the Willamette Valley take U.S. Highway 20 east over Santiam Pass. The turn to Camp Sherman is about 12 miles east of Hoodoo Ski Area. Once on County Route 14 it's about 4 miles to the turn to the headwaters, 5 miles to the Camp Sherman Bridge, 10 miles downstream to Wizard Falls Hatchery, and 14 miles downstream to Bridge 99.

ABOVE: The Metolius River is a beautiful stream with many islands of colorful vegetation.
Photo by Geoff Hill

BELOW: Churning rapids magically reflect an aqua blue at Wizard Falls.
Photo by Brian O'Keefe

CROOKED RIVER

Size:	main stem over 100 miles in length
Depth:	levels fluctuate
Main Catch:	inland redband trout, whitefish
Best Methods:	fly fishing, spinners, bait-plunking & drifting (check bait limitations)
Season:	entire year; check OSFR
Best Time:	when water temp. 40°F
Tips:	fishing best between mileposts (MP) 12 & 19 on State Hwy 27

The scenery is awesome along the Crooked River. Photo by Scott Staats

The Crooked River experience is one of rugged, dramatic canyons, enthusiastic fish, Wild and Scenic tracts, bald eagles and kingfishers, and cool, spring-fed headwaters. The river maintains a wild feeling, even in the most popular sections. Well-known locally for dependable fishing and routine rattlesnake sightings, this comparatively small river produces and supports excellent populations of trout and whitefish. In 1984, the Crooked River yielded the runner-up state record inland redband trout of 4 pounds, 9 ounces.

The main stem, formed by the South Fork and North Fork, flows over 100 miles northwest to Lake Billy Chinook and is a major tributary to the Deschutes River. In general, you will find a variety of deep pools, shallow riffles, rocky shorelines, and channels full of boulders and cobbles throughout the length of the Crooked River. A few meadow portions are the only exceptions. Water levels fluctuate with spring runoff and the irrigation season.

The North Fork of the Crooked River originates in the Ochoco Mountains 75 miles east of Prineville. Angling is fair for wild rainbow trout. The South Fork of the Crooked River begins about 60 miles east of Bend. It has been stocked annually since 1981 with Deschutes redsides and also contains a few smallmouth bass and brown bullheads. The South Fork is open only to angling with artificial flies and lures and has a 2 trout per day catch limit for trout, open to angling the Saturday of Memorial Day weekend through October 31. Check the regulations for details. The North and South Fork meet along the Post-Paulina Highway about 25 miles east of Prineville. From this point downstream to Prineville Reservoir, the river is severely affected by overgrazing and irrigation withdrawals and support only skimpy numbers of smallmouth bass and brown bullheads. Access is limited, as the river is almost entirely bordered by private land.

Without a doubt, the best fishing on the river is in the 8 miles below Bowman Dam and Prineville Reservoir. Here, the Crooked

ABOVE: The scenic highway 27 follows the Crooked River up to Bowman Dam. Photo by Geoff Hill.

RIGHT: Rainbow trout are the dominant species here. All are wild except a few escapees from Prineville Reservoir.
Photo courtesy Sunriver Fly Shop

LEFT: The silt-colored water does not affect the fishing, however, the spectacular scenery can be a distraction to anglers. Photo by Geoff Hill

BELOW: Surprise! This fish didn't want to have its picture taken. Photo courtesy flyandfield.com

CENTER: Mike Lunn holds 18" whitefish. Photo by Scott Staats

BOTTOM (left to right): A youngster has fly fishing success. Chimney Rock in background. It can be a family affair on the Crooked River. Photos courtesy flyandfield.com

River is a rich, thriving, tailrace fishery and a designated Wild and Scenic River. Don't be discouraged by the off-color water caused by fine sediment from the reservoir; it doesn't slow the fishing down. Rainbow trout are the dominant species here, combined with whitefish and occasional bass and bullhead fugitives from the reservoir. All are wild fish except for escapees through the dam. The average trout caught is 8 to 11 inches, with many from 12 to 14 inches and a few up to 19 inches. There is a nice variety of riffles, runs, pocket water, and deep pools in this stretch. The grassy, rocky shoreline generally supplies sufficient casting room. Wading is tough, slippery, with many sneaky "tripper" rocks. Weed beds and algae can frustrate the angler at times.

Paved State Highway 27 parallels the river for the 19 miles from Prineville south to Bowman Dam. The area from Milepost 12 to the dam above Milepost 19 is the most popular fishing stretch on the Crooked River, and it is all BLM land. Water levels are lowest in the winter while Prineville Reservoir is filled and highest from mid-April to mid-October during the irrigation season. Another chunk of public land lies around MP 8.

Open year-round, the river has sections that may be frozen in winter. From the Saturday of Memorial Day weekend through October 31, the catch limit is 2 trout per day with an 8-inch minimum length and no more than 1 over 20 inches. Bait may be used during this period. During the rest of the year, the river is open only to fishing for trout with artificial flies and lures; no bait is allowed during this time.

Angling is closed for 150 feet downstream from Bowman Dam.

Angling is usually excellent whenever water temperatures are above 40°F. Still-fishing and drifting bait through slower sections of the river are the most popular methods during the regular season, but fly fishing is coming up fast and is virtually the only method used during the catch-and-release season. Bait anglers commonly use Power Bait, cheese, or single eggs on size 14 hooks. Bait is most successful during turbid, high water. Spinners can be particularly productive in late summer, casting into deep pools. Fly fishers have good luck with scud imitations, bead-head nymphs, and attractor dry flies through most of the year. Midge hatches occur all winter, and there are some excellent caddis and mayfly hatches during the warmer months.

The stretch of river from Prineville west to U.S. Highway 97 is entirely private land. From Highway 97 to Lake Billy Chinook, there are plentiful public grasslands and BLM land, but the river lies at the bottom of a very deep, steep canyon. Access is limited by this terrain and a lack of roads. The water holds mainly rainbow and an abundance of whitefish in the same size range as in the river below Bowman Dam. Around Smith Rock State Park, there are a lot of rough fish but a little farther downstream, springs kick in to cool the water and support a good trout population again. Below Opal Springs, the river begins to pick up species from Lake Billy Chinook.

Most campsites along the Crooked River are primitive, except for the profusion of BLM campgrounds below Bowman Dam. Only one of these has drinking water. All have outhouses and garbage cans, and all charge a fee to camp.

The Crooked River is most easily reached from Highway 27 south of Prineville and along the Post-Paulina Highway east of Prineville. With maps, time for exploration, and 4-wheel drive, you can find your way to the North and South Forks and to the canyon section between Highway 97 and Lake Billy Chinook through the Crooked River Ranch development north of Terrebonne. To reach Prineville see directions to Prineville Reservoir (page 55).

BELOW: A spectacular view of the Crooked River downstream from Smith Rock State Park. Photo by Melinda Allen

RIGHT: This angler enjoys a pleasant winter day fishing on the Crooked River. Photo by Brian O'Keefe

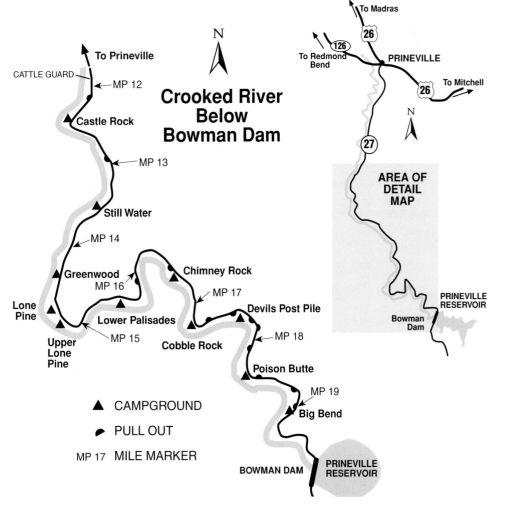

N

Crooked River Below Bowman Dam

To Prineville

CATTLE GUARD

MP 12

Castle Rock

MP 13

Still Water

MP 14

Greenwood
MP 16

Chimney Rock

MP 17

Lone Pine

Lower Palisades

Devils Post Pile

MP 18

Upper Lone Pine

MP 15

Cobble Rock

Poison Butte

MP 19

Big Bend

BOWMAN DAM

PRINEVILLE RESERVOIR

▲ CAMPGROUND

◣ PULL OUT

MP 17 MILE MARKER

To Madras

26

126

To Redmond Bend

PRINEVILLE

26 To Mitchell

N

27

AREA OF DETAIL MAP

PRINEVILLE RESERVOIR

Bowman Dam

FALL RIVER

Size:	8 miles long; 25´-50´ wide
Depth:	water levels fluctuate
Main Catch:	rainbow, brook & brown trout; whitefish
Best Methods:	fly fishing only with barbless hooks
Season:	entire year above falls; check OSFR
Best Time:	evenings; June, July, August
Tips:	access easiest in the 2 miles above and below hatchery

Fall River is a crystal clear spring-creek — its banks lined by meadows and lodge-pole pine, and its water punctuated by a wonderful waterfall. The river is open to fly fishing with barbless hooks. Fall River is an outstanding contributor of brown trout to the Deschutes River and provides excellent winter habitat for numerous species. Its pristine water supports a productive hatchery and contributes invaluable water quality to the Deschutes system. Legal size rainbow trout are stocked several times a year and merge with the naturally reproducing brook, brown, and rainbow trout. Native whitefish inhabit the river below the falls.

Fall River is located in the Deschutes National Forest close to Bend and is a very popular fly fishing stream. Emerging full-size from rushing springs, it flows east 8 miles through rolling pine forest and empties into the Deschutes River between Sunriver and LaPine. The water is very clear and cold year-round, with steady flows and temperatures. The river has a variety of depth and structure and averages 25 to 50 feet across. Some willows line the banks. The streambed is mainly of fine pumice, easy to wade, but it can be very soft in places. Many downed

TOP: Fall River holds some beauties!

ABOVE: A fat rainbow caught and released.
Photos by Brian O'Keefe

RIGHT: A calm, picturesque section of Fall River. Photo by Geoff Hill

logs in the river provide cover for the trout, and weedbeds provide insect habitat. Half of Fall River's 8 miles are bordered by private property and the remainder by National Forest land. Most of the private land is along the lower 4 miles of the stream. Watch carefully for "No Trespassing" signs and be prepared for ravenous mosquitoes.

Wild brook trout in Fall River average less than 8 inches in length. Brown trout to 8 pounds have been pulled out of Fall River, although the average catch will run up to 10 inches, and anglers will probably catch many in the 6- to 8-inch range. Rainbow trout average 8 to 12 inches, with an occasional hold-over to 20 inches. Rainbows over 20 inches are defined as steelhead in streams and must be released. Whitefish are typically 6 to 12 inches.

Evening is usually the best time to fish, and June, July, and August are the most popular months. Catch limits are 2 trout per day with an 8-inch minimum length and no more than one over 20 inches. Fall River, above the falls, is open to angling year-round. Downstream from the falls, the river is only open from the Saturday of Memorial Day weekend to September 30. There is no limit on size or number of brook trout or whitefish. Always check the current OSFR before fishing.

Successful dry-fly patterns for Fall River include Adams, Renegade, Comparadun, Blue-winged Olive, and Elk Hair Caddis. For wets, Pheasant Tail, Hare's Ear, Sparkle Pupa, Zug Bugs, and soft hackles are most effective. Long, light leaders are required to catch

Blue-winged Olive   RS2 Emerger

fish here. The most popular and most easily accessible fishing area on the river is the stretch 2 miles above and 2 miles below the hatchery. Access is easy at Fall River Hatchery and from Forest Route 42 upstream from the hatchery. Catching is tough farther upstream around the campground. There are some good areas below the falls but also an abundance of private property. Be sure to fish undercut banks thoroughly wherever they occur.

Fall River Campground, a Forest Service campground, is the only campground on Fall River. Many others are located nearby along the Deschutes River. Fall River Campground has a picnic area, outhouses, no drinking water, and a fee to camp. Other recreation options in the area include hiking, visiting the hatchery, picnicking, hunting, bird watching, and wildlife viewing.

To find Fall River take the Fall River turn from U.S. Highway 97 18 miles south of Bend and about 14 miles north of LaPine, then follow signs to South Century Drive and County/Forest Route 42. One can turn onto Forest Route 4360 about 3 miles west of the Deschutes River to access Fall River near the falls. Route 42 first parallels the river at Fall River Fish Hatchery about 8 miles west of Highway 97. From the Eugene area via Willamette Pass, follow directions to North Twin Lake (page 90), but instead of turning into the Twin Lakes continue on Route 42 another 10 miles to Fall River Campground.

ABOVE: Approach and presentation are important when fishing such clear water.
Photo by Brian O'Keefe

LEFT: Before it empties into the Deschutes River between Sunriver and LaPine, this crystal clear spring creek shows a variety of personalities, from calm, quiet water, to riffles and rapids, to a wonderful waterfall.
Photo by Geoff Hill

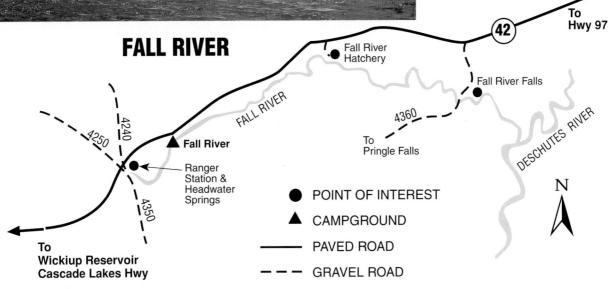

FALL RIVER

Fall River Hatchery

Fall River Falls

42

To Hwy 97

FALL RIVER

4360

To Pringle Falls

4250   4240

▲ Fall River

Ranger Station & Headwater Springs

4350

To
**Wickiup Reservoir
Cascade Lakes Hwy**

DESCHUTES RIVER

N

● POINT OF INTEREST

▲ CAMPGROUND

—— PAVED ROAD

- - - GRAVEL ROAD

LITTLE DESCHUTES RIVER

Size:	approx. 100 miles long
Depth:	water levels fluctuate
Main Catch:	rainbow, brook, & brown trout; whitefish
Best Methods:	shore fishing, floating
Season:	check OSFR
Best Time:	early and late in day; early in season
Tips:	access limited by private land; best fishing from headwaters to Crescent

The Little Deschutes River begins north of Miller Lake in the Mt. Thielsen Wilderness and flows nearly 100 miles northeast to merge with the big Deschutes River, 15 miles south of Bend. The Little Deschutes is greatly impacted by irrigation withdrawals from Crescent Creek downstream. The best fishing can be found from the headwaters to the town of Crescent. The Forest Service portion is in the best condition, supporting wild rainbow and brook trout, whitefish, and, below Highway 58, brown trout. Ninety percent of the river is bordered by private land.

Brown trout to 18 inches can be found in the lower river with the average catch 6 to 10 inches in length. Rainbow trout, scattered throughout the length of the river in small numbers, run a maximum of 10 to 12 inches in length. Brookies up to 10 inches are found mainly near the headwaters. Crayfish and whitefish are also present.

Fishing season on the Little Deschutes is open from the Saturday of Memorial Day weekend through October 31. Fishing is by all methods including bait. The catch limit is 2 trout, 8-inch minimum and only one over 20 inches. There is no limit on size or number of brook trout or whitefish.

Fishing early in the season and early and late in the day is the best time for catching the brown trout in this river. Small lures can be very productive. Use a careful approach to the browns under banks; the vibrations of your footsteps can spook them. Flies work well for rainbow and brookies in the headwaters and are excellent in the evening for browns farther downstream.

The Little Deschutes is a small, slow, meandering stream with a lot of undercut banks. The headwaters are the most wadable. The lower river has a soft bottom, beaver channels, side meander channels, and some very deep pools. Water levels fluctuate with the irrigation season from Crescent Creek, downstream. The water is tannic stained. Marshy areas border much of the river, and many areas are affected by bank erosion caused by overgrazing, but there are also some healthy, thickly vegetated riparian areas. Mosquitoes can be horrendous. The river is paralleled by roads for most of its length and is flanked mainly by private land. Many homes are situated along the river.

Anglers should ask permission to fish from private property. The upper river above the town of Crescent has the least private land. Much of this stretch of the river has good road access north and south of Highway 58. Floating the river is legal, even through private land, and would be the easiest way to fish the river. Unfortunately, put-in and take-out points are restrictively far apart.

The Forest Service's Rosland Campground, a small campground and picnic area with no drinking water and a fee, is the only official campground on the Little Deschutes and is situated about 2 miles north of LaPine. In addition to fishing and camping, the area offers opportunities for bird watching, especially in the spring, a little hunting, trapping, and wildlife viewing. The slow current here is great for floating, swimming, and canoeing.

The upper section of the Little Deschutes River is crossed by State Highway 58, 15 miles southeast of Crescent Lake. Forest roads follow the stream toward its headwaters, and many roads off of Highway 58 and 97 parallel the river downstream to its junction with the Deschutes. Heading south from Bend on U.S. Highway 97 the first public access to the river will be 30 miles south at Rosland Campground, 2 miles west of highway 97 on Route 43. From the south and from Willamette Pass the river can be reached where Highway 58 crosses it, 15 miles southeast of Crescent Lake and 5 miles west of the junction of Highway 58 and Highway 97.

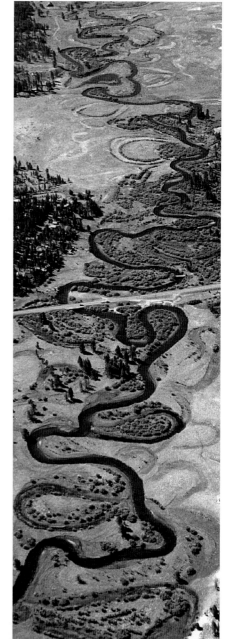

RIGHT: The Little Deschutes flows and meanders and winds 100 miles to join the Deschutes River. Photo by Jim Horyza

BELOW: The river has a lot of undercut banks and a soft bottom.
Photo courtesy Thousand Trails Campground

CREEKS

CENTRAL OREGON CREEKS

Central Oregon has a shortage of healthy, productive creeks. Most small streams here suffer severely from irrigation withdrawals and overgrazing and contain only small fish, at best. Increasing numbers of creeks are closed permanently to protect vital spawning and rearing areas. All are managed for wild fish. Habitat work continues on several important creeks, and efforts to provide better flows are on the rise. Check with ODFW and local fishing tackle outlets for more information about the water you are interested in fishing.

Most creeks are open during the regular angling season, from the Saturday of Memorial Day weekend through October 31, and have a trout catch limit of 2 per day, 8-inch minimum length, with no more than one over 20 inches. Rainbow over 20 inches in streams are considered steelhead and must be released. Many have special regulations, including decreased catch limits and special closures. Be sure to check the current Oregon Sport Fishing Regulations before fishing, since the regulations are continually changing.

BEST BETS:

Tumalo Creek – An excellent stream of great value to Central Oregon fisheries, it has good populations of wild brookies, rainbow and a few brown trout. Thirty miles of abundant, small hungry trout provide excellent fly fishing. Most of the stream is accessible, with road access possible in the burn area, 10 miles west of Bend, and from Shevlin Park, northwest of Bend. Lunkers are 10 inches in length. Tumalo Creek is now open the entire year and is restricted to artificial flies and lures only. Continuing habitat work on the stream insures excellent water quality and fish producing capabilities. Tumalo Creek currently has a reduced catch limit of 2 trout per day, 8-inch minimum. There is no limit on brook trout or whitefish.

Big Marsh Creek – A very stable stream fed by both springs and snow melt, it holds brown trout, whitefish, and small populations of rainbow and brook trout. Located 8 miles south of Crescent Lake, the creek features difficult access through marshy, brushy, and lodgepole-lined banks. Big Marsh is also a recipient of rehabilitation efforts.

Crescent Creek – This outlet of Crescent Lake is also the major tributary to the Little Deschutes River. It is a nice fly fishing stream with good access. It once had a good population of big, wild brown and rainbow trout; fish numbers are currently very low. Irrigation withdrawals leave merely a dribble of water in the creek in the fall. Brown trout are found mainly in the lower stretches of the creek and the rainbow in faster water. White-fish also populate the creek. Access is available from State Highway 58. Watch for private land. The best fishing for rainbow trout is in the riffles and pools of the canyon section east of State Highway 58. Heavy brush lines the stream from Crescent Creek Campground downstream.

LIMITED POTENTIAL:

Tributaries to Wickiup Reservoir – Browns Creek and Davis Creek. Browns Creek is now closed to angling.

Crane Prairie Tributaries – Cultus Creek, Deer Creek, Cultus River, Quinn River, and Snow Creek. Check OSFR.

Metolius Tributaries – Lake Creek and Spring Creek open to angling. All others are closed to angling. Check OSFR.

Crooked River system – Ochoco Creek, Mill Creek, Deep Creek, Marks Creek.

Odell Creek, Check OSFR. Open Memorial Day Weekend – Oct. 31.

Paulina Creek, tributary to Little Deschutes River.

Squaw Creek, Deschutes River tributary.

Three Creek, outlet of Three Creek Lake.

John Day, Klamath, and Malheur Basin Creeks

Quite literally there are more creeks than you can shake a stick at in the John Day, Klamath and Malheur basins. The John Day basin alone probably has 50 fishable creeks. The challenge, as always, is access. Many creeks flow through checkerboards of public and private property. Check with BLM, Forest Service and Fish & Wildlife for detailed maps and specific information. Respect private property boundaries. If in doubt, ask the nearest landowner for permission. Asking permission has become a lost art. It so impresses landowners they may invite you on to some amazing private fisheries. And that's what creek fishing is all about; exploring new areas, catching lots of uneducated fish, and rediscovering oneself amidst the beauty that is unique to small streams. For pure harvest and great eating, help ODFW eradicate brook trout by keeping all you want. Limits on brook trout have been rescinded in most streams to eliminate competition with native species. Make sure you know the difference between brook and bull trout, which must be released. What follows are descriptions of a few of the creeks that intrigued us while expanding Fishing Central Oregon into the John Day, Klamath, and Malheur basins.

Spring Creek (Klamath County) – This gorgeous spring-fed creek flowing past the Collier Rest Area on Highway 97, located 5 miles north of Chiloquin is a very productive fishing hole. Sixteen-thousand legal size rainbow trout are planted annually. They respond readily to drifted worms and salmon eggs; flies and lures are also good. Large native trout are present in the fall. Good trails run along both sides of the creek from the headwaters 2 miles downstream to the confluence with the Williamson. Regulations change in the Williamson so watch for the deadline between the creek and the river. Season is late May until Oct. 31. Limit is 5 trout, 1 over 20 inches. Collier State Park Campground and historic logging museum are next door.

Fourmile Creek (Klamath County) This creek is a very good trout stream flowing into Agency Lake offering a variety of trout, terrain and water types. Paved 3334 road and trail 3703 follow the creek from its source in the Sky Lakes Wilderness, offering good access to brook trout in the upper mountainous reaches. Below Nicholson Road, catch-and-release, flies and lure only regulations protect trophy size rainbow and brown trout in a meandering meadow stream environment. The creek is west of Fort Klamath on Nicholson Road and is open the entire year, one trout per day, no limit on brook trout.

Kiger Creek (Harney County) This offers an opportunity to explore the stunning Kiger Gorge on Steens Mountain, and catch native redside rainbows while doing it. Access is by hiking down from Steens Mountain Loop Rd. or up from Diamond Grain Camp Rd. Good lure and fly fishing are available as is rugged, remote but beautiful desert country for those who like to get away from it all. Similar opportunities await in most Steens Mountain canyons. Season is late May-Oct. 31. Limit is 5 trout, 1 over 20 inches.

Bridge Creek (Wheeler County) This creek offers spotty fishing but tremendous scenic variety from the north slope of the Ochocos to the impressive Painted Hills near Mitchell to its confluence with the John Day River. Best angling is after spring run-off in May and June. Standard regulations apply.

Canyon Creek (Grant County) Here, a productive, accessible rainbow trout stream flowing from the Strawberry Mountains into the John Day River at the city of John Day is available. Highway 395, forest roads 15 and 1520 provide access its entire 27-mile length. Wild trout are available above Canyon Meadows Reservoir; mostly planted fish below. Open to all methods with bait most effective until flows drop. Season is late May-Oct. 31. Stream regulations apply.

CRANE PRAIRIE RESERVOIR

Size: over 5 sq. miles
Depth: 11´ avg.; deep channels; water levels fluctuate
Main Catch: rainbow & brook trout, largemouth bass
Best Methods: still-fishing with bait, fly fishing, casting lures
Season: general trout; 4th Sat. in April to Oct. 31; check OSFR
Best Time: variable, depending on weather & water levels
Tips: best access with boat

Over the last 50 years, Crane Prairie Reservoir has produced more big trout than any other body of water in Central Oregon. At Crane Prairie, the angler can put a variety of fishing techniques to good use. And the payoff can be spectacular with rainbow, brook trout, and abundant largemouth bass measured by the pound, not by the inch.

In 1928 the upper Deschutes River was dammed below a meadow named Crane Prairie, forming a reservoir which currently covers over 5 square miles. Trees, previously bordering the channels of the Deschutes, Cultus, and Quinn rivers, were left standing as the reservoir filled and now occupy about 10% of the water's surface as silvered snags. The abundance of deadwood and comparatively shallow water has created an extremely rich environment for insects and plentiful cover for the resident rainbow, brook trout, and largemouth bass, creating an outstanding and unique fishery. One of the largest species of this bird sanctuary, the sandhill crane, for which the area was named, continue to nest here.

Rainbow trout are stocked in Crane Prairie Reservoir every spring. Rainbow trout here can grow up to 2 inches a month during the summer. The largest rainbows extracted from the reservoir push 19 pounds,

LEFT: A fly fisher poses with a Crane Prairie rainbow before releasing it.

BELOW: The calm water and reflected sunlight from silvery, standing snags provide a serene setting at Crane Prairie for this float tuber. Photos by Brian O'Keefe

with most ranging between 14 and 18 inches, and substantial numbers in the 4- to 10-pound range. In addition to trophy rainbow trout, Crane Prairie also has a self-sustaining brook trout population, with fish up to 7 pounds and the typical fish, 10 to 14 inches in length.

Sometime around 1980, largemouth bass were illegally introduced to the reservoir. These fish are flourishing and provide exciting fishing for big bass up to 8 pounds. Population surveys have produced bass that would set new state records if ever landed by an angler. Large numbers of smaller bass are also available. Crane Prairie is still primarily managed for trout, but game wardens will check for limits of bass as well as trout. Catch-and-release is now practiced by many anglers, making the game wardens job a little easier.

The ODFW has phased in a program that will plant hatchery-raised fish that are direct descendants of Crane Prairie rainbows. Eggs are taken from wild spawning fish, fertilized, and incubated in the hatchery. Fry are reared in the hatchery and planted into the lake as fingerlings and legals.

Besides the bass, bluegill and crappie were illegally introduced in 1996 and pose an even greater threat to the trout fishery. Fishermen are encouraged to keep all bluegill and crappie caught.

The shoreline of Crane is lined with snags, floating logs, and willows. Wading is

CLOCKWISE FROM TOP:
A guided trip pays dividends.
Photo courtesy John Garrison

Fly-casters enjoy a calm day.
Photo by Brian O'Keefe

Audrey Dennis, three and a-half, can barely hold the first fish she ever caught … a four-pound largemouth bass from Crane Prairie!
Photo courtesy cofishing.com

Geoff Hill, editor/publisher, with a 20-inch rainbow.
Photo by Vicki Hill

nearly impossible on the mucky bottom. Some rocky areas occur where the reservoir can be fished from the bank, mainly along the eastern shore, but overall a boat is necessary to access the best fishing areas. Weed beds and submerged logs outside of the main channels can complicate boating. A 10 mph speed limit helps reduce casualties. There are many interesting little bays to explore, a few accessible by car.

Since Crane Prairie is an irrigation reservoir, water levels fluctuate, but the change is very gradual over the entire summer. During extreme low water years, some boat ramps may be unusable. The main body of the reservoir averages 11 feet deep at full pool with the river channels, the deepest areas of the reservoir, ranging from 12 to 20 feet in depth.

All fishing methods are used on Crane, but still-fishing with bait and fly fishing are the most popular. For trout, still-fishers most often use Power Bait, or worms and a marshmallow on the bottom, or a worm or dragonfly nymph under a bobber. Some folks troll gold Thomas lures, Rapalas, and flies successfully. It is not necessary to troll very deep. For largemouth bass, fish big, shallow-diving Yakima and Luhr-Jensen crankbaits in crayfish patterns and fish-imitating patterns. Soft plastic crayfish and grubs will also produce big bass. Rig up with a sliding sinker and bury the hook in the bait to keep from pulling in weeds on every cast. Use a slow retrieve, crawling the lure along the bottom.

For flyrod bass, use big Bunny Leech patterns and cast to standing timber or submerged stumps. Flies can be trolled or cast to rising trout with excellent results. The best

fly patterns imitate damsel and dragonfly nymphs, mayfly nymphs, scuds, leeches, and midges. If you are planning on fly fishing for trout, be ready with mayfly dries in sizes 12 to 18, Woolly Buggers, and long leaders up to 25 feet in length. When catching and releasing trout, use barbless hooks and make sure you land them quickly and release them as soon as they are fully recovered. Overexertion in the warm waters of the reservoir at Crane Prairie can kill the trophy trout you release.

Fishing strategies at Crane are dependent on water level and temperature. In the early season, the trout tend to be scattered throughout the main body of the lake due to high water levels, with the brook trout favor-

BELOW: Aerial view of Crane Prairie Reservoir looking to the northeast. Photo by Vern Bartley/Aerial Images

ing the western shoreline where the stream inlets cool the water. Using masses of boats as fish locators works well this time of year. Be sure also to search the edges of the reservoir back in the snags. Later in the year, as water levels drop and temperatures rise, the trout will migrate to the deeper and cooler channels and spring-fed bays. The bass will be in shallower, warmer coves early in the season, primarily along the rugged eastern shoreline among the snags. They will disperse to the body of the lake as temperatures rise. When water temperatures reach 65 °F, bass will stay close to cover near their spawning areas in the coves. Often trout and bass will occupy the same water at Crane Prairie. In the fall look for the bass along the east shore from Big Rock to the dam. At this time of year try crankbaits, nightcrawlers, and grubs. Fly fishers, use streamers and nymphs in the fall. In terms of numbers and size of fish, the past few years have been consistently good at Crane. The "unofficial" state record whitefish (4 lbs. 14 oz.) was caught at Crane Prairie in 1994.

The reservoir is open to fishing during the general fishing season, with a limit of 5 trout per day, 8-inch minimum length, no more than one over 16 inches. The limit for bass is 5 per day, no more than three over 15 inches. The reservoir is closed to fishing for all species from one hour after sunset to one hour before sunrise. Always check the current OSFR before fishing. There is a 10

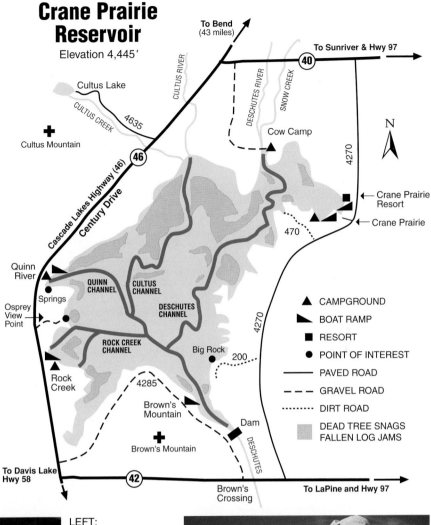

Crane Prairie Reservoir
Elevation 4,445'

To Bend (43 miles)

To Sunriver & Hwy 97

Cultus Lake

CULTUS RIVER

DESCHUTES RIVER

SNOW CREEK

CULTUS CREEK

4635

Cultus Mountain

Cascade Lakes Highway (46)

Century Drive

Cow Camp

4270

Crane Prairie Resort

Crane Prairie

470

Quinn River

Springs

Osprey View Point

QUINN CHANNEL

CULTUS CHANNEL

DESCHUTES CHANNEL

4270

Rock Creek

ROCK CREEK CHANNEL

Big Rock

200

4285

Brown's Mountain

Brown's Mountain

Dam

DESCHUTES

To Davis Lake Hwy 58

42

Brown's Crossing

To LaPine and Hwy 97

▲ CAMPGROUND
◤ BOAT RAMP
■ RESORT
● POINT OF INTEREST
— PAVED ROAD
- - - GRAVEL ROAD
· · · DIRT ROAD
▨ DEAD TREE SNAGS FALLEN LOG JAMS

LEFT:
A nice size Crane brook trout.
Photo courtesy flyandfield.com

RIGHT:
Crane Prairie is also home to some beautiful rainbows.
Brian O'Keefe photo

The Birds of Crane Prairie

LEFT: A great blue heron clings to a downed snag at Crane Prairie Reservoir … perhaps eyeing its next meal or preparing for lift-off.

BELOW: A sandhill crane stands alert, protecting the nest.
Photos by Jim Anderson

ABOVE: Nesting osprey are a common sight at Crane Prairie. They plunge straight down with an impressive splash and fly away with their catch. An osprey observation point is located on the west bank of the reservoir. Photo by Brian O'Keefe

LEFT: The majestic bald eagle can also be found at Crane Prairie.
Photo by Mary James

mph speed limit on the lake.

Many campsites are scattered around Crane with facilities ranging from completely primitive, to full hookups. The large, paved, Crane Prairie Campground and Crane Prairie Resort (full hookups) are located on the northeast shore of the lake. These have the best boat ramps. Crane Prairie Resort has guide services, rental boats, a store, and RVer's necessities. The resort opens and closes with fishing season.

Additional Forest Service campgrounds on the reservoir are Rock Creek Campground, which has improved toilet and boat ramp facilities, and Quinn River Campground on the west bank (hand pumps for drinking water, camping fees, and concrete boat ramps) and Cow Meadow Campground (no drinking water, ramp suitable for very small boats, camping fee) on the far north shore. Browns Mountain by Crane Prairie Dam in the southeast corner has a small concrete boat launch.

Crane Prairie Reservoir is a picturesque body of water with views of Cascade peaks and common sightings of osprey, bald eagles, sandhill cranes, great blue herons, and a wide variety of waterfowl. Bird watching is a popular activity, especially at Osprey Observation Point on the west bank of the reservoir. A trail out to the water's edge begins at the parking area. Summer months are best for viewing nests and feeding of the young osprey. Binoculars are helpful.

Fishing and camping are by far the main reasons to visit Crane Prairie Reservoir. Several fishing tournaments are presented each year by local clubs.

From the Eugene area Crane Prairie Reservoir is reached by taking State Highway 58 east over Willamette pass. About 3 miles past Crescent Lake Junction and .5 mile past milepost 72, turn left onto County Route 61. In another three miles turn left onto Forest Road 46 toward Davis Lake. About 18 miles north, at the junction with Route 42 from the east, you may continue north about 3 miles to Rock Creek Campground and the west shore of Crane or turn

right on 42 to access the south shore at Crane Prairie Dam/Brown's Mountain, and the east shore along Road 4270 that leads to the resort.

From Bend the most scenic route is to take Century Drive/Forest Route 46 up and past Mt. Bachelor. The shortest route from Bend is to drive south on Highway 97 for 15 miles and turn west at the Sunriver exit onto County Route 40/Forest Route 40. Continue about 22 miles to the junction of Forest Route 4270, turning left and following signs to Crane Prairie Resort. The resort and campground are about 3 miles south of the junction.

From the south, use Forest Road 43 from Wickiup Junction to the junction with Route 42. Continue on 42 to the junction with Road 4270. Bear right and follow signs to the campground and resort.

RIGHT: Fly anglers cast in rhythm, Mt. Bachelor in background.
Photo by Brian O'Keefe
BELOW: To enjoy this view of Crane Prairie, one must hike to the top of Cultus Mountain. Photo by Geoff Hill

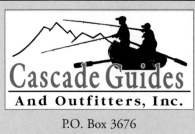

WICKIUP RESERVOIR

Size:	10,000 acres
Depth:	extreme water fluctuations; deep channels
Main Catch:	brown, rainbow, brook trout; kokanee; whitefish; chub
Best Methods:	shore fishing, trolling
Season:	general trout; 4th Sat. in April to Oct. 31; check OSFR
Best Time:	just after ice-out for browns; through July for salmon
Tips:	best access with boat

The very rich, highly productive, relatively warm water and cooler deep channels of Wickiup Reservoir generate some of the finest fishing in Central Oregon. Wickiup is renowned for its brown trout over 20 pounds and normal catches in the 5- to 8-pound range. Many large brown trout are brought into Twin Lakes Resort to be weighed and photographed, but most people never see the largest fish they hook. Long distance releases are routine. Wickiup also has a reputation for good numbers of kokanee and decent populations of rainbow trout, brook trout, whitefish, and the unwanted chub. Large numbers of fishermen and women are entertained here

each year. At full pool, Wickiup Reservoir covers 10,000 acres and is the largest of all the Cascade lakes. Located along the Deschutes River, it is the second irrigation reservoir on the Deschutes, about six miles downriver from Crane Prairie Reservoir.

The largest trout each year are usually caught the first two weeks of fishing season when the big browns are ravenous after a long winter under the ice. There are some true giants in here; a former state record brown trout from Wickiup weighed 24 pounds, 14 ounces. A brown trout caught opening day of 1998 weighed over 26 pounds. Larry Marecek of Salem caught the monster brown using a rainbow-colored Rapala. They are mostly natural reproduction, although fingerlings are stocked every spring. Numbers are excellent. There are anglers here whose lives are dedicated solely to fishing for the brown trout at Wickiup. One should try using lures or plugs that imitate fleeing baitfish to entice these predatory browns.

Very early in the season the trick to hooking the big guys is to fish fast, using floating Rapalas so that they run 2 to 3 feet deep. The best areas early are in the flats from Round Swamp to the dam and near Reservoir Campground and the Davis Arm. Later on in July, the fish move into the deep channels,

and it is important to get tackle down near the bottom. Flies can produce excellent results; use streamers, Muddler Minnows, sculpins, or anything that imitates a tasty chub or salmonid fingerling. Leeches and Woolly Buggers will produce smaller browns. Use sinking lines along the points, ledges, and shallower areas at low light. Shore fishing is popular and can be very productive early in the season along the base of the dam, in the Round Swamp area, and along the edges and ledges of the channels. Gold or bronze minnow imitations and crayfish imitations can be effective from shore.

Fishing for kokanee is the most popular pastime on Wickiup next to pursuit of lunker browns. Fishing for these salmon with spinners or bait is especially good through late July near the dam. Still-fishing with a "Wickiup Sandwich" of a piece of worm, a section of crayfish, one red salmon egg, and a single piece of white corn is a popular plan of attack. Other bait variations including red eggs work well too, fished a few feet off the bottom. Kokanee are schooling fish. Look for them in the channels and in the cooler

ABOVE: Photographed looking south, this aerial shows South Twin lake adjacent to the Deschutes Arm of Wickiup. Photo by Vern Bartley/Aerial Images

INSET: Young Cameron Bauer had a thrill catching this nice Wickiup brown trout. Photo courtesy Garrison's Guide Service

RIGHT: This beautiful brown trout was caught in Wickiup Reservoir. Photo courtesy cofishing.com

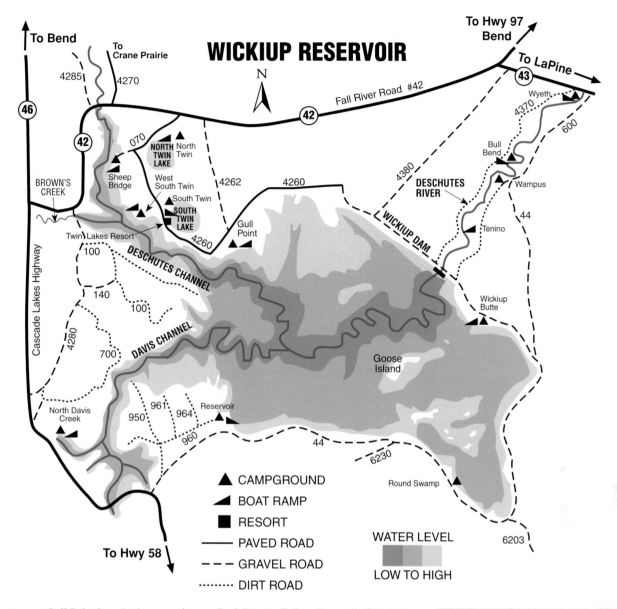

WICKIUP RESERVOIR

N

To Bend

To Crane Prairie

To Hwy 97 Bend

To LaPine

4285

4270

46

42

Fall River Road #42

43

Wyeth

070

4370

600

42

NORTH TWIN LAKE

North Twin

4380

Bull Bend

BROWN'S CREEK

Sheep Bridge

West South Twin

4262

4260

DESCHUTES RIVER

Wampus

South Twin

SOUTH TWIN LAKE

Gull Point

44

Twin Lakes Resort

4260

Tenino

Cascade Lakes Highway

100

DESCHUTES CHANNEL

WICKIUP DAM

140

100

Wickiup Butte

4280

DAVIS CHANNEL

700

Goose Island

North Davis Creek

961

950

964

Reservoir

960

44

6230

Round Swamp

6203

To Hwy 58

▲ CAMPGROUND

◄ BOAT RAMP

■ RESORT

—— PAVED ROAD

--- GRAVEL ROAD

···· DIRT ROAD

WATER LEVEL

LOW TO HIGH

water near Gull Point later in the year when trolling bait behind spinners and flashers will attract them. White corn and Buzz Bombs for jigging are an essential part of your tackle this time of year. Try different depths until you locate a school. Kokanee spawn in the Deschutes River and move closer to the river late in summer. The Deschutes above Wickiup closes September 1 to protect spawning fish. Once the kokanee have changed to their red spawning colors, they are no longer good eating. Kokanee in Wickiup are now all natural reproduction. Sizes and numbers of these small salmon fluctuate over a 3 to 4-year cycle with numbers increasing as size decreases and vice-versa. Kokanee vary from 12 to 18 inches and occasionally up to 20 inches.

Rainbow are not often fished for in Wickiup but are usually taken by kokanee and brown trout anglers. They are no longer stocked but seem to be doing just fine. An average catch will be 2 to 7 pounds but they get a lot bigger with fish up to 16 pounds.

Dark Rooster Tails or Bangtails fished along shorelines seem to work best. Fish the channels mid-day and shorelines early and late in the day. Bait commonly used in the channels includes worms, eggs, Power Bait, and crayfish. Fly fishers cast or troll nymphs near shorelines early and late in the day.

Wickiup has an abundant population of native whitefish up to 4 pounds. Monsters can be seen cruising the bottom near channel mouths. Whitefish are excellent eating and a delicacy smoked. They are good fighters and often easier to catch than the trout. They prefer the clear, cold water of the Davis Arm, where they gather before spawning. A fly fisher can have a lot of fun with a Hare's Ear. Whitefish have small mouths so use smaller bait and insect imitations.

Brook trout are not in the reservoir proper, but are concentrated toward Sheep Bridge on the Deschutes Arm. The average brookie is 10 to 14 inches, and they go up to 5 pounds. There are also largemouth bass in Wickiup that have escaped from Crane

There are some big rainbow in Wickiup also.
Photo courtesy Garrison's Guide Service

Prairie Reservoir. Bass up to 5 pounds are found around Goose Island and in the Deschutes Channel. A population of brown bullhead reside near the Round Swamp area.

Wickiup experiences extreme water fluctuations due to irrigation drawdowns. Over half of the reservoir's water can disappear over the fishing season. The deepest point in the reservoir, at the intersection of the Deschutes and Davis channels, is 60 feet maximum depth. Heavy drawdowns and very low water does not seem to have any adverse effect on the fishery. In fact, the brown trout may be even fatter after having their finny food source concentrated for them.

A boat is necessary to fish most effectively at Wickiup, although early in the season shore fishers do all right. The best boat ramp is at the west end of Gull Point Campground with another good one just east of the campground. The character of the shoreline at Wickiup is as variable as the water level. At full pool, Wickiup is a beautiful, pine-edged lake, with some willows and sandy beach areas. At low water, steep soil and gravel

banks drop abruptly to the water. Other banks become mucky hazards. Obstacles emerge at low water including many stumps and structures added in the Deschutes and Davis arms by ODFW.

Four Forest Service campgrounds are located on the shoreline of Wickiup: Gull Point Campground at the north end has drinking water, fees, boat ramps, and fish cleaning stations; Wickiup Butte Camp-

TOP: This photo of the Deschutes Arm of Wickiup was shot looking north, with South Twin Lake in the foreground and North Twin off to the right. Photo by Geoff Hill

CENTER: The character of the shoreline at Wickiup is as variable as the water level. Many stumps were left when the reservoir was filled … this one appears to be an octopus running along the beach. Photo by Don Burgderfer

BOTTOM: At full pool, Wickiup Reservoir covers 10,000 acres and is the largest of all of the Cascade lakes. The wide expanse of the main body of the reservoir can be seen from the dam. Photo by Geoff Hill

BOTTOM RIGHT: That's one big beautiful brown trout. Photo courtesy John Garrison

ground at the east end has a camping fee but has no drinking water; Round Swamp Campground in the southeast corner has no drinking water and no fee; and Reservoir Campground, with a boat ramp and fee and no drinking water, is located on the southwest corner. In addition, there are South Twin and West South Twin Campgrounds (water, fee), Sheep Bridge Campground (hand pump, fee, small boat ramp), and Twin Lakes Resort, with cabins and a full hook-up RV campground on the Deschutes Arm, and North Davis Creek (water, fee, concrete boat ramp) on the Davis Arm. Most campgrounds have boat ramps, but some may not be usable in extremely low water. Camping is also allowed above the high water mark on the west side of the Deschutes Arm and on the south side of the Davis Arm.

LEFT: Almost as big as she is! Photo courtesy John Garrison

BELOW: A boat is necessary to fish most effectively at Wickiup, although early in the season shore fishers do all right. This view is of the Deschutes Arm of the reservoir. Photo by Geoff Hill

Wickiup has a bonus limit on kokanee of 25 fish with no size limits, in addition to the trout limit. The trout catch limit is 5 per day, 8-inch minimum length and no more than one over 20 inches. There is no limit on whitefish. The bass limit is 5 per day with no more than 3 over 15 inches.

Be aware of a special closure on the Deschutes Arm September 1. Watch for the deadline markers near West South Twin Campground. General fishing season opens the fourth Saturday of April and is open through October 31 each year. One should always check the current OSFR before fishing. Restricted to artificial flies and lures, 2 trout per day upstream of ODFW marker located near West South Twin boat ramp July 15-Aug. 31. There is no boat speed limit on the main body of the reservoir, but boats are

limited to 10 mph on the arms. Boat rentals are available on the Deschutes Arm of Wickiup at Twin Lakes Resort.

Wickiup is a popular waterskiing and jet-skiing lake and is considered one of best areas in the county to windsurf with a sure bet for afternoon winds along the east end. These same afternoon winds, of course, rough up the water for waterskiers and anglers. Swimming, and relaxing along the beaches at the many campgrounds are favorite pastimes for non-fishing visitors.

The easiest way to get to Wickiup Reservoir is to take County Route 42 off of U.S. Highway 97 south of Bend or County Route 43 just north of LaPine which merges with 42 in about 12 miles. Six miles west of the junction of 42 and 43 turn toward Twin Lakes Resort and Wickiup Reservoir on For-

est Route 4260. 4260 reaches the Deschutes Arm of Wickiup at Gull Point Campground in about 3 miles and continues along the northern edge of the reservoir to the dam. Other Forest Service roads can be picked up south of the dam to continue along the southern shore and eventually to a junction with County/Forest Route 46.

From the Eugene area take State Highway 58 east over Willamette Pass. About 3 miles past Crescent Lake Junction turn left onto County Route 61. In another 3 miles turn left onto County/Forest Route 46 toward Davis Lake. About 13 miles north you reach the junction to the unpaved routes along the south shore of Wickiup. The junction with Route 42 is another 7 miles north. A turn to the east on 42 brings you to the turn to Wickiup Reservoir in about 5 miles.

LAKE BILLY CHINOOK

Size:	3,997 acres
Depth:	max. depth 415´
Main Catch:	bass, kokanee, rainbow & bull trout
Best Methods:	shoreline trolling for bull trout, still-fishing for other species
Season:	special regulations; check OSFR
Best Time:	April through June and fall for kokanee
Tips:	Crooked & Deschutes arms open year-round; popular recreation area

In the middle of some of the best agricultural land in Central Oregon and at the bottom of 400 feet of basalt rimrock lies Lake Billy Chinook. This is big water: 3,997 surface acres and 415 feet deep, formed by Round Butte Dam. The lake has filled the canyons of the Crooked, Metolius, and Deschutes rivers, forming the three "arms" of the reservoir. Each arm is 6 to 12 miles long, creating 72 miles of shoreline at full pool. Lake Billy Chinook holds largemouth and smallmouth bass, kokanee, and rainbow, brown and bull trout to test your angling skills year-round. Whitefish, a few landlocked chinook salmon, a very small population of bluegill and black crappie, pikeminnow, chiselmouth chubs, and two types of suckers complete the species list.

Lake Billy Chinook is best known for its trophy bull trout of over 20 pounds. The first, second-, and third-place bull trout state records have all come out of Lake Billy Chinook in recent years. All were over 20 pounds; the largest was 23 pounds, 2 ounces. The average bull trout caught is 14 to 20 inches in length and 4 to 5 years old. At the age of 7 or 8, these fish should weigh 10 to 20 pounds; they can live to be 10 to 12 years old. The bull trout, with a federal listing as a "threatened and endangered" species, currently holds a "sensitive" status in Lake Billy Chinook. A small but stable spawning population survives in the lake. Anglers are encouraged to release all bull trout unharmed. Currently, the catch limit on the lake is 1 bull trout over 24 inches per day.

Lake Billy Chinook is also well-known for its large numbers of kokanee. The cyclical abundance of kokanee results in good years, with many fish of a smaller size, and less productive years, with fewer but larger fish. Currently, kokanee average 12 to 14 inches and range up to 16 inches and 1 pound. The kokanee are all naturally reproducing fish.

Smallmouth bass grow slowly in the cool waters of Lake Billy Chinook. Most fish are about 10 inches in length and weigh around one pound, with a few in the 2- to 4-pound range. The Crooked Arm tends to have a lot

RIGHT: The Deschutes River Arm of Lake Billy Chinook (right) merges with the Crooked River Arm and main body of the lake. The Three Sisters rise in a hazy backdrop. Photo by Geoff Hill

BELOW: Before releasing this beauty back into the water, Brett Dennis holds this 34-inch-long, 23-pound bull trout with a 22-inch girth. The fish was just shy of the State record. Photo courtesy cofishing.com

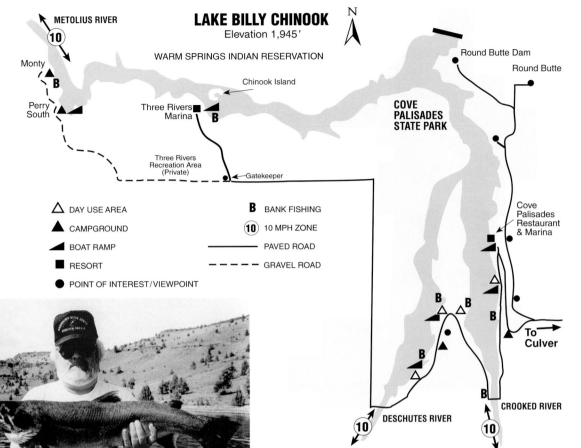

LAKE BILLY CHINOOK
Elevation 1,945'

WARM SPRINGS INDIAN RESERVATION

N

METOLIUS RIVER
10
Monty
B
Perry South
Chinook Island
Three Rivers Marina
B
Three Rivers Recreation Area (Private)
Gatekeeper

Round Butte Dam
Round Butte

COVE PALISADES STATE PARK

Cove Palisades Restaurant & Marina

B
B
B
B
B
B

To Culver

10 DESCHUTES RIVER
10 CROOKED RIVER

△ DAY USE AREA
▲ CAMPGROUND
◣ BOAT RAMP
■ RESORT
● POINT OF INTEREST/VIEWPOINT

B BANK FISHING
10 10 MPH ZONE
—— PAVED ROAD
----- GRAVEL ROAD

TOP: John Garrison of Bend with his 14-pound bull trout.
ABOVE: This fishing guide provides knowledge as well as pontoon boat comfort. Photos courtesy John Garrison

of little smallmouth, with the biggest, but fewer, in the Metolius Arm. Large-mouth bass are present but not in great numbers and prefer weedy, brushy habitat. Rainbow and brown trout reach 20 inches in the reservoir, with the average trout 12 to 13 inches. A few browns up to 10 pounds are in the lake but are few and far between. The best fishing for all of the species and for the largest of all the fish is in the Metolius Arm.

For bull trout, the most commonly used lure is a Rapala, split back or not, up to 8 inches in length. Shoreline trolling, especially around the head of Metolius, is most effective. Several different colors of Rapalas work well. The largest fish are usually deepest.

For the kokanee salmon, the most important fish-finding factor is to get the lure down to 45°F water. The river channels hold the coldest water, and the Metolius is the coolest of the three. The kokanee follow the plankton, their food source, which are usually found at depths of 60 to 100 feet as water warms. One popular area to fish for kokanee is at the confluence of the Deschutes and Metolius arms. Usually, the best fishing for kokanee, which prefer cold water, occurs in April through June, when the fish are in relatively

LEFT TO RIGHT: Brooke Snavely, displays a stringer of good eating kokanee.

These anglers have located a school of kokanee on the upper end of the Metolius Arm. Brooke Snavely photos

Trolling lures produced this beautiful bull trout. Photo courtesy Garrison's Guide Service

shallow water, and again in the fall. Early in the year, use small lures, such as red wedding rings with white corn, or troll hardware; Ford Fenders are preferred. Troll as slowly as possible in S-curves until you catch one, usually indicating that you have located a school. Once you find the school, continue to troll in that area. During the kokanee's spawning run, the last week of August and the first week of September, bait is not needed to hook these feisty little salmon. Often a Buzz Bomb or treble hook with different color weights in 15 to 20 feet of water is adequate. This method only works during the two weeks of spawning. Jigging with Buzz Bombs and white corn is the most popular method for catching kokanee late in the year. The Metolius Arm, with its cleaner, cooler swifter water, is usually the best arm for kokanee.

Smallmouth bass and rainbow and brown trout are found mostly along the shorelines in all three arms. The best trout stretches are at the heads of each of the three arms. Another good spot is at the confluence of the Deschutes and Crooked arms. About the only place to fish from shore on Lake Billy Chinook is between the two boat ramps on the Deschutes Arm and near bridges and docks. Most of the shoreline is pretty steep elsewhere on the reservoir. Still-fishing a nightcrawler under a bobber or fishing a nightcrawler or Rooster Tail with a slow

retrieve is the most successful method for smallmouth bass and rainbow and brown trout. Trolling with a nightcrawler or Rooster Tail is also effective. Fly fishers need to hike up the arms and fish the rivers before they hit the reservoir or work submerged structure along shorelines in the reservoir. The best bass catching is along the shoreline, casting plugs and lures. Look for rocky points, submerged rocks and bars, and grassy shorelines as cover for smallmouth bass. Lures and flies imitating crawfish and fingerlings of any species present in the lake will usually interest the bass. Rapalas work well. Some fishermen successfully pop plugs along the cliffs, but this is not nearly as effective as the other methods.

Water levels fluctuate very little at Lake Billy Chinook and change no more than 10 to 15 feet during wintertime drawdown in the

worst of the drought years. The lower elevation of this area and protection from wind make for warm, pleasant days on the lake. Waterskiing, boating, swimming, picnicking, and sightseeing are popular activities. The area has interesting geological features, the Palisades being named for distinctive columnar basalt formations. There is a petroglyph site between the Deschutes and Crooked arms. Sandy beaches, excellent campgrounds, picnic areas, and houseboats for rent add to the many recreational opportunities.

The Crooked and Deschutes arms of Lake Billy Chinook are open year-round. The Metolius Arm is administrated by Warm Springs Confederated Tribes and is open to fishing only from March 1 to October 31 each year. A tribal permit is required to fish the Metolius Arm. It is illegal to land a boat on reservation land which lies along the north shore of the Metolius Arm. The Metolius Arm is also closed to the taking of crayfish, except for tribal members.

The generous kokanee limit throughout the reservoir is 25 per day with no size limit, in addition to the trout limit. The trout limit is 5 per day, 8-inch minimum length, with no more than one over 20 inches, including bull trout (minimum 24"). There is a possession limit of one bull trout, and no live bull trout may be held while angling. If you catch a bull trout with a tag, leave the tag in the fish if you are releasing it but write down the

LEFT TO RIGHT: Fishing from a boat on a guided trip is a good way to learn the lake.

Jeff Puller proudly holds his prize 10-pound bull trout.

Photos courtesy Garrison's Guide Service

information from the tag and turn it into the Oregon Department of Fish and Wildlife. If you keep the fish, the tag needs to be returned to ODFW. A special sanctuary for bull trout, managed by the CTWS, extends 350 yards downstream from the cable crossing on the Metolius Arm. Bull trout caught in the area must be released unharmed; however, kokanee may be kept. Always check the current OSFR before fishing. A speed limit of 10 mph is in effect above the bridges on each arm of the reservoir. There is also a speed limit on the waterskiing course on the Crooked River Arm.

Cove Palisades State Park begins at the top of the rimrock and extends down to Lake Billy Chinook. There are approximately 300 campsites in the state park, a trailer dump, and boat launches (one on the Crooked Arm and two on the Deschutes Arm). The state park also offers picnic areas, swimming beaches, and fish cleaning stations. Supplies and boat rentals are available at the Cove Palisades Restaurant and Marina which opens about April 15 each year and closes in mid-October. The Three Rivers Recreation Area is a day-use area and private marina on the Metolius Arm. Perry South Campground, on the upper-end of the Metolius Arm, is a primitive Forest Service campground. Perry South has a boat ramp and dock, drinking water, and a fee to camp. Monty Campground is 3 miles farther up on the Metolius River and also offers primitive camping with drinking water and no fee.

From the Portland area, take U.S. Highway 26 to Madras. From Madras follow the Cove Palisades Tour Route from the south end of town for an enjoyable 11-mile drive to the lake.

From Bend, drive north on U.S. Highway 97 through Redmond and Terrebonne. Take the left turn to Culver, about 10 miles south of Madras, and follow the Cove State Park/Tour Route signs

about 8 miles to the lake.

From the Eugene area, take U.S. Highway 20 to Sisters, then State Route 126 to Redmond, and U.S. Highway 97 north through Terrebonne to the turn to Culver.

TOP: Mt. Jefferson reigns over the Metolius Arm of Billy Chinook. Chinook Island appears in the foreground. Photo by Lowell Heydon

BOTTOM: This view includes the island straight ahead, the Deschutes Arm to the left, and the Crooked Arm to the right. Photo by Scott Staats

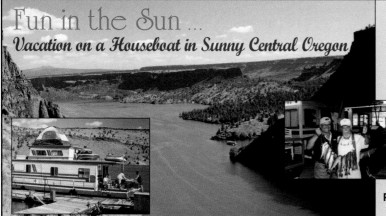

LAKE SIMTUSTUS

Size:	7 miles long
Depth:	very deep
Main Catch:	stocked kokanee & rainbow, brown trout, & stocked steelhead
Best Methods:	still-fishing & trolling from a boat
Season:	general trout; 4th Sat. in April to Oct. 31; check OSFR
Best Time:	early & late in season
Tips:	boat necessary for access; tribal permit required

TOP: Located just north of Lake Billy Chinook, this deep, narrow reservoir passes through some beautiful high desert scenery.

BOTTOM: An RV park with tiered sites overlooks a cove of the lake.
Photos by Geoff Hill

Lake Simtustus is a deep, cold, and narrow body of water 7 miles long, formed by Pelton Dam on the Deschutes River, backing up to Round Butte Dam below Lake Billy Chinook. It has good fishing for kokanee, massive rainbow and brown trout, bull trout, steelhead, smallmouth bass, and pikeminnow. The reservoir was named after a Warm Springs warrior who served as an Army scout in the Paiute wars of the 1860s and lived on the Warm Springs Reservation until his death in 1926. The lake is located 7 miles west of Madras.

The main fishery here is for kokanee, but there are also some huge rainbow and remnant brown trout that mostly hang out at the upper end of the lake. The last brown trout were stocked in 1996. In 1997, annual stocking of hatchery steelhead began. Simtustus is stocked annually with kokanee and legal size rainbow trout. A few bull trout immigrants from Lake Billy Chinook, smallmouth bass, and a profusion of pikeminnow round out the menu. Fishing is usually best early and late in the season. Angling is almost entirely from boats; the steep, rocky gorge makes shore fishing possible only at the two campgrounds on the lake.

Two-pound kokanee are common at the log boom on the upper end of the lake. Trolling is the most popular technique for taking them, although some anglers jig at the boom with bait combinations. The average kokanee is in the 15- to 22-inch range and is included in the trout catch limit. Rainbow trout average 12 to 16 inches, but Simtustus holds the runner-up state record for rainbow trout at 24 pounds, 2.25 ounces, and there are more like it lurking in the depths. In fact, another 24-pound rainbow was caught in the summer of 1996. The 1998 season produced a 17-pound German brown and a 14-pound rainbow, plus many more over 5 pounds. The big fish are usually deep and toward the head of the reservoir, where they feed on the remains of the not-so-lucky that have gone through the turbines of Round Butte Dam. The "big lures for big fish" principle holds true on Simtustus. A #9 countdown, rainbow Rapala is a favorite for browns. Any color of Nordic works for jigging. A fish finder can be a blessing.

Bull trout are occasionally taken by trolling or still-fishing bait. As of 2005, brown trout were still present in good numbers, and angling for them can be fair in the colder and more turbid water conditions of spring. Browns from 10 to 15 pounds are not uncommon: the average being 14 to 20 inches. Pikeminnow on the dry fly can be great sport for beginning fly fishers.

The upper section of the reservoir is known as "the narrows" as the near vertical canyon walls come together. It is quite spectacular, and numerous picturesque waterfalls cascade out of seams in the shear rock.

A tribal permit is required to fish Lake Simtustus. These are reasonably priced and can be purchased at any outlet for fishing licenses in Central Oregon for the day or the entire season. Fishing season opens the last Saturday in April and is open through October 31 each year. The trout limit is 5 per day, with a 8-inch minimum length, and of these no more than 1 over 20 inches, including bull trout (minimum 24"). There is a possession limit of one bull trout, and no live bull trout may be held while angling. Kokanee are part of the trout limit. Always check the current OSFR before fishing.

A 10 mph speed limit is in effect on the upper 6.5 miles of the reservoir. Boat landing on the western shore (Warm Springs Reservation) is prohibited except at Indian Park. Boat launches are available at Pelton Park, Lake Simtustus RV Park, and Indian Park.

Other recreation on the lake includes jet-skiing, waterskiing, picnicking, swimming, and lounging. There is a small wading area at Indian Park. Water fluctuations are minor, and there are fewer waterskiers than at Lake Billy Chinook and less wind. Occasional algae blooms turn the water to pea soup.

The camping experience at Indian Park on the Warm Springs Reservation includes pit toilets, a hand pump for drinking water, a fee to camp, and a long bumpy ride along the west side of the Deschutes River. You must have tribal fishing permits to camp here. Camping is also available at Pelton Park on the east side of the lake. This campground is run by Portland General Electric and has drinking water, a picnic area, modern bathrooms (some with pay showers), a boat launch and dock, boat rentals, and a fee for camping. There is also a small store nearby.

In addition, a privately operated RV park and campground is situated along a cove on the east side of the reservoir. This facility has a boat launch and dock, boat rentals, showers, and a bait and tackle shop. All parks are open during the general fishing season.

To reach Lake Simtustus from Bend drive north on U.S. Highway 97 to Madras, connecting with U.S. Highway 26 toward Warm Springs at the north end of town. The turn toward Pelton Park is about 7 miles north of Madras. From the Portland area take Highway 26 to Warm Springs. The turn to Pelton Park is 3 miles south of town. From the Eugene area take U.S. Highway 20 to Sisters, then State Highway 126 to Redmond and Highway 97 north to Madras. The Pelton Park turnoff gives access to the east shore. The west shore access road to Indian Park begins on the west side of the bridge over the Deschutes River at Warm Springs. This gravel road heads back upstream and reaches the lake in 15 miles.

BELOW: The canyon walls come together on the approach to "the Narrows."
Photo by Geoff Hill

LEFT TO RIGHT: A boat is required to get to the best fishing areas in this 7-mile long lake. Numerous waterfalls flow down the canyon walls
Photos by Geoff Hill

PRINEVILLE RESERVOIR

Size: 3,000 acres at full pool
Depth: 60´ average; extremely variable
Main Catch: stocked rainbow trout, bass, brown bullhead, black crappie
Best Methods: shore fishing, trolling
Season: entire year; check OSFR
Best Time: bass & bullheads in early spring; trout when water levels lower mid-summer
Tips: popular for ice fishing

Prineville Reservoir is situated 15 miles south-southeast of the town of Prineville in the heart of high desert juniper and sage country. This irrigation and flood-control reservoir is 15 miles long and .5 mile wide, covering about 5 square miles at full pool. The reservoir averages 60 feet in depth, and, at the dam, is over 130 feet deep. Planted rainbow trout, large- and smallmouth bass and brown bullhead are the main game here. The reservoir also has pikeminnow and cray-fish to amuse the visitor. Black crappie, extremely competitive with trout, were illegally introduced to the reservoir and may affect the trout fishery in years to come.

In mid-May of each year, 170,000 rainbow trout fingerlings are stocked in Prineville Reservoir. The average size trout caught by the angler is 10 to 12 inches with the largest up to 16 inches in length. There are believed to be larger ones lurking about. Both species of bass naturally reproduce in the reservoir, and 6- to 7-pound fish are taken out every season. Brown bullheads up to 12 inches. Crappie average 6 to 7 inches. Crayfish are abundant enough to be harvested commercially, but numbers have decreased in recent years.

Most folks on the reservoir fish for trout with some sort of cheese combination. Some swear that garlic flavored cheese is the best, and others combine it with a worm or egg. Shore fishing is easy and very productive. Trout fishing gets better as the water level lowers in the summer. Trolling catches trout, too, using flashers and worms or lone spin-

ners. Some of the more popular areas to fish for trout are along the cliffs across from the resort and around Big and Little Island. Fly fishers troll black Woolly Worms, scud imitations, and Prineville Specials, trolled shallow with a lot of line out. As the water warms, the trout move to deeper water. In the fall, the channel above the 5 mph markers in the upper mile of the reservoir can be very good. A fish finder is a very useful item to have when cruising Prineville's 3,000 acres of water.

Prineville Reservoir has a very good bass fishery. The reservoir formerly held the state record for smallmouth bass with a 6-pound, 6-ounce entry. Largemouth reach 8 pounds, with fair numbers in the 4- to 6-pound range caught every year. Bass fishing is often best early in the spring in the upper end of the reservoir where the largemouth are spawning in the shallower, brushy, warmer water, like around Owl Cove. Throughout the year, look for

largemouth in submerged brush and stumps and in the willows along shorelines. Smallmouth bass prefer cooler temperatures than the largemouth and live and breed along rocky points, rocky shorelines, and submerged gravel bars. One of the best smallmouth bass spots is right at the base of the dam, although a lot of these will be small fish.

Plugs, spinnerbaits, flies, real and artificial worms, and spinners will all catch bass at one time or another. Keep trying different methods until you find the one they want that day.

More cover-oriented than the trout, the brown bullhead and the bass tend to be found along the edges of the reservoir. Fishing for bullheads is usually best March through June when they are spawning in the shallower, warmer water coves. Another very good time to fish for bullheads is when the pool is rising and the water is warming. Look for them in mud-bottom bays and in

Boat docks at the State Park get heavy use during the busy summer season. This photo was taken during the off-season. Photo courtesy Oregon Department of Transportation

the upper end of the lake in 2 to 4 feet of water. Worms are the most commonly used bait. Bullheads here average 8 to 10 inches, with an occasional one up to 12 inches in length. Their population numbers tend to fluctuate, with some years of great production and others not so great.

Prineville Reservoir is a popular ice fishing spot in the winter for rainbow trout. The most commonly used method is some kind of bait combination of cheese, eggs, and worms. Day Beach, Jasper Point, the county boat ramp, the state park and resort areas on the north shore, and Powder House Cove and Bowman Dam at the west end of the reservoir are all good ice fishing areas.

Much of the shoreline of Prineville Reservoir has a gradual slope.

ABOVE: A view of Prineville Reservoir in the area of the Prineville Reservoir Resort.
Photo courtesy Prineville Reservoir Resort

RIGHT: Bass fishing has become increasingly popular at this body of water.
Photo by Brian O'Keefe

There are a few areas of steep cliffs and talus. Some of the most popular shore fishing areas are at Jasper Point, the State park, and Bowman Dam. As many people fish from shore as from boats most of the year, although more people fish from shore in the fall. Water levels are extremely variable due to irrigation drawdown, and as water levels fall, many boat ramps become unusable. The best boat ramps are at Jasper Point and the State park. Primitive boat ramps exist at Roberts Bay on the south shore across from resort, Powder House Cove on the west end, and Prineville Resort and Crook County Park on the north shore.

The reservoir has some good beaches, and quite a few people boat into secluded areas for a day of sunbathing, picnicking, and waterskiing. Visitors enjoy sailing on the lake or showing up for a bass tournament. There are many primitive campsites along the banks of the reservoir. The best camping facilities on the reservoir are at the resort and Prineville Reservoir State Park. Advanced reservations are necessary for both. The state park has campsites, a boat ramp, drinking water, restrooms (some with showers), and a camping fee. The resort offers rooms, camping, RV hookups, a store, restaurant, boat rentals, and boat moorage. It opens the first of April and closes around the end of September. Jasper Point, in the same area, has a primitive camping area.

Prineville Reservoir is open to fishing year-round. The catch limit for trout is 5 per day, 8-inch minimum length, and of these no more than 1 over 20 inches. For bass, the limit is 5 per day, no more than 3 over 15 inches with a minimum length of 12 inches. Always check the current OSFR before fishing.

To reach Prineville Reservoir from the Portland area, travel U.S. Highway 26 east through Madras to the town of Prineville. From the Eugene area take U.S. Highway 20 east to Sisters, then State Route 126 through Redmond to Prineville. From Bend drive U.S. Highway 97 north to Redmond and then State Route 126 east to Prineville.

From the town of Prineville there are several routes to the reservoir. From Third Street in the middle of downtown Prineville take the turn onto Main Street at the sign to Bowman Dam and follow the Crooked River upstream 19 miles to the west end of Prineville Reservoir. At the eastern edge of Prineville, past the turn to Bowman Dam, turn right on Combs Flat Road toward Paulina and in a few miles turn right toward Prineville Resort on Juniper Canyon Road. It's 14 miles on this paved road to the northern shore of the reservoir and Prineville Reservoir State Park and 16 miles to Prineville Resort. There is a primitive, unmaintained road into the extreme upper end of the reservoir farther east off of Combs

FROM TOP:
Highway 27 was constructed on top of Bowman Dam.
Prineville Reservoir from the road between State park and resort.
Photos by Geoff Hill

Scott Staats displays a hefty largemouth bass.
Photo by Howard Abshere

PRINEVILLE RESERVOIR

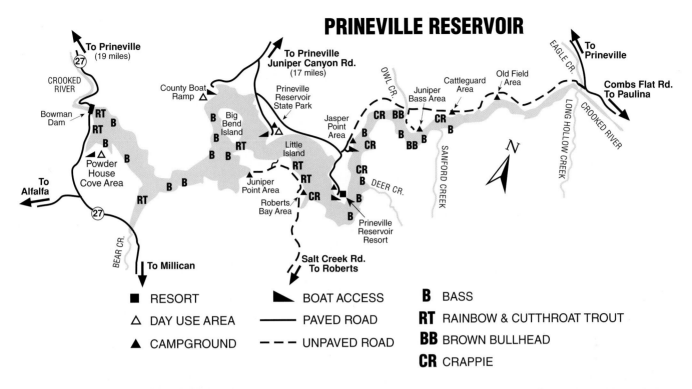

RESORT
△ **DAY USE AREA**
▲ **CAMPGROUND**

◤ **BOAT ACCESS**
— **PAVED ROAD**
--- **UNPAVED ROAD**

B BASS
RT RAINBOW & CUTTHROAT TROUT
BB BROWN BULLHEAD
CR CRAPPIE

Flat Road and the Paulina Highway, but at times this access road is impassible even with 4-wheel drive.

There are also several routes into the southern shore of the reservoir off of U.S. Highway 20 east of Bend. About 30 miles east of Bend take a left turn onto State Route 27 to the reservoir. This road ends up at the dam in around 20 miles. There are a couple of turns off of Route 27 that lead to Roberts Cove and Bear Creek along the south shore of the reservoir. It's a good idea to have a BLM map to follow these circuitous routes.

LEFT: Howard Abshere reeled in a nice largemouth bass.

RIGHT: The upper end of Prineville Reservoir near the resort is a popular place to catch the tasty crappie.
Photos by Scott Staats

OCHOCO RESERVOIR

Size: surface acreage varies from 120-1,200 acres depending upon irrigation draw-off
Depth: 30´ average; 100´ max.
Main Catch: stocked rainbow trout, black crappie
Season: entire year; check OSFR
Best Methods: trolling
Best Time: early spring
Tips: popular for ice fishing

At full pool, Ochoco Reservoir is 3 miles long and about .5-mile wide and is open to fishing year-round. Fishing is excellent for stocked and wild rainbow trout. The average catch is 12 to 14 inches with lunkers up to 6 pounds. Ice fishing is very popular at Ochoco, especially down by the dam and near the state park. Ice fishers use cheese, eggs, worms, and Power Bait successfully, fishing just off the bottom. At ice-out until water levels start to rise in the spring, fishing is very good along the north shore using bait, but trolling is the most productive method year-round. Rooster Tails, Mepps, and flashers are good choices on Ochoco. As the year progresses, the water warms, and the trout move into deeper water. Anglers will have better success fishing nearer the dam with flashers and bright lures close to the bottom. Some folks jig in the deepest areas of the reservoir near the dam.

Illegally introduced black crappie and a small number of brown bullhead are the only other game in Ochoco Reservoir. Also present are non-game species, such as suckers. The trout limit is 5 per day, 8-inch minimum, and of these no more than 1 over 20 inches. Always check the current OSFR before fishing.

Because it is an irrigation reservoir, water levels at Ochoco change dramatically over the year, and surface acreages vary from 120 to 1,100 acres. At full pool, Ochoco averages 30 feet in depth with a maximum of 100 feet near the dam. A few lava outcroppings occupy the banks but, because of lowering water

CLOCKWISE:

Ochoco Reservoir, seen here from the air, is only about half full. At full pool, the reservoir is 3 miles long and about a half-mile wide. Photo by Lyle Cox, *The Bulletin*

Black crappie provide lots of action once located. Photo by Scott Staats

Rainbows are the main attraction at Ochoco. Photo by Tiffany Lewis

OK, who's going to fillet all these? Crappie are fun to catch, and provide many a tasty dinner. Photo by Scott Staats

levels, shorelines will usually be composed of exposed silty bottom and muddy flats. Mill Creek and Ochoco Creek form channels in the reservoir. In the spring and summer afternoon winds can be substantial.

When targeting Ochoco's rainbows with a fly rod, try trolling from a float tube, canoe, or a pontoon boat. Try fishing along the riprap near the dam or on the east end of the lake near the inlets. Use an intermediate sinking line and troll leech patterns like the Woolly Bugger, Lake Bugger and Mohair Leech or a soft hackle wet fly like the Carey Special.

Crappie are often in large schools and may hold at specific depths around sunken structure. The challenge lies in locating them and plumbing the precise depth where the school is holding.

Small rubber-skirted jigs are a favorite lure for crappie fishermen. Red and white, and yellow are top producers. Small spinners, small plugs, and spoons also work well. Fly rodders can also get in on the act, casting or trolling small, weighted streamers. Fish the lure or fly like a wounded baitfish, trolling slowly or casting and retrieving with stops and starts.

There are two boat ramps on the reservoir, one at Ochoco County Park and one at Lake Shore RV Park. Anglers manage to get small boats in the reservoir during low water, but it takes much caution on muddy approaches and can require 4-wheel drive.

Although most visitors fish, others come to bird-watch, photograph, swim, sun, picnic, hunt, or sailboard. At full pool, a few waterskiers or jetskiers may be on the water.

Anglers may want to be aware of elevated mercury levels at Ochoco. Fish have not exceeded DEQ standards for mercury, but you might not want to feast regularly on your catch from this site.

Camping facilities on Ochoco Reservoir include Ochoco Lake Campground, open from April though October, which charges a fee and has drinking water, flush toilets, showers, a boat ramp, and a day-use area. The Crystal Corral has an RV park with 17 full hookups, a cafe, and a store. Lake Shore RV Park and Store offers full hookups, a marina, store, boat rentals, and a boat ramp.

Ochoco Reservoir is located 6 miles east of Prineville on U.S. Highway 26.

This photo was taken from the dam. Photo by Geoff Hill

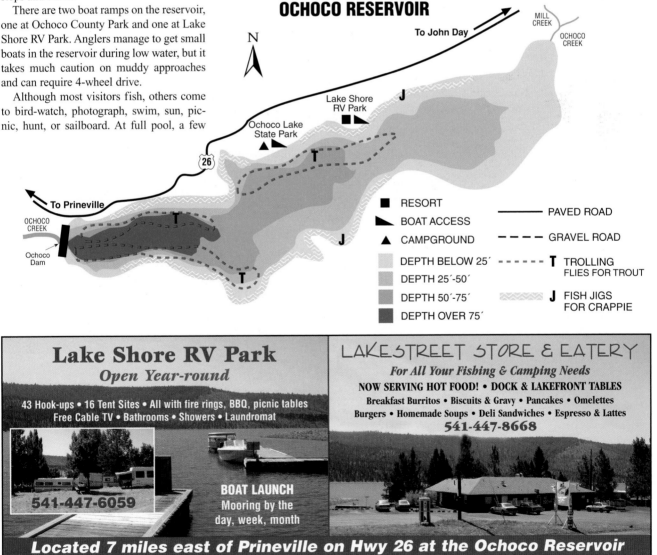

WALTON LAKE

Size:	18 acres
Depth:	12 feet average; max. 21 feet
Main Catch:	rainbow trout
Best Methods:	fly, bait
Season:	entire year
Best Time:	spring
Tips:	electric motors only

Walton Lake is a popular put-and-take fishery, nestled high in the Ochoco National Forest. In the 1940s, the Isaac Walton League dammed spring-fed Ochoco Creek, creating this 18-acre lake with constant water levels and clear, green water.

Walton Lake has a maximum depth of 21 feet, with an average depth of 12 feet and .8 mile of shoreline. Stocked several times a year with rainbow trout, the lake offers catches averaging 8 to 11 inches, with a few holdovers of up to 19 inches. A few accidental brook trout also inhabit the lake.

A trail circling the lake provides good bank fishing opportunities. Fishing from float tubes and small rafts is popular, and only electric motors are allowed. There is a gravel boat ramp, handicapped fishing access, and a small beach and swimming area located near the boat ramp. Fees are charged for both campsites and for day-use.

Take U.S. Highway 26 east out of Prineville for about 14 miles, then take the right-hand fork onto Forest Route 22 toward Walton Lake. Take a left-hand turn in another 8 miles to continue on Road 22, following signs to the lake for another 7 miles. The road is paved all the way to Walton and continues clear around the lake.

FROM TOP TO BOTTOM:
This 18-acre lake has constant water levels and clear, green water.
Photo by Joyce Williams/USFS

Fishing from the bank is popular at Walton Lake.

It's Senior Derby Day at Walton Lake, and life is good!
Photos courtesy Barb Franano

ANTELOPE FLAT RESERVOIR

Size: 170 acres
Depth: 15 feet average
Main Catch: rainbow trout
Best Methods: fly fishing, bait fishing
Season: entire year
Best Time: spring
Tips: good fishing at ice-out

With 170 surface acres at full pool, Antelope Flat Reservoir has plenty of room for anglers to spread out. The boat launch area is shown here. Photo by Gary Lewis

Antelope Flat Reservoir is a remote mountain irrigation reservoir set in the high desert east of Alfalfa and southeast of Prineville. The lake's rainbows thrive in years with average or greater moisture and are capable of growing fairly fast over the course of the summer and fall.

With 170 surface acres at full pool, Antelope has plenty of room for anglers to spread out. Shrouded by pines and junipers, it is a peaceful place to camp. A boat is recommended, but is not necessary. Good bank angling is available from the boat launch around to the dam.

Troll suggestive leech patterns like the Woolly Bugger, Lake Bugger, Carey Special and Mohair Leech. Other effective patterns include the Tellico, Zug Bug and Prince Nymph. Search out rocky points and the transitions from the shallows to deeper water. Fish chironomid patterns (small midge larvae and pupa) with a floating line, strike indicator and a long leader. Set the indicator to hold the fly above the top of the weeds. Cast downwind, keep your line tight and your eye on the indicator.

A paved launch, suitable for smaller boats, is provided near the campground. There is no dock. A handicap-accessible restroom is nearby.

Managed by the Forest Service (541-416-6500), the campground at the lake has 25 basic sites with no hookups and a maximum length of 30 feet. Tables, grills and vault toilets are provided. Bring your own drinking water.

From Prineville, head south on North Combs Flat Road (Paulina Highway). Drive 30 miles, then turn right on Forest Road 17. After 10 miles, FR17 merges with FR16. Continue on, following the signs to the reservoir in about 3 miles.

From Alfalfa, take the Reservoir Road to the Crooked River Highway and turn right. Turn left on Bear Creek Road, follow it for 14 miles, then turn left on S. Kloochman Road. Proceed uphill past Kloochman Reservoir, then turn right on Forest Road 16 and follow signs to Antelope Flat.

ALLEN CREEK RESERVOIR

Size: 200 acres
Depth: varies
Main Catch: redband rainbow trout
Best Methods: bait fishing, fly fishing
Season: entire year
Best Time: when road opens
Tips: Troll leech patterns from an inflatable raft or float tube

Allen Creek Reservoir is a 200-acre irrigation impoundment high in a remote corner of Summit Prairie, in the Ochoco Mountains. Pine trees, manzanita, and junipers surround this cattle country lake. Private lands are mixed among publicly owned Bureau of Land Management lands.

Redband rainbows, which average eight to 14 inches, offer good fishing. Trout of 20 inches and more are available. The limit is five trout per day with no more than one over 20 inches. Access to this remote lake is blocked by snow, most years, until mid-June.

Allen Creek Reservoir has plenty of room for anglers to spread out. An inflatable boat is recommended, but is not necessary. Good bank angling is available.

Power Bait is a good bet for the bait fisherman. Run a sliding sinker to a barrel swivel and 28 inches of leader terminating at a No. 14 treble hook. Mold a pinch of Power Bait around the hook. The bait will float off the bottom. Leave your bail open and set the hook when the line starts to move.

Fly fishermen should troll suggestive Lake Bugger and similar leech patterns near submerged timber, rocky points, and the transitions from the shallows to deeper water. Fish chironomids (small midge larvae and pupa) with a floating line, strike indicator and a long leader. Set the indicator to hold the fly above the top of the weeds. Cast downwind, keep your line tight and your eye on the indicator.

Allen Creek Campground offers the nearest place to pitch a tent. Picnic tables, grills, and a vault toilet are provided. Bring your own drinking water. Some primitive camping is available close to the lake, but stay away from private lands.

You'll need a navigator, a compass and an Ochoco National Forest map to make sense of the roads. From Mitchell, take Upper Bridge Creek Road to Badger Creek Road and follow it southeast to South Howard Road. From Walton Lake, take Forest Road 22 east. Bring a high clearance, four-wheel drive vehicle, along with a shovel and a winch. Expect a hike of over a mile to reach the water.

Judith O'Keefe nets an Antelope Flat Reservoir rainbow. Photo by Brian O'Keefe

The effect of a drought year is seen in this photo of Allen Creek Reservoir.
Photo by Joyce Williams, courtesy USFS

HAYSTACK RESERVOIR

Size:	240 acres
Depth:	27´ average
Main Catch:	brown & rainbow trout; kokanee, bass, crappie
Best Methods:	trolling deepest areas, shore fishing
Season:	entire year; check OSFR
Best Time:	spring & summer
Tips:	fish shallows for brown trout in early spring

Haystack Reservoir is a re-regulation facility, situated 8 miles south of Madras in the juniper and sage desert. Most of the fishing at Haystack is for kokanee, rainbow trout, and bass, but there are also trophy-size brown bullhead, black crappie, brown trout, and bluegill.

Haystack is open to fishing year-round, but the angling is usually on the slow side. Water quality is good, and fish grow fast, but continual losses through the unscreened outlet and nearly daily influx of cold water take a bite out of fish numbers and successful reproduction. Ice fishing is not very good here, as the climate is too mild for good ice formation. Spring and summer are the best times to fish for the warm water species, and the salmonids can be caught year-round. Maximum depth of the reservoir is 75 feet with an average depth of 27 feet. There are great views of Mt. Jefferson from the water.

Kokanee catches range from 2 to 3 pounds, 14 to 18 inches in length, with catches up to 20 inches. Thirty-thousand kokanee fingerlings are planted each year. Trolling the deepest areas of the lake with flashers, a Wedding Ring, and a piece of corn or worm is the most effective technique. Vary the trolling depth until a school is located and then stay in the school. Still-fishing with bait can be productive once a school is located. Kokanee are also caught from shore using a variety of bait, including worms, white corn, and red eggs.

Legal-size rainbow and brown trout are planted annually. Fishing is usually pretty slow for the trout, but it is possible to catch them from shore year-round on Power Bait, eggs, cheese, or worms. From the west boat ramp around to the inlet and near the dam are the best areas for shore anglers. Try for the browns and rainbow early in the spring while they are still cruising the shallows and ravenous after the long, cold winter. Trollers will occasionally take rainbow while fishing for kokanee.

Fishing for largemouth bass is fair. Most bass anglers here use spinnerbaits, plugs, spoons, and worms. The best bass catching areas of the reservoir are in the shallow bays along the south shore, particularly near the vegetation in the southeast and southwest corners. The best time to fish is mid-spring. An average catch is 12 to 14 inches, with the largest bass ranging from 3 to 5 pounds.

Haystack is one of the few fishing spots in Central Oregon with black crappie. These sunfish reach admirable sizes up to 12 inches in length, with the average catch at 8 to 10 inches. The best fish are taken near vegetative cover in the southeast corner of the reservoir in late May through June. Bluegill transplanted into Haystack in the summer of 1993 are hanging on, but their numbers are small. The few bullheads in Haystack are usually caught from shore by anglers fishing for other species. Nightcrawlers are the standard bait for those intending to catch the catfish. The bullhead average 1 to 2 pounds with the big guys at 3 pounds.

The trout and kokanee catch limits are 5 per day, with an 8-inch minimum, and of these no more than 1 over 20 inches. The catch limit for bass is 5 per day, with no more than 3 over 15 inches. There is no limit on bluegill, crappie, or bullhead.

An excellent Forest Service campground occupies the east shore and has a boat ramp, drinking water, and facilities for day-use and

Ten-year-old Chris Henderson pulled this monster fish in all by himself with Dad's four-foot ultra-lite pole. This beauty weighed in at 12.5 pounds and was 30 inches long!
Photo courtesy Mark and Sherri Henderson

overnight camping (with fees). In mid-summer, Haystack becomes a center for water-skiing, and anglers disappear to avoid conflicts. Even though there is a 5 mph speed limit in the west corner of the lake, the reservoir really is not large enough to handle

TOP: A fisherman works the shallow south end of Haystack for the warm water species.
Photo by Anne E. Davidson, courtesy USFS/Ochoco National Forest

RIGHT: An aerial view of the reservoir.
Bend Mapping & Blueprint file photo

both forms of recreation. There are two good boat ramps on the lake. As the water level drops over the summer, the east shore ramp may become unusable. The west shore ramp is good year-round.

Haystack is located 7 miles south of Madras and about 2 miles east of U.S. Highway 97. From the Portland area take U.S. Highway 26 to Madras, then Highway 97 south 7 miles to the turn toward Haystack. To get there from the Willamette Valley take U.S. Highway 20 east to Sisters, then State Route 126 through Redmond to U.S. Highway 97. Drive north on Highway 97 through Terrebonne. The turn into Haystack is about 8 miles north of Terrebonne. From Bend take Highway 97 north to Redmond and continue on as described above.

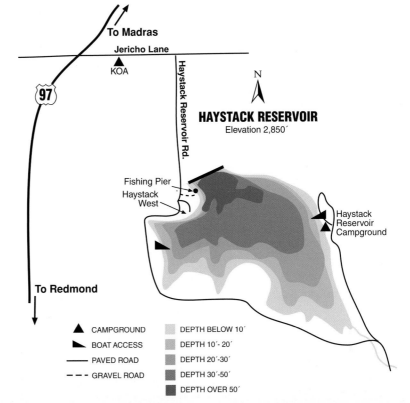

CLOCKWISE: The fishing platform at Haystack Reservoir is handicap accessible.
Photo courtesy ODWF; by Joyce Williams

A nice brownie for GL.
Gary Lewis photo

A view of Mt. Jefferson is available from the reservoir. Note the low water level. This photo was taken during a drought year.

Fishing Haystack Reservoir from your boat is the most popular way to fish.
Photos courtesy ODWF; by Joyce Williams

PAULINA LAKE

Size: 1,320 acres
Depth: max. depth 250´
Main Catch: kokanee,
rainbow & brown trout
Best Methods: trolling, still-fishing,
jigging, fly fishing
Best Time: varies each of
"four seasons" – ice-out,
spring, summer, fall
Season: general trout;
4th Sat. in April to Oct. 31;
check OSFR
Tips: renowned for
trophy browns

On October 4, 2002, a 28-pound, 5-ounce brown trout was landed, eclipsing the former state record set in 1993. Paulina Lake has long been famous for its trophy brown trout and, it is generally believed that, if the record should fall again, it will be a fish from Paulina Lake that replaces it. Paulina first grabbed the state brown trout record in 1965 with a 35-pound, 8-ounce behemoth and has held it ever since. However, there is an asterisk behind that record, indicating it was not a legal catch. It was wallowing in the lake with a broken line and tackle hanging from its mouth and was scooped up with a net. Earlier, a fisherman had hooked the fish and tired it out before it broke the line. But Paulina is not only famous for its brown trout, it grows big rainbows and kokanee as well. For over a decade, Paulina owned the kokanee state record with a 4-pound, 2-ounce fish. Rainbows that range in size from 6 to 12 pounds are not uncommon.

Paulina Lake shares the caldera of Newberry National Volcanic Monument with East Lake. This is a fascinating geologic area formed by the collapse of Mt. Newberry 10,000 years ago and includes the largest obsidian flow in North America, pumice fields, and cinder cones. Paulina Peak, the remnant rim of Mt. Newberry, overlooks the crater from 7,998 feet above sea level. After Mt. Newberry's collapse, the two craters filled with snow-melt, rainwater, and seepage from hot springs to form two fishless lakes. Many years of stocking have created two of Central Oregon's finest lake fisheries. Paulina is a big lake, covering about 1,300 surface acres and obtaining depths to 250 feet. Fish of each species are stocked every year. Paulina is mainly a kokanee fishery, with fish up to 23 inches in length. Brown trout catches typically range between 12 and 20 inches, with fish in the 7- to 10-pound range not uncommon. The lake also holds rainbow trout averaging 10 to 14 inches and a few larger.

Fishing techniques in the Newberry Crater revolve around four "fishing seasons:" ice-out, spring, summer, and fall. These "seasons" will affect one's trolling speed, leader length, depth, presentation, and location. Ice-

LEFT: This view is from Paulina Lake Resort moorage looking east.
Photo by Geoff Hill

BELOW: Aerial view of Paulina Lake looking south. Photo by Vern Bartley/Aerial Images

out is the time to pursue big browns by trolling big plugs. Anglers should try different depths and various parts of the lake. In the spring, kokanee schools are scattered in 24 to 100 feet of water. Trolling with bait and jigging are the most popular techniques for catching kokanee this time of year. Still-fishing, trolling or casting close to the shoreline are the best bets for the early season. Anglers should concentrate their efforts close to the bank and within 35 feet of the surface for the rainbows and browns. Casting lures from shore in early spring and in the fall is an effective method for catching large brown trout and rainbows. Use a 3- to 4-inch P.J. Shiner or a Krocodile spoon. The Kroc is a favorite in windy conditions because of its tremendous castability. Change the speed of the retrieve often, as a stop-and-go technique is very enticing to large, predator fish. Spinners, such as brown Bangtails with a gold blade, are good for catching browns; and black Rooster Tails, with a silver blade, are good for rainbows.

When still-fishing for rainbows, one should fish near the bottom with salmon eggs, worms, Velveeta cheese or Power Bait in green or rainbow colors. Dodgers, Cow-bell, or Bear Valley lake trolls make excellent attractors. Probably the most critical aspect of setting up a trolling outfit is to use a rather long leader from the attractor to the lure or bait. Because of the lake's crystal-clear water, a longer leader is needed between the lake-troll flasher and lure or bait. A leader length of at least 30 to 72 inches is recommended. Trolling for big brown trout with rapalas or Floating Power Minnows often brings success.

The hot summer days push fish into deeper water but fishing remains good if anglers concentrate their efforts where the fish congregate. Rainbows can be caught from mid-depth (20–60 feet) and browns caught shallow in the early morning and late evening. They are found around steep drop-offs, rock shelves in 40-ft. or deeper water. Kokanee will school up, usually at or around the 40-ft. depth and may be found throughout the

LEFT: Guy Carl of Napa, California, holds second place for the state record for a "rod and reel" caught brown trout. The 36" long fish weighed 27 pounds, 12 ounces.
Photo by Ross Martin

BELOW: Paulina Lake as seen from Paulina Peak.
Photo by Don Burgderfer

Paulina Peak, the remnant rim of Mount Newberry, rises in the background. Photo by Geoff Hill

middle of the lake. Fall fishing finds cooler water conditions and more active fish as winter approaches. Spring tactics again become most popular as the fish move into shallower water to feed, in preparation for the cold weather ahead. German browns and kokanee spawn in the fall, so efforts should be concentrated in shallower water areas. Gravel lake bottom or underwater springs are the best bets. Fish at this time of year become very irritable and will strike out at anything that passes near them.

Trolling flashers is by far the most popular fishing method on Paulina Lake, still-fishing the second, and fly fishing third. For kokanee, trolling a Wedding Ring with corn or a piece of worm on the end is very effective. Jigging is increasing in popularity, using Buzz Bombs, Zingers, Crippled Herring, and Nordic lures. Another kokanee-producing method is to first locate schools with a fish-finder and, depending on their depth, troll with a downrigger, flashers and corn, or red flies. Along Paulina Lake's 8 miles of shoreline, the easiest bank fishing is

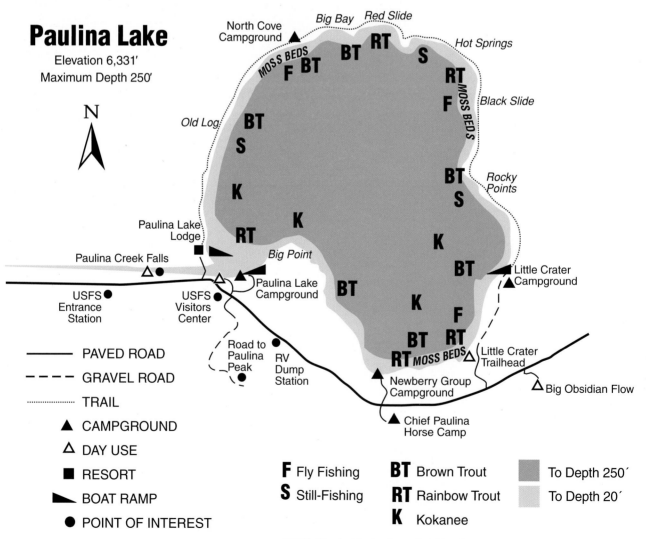

Paulina Lake

Elevation 6,331′
Maximum Depth 250′

N

PAVED ROAD
GRAVEL ROAD
TRAIL
▲ CAMPGROUND
△ DAY USE
■ RESORT
◣ BOAT RAMP
● POINT OF INTEREST

F Fly Fishing
S Still-Fishing
BT Brown Trout
RT Rainbow Trout
K Kokanee

To Depth 250′
To Depth 20′

NOTE: Check at Lodge for updated locations

in the northeast corner of the lake by the black slide. Weedbeds often offer excellent fishing in front of Paulina Resort on the southwest shore of the lake, in front of the summer homes on the south bank, and in front of the black slide. Logs along the east shore and logs and stumps close to shore on the west side create good cover for shy fish. Wading is not easy along Paulina's shores; float tubes are very popular. Water levels fluctuate little.

Opening day is with the general trout season, the last Saturday in April. However, anglers should check to be sure the ice has thawed enough to allow open fishing water. The fishing season remains open through October 31. The catch limit is 5 trout per day, with a 8-inch minimum length and no more than 1 over 20 inches. The lake has a 10-mph speed limit. Several boat ramps are available. Also note that winds can be bad especially in the afternoon. Other recreational opportunities in Newberry National Volcanic Monument include sightseeing, photography, bird watching, hiking, and canoeing in the summer; and snowmobiling and cross-country skiing in the winter. There are several good hiking trails in the Newberry Monument, including one, which traverses the entire rim of the crater. A road leads to the top of Paulina Peak, where there are fantastic views of the Cascade Mountains to the west, the high desert to the east, and the entire Newberry volcano.

Several good Forest Service campgrounds are located on the lake. These include Paulina Lake Campground on the southwest shore (drinking water, fees, picnic facilities, and boat launch), North Cove Campground on the north shore (primitive, boat or hike-in), Little Crater Campground on the east shore (drinking water, fees, picnic facilities, boat ramp), and Newberry Group Camp on the south shore (water, fee, picnicking, reservations). In addition, there is Paulina Creek Falls picnic area just west of the lake and Chief Paulina Horse Camp just across the highway from the lake. More campgrounds are located around East Lake. Paulina Lake Resort has a store, restaurant, cabins, moorage, boat rentals, and a fee boat ramp. The resort is open late April through October 31 and mid-December through mid-March.

To get to Paulina Lake drive south on U.S. Highway 97 from Bend about 22 miles, or about 6 miles north of LaPine if coming from the south. Turn east on County Route 21 to East Lake, Paulina Lake, and Newberry National Volcanic Monument. Paulina Lake is 13 miles up the road, East lake an additional 5 miles.

From the Eugene area take State Highway 58 east over Willamette Pass, then County Route 61 to the town of Crescent and Highway 97 north to LaPine. Continue north of LaPine to County Route 21 and turn east to the lakes.

ABOVE: John Hofferd shows off his 24-pound brown trout taken in 1998 from Paulina. Photo courtesy John Hofferd

RIGHT: Ronald Lane holds his Oregon State Record 28-pound, 5-ounce brown trout caught October, 2002. Photo courtesy Ronald Lane

EAST LAKE

Size:	1,050 acres
Depth:	max. depth 200´
Main Catch:	brown & rainbow trout; kokanee, Atlantic salmon
Best Methods:	still-fishing;, trolling; fly fishing; jigging, casting
Season:	general trout; 4th Sat. in April to Oct. 31; check OSFR
Best Time:	early & late for trophy browns; all season for other species
Tips:	best fished from a boat or float tube

East Lake is one of two exceptional trout lakes nestled in the caldera of the Newberry National Volcanic Monument, the largest ice-age volcano in Oregon. About 37 miles south of Bend, East Lake occupies 1,050 acres and has a maximum depth of 200 feet. East Lake shares this outstanding geologic area with Paulina Lake, both well-known for their large brown trout.

East Lake is 6,381 feet above sea level, is approximately a mile in diameter, and the average depth is just over 67 feet. The lake is fed by snow-melt and underground springs.

Covering over 500 square miles, Newberry Volcano is one of the largest shield volcanoes in the lower 48 states. The area was named after J. S. Newberry, a scientist attached to the 1853 railroad surveying party. The volcano's summit contains a seventeen square mile caldera, formed as the top of the volcano collapsed when the magma chamber beneath emptied out. The caldera, also referred to as Newberry Crater, may have once contained only one lake, like Crater Lake. However, more recent eruptions divided the crater into two crystal clear lakes, separated by pumice, ash, and lava flows.

East lake is one of the finest and most traditional fisheries in Oregon, regularly producing brown trout over 10 pounds. The lake record is a 22-1/2 pound Brown. Rainbow trout are the backbone, being brought in using all techniques: trolling, still-fishing, wet and dry flies, jigging, and casting. Kokanee, introduced in 1993, have been caught up to 20 inches. Atlantic salmon, one of the few lake trout species that will rise on a dry fly, are particularly popular with flyfishers. Unfortunately, chub have become a pest ... but then, they are the food source for the big brown trout.

TOP: East Lake grows some beautiful fish ... Brett Davis caught this nice 12-pound brown trout, summer 2004.
Photo courtesy cofishing.com

CENTER: In this aerial, East (front) and Paulina lakes are viewed from the northeast.
Photo by Vern Bartley/Aerial Images

RIGHT: A number of boat ramps, docks, and campgrounds are available at this outstanding geologic area.
Photo by Geoff Hill

The catch limit at East Lake is 5 trout per day (any species) and two catches in possession. The minimum length is 8 inches, and only one fish over 20 inches is allowed. Because of East Lake's high altitude, it may be partially ice-covered at season opening. The ice recedes from the southeast corner where an underground hot springs warms the water a few degrees providing the angler the best chance of catching a trophy-sized brown trout. The wily browns prowl the south and east shores. Casting and retrieving or trolling minnow-type lures such as floating Rapala minnow imitators in the perch, rainbow, gold or silver color, or 1/4 or 3/8 oz. Krocodile spoons imitating chub patterns, in shallow water, should produce.

The early season is also an excellent time to fish for the other species. Rainbows, especially, are found in large numbers along the ice's edge until the lake has completely thawed, at which point they disperse more evenly throughout the lake. Trolling is probably the most effective means of catching fish at East Lake. Ford Fender, Cowbell, Flashlites, Dodgers, and Jack-O-Diamonds make excellent attractants. The most critical aspect of setting up a trolling outfit is to use at least four to six feet of 4 lb. test leader. East Lake is very clear. A bare worm will catch fish, but Number 1 and 2 Needlefish, Wedding Ring, Triple Teazer can also be productive, especially when augmented with a worm. Try Kwikfish or FlatFish in Frog, Coach Dog, and Black Glitter patterns, too.

Still-fish with Velveeta cheese, Power Baits (rainbow, chartreuse, pink or orange), worms, single eggs, or canned shrimp. Eggs on a #8 hook tipped with white corn works well. Anglers can enhance their success by anchoring boats from both ends facing into the wind to reduce movement. Try to keep bait just off of the mossy, weed-covered lake bottom. Use a 2-pound leader with number

TOP: Joe Shockley with his 30", 10-pound brown trout caught in July of 1998 with an AP Olive Emerger fly pattern. Mom and dad proudly look on.
Photo courtesy Sunriver Fly Shop

BELOW: A young angler proudly holds her East Lake kokanee.
Photo courtesy flyandfield.com

14 to 18 hook. Doughbait treble hooks for cheese and Power Bait, or a single hook tucked completely inside a salmon egg, are recommended. Either split shot or sliding sinkers should be used to maintain the bait from 18 to 24 inches off of the bottom. Some folks do well with bait under a bobber … best results before the wind comes up.

The prize catch during the summer months is the Kokanee. This red meated, land-locked sockeye is the most delicious freshwater fish available, especially when smoked. Kokanee fishing is exciting, as they are fighters, but very soft mouthed. It takes skill to land Kokes. By mid-summer, the Kokanee will be deep, sometimes 40 to 50 feet. To reach that depth without a downrigger, one must troll with up to four ounces of lead. Stick to the northern half of the lake where water depth exceeds 80 feet. Trolling outfits for Kokanee are similar to those used for Rainbow, with the addition of white

shoepeg corn to the bait. Try Kokanee King or Krocodile, without the worm, but with the corn. Jensen Dodgers in size 000 and Flashlights make excellent attractants for the Kokes because their low drag does not require as much weight to get deep. Jigging with a Nordic Jig or Buzz Bomb can also be deadly against Kokanee, especially with the aid of a fish-finder.

Ounce for ounce, and sometimes pound for pound, there isn't a better fighting fish than the Atlantic salmon, especially on the end of a fly rod. Unlike any other lake in Oregon, this species can be kept here — if you can land them. Slim-bodied, silver-sided with a black spot or series of spots on the gill plate, and forked tail, Atlantic salmon may be caught still-fishing, casting or trolling, but for pure sport, go after them with flies. Adams, midge, mosquito, mayfly, and cal-

libaetis are the preferred dries, and nymphs, leeches, Hare's Ear, and Woolly Buggers are the best wet flies.

There are some excellent midge hatches early and callibaetis hatches throughout the summer, especially in the northeast corner of the lake. Often there is decent fly fishing within wading distance of the northeast shore in late afternoon to evening. Generally, nymph patterns are most often used throughout the lake.

For casting, Super Dupers, Bang Tails, and Rooster Tails in frog, white, and black are recommended. Although 95% of the fish caught at East Lake are from boats, casting from shore can be effective. The three best shore fishing spots are off the launching dock at the Hot Springs Campground, as close as one can get to the bluff on the north shore (hike from the Cinder Hill Campground), or all along the west shore where the white slide is located. The west shore can even produce browns late

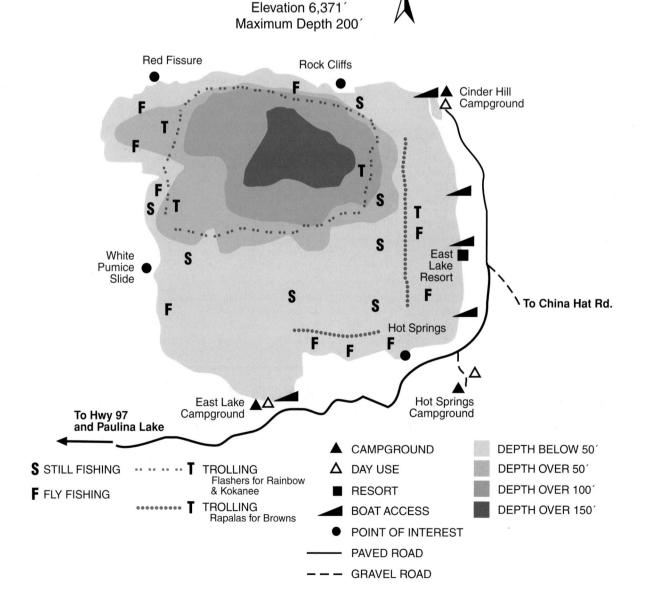

East Lake

Elevation 6,371′
Maximum Depth 200′

N

Red Fissure

Rock Cliffs

Cinder Hill Campground

White Pumice Slide

East Lake Resort

To China Hat Rd.

Hot Springs

East Lake Campground

Hot Springs Campground

To Hwy 97 and Paulina Lake

S STILL FISHING

F FLY FISHING

····· **T** TROLLING
Flashers for Rainbow & Kokanee

•••••• **T** TROLLING
Rapalas for Browns

▲ CAMPGROUND

△ DAY USE

■ RESORT

◤ BOAT ACCESS

● POINT OF INTEREST

——— PAVED ROAD

– – – GRAVEL ROAD

DEPTH BELOW 50′

DEPTH OVER 50′

DEPTH OVER 100′

DEPTH OVER 150′

into the season, and has the added advantage of having the predominately westerly wind at the fisher's back to aid in casting.

East Lake has many weedbeds located near the hot springs, in front of the white slide and along the cliffs on the north side. These weedbeds, full of freshwater shrimp, are good sites for both trolling and still-fishing. Shoreline character of the lake varies from gradually sloping beaches and weed-clogged shallows to steep, rocky cliffs. Winds can be bad in the afternoon.

Three Forest Service Campgrounds on East Lake have nearly 200 campsites. East Lake, Hot Springs, and Cinder Hill Campgrounds have overnight camping, drinking water, toilets, boat launches, and day-use picnic tables. Reservations are not required in these National Forest campgrounds, but can be made (for an additional fee) by calling 1-800-280-CAMP. East Lake Resort, on the east shore, features rustic cabins, an RV park with electricity and water hook-ups, rental boats (with or without motors), laundromat, public showers, gasoline, propane, cafe, and a store with sundries, snacks, bait, tackle, and fishing advice.

There is a 10-mph speed limit for motor boats on East Lake. Anglers should be aware of a mercury advisory for East Lake. Water levels fluctuate 2 to 3 feet over the year, changing the configuration of boat ramps, docks, and fishable shorelines. The weather is extremely variable at this altitude (6,380 feet), so be prepared. Opening day is the last Saturday in April; closing is October 31. Always check the current OSFR before fishing. Roads are usually plowed into East Lake Resort prior to opening day. The resort is open mid-May each year and closes in early October.

To reach East Lake travel 22 miles south of Bend on U.S. Highway 97 (9 miles beyond the Sunriver turn-off), then 18 miles east on East Lake-Paulina Lake Road (County road 21).

ABOVE: This 16.5-pound brown trout was caught September 22, 1992 by John Hofferd. Photo courtesy John Hofferd

LEFT: This brown trout is a fine example of the beauties to be found in East Lake. Photo courtesy Sunriver Fly Shop

BELOW: Even with 6.5 miles of shoreline, most of the fish at East Lake are caught from a floating device.

Views of Paulina Peak are visible from many points along the shoreline. Photos by Geoff Hill

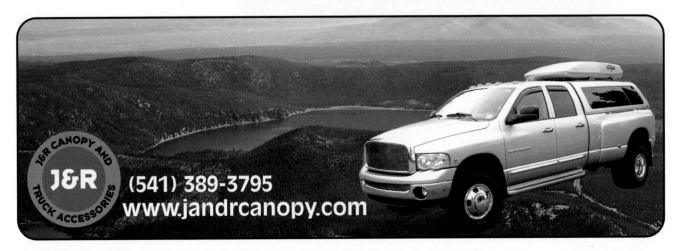

THREE CREEK LAKE

Size:	76 acres
Depth:	28′ max.
Main Catch:	stocked rainbow trout, brook trout
Best Methods:	shore fishing, trolling & still-fishing from a boat
Season:	entire year; check OSFR
Best Time:	mornings & evenings after ice-out

Three Creek Lake, elevation 6,550 feet, is an alpine gem resting at the base of Tam McArthur Rim south of Sisters. This 28-acre lake has planted rainbow trout and a self-sustaining population of brook trout, ranging from 8 to 15 inches. Most catches average around 10 inches. Trolling flies and lures, fishing from shore, and still-fishing with bait are all successfully used methods.

The shoreline of Three Creek Lake varies from gentle slope to rocky cliff, surrounded by old growth forest. Maximum depth is 28 feet down the center and near the cliff on the south end of the lake. Early in the season, many logs lie in the water along the west shore. As summer progresses, weed beds begin to appear along the edges of the lake, water level lowers gradually, and the logs become high and dry

Most of the lake is easy to fish from shore or by wading, but fishing from a boat is by far the most popular method. Motors are not allowed on Three Creek Lake, contributing to the serenity of the setting. There is a prim-itive boat ramp on the east shore as well as a small store which rents boats.

Soon after the lake is stocked every spring, spin and bait fishermen do well near the dam on the northeast corner of the lake. A little later in the season, try still-fishing the deep water along the cliffs on the south end of the lake and along the campground on the southeast shore. The largest fish are usually taken from these areas. Trollers do well near the dam, the boat ramp, and along the south end with both spinners and lures. The west shoreline between the two inlet creeks is also a popular trolling lane. Fly fishing can be rewarding during evening hatches or while trolling nymphs along the west shoreline. Try black and green streamers or large Gold Ribbed Hare's Ears. Zigzag trolling patterns and changes in speed can sometimes entice otherwise wary brook trout. Morning and evening are the best times to fish water this clear.

There are two primitive Forest Service campgrounds: Three Creek Lake Campground and Driftwood Campground on the lake. These sites have outhouses but no drinking water, and a fee is charged. Another similar campground, Three Creek Meadow, is a mile back toward Sisters.

The most popular activities at Three Creek Lake are camping, fishing, and swimming, but there are also excellent hiking trails near the lake. Several trailheads originate on the perimeter of the lake as well as back along the road toward Sisters.

From Highway 20 in Sisters turn south onto Elm Street which becomes Forest Route 16. The road is paved for about 15 miles and is one of the most beautiful drives in Central Oregon, climbing 2,400 feet through towering ponderosa pines and past vistas of Cascade peaks. The last 2 miles to the lake are on a fair gravel and cinder road. Due to the elevation the road is often not open until July. Call the Sisters Ranger District of the Deschutes National Forest for information regarding road conditions and progress of ice-out on the lake.

LITTLE THREE CREEK LAKE

A .5-mile trail leads from Driftwood Campground on the north shore of Three Creek Lake to Little Three Creek Lake. This modest lake is 14 acres, about 10 feet deep, and holds a good population of wild brook trout, averaging 6 to 8 inches in length. Cast-

Surrounded by old growth forest, Three Creek Lake is easy to fish from shore; however, fishing from a boat is the most popular method.
INSET: A trail along the Tam McArthur Rim offers a nice view of Little Three Creek Lake. Photos by Geoff Hill

LEFT: Aerial view looking west.
Photo by Geoff Hill
ABOVE: Lakeside at
Three Creek Lake.
Photo by George Linn

ing from shore is possible, but the fish are often out of range. Packing in a lightweight tube or raft makes access to fish complete. Due to a large number of small fish, spinners, attractor dry flies, and nymphs in the 12 to 16 size range are most successful.

Many people make the trip to the end of the road at Three Creek Lake, but miss the alpine beauty of this little gem nestled beneath the Tam McArther Rim in the Three Sisters Wilderness. The Department of Fish and Wildlife stocks this and other wilderness lakes by helicopter every other year, ensuring an abundance of fish.

Bring a boat when you come to Little Three Creek Lake. Casting from shore, you will almost reach the rising fish. And almost isn't good enough. The best bet is to pack in a float tube or an inflatable raft. If you must fish from the bank, walk around to the west side where the water is a little deeper.

Small Rooster Tail spinners or wobbling spoons can take brookies here and bait works well, but fly fishing can be the most productive. Use a red-tag Woolly Worm or a Prince Nymph or a Brown Hackle when searching for subsurface feeders. Be ready with a selection of small dry fly patterns such as the Adams, Light Cahill and Spider. In September, you may find fish feeding on windblown ants and grasshoppers.

To target bigger brook trout to 20 inches (there are a few), troll big leech patterns or baitfish imitations close to the bottom.

Two trails lead from Three Creek Lake into Little Three Creek. From Three Creek Campground, follow the lake trail around the south end of the lake, skirting the shoreline and heading away from the lake due west. The trail from Driftwood Campground will bring you to the lake in about a mile. Follow the creek upstream to the lake or start at the trailhead.

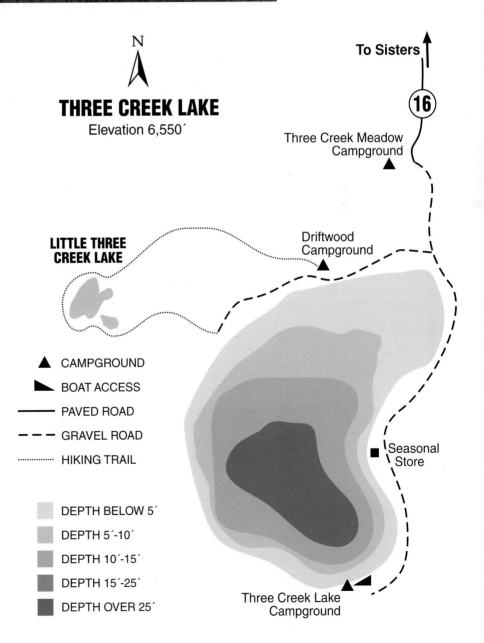

N

THREE CREEK LAKE
Elevation 6,550′

To Sisters

16

Three Creek Meadow
Campground ▲

LITTLE THREE
CREEK LAKE

Driftwood
Campground ▲

▲ CAMPGROUND

◤ BOAT ACCESS

——— PAVED ROAD

– – – GRAVEL ROAD

············ HIKING TRAIL

■ Seasonal
Store

DEPTH BELOW 5′

DEPTH 5′-10′

DEPTH 10′-15′

DEPTH 15′-25′

DEPTH OVER 25′

Three Creek Lake
Campground

SUTTLE LAKE

Size:	250 acres
Depth:	75′ maximum
Main Catch:	kokanee, brown trout, whitefish
Best Methods:	still-fishing from boat, fly fishing
Season:	entire year; check OSFR
Best Time:	kokanee: May & June trout: early & late in season

Fifteen miles northwest of Sisters and easily accessible from U.S. Highway 20, Suttle Lake sits in a pretty setting of mixed conifer forest with views of Cascade peaks. The 250-acre lake is 75′ deep at its maximum depth and has an excellent population of naturally reproducing kokanee, plus brown trout, whitefish, and crayfish.

Kokanee fishing at Suttle Lake is best in May and June using bait. The most commonly used baits are periwinkles and caddis larva, but nightcrawler and red egg combinations are also popular. Kokanee sizes currently average 9 to 10 inches with the numbers of kokanee up and sizes down. Still-fishing from a boat is the best approach, fishing closer to shore early in the season and in the deeper water during mid-summer. The same baits work throughout the season when presented just off the bottom. It is possible to fish from the bank for kokanee near the Suttle Lake picnic area on the northeast corner of the lake.

Brown trout from 10 inches to 10 pounds hide out here, with many in the 3 to 5 pound range. Most are taken early in the season trolling a Rapala near the surface. Late in summer, the brown trout head for the depths. Flashers, lures, and Rapalas need to run deep this time of year. Late in the season is another good time of year for catching brown trout. When late in the day, or anytime light intensity is low, chances of catching a big brown increase. Mid-summer fly fishers troll nymphs and Woolly Buggers near the surface. Early evenings are especially good fly fishing. Any lure, spinner, or

TOP: Suttle Lake produces some nice brown trout. Jon Wiley fooled this one with an "AC" plug. Photo by Megan Wiley

ABOVE: Located northwest of Sisters, Suttle Lake is paralleled by Highway 20. To take advantage of the lake's wide expanse, fishing by boat is the most productive method. Photos by Geoff Hill

Aside from fishing, Suttle Lake offers numerous other activities including camping, hiking, sailing, and waterskiing. Photo by Geoff Hill

fly that looks like a succulent kokanee fingerling will appeal to the big browns. Crayfish patterns are worth a try, too.

Native whitefish of 10 to 12 inches are usually an incidental catch when fishing for the other species. The fry are a favorite snack of brown trout.

Boats are most commonly used on Suttle Lake, float tubes are adequate, and wading is possible in some areas. There are few areas fishable from shore. Suttle Lake has a kokanee catch limit of 25 with no size limits, in addition to the trout limit of 5 per day, with an 8-inch minimum, and of these no more than 1 over 20 inches. There is no limit for whitefish. Check the current OSFR before fishing.

About 1.5 miles long and half-a-mile wide, Suttle Lake is a great place for family outings. Excellent campgrounds and boat ramps and opportunities for horseback riding, hiking, sailing, and windsurfing give the visitor a wide choice of activities. Good swimming areas and designated areas for waterskiing round out the excellent recreational facilities at Suttle Lake. Other fishing opportunities are nearby.

Three Forest Service campgrounds are located on the lake: Blue Bay Campground, South Shore Campground, and Link Creek Campground. All three have drinking water, boat ramps, and charge camping fees. Suttle Lake Picnic Area is on the northeast corner of the lake. Scout Lake Campground is about .5 mile south of Suttle Lake. Suttle Lake Resort, on the east end of the lake, offers a new lodge with rooms, cabins, camping, boat rentals, a restaurant, and store. (Nearby Blue Lake is no longer open to the public.)

To reach Suttle Lake from the Willamette Valley take U.S. Highway 20 east over Santiam Pass. About 7 miles east of Hoodoo Ski Bowl take the Suttle Lake turn south off of Highway 20. From Bend take Highway 20 west through Sisters and about 16 miles west of Sisters turn left at the Suttle Lake sign. The entry road to the resort is just to the west.

Views of the marina and lake can be seen from one of the resort's cabins.
Photo by Ali Geraths

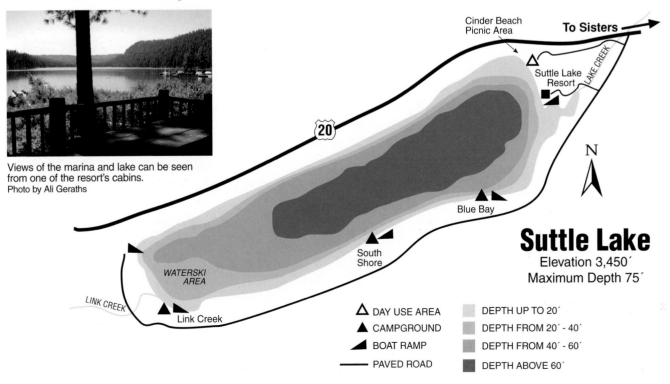

Cinder Beach Picnic Area

To Sisters

LAKE CREEK

Suttle Lake Resort

20

N

Blue Bay

South Shore

Suttle Lake
Elevation 3,450´
Maximum Depth 75´

WATERSKI AREA

LINK CREEK

Link Creek

△ DAY USE AREA

▲ CAMPGROUND

◢ BOAT RAMP

— PAVED ROAD

DEPTH UP TO 20´

DEPTH FROM 20´ - 40´

DEPTH FROM 40´ - 60´

DEPTH ABOVE 60´

BIG LAKE

Size: 225 acres
Depth: max. depth 66´
Main Catch: stocked rainbow trout, brook trout, kokanee, & cutthroat
Best Methods: still-fishing from a boat or the bank, trolling
Season: entire year; check OSFR
Best Time: early spring for cutthroat & rainbow; fall for brook trout & kokanee

Big Lake is perched at the top of Santiam Pass at 4,645 feet elevation, right next to Hoodoo Ski Area. The lake covers 225 acres and has a maximum depth of 66 feet. Water levels fluctuate a few feet during the year, with the lowest point in September, at which time the boat ramp may not be useable by big boats. Big Lake has gently sloping shorelines surrounded by forest. Winds can get nasty in the afternoon.

Fishing is not the biggest draw at Big Lake; most people come here to enjoy the cool mountain air, the camping and nearby hiking on the Pacific Crest Trail, swimming, waterskiing, and jetskiing.

Nonetheless, Big Lake holds decent numbers of kokanee, cutthroat, rainbow, and brook trout. Kokanee are stocked every year and rainbow and brook trout every few years. In 1995, 2,200 rainbow trout fingerlings were planted, 2,000 kokanee, and 1,400 brook trout. Cutthroat were last planted in 1993. Brook trout average 12 inches in length, rainbow trout 6 inches, and kokanee 11 inches in length. The catch limit is 5 per day, 8-inch minimum length, and of these no more than 1 over 20 inches. The fishing season is open year-round.

Big Lake is what is known as an "oligotrophic" lake in the trade, meaning that it is less than rich and doesn't grow fish very well. Fishing, or catching, is only fair. Instead, the water is very clear, and there are few weedbeds or other obstructions in the water. The main catches are cutthroat and rainbow trout, and the best time to catch them is in early spring, although access by car can be impossible at that time of year. Big Lake is easy to fish from either the bank or from a boat, using the usual methods: still-fishing with bait and casting and trolling lures or flies. Fall is the best time to catch the brook trout and kokanee. Trolled flashers work best for the kokanee.

There is an excellent campground here with tremendous views of 7,794-foot Mt. Washington. Big Lake Campground has over 60 sites, 5 day-use sites and charges a fee to camp. It has a pressurized water system, swimming area, and picnic area and is entirely paved except for the gravel boat ramp.

To get to Big Lake, take U.S. Highway 20 from either the east or the west to the turn into Hoodoo Ski Area, Big Lake Road, and Benson Sno-Park at the top of Santiam Pass. It's 3 miles into Big Lake Campground on Road 2690 which is paved all the way.

TOP: Mt. Washington dominates the view at Big Lake. Photo by George Linn
BELOW: From the sky, the forested shoreline is apparent. Photo by Geoff Hill

LOST LAKE

Size:	50 acres
Depth:	shallow with deeper potholes
Main Catch:	rainbow & brook trout
Best Methods:	fly fishing
Season:	entire year
Best Time:	spring, fall
Tips:	Use a small boat or float tube to reach the deepest water.

Nestled in a basin between snow-capped Mt. Washington and Three-Fingered Jack, Lost Lake may be one of the most accessible of the high country lakes. Green firs, twisted hemlocks and mountain peaks are mirrored in the blue water and bend with each dip of your paddle. Ignore the cars rushing by and you will marvel at the scenery surrounding one of the Cascade's most beautiful jewels.

Several small tributaries feed the lake, which sits on a bed of leaky lava. In drier years, the water level drops, leaving the fish no choice but to take refuge in the deepest holes. Rainbows that average eight to ten inches make up the bulk of the catch, but wild brook trout are available. Fishing is restricted to catch and release with artificial flies or lures.

Early in the spring, trout can be found feeding in the shallows as the sun warms the water. Paddle a float tube or a small boat to troll small spinners or flies such as the No. 8 Woolly Bugger or Spruce. Use minnow imitations like the Zonker to spark the predatory instinct in the bigger brook trout and rainbows. While trolling baitfish imitations, change direction, speed and depth to simulate the escape tactics of a worried minnow.

When fishing from the bank, consider using a float and two small wet flies such as the Soft Hackle Hare's Ear, Brown Hackle, or red-tailed Woolly Worm. Vary the retrieve and keep moving until you find the fish.

Later in the spring and summer, seek out the deepest channels and pockets where the trout tend to congregate. Probe the depths with weighted nymphs like the Beadhead Hare's Ear and Prince Nymph, or fish chironomid imitations such as the Bloodworm, San Juan worm or Rainbow Warrior on a long leader beneath a strike indicator.

ABOVE: Lost Lake, ringed by green firs and twisted hemlocks is a familiar sight to travelers on the Santiam Pass. Three Fingered Jack peeks over the foothills.

BELOW: The east side of the lake provides a view of Hayrick Butte. Photos by Geoff Hill

The campground is located on the western shore of Lost Lake. A boat launch provides easy access for the car-topper or canoeist. No motors are allowed on the lake.

From Sisters, head north and west on Highway 20-126 past Suttle Lake. Lost Lake is located in the Santiam Pass in the Willamette National Forest. Look for it on the north side of the highway, near milepost 77.

TODD LAKE

Size: 45 acres
Depth: 56´ max.
Main Catch: stocked brook trout
Best Methods: shore fishing, trolling
from float tube or raft
Season: entire year; check OSFR
Best Time: just after ice-out

Todd Lake is the first of many lovely alpine lakes accessed from the Cascade Lakes Highway west of Mt. Bachelor. At 6,150 feet, it is also the highest. Lying near the base of Broken Top mountain a half-mile off the highway, the 45-acre lake is encircled by alpine meadows and fir forests and is dominated by spectacular views of Broken Top and Mt. Bachelor.

Stocked brook trout are the only game here, but the angling can be invigorating. Fish average 8 to 10 inches with some as large as 15 inches. The best action is usually right after ice-out, a late event at this elevation, but it's also possible to hit some lively fishing anytime during the season.

Small spinners, bait, and flies are all effective on Todd Lake. It is a very pleasant experience to carry in a float tube or small raft and slowly troll around the lake on a warm summer evening. Fly fishers, try trolling green Woolly Buggers if nothing is rising.

ABOVE: Looking north in this aerial view, Broken Top (right), Middle and North Sisters loom above Todd Lake. INSET: Stocked brook trout are the only game here. Photos by Geoff Hill
LEFT: A float tuber enjoys the solitude at Todd Lake.
Photo by Brian O'Keefe

Most of the shoreline of Todd has a very gentle slope and can be fished from shore or easily waded. Rock outcroppings are rare. No major obstacles occupy the water, and the nourishing weed beds are always a good place to fish. A decent trail runs around the lake, but swampy areas exist in the north meadow. There is a small campground with four tent sites and a picnic area on the west shore of the lake. No fee is charged to camp here.

Catch limits on Todd Lake are 5 trout per day, 8-inch minimum length, and of these no more than 1 over 20 inches. Motors are prohibited on the lake. Always check the current OSFR before fishing.

To reach Todd Lake from Bend, follow the signs 22 miles to Mt. Bachelor on Forest Road 46 (Century Drive). Two miles past Mt. Bachelor Ski Resort, turn right onto Road 370 and drive .5 mile on the gravel and cinder road to a large parking area. The trailhead to the lake (and several other destinations) starts here. It's a .25-mile hike into the lake. Early in the season the road past Mt. Bachelor may still be blocked by snow, and Todd Lake will not be accessible by car. To check whether the roads are clear of snow, call the Bend Ranger District of the Deschutes National Forest or Deschutes County Highway Maintenance.

Coming into Todd Lake from the south, take the turn to Sunriver from Highway 97, 15 miles north of LaPine. Follow County Route/Forest Route 40 west to Forest Route 45, follow 18 miles to its junction with County Route 46. Turn left (west) and drive about 5 miles to the turn into Todd Lake on Road 370.

From the Eugene area take State Highway 58 over Willamette Pass, turning left toward Crescent on County Route 61. In approximately 4 miles turn left (north) onto Forest Route 46 toward Davis Lake. It's a long (nearly 50 miles) and very scenic drive up most of the length of the Cascades Lakes Highway to Todd Lake.

SPARKS LAKE

Size: 400 acres
Depth: 10´ max.; levels fluctuate
Main Catch: cutthroat & brook trout
Best Methods: fly fishing only with barbless hooks
Season: entire year; check OSFR
Best Time: just after ice-out
Tips: canoes helpful

A large, shallow, trout lake located on the northwest edge of Mt. Bachelor, Sparks Lake is the first of the high lakes you see from the Cascade Lakes Highway west of Bend. Views of South Sister, Mt. Bachelor, and Broken Top are breathtaking. Prior to 1997, Sparks Lake was a brook trout fishery and, although brookies may still be available, the lake's stocked and featured species is cutthroat trout.

Sparks Lake covers 400 acres and has a maximum depth of 10 feet. The lake is surrounded by fascinating lava formations. At several points along the shore, the lake's water disappears into the edges of the lava, producing exotic noises as the water drains out. The deepest area of the lake is the far south end.

Brook trout average 11 inches with a few to 18 inches, but numbers are small. The main (northern) body of the lake is very shallow, and the extremely clear water requires long, light leaders and stealth.

A narrow channel about a half-mile long connects the north and south portions of the lake. Smaller fish are usually caught in the channel and larger fish in the lower lake. A 2.5-mile trail leading to the southern portion of the lake starts near the highway. This lower portion of the lake is almost completely surrounded by lava flows, making shore access difficult except by the trail. Sparks is most easily accessed by boat.

Sparks Lake is open to fly angling with barbless hooks only. Debarbing hooks helps reduce injuries to released fish. Streamers are frequently fished during the day and dry flies in the evenings, with bucktails and Mickey Finns popular for trolling. The brook trout often prefer the brighter colors of yellow and orange tied-down Caddis in sizes 8 to 14; Royal Wulffs, Royal Coachmen, Adams, and Humpys in sizes 12 to 18, all fished with fast retrieves. Sometimes realistic nymphs are more effective. Mornings and late afternoons usually provide the best results, and during some late afternoons, there are often some good hatches.

At an elevation of 5,400 feet, access to Sparks Lake can be blocked by snow until quite late in the year. Like most of the high lakes, some of the very best fishing is right at ice-out, and some fly fishers will don snowshoes or skis in order to take advantage of hungry trout.

Low water levels at Sparks Lake late in the season can cause difficulties for boaters. Motors are allowed on the lake but cannot be operated while fishing. Consequently, canoes are a popular form of transportation. A good boat ramp is located at the end of the main road into the lake but may not be usable during low water. There is a 10 mph speed limit for motor boats. The catch limit is 5 trout per day, 8-inch minimum, and of these no more than 1 over 20 inches. Always consult the current OSFR before fishing.

There are two small campgrounds on the lake: Soda Creek Campground and Sparks Lake Campground, with no drinking water and no fees. Many people come to Sparks Lake just to canoe, picnic, hike, or camp, and to enjoy the beautiful surroundings. The trailhead located .1 mile off the highway is also a designated mountain bike trail. The Ray Atkeson Memorial offers a barrier-free interpretive trail, wayside, and toilet.

From downtown Bend follow the signs 22 miles to Mt. Bachelor on Forest Route 46 (Century Drive). About 4 miles past the ski resort a small sign indicates a left turn to Sparks Lake, onto spur road number 400. After the turn a fork to the right continues .2 mile in along Soda Creek to several primitive campsites. Along the left fork you will reach the trailhead in .1 mile and the first primitive campsites of Sparks Lake Campground are 1 mile down the road. The road ends in 1.7 miles at the boat ramp and turn-around.

For access from the Eugene area, see directions to Todd Lake (page 76).

CLOCKWISE FROM TOP LEFT: Snow-capped mountain views are hard to beat from Sparks Lake … Devils Flow and South Sister, Broken Top, Mount Bachelor. Photos by Geoff Hill

Several small creeks flow through the meadow into Sparks Lake. Photo by Brian O'Keefe

Aerial looking north. Photo by Geoff Hill

DEVILS LAKE

Size:	35 acres
Depth:	9´ max.
Main Catch:	stocked rainbow trout, brook trout
Best Methods:	still-fishing from floating device, shore fishing
Season:	entire year; check OSFR
Best Time:	summer season
Tips:	good place for children

Devils Lake is first glimpsed from the Cascade Lakes Highway 1 mile west of Sparks Lake. Its extraordinary turquoise color will stop you in your tracks. Fortunately, there is a large pull-out along the highway designed for this purpose. Spring-fed Devils Lake is absolutely crystal clear, giving the viewer an eerie feeling of looking deep into another world. Both brook and rainbow trout inhabit that world.

One reason these 35 acres of water are so clear is lack of nutrients. The second reason is that it is shallow, 9 feet at its deepest. This cold, clear lake does not grow fish rapidly, and the self-sustaining brook trout are quite small, averaging 6 to 7 inches. Rainbow trout are planted several times during the summer, making this an excellent place to take children. The average size rainbow trout in the lake is 8 to 11 inches in length.

Devils Lake has very little bottom structure, making fishing both easy (nothing to hang up on) and difficult (spooky fish). Light leaders are essential. Small spinners, bait, and flies will all work here; these hatchery fish are not picky. For spinners, try gold Thomas lures, Mepps, or yellow Rooster Tails. Red salmon eggs work well for the rainbow and worms for the brookies. Fly fishers cast Adams or attractor dries if fish are rising, caddis, mayfly or damsel nymph imitations if they're not. The northern shore of the lake can be fished from the bank. Most fish are caught in the northeast corner, the deepest part of the lake.

The catch limit is 5 trout per day, 8-inch minimum length, and of these no more than 1 over 20 inches. Always consult the current OSFR before fishing. No motors are allowed on the lake. This is a great place to take a small boat or raft.

Devils Lake Campground offers walk-in tent sites along a winding, wooded trail by the lake. No drinking water is available, but there are outhouses. There is no charge to camp here. Picnic facilities are also available.

Several trailheads nearby include one to the south shore of the lake and several others that take off into the Three Sisters Wilderness (overnight wilderness camping permit required as well as Northwest Forest Pass). There is also a horse camp, parking for stock trailers, and horse access to the wilderness trails at Wickiup Plains trailhead.

To find Devils Lake from downtown Bend drive on the Cascade Lakes Highway 6.5 miles past Mt. Bachelor Ski Resort to the left turn into the Devils Lake Campground/Wickiup Plains Trailhead. From the Eugene area and areas south of Bend, see directions to Todd Lake (page 76).

Aerial view from above Devils Garden lava flow on the flanks of South Sister. Easily viewed from the Cascade Lakes Highway, this cold, clear, blue lake is a popular wayside attraction as well as a scenic place to fish. Photo by Geoff Hill

GREEN LAKES

Size:	South: 8 acres
	Middle: 85 acres
	North: 10 acres
Depth:	South: 26 feet
	Middle: 55 feet
	North: 20 feet
Main Catch:	rainbow trout, brook trout
Best Methods:	fly fishing, bait fishing
Season:	entire year
Best Time:	July
Tips:	Fish dark, weighted wet flies.

Hiking trails lead to this cluster of three small lakes at the base of South Sister … Middle and North Sisters in background. Aerial photo by Geoff Hill

West of Broken Top Mountain and east of South Sister, you'll find the Green Lakes, at 6400 feet above sea level, nestled in a saddle between the two mountains. Deep within the Three Sisters Wilderness, a five-mile hike will put the angler within casting range of his quarry.

South Green is the first lake you come to on the main trail. This eight-acre lake is 26 feet deep and is stocked with rainbows to supplement the fishing for the wild brook trout.

Of the three lakes, Middle Green offers the best fishing. At 85 acres and a depth of 55 feet, there's more room for anglers to spread out. Fish aren't as spooky as they are in the shallower water. Rainbow and brook trout are present. Rainbows average 10 to 12 inches with some holdovers running to 18 inches. Brook trout average 6 to 14 inches.

North Green, at 10 acres and 20 feet deep, has both rainbow and brook trout.

A float tube or a raft is a good choice for the fly angler, but five miles is a long way to pack your boat. Instead of a fly rod and watercraft, consider bringing a small spinning setup. Rigged with four-pound line and a casting bubble, you can cover a lot of water. The lack of brush at the water's edge makes navigating the shoreline on foot a simple task.

The casting bubble provides the weight necessary for long-distance casting. Whether fishing on the surface or below the surface, the best choice is the medium-size, clear plastic bubble.

Slide the bubble over your main line and tie on a No. 14 black barrel swivel. Knot a three-foot, four-pound test leader to your barrel swivel, then tie on the fly. For starters, use a No. 8 black Woolly Bugger, or No. 10 Woolly Worm. A second, smaller fly, such as a Pheasant Tail or soft hackle Hare's Ear tied in tandem may spark reluctant feeders. Vary the depth and retrieve until you find the fish.

Most hikers reach Green Lakes via the main trail from North Century Drive (Highway 46). Find the trailhead across the road from Sparks Lake. Beginning at an elevation of about 5400 feet, the trail climbs 1000 feet in five miles, following Fall Creek up through the pine and fir forest and up into the alpine saddle. Bring mosquito repellent and sunscreen.

Another five-mile route brings the hiker to Green Lakes from Crater Ditch Creek. From Century Drive, take the turn-off to Todd Lake and drive past Todd Lake on Forest Road 370. Turn left on Forest Road 380 and follow to the trailhead (Trail 10).

Trails from Pole Creek and Three Creek Lake reach Green Lakes from the north.

ELK LAKE

Size:	390 acres
Depth:	25´ – 35´ avg.; 75´ max.
Main Catch:	kokanee, stocked brook trout
Best Methods:	still-fishing and trolling from boats
Season:	entire year; check OSFR
Best Time:	early season (June) for brook trout; late fall evenings for fly fishing

Most visitors come to Elk Lake for the beauty of its cold, clear, deep blue water, views of South Sister, Broken Top, and Mt. Bachelor, sandy beaches, and afternoon winds. Little is heard about the fishing at Elk Lake, which is actually alive and well. The lake has a surface area of 390 acres, a maximum depth of 75 feet, and supports both stocked and naturally reproducing kokanee and brook trout. Elk Lake is located 4 miles south of Devils Lake.

Elk Lake is not a rich lake but, instead, is so transparent you can see the bottom clearly from any location on the surface. It has an average depth of 25 to 35 feet. The many kokanee in the lake, commonly 7 to 10 inches in length – not large but abundant – make excellent eating because of the cold water. These fish are mainly found in the "Kokanee Hole" at the south end of the lake near the lava flow, also the deepest part of the lake. Nightcrawlers, eggs, and periwinkles; still-fishing, wind drifting, and jigging are the methods most often used. Few kokanee are caught elsewhere on the lake.

Twenty-thousand brook trout fingerlings are planted every summer. The average catch is about 12 inches in length with fish up to 18 inches, and good numbers in the 2- to 3-pound range. Commonly used methods are still-fishing worms, trolling, or fly fishing with black flies and lures. Gold flashers with worms on a long leader works well, never silver. Ask at the lodge for tips. The best shore fishing is off the south end using worms. Early season fishing for brook trout is best – these fish are wonderfully hungry in June. Most are caught in shoal areas, usually in water no deeper than 20 feet. Late fall evenings can be very good fly fishing.

Catch limits on Elk Lake are 25 kokanee per day with no size limit, in addition to a trout limit of 5 per day, 8-inch minimum length, and of these no more than 1 over 20 inches. Always check the current OSFR before fishing. There is a boat speed limit of 10 mph.

The water level at Elk can fluctuate as much as 15 feet through the year, but the boat ramps remain usable. There are no obstacles to boating on the lake, and the few weed beds stay pretty short. Summer homes line the north and northwest shores. Boat launches can be found at Elk Lake Resort, Little Fawn Campground, and Point Campground.

As mentioned before, fishing is not the main activity on Elk Lake. The sandy beaches, good breezes, and great scenery are con-

Beautiful mountain views and lots of water greet anglers at Elk Lake. Photo by Geoff Hill

ducive to sailing, windsurfing, picnicking, swimming, and just plain relaxing. The Pacific Crest Trail is 1 mile to the west of Elk Lake. Trailheads are just on the other side of the Cascade Lakes Highway from the lake. Hosmer Lake and many other excellent fishing spots are close by. In the winter, Elk Lake is a popular destination for cross country skiers and snowmobilers.

Forest Service day-use facilities on the lake include Beach on the southwest corner, Little Fawn on the southeast corner, and Sunset View on the east shore. Three campgrounds are on the lake: Elk Lake Campground and Point Campground on the west shore, both with pressurized water systems, latrines, and use fees; and Little Fawn

Campground on the southeast corner with a hand pump, latrines, and fees. Little Fawn also has a group camp that can be reserved in advance. Elk Lake Resort on the west shore is open most of the year.

Four miles south of Devils Lake (directions on page 78), a turn east on Forest Route 4625 will bring you to Sunset View in a little over a mile of bumpy gravel road. In another mile you will arrive at the turn into Little Fawn. The turn into Elk Lake Resort off the Cascade Lakes Highway is a .5 mile south of the turn to Sunset View. Elk Lake Campground is .1 mile south of the resort, Point Campground 1 mile farther, Beach Day Use Area another .3 mile south. About a mile south of Beach, turn onto Forest Route

ABOVE: Though most well-known for its sandy beaches and beautiful views, Elk Lake offers some excellent fishing opportunities. Photo by Geoff Hill

INSET: This late fall brook trout was fooled by an artificial fly, photographed and released only to be fooled again. Photo by Brian O'Keefe

4625 toward Hosmer Lake and East Elk Lake to reach Little Fawn in 1.7 miles. The pavement ends 1.2 miles off the Cascade Lakes Highway.

Coming from the south the turn to East Elk Lake on Forest Route 4625 is 5 miles north of Lava Lake (directions on page 85).

HOSMER LAKE

Size:	160 acres
Depth:	8 1/2´ max.
Main Catch:	Atlantic salmon, brook & rainbow trout
Best Methods:	fly fishing only with barbless hooks
Season:	entire year; check OSFR
Best Time:	good hatches generally all season
Tips:	floating devices useful

Hosmer Lake, just east of Elk Lake, is 160 acres of water well-known for its big fish and its beautiful surroundings. This is an idyllic setting with views of Cascade peaks, heather-covered islands, and abundant wildlife. Eight and one-half feet at its deepest, the lake attracts anglers who are often heard muttering to themselves as monster brook trout and Atlantic salmon cruise in the crystal clear water a few feet below their rod tips. Of course, the fish can see them too. Hosmer Lake is restricted to fly fishing with barbless hooks only and catch-and-release on all salmon.

The average brook trout catch here is 14 inches and many have grown into lunkers over the years. The second place state record brook trout, at 6 pounds, 12 ounces, came out of Hosmer in 1977, and there are more like it still in there. The landlocked Atlantic salmon in Hosmer average 16 inches in length, with the largest currently about 22 inches. Three-thousand half-pound Atlantic salmon are planted annually. The stocking of brook trout was discontinued in 1997. Catching fish is a challenging proposition at Hosmer, particularly as its popularity continues to increase. These are double PhD fish.

There are good hatches most of the time on Hosmer. Nonetheless, nymph patterns are used 90% of the time. Leech, damsel, mayfly, and scud imitations are best. For dries, be prepared with Elk Hair Caddis in sizes 8 to 14. Tied-Down Caddis and Salmon Candy patterns are good when used with a floating line. Use a sink tip or full intermediate sinking line when fishing nymphs.

Hosmer Lake's two major pools are connected by a weed-lined channel nearly a mile

TOP: Hosmer is noted for its shallow, clear water and heather-covered islands. Photo by Geoff Hill

INSET: Hosmer is known for its Atlantic salmon. Photo by Gary Weber

RIGHT: Broken Top is among the peaks visible from the heavily vegetated shoreline at Hosmer. Photo by Don Burgderfer

BELOW: For dry flies, caddises can be productive, however, 90% of the time, nymph patterns such as leech imitations do best. Flies courtesy www.umpqua.com

Elk Hair Caddis

Bunny Leech

long. The channel runs from the northern portion of the lake down through Mallard Marsh to the southern pool. About halfway down the channel, there is a small cove with an outlet into a lava flow where a rock dam has been built to keep the fish in. Besides the massive amount of shoreline vegetation, there are very few obstacles in the water.

The northern pool is the largest and also the shallowest part of Hosmer Lake, averaging 3 to 4 feet deep. It is fed by Quinn Creek, a crystal clear spring-creek. The bottom has very little structure. A channel running through this portion of the lake is the deepest area within it. The smaller southern pool has the deepest water in all of Hosmer. Water levels are very stable, even in low water years.

The shoreline of Hosmer is heavily vegetated, and there are only a few spots where one can fish from shore with difficulty. However, the fish are seldom anywhere close to shore. It is by far best to fish from a boat. Float tubes and canoes are very popular here. In the fall, many fish move down into the deeper southern portion of the lake. A good caster could conceivably reach fish with a long cast from the boat ramp.

Canoes are the most popular method of conveyance on Hosmer Lake. As many people come to canoe as to fish. It's a pleasant lake to paddle; watch otter, osprey, and endless waterfowl; and drool over big fish.

The catch limit on Hosmer is 5 trout per day, 8-inch minimum length. All Atlantic salmon must be released unharmed. Only fly angling is allowed. Angling from motor-propelled craft while the motor is operating is prohibited, and only electric motors are permitted. Check the current OSFR before fishing.

There are two good campgrounds on the lake. South Campground along the southern portion of the lake has outhouses, a concrete boat ramp, and some pull-throughs. Mallard Marsh Campground is a little farther north with similar facilities and a small slip in the weeds to launch canoes or other small boats. No drinking water is available at the Hosmer campgrounds, and fees are charged to camp here. The nearest drinking water is at Little Fawn Campground on the southeast shore of Elk Lake, about a mile away.

From Bend, travel the Cascade Lakes Highway past Mt. Bachelor about 13 miles to milepost 35. Turn left onto paved Road 4625 at the East Elk Lake/Hosmer Lake sign. In just over a mile, take the right hand turn toward the boat ramp, the southern end of Hosmer Lake and South Campground. The turn toward Mallard Marsh Campground on Road 600 is another .1 mile down Road 4625. The pavement ends here.

For access from the south, see directions to Lava Lake (page 85). The turn into Hosmer is 3 miles north of Big Lava Lake.

TOP: Aerial view looking to the southwest. Photo by Geoff Hill

BOTTOM: Canoes and float tubes are the most popular method of conveyance for anglers and sightseers on Hosmer Lake. Mt. Bachelor in the background.
Photo courtesy carbonesflyfishing.com

LAVA LAKE

Size:	1/2 sq. mile (320 acres)
Depth:	30´ max.
Main Catch:	stocked rainbow & brook trout, chub
Best Methods:	still-fishing with bait, fly fishing
Season:	general trout; 4th Sat. in April to Oct. 31; check OSFR
Best Time:	early and late in season
Tips:	floating devices useful

"Big" Lava Lake is one of several high Cascade lakes with excellent trout fishing as well as beautiful surroundings. The view from the lake is dominated by Mt. Bachelor, South Sister, and Broken Top. Lava Lake is located about six miles south of Elk Lake along the Cascade Lakes Highway, a National Scenic Byway.

Big Lava Lake covers approximately one-half square mile and is 30 feet deep, maximum. This rich, spring-fed lake grows fish rapidly. Brook trout are no longer stocked, and the lake is managed primarily for rainbow with annual plantings. Rainbows are currently the most plentiful species, the fish ranging from 6 inches to 5 pounds, averaging 13 to 15 inches with generous numbers in the 16- to 17-inch range. Brook trout in the lake run to 19 inches, averaging 12 inches in length.

Peak fishing at Lava Lake takes place early and late in the season. Still-fishing with bait is the most popular fishing method throughout the season, and Power Bait or cheese are most often used. One particular brand of cheese is so popular here that a peninsula on the northeast shore is known locally as Velveeta Point. Trolling with Thomas brand and FlatFish lures, about 50 feet off shore, is another productive method in the spring and fall. Fly fishing is most effective these same times of year, when fish

The scenery is a bonus as the fish grow big in this rich, spring-fed lake, making it an excellent trout fishery. Photo by Geoff Hill
BOTTOM: Eric Olson and son David came from Round Rock, Texas to catch this 4 lb. 9 oz. Lava Lake rainbow. And, yes, David caught it!
Photo courtesy Garrison's Guide Service

are in the abundant shoal areas of the lake. Try Careyflashers any time of year or Mickey Finns in the fall, especially in the southeast corner of the lake and along the bull rushes around the lake. When in doubt, try green lures and flies.

Small hooks are a must with all methods, and when trolling, leaders up to 7 feet long and not over 4-pound test should be used. Be forewarned, the Lava Lake fish seem to have a particular dislike for brown leader material. But the most important fact to consider when fishing this lake is that the fish are almost always right on the bottom.

Rushes line most of the shore of Lava Lake, and plentiful shoal areas are easily accessible from the water. Most fish are caught from floating devices. A few rock outcroppings around the lake and the shallow area on the north end of the lake can be fished from shore.

The water level of Lava Lake fluctuates with annual snow melt, the lowest level occurring in April and the highest water levels in early September. The deepest area of the lake runs from the northernmost point of the lake along the east shore down two-thirds the length of the lake.

The view from the boat dock at Lava Lake Resort is worth the trip. Photo by Geoff Hill

There is a 10 mph speed limit on the lake. Fishing season begins the fourth Saturday in April and is open through October 31. The catch limit is 5 trout per day, 8-inch minimum, and of these no more than 1 over 20 inches. Always check the current OSFR before fishing.

Most visitors at Lava Lake come to fish, although some come just to camp, enjoy the sights, or canoe this popular scenic area. There are several trailheads near the lake for those who wish to do some hiking. Lava Lake Resort is open during fishing season when the snowpack permits. The resort offers an RV park with full hookups. A Forest Service campground on the lake has drinking water, latrines, a fish cleaning station, and a good boat ramp. There is also a Forest Service campground on Little Lava Lake, a half-mile off the access road into Lava Lake.

From downtown Bend, take Century Drive (Cascade Lakes Highway) past Mt. Bachelor. The turn into Lava Lake on Road 500 is at milepost 38, 16 miles south of Mt. Bachelor. The lake is 1 mile in on a paved road. Lava Lake is just as easily reached from Bend by taking the turn to Sunriver off of Highway 97, 15 miles south of Bend and 15 miles north of LaPine. Follow County Route/Forest Route 40 west 22 miles to its junction with County Route 46. Turn right (north) and drive about 6 miles to the turn into Lava Lake.

The lake can also be accessed from the Eugene area via Willamette Pass. See directions to Todd Lake (page 76).

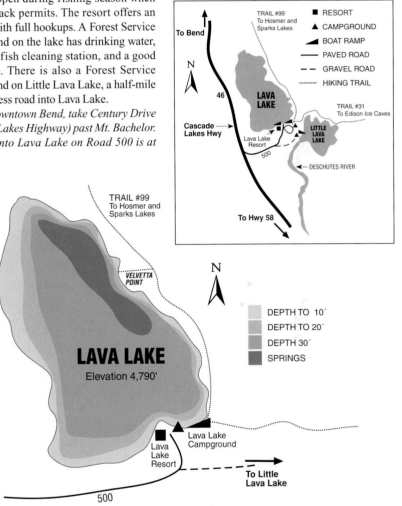

LITTLE LAVA LAKE

Size: 130 acres
Depth: 20′ max.
Main Catch: stocked rainbow trout; brook trout; whitefish; chub
Best Methods: still-fishing; trolling
Season: entire year; check OSFR
Best Time: variable
Tips: most fish from boats

Little Lava Lake is a small forest lake about a half-mile south of "Big" Lava Lake. This 130-acre lake has a maximum depth of 20 feet and supports planted rainbow trout, some brook trout, and self-sustaining populations of whitefish and chub. The fishing here is not as good as at Lava due to competition from the chub population. Rainbow trout average 8 to 12 inches. Little Lava has a catch limit of 5 trout per day, 8-inch minimum length, and no more than one over 20 inches. Always check current OSFR before fishing.

All fishing methods work here: bait, lures, and flies, both still-fished and trolled. Trolled flies are often most effective. As in Big Lava, lead or sinking lines are mandatory. The shoreline is similar to big Lava's with bull rushes and some lava outcroppings, surrounded by forest. The best spot to fish from shore is just north of the boat ramp, but most people fish from a boat. There is a 10 mph speed limit on the lake.

Little Lava's biggest claim to fame may not be its fishing, but that it is the source of the mighty Deschutes River which, at this stage of its life, emerges from Little Lava Lake as a demure brook. Occasionally larger fish from the river will migrate into Little Lava Lake. The state record brook trout, at 9 pounds, 6 ounces, was taken from the river below the lake in 1980.

There is a small Forest Service campground at Little Lava with a hand pump, outhouses, and a small concrete boat ramp. This is a good lake for small boats and rafts. It also has a shallow wading area for children near the boat ramp. Additionally, there is a trail head about .1 mile south of the junction with the road to Lava Lake.

To get to Little Lava Lake from downtown Bend, follow the directions to Lava Lake (page 85). About a half-mile in toward Lava Lake on Road 500, turn right toward Little Lava Lake on Road 520. The graveled road reaches the lake in another .5 mile.

TOP: Best known as the source of the Deschutes River, Little Lava Lake lies just south of "Big" Lava.

CENTER: Looking south in this aerial, the mighty Deschutes is seen emerging from Little Lava Lake as a demure brook.

LEFT: The Cascades dominate the skyline in this view looking north. Photos by Geoff Hill

LITTLE CULTUS LAKE

Size: 175 acres
Depth: 60′ max.
Main Catch: rainbow & brook trout
Best Methods: trolling, bank fishing
Season: entire year; check OSFR
Best Time: early & late in day

Little Cultus Lake is a 175-acre lake nestled in the pines a few miles off the Cascade Lakes Highway, 2 miles south of "Big" Cultus Lake. With good fishing for rainbow and brook trout, Little Cultus is a great place to take the family for a quiet weekend of fishing and camping. Rainbow trout, 8-12 inches, are the primary fishery. Brook trout stocking ended in 1997; however, some up to 16 inches are still available.

Little Cultus' gently sloping shorelines are easily wadable. The deepest spots, up to 60 feet deep, are in the center of the lake. Trolling flashers with a trailing nightcrawler or single lures, such as a gold Thomas lure or yellow Rooster Tail, along drop-offs is a commonly used technique here. Anglers should troll slowly to get down to the fish. Bank fishing is best along the north shore of the lake, using bobbers and worms or spinners, spoons, or a marshmallow and worm fished near the bottom. The fish at Little Cultus Lake often surface feed on emerging damselflies and mayflies. Fly fishers can be well-prepared with mayfly dries, ant imitations in sizes 10 to14, damsel nymph imitations, and Woolly Buggers. Searching the shallower areas of the lake with wet flies, early and late in the day, is especially effective.

Catch limits on the lake are 5 trout per day, 8-inch minimum length, and of these no more than 1 over 20 inches. Always check the current OSFR before fishing. There is a 10 mph speed limit on the lake.

Little Cultus Lake offers a quiet, wooded area with primitive camping. Road surfaces are dirt or gravel. Little Cultus Campground, on the southeast corner of the lake, charges a fee and has a picnic area, outhouses, a hand pump for drinking water, and a paved boat ramp. There are more primitive campsites farther west. Part of the northeast shore of Little Cultus Lake, with a few additional campsites, is accessible by the road into Deer Lake. There is no fee to camp in the primitive areas. In addition to fishing, the lake is a popular spot for swimming and boating.

To find Little Cultus Lake follow directions to Cultus Lake (page 89). About 1.5 miles in toward Cultus Lake on Road 4635, turn left onto Road 4630, following signs to Little Cultus Lake and Irish and Taylor lakes. Little Cultus Lake is about 3 miles, at the junction with Road 640 to Deer Lake. Turn left to reach Little Cultus Campground (.5 mile).

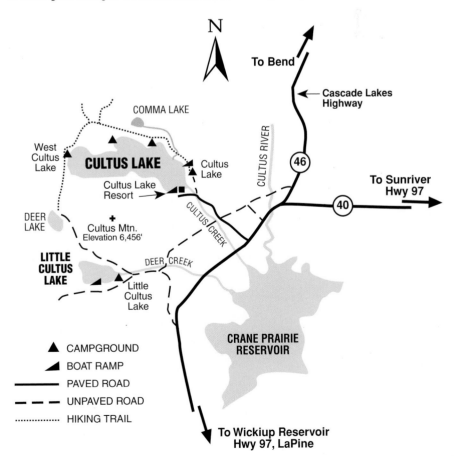

Off the beaten track, nestled in the forest, Little Cultus Lake offers a quiet, peaceful setting for some good fishing for brook and rainbow trout. Photo by Geoff Hill

CULTUS LAKE

Size:	791 acres
Depth:	200´ max.
Main Catch:	mackinaw, rainbow & brook trout
Best Methods:	trolling the depths for mackinaw & shallower areas for trout
Season:	entire year; check OSFR
Best Time:	just after ice-out
Tips:	very popular summer recreation area

Cultus Lake is known throughout the state for the trophy mackinaw (lake trout) lurking in water up to 200 feet deep. This 791-acre lake is located in the heart of the high Cascades 50 miles southwest of Bend and 4 miles east of the crest of the Cascade Mountains. Cultus Lake's sapphire blue water is surrounded by pine and fir forest and is bordered on the north and west by the Three Sisters Wilderness.

The mackinaw here range from 12 inches in length to over 20 pounds in weight, with many fish over 10 pounds taken every season. Early in 1996, a 17.5-pound mackinaw was recorded at the resort. In addition to those naturally reproducing, rainbow trout are planted every spring and average 8 to 11 inches throughout the season. Occasionally, a few larger holdovers are taken. A small population of self-sustaining brook trout reach lengths of 10 inches and average 6 to 7 inches. Whitefish are also available.

The water level in Cultus Lake fluctuates about 3 feet every year from its low at the end of winter to a high around the beginning of September. The "mack zone," the deepest water in the lake, runs in a line between the mouth of the big bay on the north shore to the cabins just east of the resort's lodge. Many of the big macks landed come from this part of the lake. Water up to 120 feet in depth runs down the center of the lake from west to east and is also fished for mackinaw. The most popular methods for catching macks are flasher systems trailing a worm, or downrigger systems with a FlatFish or Rapala trolled at depths of 100 to 200 feet. At ice-out, large mackinaw are known to prowl near the edge of the ice, feeding in the ice-free shallows. Every spring, some big fish are taken after the angler has struggled through remaining snow to reach the lake. Any lure or fly resembling a minnow is a good bet to initiate violent strikes at this time of the year.

Any lure resembling a minnow such as this power minnow is a good bet.
Photo courtesy Luhr Jensen

For rainbow trout, fish in the shallower shoal areas. Try trolling and casting small green or black lures early in the season and switch to silver and gold in the fall. Lures such as Rooster Tails and Mepps can be productive. Another good method is to troll, wind drift, or use a very slow retrieve with trout Power Bait, flies, worms, or red eggs. Still-fishing bait with a bobber is a good bet. Fly fishers, try trolling Woolly Worms or Hare's Ears, and for dries, Elk Hair Cad-

Dry flies such as comparaduns (left) and elk hair caddis (right) work well in the shoal areas.
Photos courtesy www.umpqua.com

dis, ants, or comparaduns, again, in the shoal areas. Catch limits on Cultus Lake are 5 trout per day, 8-inch minimum length, and of these no more than 1 over 20 inches, including mackinaw. Always check current OSFR before fishing.

Cultus Lake is a very popular summertime recreation area with large campgrounds and a good boat ramp. Long, sandy beaches with shallow water along the eastern and western shores are ideal for sunbathing and swimming. The lake is a very popular water-

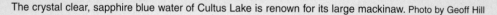

The crystal clear, sapphire blue water of Cultus Lake is renown for its large mackinaw. Photo by Geoff Hill

skiing area in mid-summer. Trail-heads nearby offer opportunities for horse-packing, backpacking, and day-hiking in the Three Sisters Wilderness. Many other good fishing spots are close to Cultus. Also popular at Cultus are windsurfing, kayaking, canoeing, sailing, and nature photography.

Two Forest Service campgrounds rest under large conifers along the shore of the lake. Cultus Lake Campground is a 55-site drive-in campground with drinking water, boat ramp, trailer parking, and a picnic area. There is a fee for camping. West Cultus Lake Campground, at the far west end of the lake, is accessible only by boat, hiking, or horseback. There is a fee to camp there. The 3-mile trail into West Cultus begins at the north end of Cultus Lake Campground. Cultus Lake Resort also has accommodations, plus boat rentals, a store, and a restaurant.

To reach Cultus Lake take the turn to Sunriver off of Highway 97, 15 miles south of Bend and 15 miles north of LaPine. Twenty-two miles west of Sunriver, Route 40 reaches a junction with Route 46. Turn left (south) here and in a little over a mile turn right onto Road 4635 toward Cultus Lake Resort and Cultus Lake. It's about 3 miles into Cultus Lake.

For access from the Eugene area, see directions to Todd Lake (page 76) via Willamette Pass. It's about 32 miles north on Route 46 from County Route 61 to the left turn into Cultus Lake.

ABOVE: Cultus Lake is a popular summer recreation area. Photo by Geoff Hill

LEFT: Mike Myers of Portland shows off a 15-pound Cultus Lake mackinaw which he caught on opening day.
Photo courtesy
Garrison's Guide Service

NORTH TWIN LAKE

Size:	130 acres
Depth:	60´ max.
Main Catch:	stocked rainbow trout
Best Methods:	shore fishing, fly fishing
Season:	entire year; check OSFR
Best Time:	early & late in day
Tips:	limited space for backcasting

The near-perfect circles of North Twin Lake and South Twin Lake were formed in prehistoric times by explosive volcanic eruptions when molten lava met ground water. The filled crater of North Twin, at 130 surface acres and a maximum depth of 60 feet, is slightly larger than South Twin. North Twin is ringed by pine forests with the only open area at the beach and boat ramp on the north shore. The lake harbors healthy numbers of stocked rainbow trout and illegally introduced bullhead.

Fishing for rainbow trout here can be very good. The average catch is 8 to 12 inches in length, due to competition with the catfish.

Occasionally a larger fish is extracted. Locals do well angling near the shorelines early and late in the day using bait, flies, or lures. The best bait fishing is along the west shore in the deeper holes using red eggs, Power Bait, or marshmallows and worms suspended just off the bottom. Rooster Tails, Panther Martins, and dark flies trolled slowly or cast toward shore catch many fish. Fly fishing is most effective near shore. There are some good hatches of mayflies, caddis, damsels, and flying ants. A boat or float tube is best for fishing on the lake, due to limited space for backcasts.

Water levels fluctuate slightly during the year but not enough to affect fishing. The lake supports extensive weedbeds, prime trout territory. The majority of shore fishing is done from the west shore where the dropoff is steepest. No motors are allowed on the lake. The trout catch limit is 5 per day, 8-inch minimum length, and no more than one over 20 inches. Always check the current OSFR before fishing. Additionally, ice fishing may

be a possibility when access is available.

North Twin offers quiet, primitive camping in the pines, a good swimming beach, a dirt boat ramp, and other excellent fishing opportunities nearby. North Twin Campground has latrines, no drinking water, and charges a fee. The closest resort is at South Twin.

North Twin Lake is located about 45 miles southwest of Bend. From U.S. Highway 97 take the Fall River turn 3 miles south of Sunriver onto County Route 42, or 2 miles north of LaPine turn onto County Route 43 at the sign to Wickiup Reservoir. The two routes merge 6 miles east of the turnoff onto Forest Route 4260 to Twin Lakes Resort/Wickiup Reservoir. A dirt spur road turns into North Twin Lake about 100 yards off the highway and reaches the lake and campground in about .25 mile.

From the Eugene area over Willamette Pass, follow directions to Todd Lake (page 76). About 20 miles north of County Road 61, turn east onto Route 42. The turn into the Twin Lakes is about 5 miles east.

Ringed by pine forests, the only open area at North Twin is the beach and boat ramp on the north shore. Photo by Geoff Hill

SOUTH TWIN LAKE

Size: 120 acres
Depth: 55´ max.
Main Catch: stocked rainbow trout
Best Methods: trolling & still-fishing with bait, fly fishing
Season: general trout; 4th Sat. in April to Oct. 31; check OSFR
Best Time: variable
Tips: bait fishing from boats most popular method

The Deschutes Arm of Wickiup Reservoir flows by South Twin Lake. Photo by Geoff Hill

A lure's toss from the Deschutes Arm of Wickiup Reservoir, less than a mile south of North Twin, pinpoints South Twin Lake. The fishing at South Twin has been very good the past few years. Consistent stocking of fingerlings and legal-size rainbow trout several times a year has resulted in an excellent fishery. The largest recorded rainbow to come out of South Twin was over 13.5 pounds.

The trout average 10 to 14 inches, with 18-inch fish common. Most anglers fish from boats and use bait. The deeper south end of the lake, the northeast corner, and the entire north shore along the weedbeds are especially good areas. Ten feet off of the resort's dock is another excellent spot. Depths of 15 to 30 feet are the best producers. The 120-acre lake has a maximum depth of 55 feet. Trolling slowly with a flasher and a piece of worm or egg or with a very small lure are productive methods throughout the season. Still-fishing with eggs, worms, and a marshmallow or Power Bait far enough off the bottom to stay out of the weeds is also a popular method. Successfully used lures are FlatFish, Rooster Tails and various small spoons, or small lures like Needlefish.

For best results, fly fishers use sinking or sink-tip lines and sizes 10 and 12 dark nymphs, including Hare's Ears, Twin Lakes Specials, or dark leech and streamer patterns. Nymph fishing is good all day around the edge of the lake. Make sure you try the shallows near the campground, too. The best fly hatches usually occur mid-day.

One more winning characteristic of South Twin Lake is its calm water when winds are howling over other Cascade lakes. South Twin is completely tree-lined except for the beach day-use area. Water levels vary just a little over the season. The lake is rich with weedbeds. No motors are allowed on the lake. Fishing season opens the last Saturday of April and is open through October 31 each year. The trout catch limit is 5 per day, 8-inch minimum length, and no more than one over 20 inches. Always check the current OSFR before fishing.

South Twin is a more "developed" lake than North Twin. South Twin Campground on the lake and West South Twin Campground on the Deschutes Arm of Wickiup Reservoir both have drinking water, boat launches, toilets, beach areas, and fees. South Twin Campground also has a day-use area. Twin Lakes Resort on South Twin Lake is a cozy resort with cabins, a restaurant, store, marina, and full RV hookups. Mountain bike trails originate near the resort. There are also excellent hiking opportunities, wildlife viewing, and good swimming beaches at South Twin. Exceptional fishing opportunities are close-by at Crane Prairie Reservoir and Wickiup Reservoir.

To get there, follow directions to North Twin Lake (page 90). Instead of turning onto the spur road into North Twin continue on Forest Route 4260, 2 miles farther to South Twin Lake.

DAVIS LAKE

Size: 3,000 acres at full pool
Depth: very shallow; max. 25′
Main Catch: Klamath rainbow, largemouth bass
Best Methods: fly fishing only with barbless hooks
Season: entire year; check OSFR
Best Time: spring & fall
Tips: floating devices useful

Davis Lake is one of Central Oregon's most resilient fisheries. Dogged by drought and fire, this blue-ribbon water seems to bounce back from every blow.

At full pool, this large, shallow lake located 10 miles south of Crane Prairie covers 3,000 acres and is 25 feet at its deepest. At its best, 2- to 5-pound rainbows are common. Davis Lake is open to fly fishing only with barb-less hooks.

In the past, Klamath strain rainbow trout were planted to supplement natural reproduction. No stocking is being done at present. Chub have been a problem in the lake and the rainbows and introduced largemouth bass are controlling them to some extent.

Habitat and structure restoration in Odell Creek has contributed to the health of Davis Lake. Wild rainbows spawn in the creek and their fry migrate back into the lake. Atlantic salmon were planted in the lake until 1995. Few, if any, survive ten years later. Largemouth bass were illegally introduced somewhere around 1995 and are thriving. Fishing at Davis is usually good throughout the season, although some fishermen would say it's a little better in the spring and fall. Some of the most popular flies on the lake are black and dark olive Woolly Buggers in sizes 4 to 10, Peacock Herl nymph patterns, Black Montana Nymph, and leech and damsel imitations in black, drab olive, and brown. For hatches, be prepared with Pale Morning Dun and Callibaetis imitations. The lake usually fishes well throughout the day.

Largemouth bass in Davis Lake's rich waters, grow to 8 pounds or more. To target bass, cast large poppers or eight- to ten-inch white, black or olive Bunny Leeches to shoreside structure or lily pads.

Reeds, marsh grasses, and other thick vegetation along the shoreline, plus a mucky bottom, make it very hard to wade and difficult to fish Davis from shore. (It also makes for a very rich aquatic life). A person could fish from the lava flows if the fish are in shallow water, but normally the fish will be nowhere near shore. Float tubes are good here, and some sort of boat or floatation device is normally necessary to fish

When water conditions are good, Davis Lake can provide excellent fishing. Float tubing is a popular method to access the abundant Klamath rainbows.
Brian O'Keefe photos

CLOCKWISE FROM TOP:

Open for fishing year-round, Davis Lake attracted this angler despite chilly conditions.

Eagles spend spring and summer nesting at Davis Lake.

An underwater photo of a Davis rainbow.
Photos by Brian O'Keefe

Aerial view before fire.
Photo by Geoff Hill

Howard Abshere holds a nice largemouth bass. Bass fishing is fast becoming a viable fishery at Davis.
Photo by Scott Staats

effectively. There previously was very little structure in the lake, but recently the Forest Service and ODFW added logs to the creek channel to provide cover for fish.

Davis is open for fishing year-round. The catch limit is 2 trout per day between 10″ and 13″. There are no bag limits on warm water fish. Watch for the angling deadline signs at the West Davis Campground boat ramp. Motors are allowed on the lake, and fishing is allowed with the motor running.

There is a primitive boat launch at West Davis Campground and a good boat ramp at Lava Flow Campground on the northeast corner of the lake. However, due to nesting eagles, Lava Flow is open only from September 1 to December 31 of each year.

The Davis Lake area was a pretty one before the big forest fire of 2003, with very good campgrounds. East and West Davis Campgrounds are located on the south end of the lake and have drinking water and camping fees. Lava Flow Campground has no drinking water, no fee, and a boat ramp. Waterfowl abound here, and bird watching is a popular pastime. The grebes do their dance on Davis Lake. A hiking trail runs along the west shore of the lake.

Salvage logging and clean-up from the fire

is underway, and in time it will once again be a beautiful area.

From the Eugene area Davis Lake is reached by taking State Highway 58 east over Willamette Pass. About 3 miles past Crescent Lake Junction turn left onto County Route 61. In another 3 miles turn left onto Forest Route 46 toward Davis Lake. The turn toward West Davis Campground is in another 3 miles onto Forest Route 4660. After traveling about 3 miles on 4660, make a right turn onto Forest Route 4669 which reaches West Davis in about 2 miles. East Davis Lake Campground and Lava Flow Campground are both accessed 5 miles farther north on Forest Route 46 (a total of about 8 miles from County Route 61) by turning left onto Forest Route 62 to spur road 855. East Davis is then about 2 miles south (left) and Lava Flow is 3 miles north on the 855 spur.

From Bend take U.S. Highway 97 south about 18 miles to the turn to Fall River on County Route 42. Follow 42 west to its junction with County Route 46, about 26 miles. A left onto 46 will bring you to the turn into East Davis and Lava Flow Campgrounds in about 10 miles.

CRESCENT LAKE

Size: 3,600 acres
Depth: 280´ max.
Main Catch: kokanee; mackinaw;
rainbow & brown trout;
whitefish; chub
Best Methods: trolling
Season: entire year; check OSFR
Best Time: early in the season
Tips: fish finders helpful
in mid-summer

Crescent Lake is a popular recreation area in an attractive setting of wooded shorelines and sandy beaches. Its brilliant blue-green water shelters kokanee, mackinaw, rainbow trout, brown trout, whitefish, and chub, all waiting to tease your tackle. The lake covers 3,600 acres and is 280 feet deep. Numerous picnic, camping, and swimming areas sprinkled along the shoreline make this a great family spot. Crescent Lake is located 60 miles southwest of Bend and 75 miles southeast of Eugene.

The best fishing at Crescent Lake is early in the spring. At ice-out, the mackinaw (lake trout) are in very shallow water near the resort on the northern tip of the lake. As the season progresses, the fish move deeper, eventually cruising at depths as great as 180 feet by mid-summer. The lake is being managed as a trophy mackinaw fishery. An average mackinaw is in the 8- to 9-pound range, and there's a very good chance of landing one over 10 pounds and even connecting with something over 20 pounds. In 1996, a fish of 31 pounds is rumored to have been pulled out of Crescent Lake.

To catch mackinaw, most anglers troll Rapalas and FlatFish. By July, the fish are in water deep enough that downriggers, lead lines, and heavy weights are necessary. Effective trolling depth depends on the bottom structure and time of year; in mid-summer, the macks can be anywhere from 60 to 180 feet down. Fish finders are very helpful, to put it mildly. Popular fishing areas for mackinaw are along the northwest shore near the summer homes and along underwater ledges near Spring and Contorta Point campgrounds on the south side of the lake. Jigging with lures, such as Nordics, once the fish have been located is growing in popularity. Also, locating a school of kokanee and jigging underneath them for mackinaw can achieve results, as the big macks feed on the kokanee. A less common technique is casting spoons or Rapalas from shore early in the spring, but bank fishing is mainly limited to two rocky points near Simax Beach. Fly anglers can use big streamers successfully on Crescent Lake.

Kokanee are stocked annually and currently average 14 inches in length, with a few up to 20 inches. Again, early season offers the best fishing, and trolling the usual kokanee lures is the most popular method. Jigging in pinpointed schools and trolling spinners and flashers can also be effective. Running a downrigger at depths of 35, 60, and 90 feet is another method to try. A few of the best kokanee catching areas are off the resort along the northeast shore and out from the summer homes near the island. The larger-than-usual size of these little salmon make this lake a popular kokanee fishing spot.

Annually stocked brown trout average 16 to 24 inches in Crescent Lake, and there are some large browns up to 12 pounds. Fishing the shorelines early and late in the day and trolling Rapalas, Rebels, or floating Power Minnows are the most common techniques, but all methods are used to catch the brown trout. Rainbow trout naturally reproduce in Crescent Lake and are stocked annually as well. The numbers are not large, and the average size is around 16 inches with a few as large as 6 to 8 pounds. Techniques are the same as for brown trout. Anglers should look for the rainbow near the creek inlets on the south shore.

Whitefish abound in Crescent Lake. This native species can grow to be quite large. They are good eating, especially delectable when smoked. There is no catch limit on whitefish. They are liable to end up on the end of your line when you are fishing for any of the other species.

Catch limits on Crescent Lake are 5 trout per day, 8-inch minimum length, and of these no more than 1 over 20 inches, including mackinaw (30-inch minimum).

Steve Kroll holds this 9.5-pound brown trout before releasing it. Photo by Rick Arnold

One should always check the current OSFR before fishing.

Crescent Lake is used for irrigation and suffered from low water levels for many years. It has been slow to refill but continues to be a quality fishery. Some boat ramps which are unusable at low water include Spring Camp-ground and Crescent Lake Campground's new ramp, although the old one at Crescent can still be used successfully. A few obstacles in the form of protruding rocks are present at low water, near the points

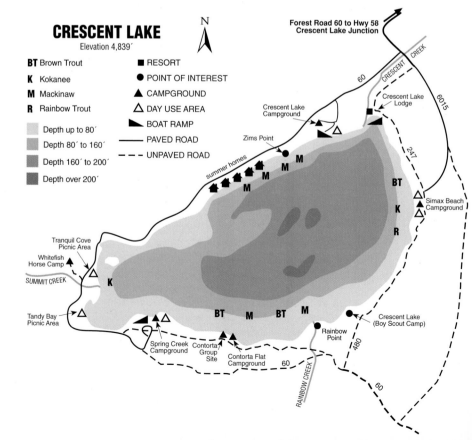

CRESCENT LAKE
Elevation 4,839´

N

BT Brown Trout
K Kokanee
M Mackinaw
R Rainbow Trout

■ RESORT
● POINT OF INTEREST
▲ CAMPGROUND
△ DAY USE AREA
◤ BOAT RAMP
— PAVED ROAD
--- UNPAVED ROAD

Depth up to 80´
Depth 80´ to 160´
Depth 160´ to 200´
Depth over 200´

Forest Road 60 to Hwy 58
Crescent Lake Junction

CRESCENT CREEK
60
6015
Crescent Lake Lodge
247
Crescent Lake Campground
Zims Point
summer homes
Simax Beach Campground
BT
K
R
Tranquil Cove Picnic Area
Whitefish Horse Camp
SUMMIT CREEK
K
Tandy Bay Picnic Area
Spring Creek Campground
Contorta Group Site
Contorta Flat Campground
BT   M   BT   M
60
Rainbow Point
480
Crescent Lake (Boy Scout Camp)
RAINBOW CREEK
60

ABOVE: The brilliant blue-green water of a "low" Crescent Lake is evident in this aerial shot, photographed looking east. Photo by Geoff Hill

off of the summer homes and Contorta Point.

The bottom structure of Crescent Lake is a variable topography of humps and bumps that are great for hiding mackinaw. The wind can be bad here, though not quite as strong as at Odell Lake. The north shore is the most sheltered, and the lake's west end tends to have the calmest water. Summer homes line much of the northern shore. Makualla Boy Scout Camp resides on the south shore.

Hobie cats are prevalent on Crescent Lake as are jetskis, waterskiers, swimmers, and windsurfers. Gently sloping, sandy beaches have pleasantly warm water for swimming in the summer. Trailheads located at Crescent Lake Campground and Tranquil Cove lead into the Diamond Peak Wilderness. Trailheads near Spring Creek Campground give access to the Oregon Cascades Recreation Area where mountain bikes are allowed, unlike in the Wilderness Area. Bikes are not allowed on the Pacific Crest Trail regardless of its location. In the winter, cross-country skiing and snowmobiling are popular activities, although Crescent Lake tends to have

more snowmobilers, and Odell Lake is more attuned to cross-country skiers. Good Forest Service roads circle the lake but, at times, are quite a distance from the shore.

Five Forest Service campgrounds are on the lake. Crescent Lake Campground on the northern tip of the lake and Spring Campground on the southwest corner of the lake have boat ramps, drinking water, and fees. Contorta Point Campground on the south shore has been improved and now offers one site for groups of up to 40 called Contorta Group Site. The fee in 2005 is $45 per day, per group. The second site, called the Contorta Flat Campground, has 18 camping sites available on a first-come, first-served basis and has a fee to camp. Whitefish Horse Camp is located on the west end where campsites can be reserved. Simax Group Camp on the northeast shore is paved; has electricity to all sites, flush toilets, showers, and a reservation system. Picnic facilities are available at Crescent Lake Campground and Simax Beach on the northeast shore, at Spring Creek

Campground, and at Tandy Bay and Tranquil Cove on the west end. Crescent Lake Lodge and Resort is situated at the most northern point of the lake.

Crescent Lake lies 75 miles southeast of Eugene just off State Highway 58 about 10 miles east of Willamette Pass. At the small community of Crescent Lake Junction, National Forest Route 60 heads southwest and reaches the lake in 2 miles, then runs along the northwest and south shores for about 11 miles to its junction with Forest Route 6015. Forest Route 6015 then heads north to join back with Route 60 near the northern tip of the lake.

Coming from Chemult, Crescent Lake Junction is 18 miles northwest of the junction of Highway 58 and Highway 97. A shortcut from Bend is available by turning west onto the Crescent cut-off road (County Route 61) at Crescent and follow to its junction with Highway 58 in 12 miles. It is then 3 miles west on Highway 58 to Crescent Lake Junction.

ODELL LAKE

Size: 3,600 acres
Depth: 305´ max.
Main Catch: kokanee, mackinaw, rainbow trout, whitefish
Best Methods: trolling or jigging for kokanee & mackinaw; still-fishing, fly fishing, & casting spinners or lures for rainbows
Season: end of April to Oct. 31; check OSFR
Best Time: mackinaws best April, May, early June & October
Tips: fish finders, depth gauges & downriggers helpful

Diamond Peak stands as a sentinel over Odell Lake, one of the blue giants of the Deschutes National Forest. A twin to Crescent Lake just a few miles east, Odell Lake covers 3,600 acres, and its cold waters reach a maximum depth of 305 feet. Surrounded by beautiful campsites in thick forests, Odell Lake offers camping, fishing, and windsurfing. Mackinaw, rainbow trout, kokanee, bull trout, and whitefish all naturally reproduce in the lake. Odell Lake is being managed as a trophy mackinaw fishery and holds the state record for mackinaw (lake trout) with a 40-pound, 8-ounce entry in 1984. The fish was 45.5" long and was caught with a homemade jig by Kenneth Erickson, fishing in water 100 to 110 feet deep. The previous state record also came from Odell Lake, a 36-pound, 8-ounce entry in 1976.

A mackinaw weighing 37 pounds was taken out of Odell Lake during the 1998 season, and the lake holds many more in that size range. The average catch is 8 to 9 pounds with many larger. The mackinaw have lots to eat in Odell, preying on smaller fish, including kokanee and whitefish. Many anglers use the strategy of locating the kokanee schools first to find the macks they are really after. Mackinaw should be fished for just below the school of kokanee, on which they may be feeding. The macks also prowl along humps and ledges. Some good mack areas are located east of Princess Creek boat ramp, east of the Highway 58 viewpoint, east of Chinquapin Point boat ramp on the east end, near the railroad slide on the south shore east of Serenity Bay, and off Burley Bluff near Shelter Cove. These fish are found deep most of the year, at depths up to 160 feet. Productive tackle includes weights up to 8 ounces or downriggers (weighted with balls up to 8 pounds) with terminal Rebels, Rapalas or FlatFish in red, fluores-

Surrounded by beautiful campsites in thick forests, Odell Lake is one of the blue giants of the high Cascade lakes. Photo by Geoff Hill
INSET: Jennifer Lewis holds a 17-pound mackinaw she caught at Odell. Photo by Gary Lewis

In this view of Odell Lake looking south toward Shelter Cove, Diamond Peak dominates the horizon. Photo by Geoff Hill

INSET LEFT: Sometimes even a smooth water day will produce a prize catch. Photo by Del Stephens

INSET RIGHT: Crescent and Odell lakes guide, Steve Kroll holds a 30-pound male lake trout before releasing it back into the water. Photo courtesy Steve Kroll

RIGHT: Before releasing his trophy bull trout, an endangered species, this angler posed for the camera. Photo by Steve Kroll, Odell Guide Service

cent colors, blue, or green. Troll off shoals and bottom contours at the correct depth.

One technique perfected by the Luhr Jensen fishing team which has produced consistent mackinaw results (after a concentration of fish has been located using a depth sounder) is jigging with the Nordic or Crippled Herring jigs. Some of the team's favorite jigging areas are out from Princess Creek, viewpoint, and the railroad slide. Glo/Fluorescent Green Stripe and Chartreuse/Green Stripe have been the top colors. See the diagram for jigging instructions *(on page 228)*.

Strikes which come when working a jig almost always occur as the lure is falling. Hesitation in the descent of the jig, a twitch of the line, a "tap" or anything else unusual as the lure is falling is immediate reason for setting the hook. Many times it is not possible to detect a "strike" but resistance is felt when the rod is raised. This, too, signals "set the hook." The use of a premium quality, high-visibility line such as Trilene XT (which also has high knot strength and thin diameter in relation to pound test) is one thing that will aid anglers in detecting strikes as the jig is falling.

The success rate averages 2 mackinaw per day for those with the know-how, with fish finders, and experience. There are many good mack areas in the center of the lake. Look for the right depth once you know how deep they are holding. The fish will move deeper as the water warms in spring. At first ice-out, try north of the lodge where they will be in relatively shallow water. Mack fishing is usually best early in the spring, mainly in April and May, sometimes into June, and will pick up a little again in Octo-

ber. In October, the lake trout spawn near the dock at the lodge.

Kokanee average 10 to 12 inches with a few up to 14 inches in length. Most fishermen jig lures or troll flashers followed by a lure with corn or worm. Ford Fenders, Wedding Rings, and Nordics are popular. A fish finder helps to locate schools.

Trolling techniques work well, with most anglers using lead core line, a lake troll, and a small spoon such as Needlefish, Super Duper, or Kokanee King.

Odell has very clear water, so it is recommended to use a 24- to 48-inch, 4- to 8-pound test leader between troll and lure. During warm weather, when kokes can be found near the bottom, a size 025 Nordic jig or Crippled Herring in Mother-of-Pearl, Silver/Blue Stripe/Silver Prism-Lite or Chartreuse/Green Stripe can be very effective. Seasons seem to change the color schemes. Early in spring, most success is with flame orange; late in the summer, it is pink and white.

One of the biggest mistakes made by anglers is working a lure too fast. Most will not perform correctly at fast speeds and kokanee generally will not hit a fast-moving lure … they need to be tantalized by it. The best advice is to troll S-L-O-W-L-Y — the slower the better.

Kokanee have very delicate and tender-mouths. Care must be taken to make sure the shock of the initial strike is absorbed by using a rubber snubber or having a flexible

rod tip and that they are carefully played and landed with the aid of a net to prevent hooks from tearing out.

Early in the spring, the kokanee will be in water 10 to 30 feet deep often along the north shore and can be caught with worms and corn. In late summer, downriggers may be necessary as the fish are often as much as 100 feet down. The kokanee prefer water temperatures of 60°F or cooler, so be looking for these temperatures as water warms throughout the season. The best fishing for kokanee is usually early and late in the day. In fall, toward their spawning season, the kokanee move into shallower areas of the lake seeking inlets.

Odell has a good population of rainbow trout averaging 12 to 16 inches with some to 18 inches and over. Recently a 22-inch, 5-pound rainbow was recorded; and several over 20 inches were caught. Good techniques include fishing along the shorelines trolling spinners, Wedding Rings with corn or worm, or Rooster Tails in brown or black. Still-fishing with crayfish is also an effective method. There is good fly fishing for rainbow trout around the edges of the lake, near Odell Lake Resort, and on the extreme east end of the lake. The rainbow are active all day; and some mornings and evenings, there is dry fly action in the shallows. They can also be caught off the dock on the east end with worms and bobbers or a fly with a bobber. The south shore can be fished for rain-

bow from the bank.

Odell Lake is closed to the taking of bull trout throughout the season, but they are sometimes caught by mack fishermen. Please release the bull trout carefully. They are listed in the state of Oregon as a threatened and endangered species, and only a small population survives in Odell Lake.

There generally is not much shore fishing at heavily forested Odell Lake. A boat is necessary to fish most effectively. Small boaters beware of the afternoon winds; the lake can get dangerously rough.

Water levels vary little over the year, with many springs and creeks continually feeding the lake. Average depth is 80 to 120 feet. Algae blooms can sometimes slow fishing.

Odell Lake is open late April to October 31. Catch limits are 25 kokanee per day. The trout catch limit is 5 per day, 8-inch minimum length and no more than one over 20 inches. This includes mackinaw (30-inch minimum). Odell is closed to the taking of bull trout and is closed to angling within 200

RIGHT:
Anglers proudly display a 32 lb., 8 oz. big mack.

FAR RIGHT:
A happy fisherman has this catch to smile about … a 28-pounder!
Photos by Del Stephens

feet of the mouth of Trapper Creek. Always check the current OSFR before fishing.

Odell's dependable afternoon winds make it an excellent and popular windsurfing area. An annual canoe race is sponsored by Odell Lake Resort. The lake is bordered on the south by the Diamond Peak Wilderness, with trailheads along the south shore. Skyline Trail skirts the west end of Odell Lake.

Forest Service campgrounds on the lake include Sunset Cove Campground on the northeast corner of the lake with picnic and camping facilities, a boat ramp, drinking water, and fees; Odell Creek Campground on the southeast corner with a trailhead, drinking water, camping, and fees; Trapper Creek Campground on the southwest corner with a boat ramp, camping, water, fees, and a trailhead; and Princess Creek Campground on the north shore with camping, picnicking, drinking water, a boat ramp, and a fee. Pebble Bay Campground, on the south shore, is accessible by boat only and has a very small picnic and camping area, no drinking water, and no fees. During the winter, the area is enjoyed by cross-country skiers.

Odell Lake Resort on the southeast corner of the lake has accommodations, restaurant, marina, guide service, and boat rentals and is open year-round. Shelter Cove Resort, also open year-round, offers a restaurant, cabins, a marina, an RV park, and a store.

Odell Lake is situated along State Highway 58 about 70 miles southeast of Eugene and just a few miles west of Crescent Lake. Highway 58 parallels the northern shore for most of the length of the lake. There are two roads into Odell Lake: the farthest west, Forest Route 5610, leads from Willamette Pass to the west end of the lake and continues along 1/3 of the southern shore; on the east end of the lake, a well-marked paved road leads into Odell Lake Resort and Odell Creek Campground.

Coming from the east, follow directions to Crescent Lake Junction but continue on Highway 58 for 2 miles farther to Odell Lake.

Dean Lewis proves the fishing is great when it's cold and miserable with this 34-pound Mack. Photo by Del Stephens

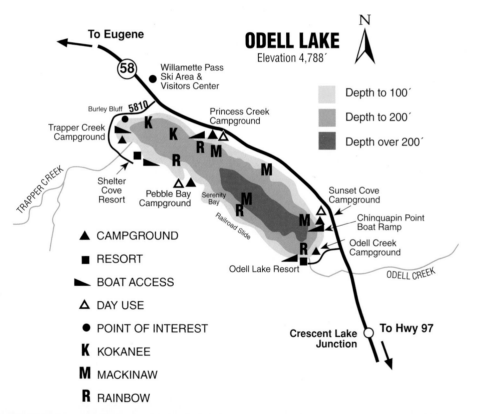

GOLD LAKE

Size: 96 acres
Depth: 43´; 12´ average
Main Catch: brook & rainbow trout
Best Method: fly fishing
Season: Saturday of Memorial Day
weekend to October 31
Tips: fly fishing only

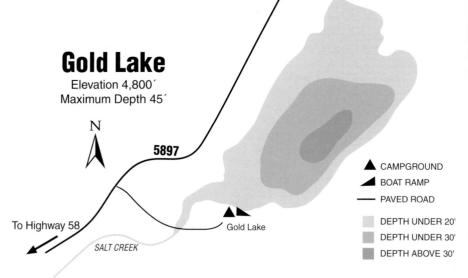

Gold Lake

Elevation 4,800´
Maximum Depth 45´

N

5897

To Highway 58

SALT CREEK

Gold Lake

▲ CAMPGROUND
◣ BOAT RAMP
— PAVED ROAD

⬜ DEPTH UNDER 20'
⬛ DEPTH UNDER 30'
⬛ DEPTH ABOVE 30'

Named for its brown stained water that looks gold in certain conditions, Gold Lake is a productive fly fishing lake on the Willamette Pass just west of Odell Lake. Small, easily accessible, loaded with spunky brook and rainbow trout and constantly changing insect hatches, Gold lends itself to fly fishing from float tubes, canoes and rowboats. Fly fishing only with barbless hooks and no boat motors (gas or electric) are allowed, preserving the serenity of the high Cascade setting.

At 96 acres, Gold Lake is big enough to accommodate a fair number of anglers, but small enough to fin all the way around in a float tube, although it will take awhile. With trees and brush to water's edge, the shore is not very friendly to bank fishers. Likewise, the lakebed's soft muddy bottom make wading difficult. The best fishing is from boats around the lake's extensive weed beds and in the 40-foot depths.

With only the Salt Creek outflow breaking its otherwise oval shape, Gold Lake is pretty easy to read. Just go to where fish are rising, typically along the deep edges of weed beds, and fish with floating lines, dry flies and nymphs. If there is no rise activity, use Woolly Buggers on full sink lines in the center of the lake to reach fish resting near the bottom.

The catch rate is about 2-to-1 brookies over rainbows. The brook trout average 12

inches stretching beyond 20. Rainbows run 11-22 inches with a 13-inch average. Both species are fat, hard fighting fish. Gold Lake is a good place to keep some fish. ODFW wants the brook trout eliminated, so there is no size restriction. Even if everyone caught and kept that many, it will take awhile to trim down the brook trout population. Rainbows must be released unharmed. Apparently, the state is trying to create a quality rainbow trout fishery. Not that it isn't good already.

After Crane Prairie, Gold may be one of the buggiest lakes in the state. There are nearly constant hatches providing myriad opportunities to present nymphs, emergers, dries and spinner patterns. The lake has strong ant, caddis, damsel, mayfly, midge and mosquito hatches. Correct size, color and action matches are critical when fish key in on a particular insect. Fish preferences change frequently so be prepared with a well-equipped fly box and don't hesitate to experiment with leader length and retrieves. Gold Lake fish display split personalities, favoring motionless dries, but

otherwise like actively moving wet flies. Fly sizes tend to be small, with 12-14's common for dries, 8-12's for nymphs and 6-8's on leech and streamer patterns.

There is a nice Forest Service campground with several lake front campsites, restrooms, recycling station and boat ramp on the west end of the lake. A faint trail leads most of the way around the lake, petering out in a boggy area on the east shore. There is some stream fishing opportunity in the Salt Creek outflow a short distance below the lake, but watch OSFR for special closures. Well-marked trails that double as cross-country ski routes in winter lead to the nearby Marilyn and Rosary lakes, Gold Lake Sno-Park and Willamette Pass Ski Area.

From Eugene, travel 70 miles East on State Highway 58, then 2 miles up Forest Road 500. The signed turn-off is about 1 mile west of Willamette Pass Ski Area.

From Bend, travel 80 miles south to Willamette Pass via Century Drive or U.S. Highway 97, connecting with Highway 58. Travel west past Willamette Pass Ski Area, then 2 miles up FSR 5897.

ABOVE: Author Brooke displays his brook. Gold Lake brookies are plentiful, and there is no limit on size or number per day.
RIGHT: Some sort of watercraft is helpful in locating fish.
Photos by Brooke Snavely

BEST PONDS AND LAKES FOR KIDS (AND ADULTS)

Several of Central Oregon's lakes and ponds are managed for accessibility and opportunity. A few are limited to kids under a certain age. Refer to the Oregon Sport Fishing Regulations as the rules are subject to change.

When fishing with kids, start off with tackle matched to their size, but choose it carefully. A light five to six foot rod is about right for a three to four foot child. Don't skimp on the rod or reel. A good reel will help keep tangles to a minimum.

Fill the reel with good line. Four- to six-pound test is perfect for trout. It casts easier than heavier line and won't spook as many fish. Put a few barrel swivels in with their tackle. You will tie a swivel on the end of the main line and then tie a twenty inch leader on the end of that. Knot a No. 10-12 bait hook to the leader. Buy hooks with a non-reflective finish and barbs to hold the bait.

For bait fishing, it doesn't get much better than worms but you will do well to experiment with some of the other trout baits. Sometimes one bait or combination of baits will work when nothing else does.

The weather can change quickly early in the season so bring warm clothes and something to change into if someone falls in. Bring something to eat and drink as well. Allow children the freedom to play on the bank and spend a little time looking at the bugs that live under the rocks. Explain that the trout don't just eat worms, but that their diet consists mainly of insects. Make it interesting and fun.

With a little patience and preparation, even parents who aren't fishermen can teach and enjoy fishing with their children. Not only are you ensuring that you'll have someone to go fishing with, you're ensuring that the next generation will appreciate and enjoy the outdoors as much as you have.

Oregon lists their stocking schedule on its web site (www.dfw.state.or.us). Some lakes are stocked with only eight- to ten-inch fish. Other waters receive plantings of brood-stock trout, weighing up to five pounds. The great thing about hatchery trout is that they are used to regular feedings. They're hungry by opening day.

SHEVLIN POND

Size:	1 acre
Depth:	4 feet
Main Catch:	rainbow trout
Best Methods:	fly fishing & spin fishing
Season:	entire year
Best Time:	April through November
Who can fish:	children 17 and under
Tips:	Use a fly and bubble on a spinning rod. Best flies are Prince Nymph, Woolly Bugger, baitfish patterns.

Nestled in a grove of pine trees in the Tumalo Creek drainage, Shevlin Pond is one of the friendliest of the kid-friendly ponds in Central Oregon. A small pond, about an acre in size, it is stocked regularly throughout the fishing season with catchable rainbow trout.

Shevlin has an average depth of about three feet and is completely accessible all the way around. Fish will move from one end of the lake to the other dependent on depth and feed conditions.

All methods work well here, but fly fishing is very productive. One effective technique for taking trout combines the simplicity of the spinning rod with the subtleties of fly fishing.

The casting bubble is the key to making this technique effective. It must be the type that can be filled with water, which provides the weight necessary for long-distance casting. Whether fishing on the surface or below the surface, the best choice is the medium size, clear plastic bubble that is the approximate size of a chicken egg.

Slide the bubble over your main line and tie on a No. 12 or 14 black barrel swivel. Knot a three-foot, four-pound test leader to your barrel swivel, then tie on the fly. For starters, use a wet fly such as a No. 8 Woolly Bugger, or No. 10 Woolly Worm. Good nymph patterns are flies like the beadhead Hare's Ear, Pheasant Tail, or Prince Nymph. When fishing for bigger fish, try patterns such as the No. 8 Muddler Minnow, Zonker, or crayfish imitations.

Cast, tighten up the line, and begin to reel — slowly. Vary the depth and retrieve until you find the fish. A slow retrieve is usually the most effective.

For best success, check the stocking schedule before heading to Shevlin Pond. Oregon lists their stocking schedule on its website (www.dfw.state.or.us).

Shevlin Park is located about 3 miles west of Bend. Drive west on Newport Avenue, which becomes Shevlin Park Road as you leave town. Shevlin Park Road drops down into Tumalo Creek canyon. Cross the creek and turn right into the parking lot at Shevlin Park. The pond is a short walk north from the parking area.

LEFT: Shevlin Pond is a great beginner pond for kids.
Photo by Gary Lewis

LOWER LEFT: Kids love to go fishing from a boat. Always make sure they wear a lifevest.
Photo by Mark L. Armstrong

BELOW: Grandpa shared his love for fly fishing with granddaughter Ashley.
Photo courtesy carbonesflyfishing.com

CENTURY GRAVEL PIT

Size: 3 acres
Depth: 6 feet
Main Catch: rainbow trout
Best Methods: spin fishing
Season: entire year
Best Time: May through October
Who can fish: all ages
Tips: Use a small spoon tipped with bait. Cast and make a slow, somewhat erratic retrieve.

Century Gravel Pit is located off the road between Big Cultus and Little Cultus Lakes. Lacking the ambience of most of the nearby waters, it offers, nonetheless, access and opportunity for anglers who need to put some trout on the table.

Stocked with rainbow trout throughout the season, fishing improves as the shallow water warms in the spring. Fish the deepest water for the best success. Minnow imitations work well at Century Gravel Pit. Use a small spoon or a floating Rapala or similar lure in a rainbow pattern. Check the stocking schedule before you go. Oregon lists their stocking schedule on its web site (www.dfw.state.or.us).

To reach the Century Gravel Pit, follow the Cascade Lakes Highway west out of Bend, then south past Elk Lake and Lava Lake. Continue past the junction with Road 40 and turn right on Road 4635 toward Big Cultus Lake. Turn left on Road 4630 and left again on the road to the gravel pit.

FIREMAN'S POND
(A.K.A. LIONS' POND)

Size: 1 acre
Depth: 3 feet
Main Catch: rainbow trout, largemouth bass, bluegill, catfish
Best Methods: spin fishing
Season: entire year
Best Time: April through July
Who can fish: all ages
Tips: Use sliding sinker to bring bait down. Slide bullet sinker on main line, then tie on 18–36" leader. Suspend bait off bottom with Berkeley Power Bait or marshmallow in front of a piece of worm.

Fireman's Pond (a.k.a. Lions' Pond) is a small pond in a park within the Redmond city limits. A paved peninsula offers wheelchair access and a grass bank puts anglers close to the water. Because you have the opportunity to hook bass, trout, or bluegill, fish a fly and bubble combination, or a nightcrawler under a float for the most consistent action.

Cut 20 inches of four-pound line to use as a leader and connect it to the main line with a swivel. Tie a No. 8–12 hook to the end of the leader. The float will attach to the main line above the swivel. You may need to add some lead weight above the swivel, depending on the type of bait you use.

From Redmond, head east on SE Veteran's Way. Cross the railroad tracks and turn left on SW Lake Road. Proceed less than 1/2 mile. The pond is on the left.

REYNOLD'S POND

Size: 20 acres
Depth: 6 feet
Main Catch: bullhead, sunfish, largemouth bass
Best Methods: bait fishing
Season: entire year
Best Time: April through October
Who can fish: all ages
Tips: For bullhead, fish late in the evening. Use a sliding sinker and a single hook baited with a nightcrawler.

Reynold's Pond is a quiet lake hidden away in the sagebrush and junipers east of Alfalfa. Largemouth bass, bullhead catfish and redear sunfish make up the bulk of the catch here. Access along the bank is good and most of the best water is within casting range. The pond is a short walk from the parking area, and though there is no boat launch, you can carry in a raft, canoe, or a float tube to help you explore more water.

For the bass, fish close to structure with plastic worms or grubs. For bullhead, fish late in the evening. Use a sliding sinker and a single hook baited with a nightcrawler. To catch the sunfish, use a fly and bubble or a single hook baited with a grasshopper.

To find Reynold's Pond, drive east of Bend on Alfalfa Market Road toward the town of Alfalfa. Continue east to Johnson Market Road and head south. The lake about 1/2 mile past the landfill.

LEFT: Success puts a smile on the face of this young angler.
Photo by Mark L. Armstrong

ABOVE: Many of the smaller ponds hold some nice bluegills.
Photo by Brian O'Keefe

MIRROR POND

Size:	20 acres
Depth:	6 feet
Main Catch:	rainbow trout
Best Methods:	spin fishing
Season:	entire year
Best Time:	April through October
Who can fish:	all ages
Tips:	Concentrate on fishing the river channel (visible at low water).

Downtown Bend offers an underutilized fishery in the Deschutes River. Mirror Pond, the centerpiece of Bend's Drake Park, is open to fishing for rainbow trout and whitefish. Bait is permitted on this section of the river and a limit of two rainbow trout is permitted.

Fish the holes in the old river channel with bait for the best success. There are two ways to fish with bait: either suspended from a float, or on the bottom. Cut 20 inches of four-pound line to use as a leader and connect it to the main line with a swivel. Tie a No. 8 - 12 hook to the end of the leader. The float will attach to the main line above the swivel. You may need to add some lead weight above the swivel, depending on the type of bait you use.

Worms or salmon eggs work well for trout when fished under a bobber. Berkeley Power Bait and similar "jar baits" are best used when fishing off the bottom.

To fish off the bottom, slide a bullet sinker on your main line. Tie on a barrel swivel, then tie on a 24-inch leader. Power Bait or a marshmallow in front of a piece of worm will keep your bait suspended above the vegetation.

To fish Mirror Pond, drive west on Franklin Avenue past the intersection with Wall Street and find a place to park along Drake Park.

SPRAGUE PIT

Size:	3 acres
Depth:	7 feet
Main Catch:	rainbow trout
Best Methods:	spin fishing
Season:	entire year
Best Time:	May through October
Who can fish:	all ages
Tips:	Worms or salmon eggs work well for trout when fished under a bobber. Berkeley Power Bait and similar "jar baits" are best used when fishing off the bottom.

Sprague Pit is a shallow lake close to Crane Prairie Reservoir. Stocked with trout throughout the season, it can be a good bet after the water warms in the spring. Bait-fishing is the preferred method here.

Spoons that imitate baitfish work well at Sprague Pit. Little Cleos, Triple Teasers, and Kastmasters are some of the more popular models. Smaller is better when targeting hatchery trout. Add a snap swivel, then tie the spoon directly to your main line and add a little weight if needed. Add a chunk of worm to provide a scent trail. Cast, let it sink, and retrieve just fast enough to keep your lure wobbling, not spinning.

The best plugs for catching hatchery trout are minnow and crayfish imitations. Try small Rapalas, FlatFish, or Hot Shots. You will need to add some weight for casting. Vary your retrieve and depth until you start hooking rainbows.

To reach Sprague Pit, follow Road 40 west from Sunriver. Drive past the Crane Prairie turn-off and head south on Road 970. Turn left at the cattle guard.

ABOVE: the reason for the name Mirror Pond is evident in this photo. Photo by David Morris

LEFT: These kids are old enough to venture out on their own, and smart enough to wear their lifevests. Photo by Mark L. Armstrong

ANTONE RANCH LAKES

Size:	186 surface acres 6 lakes
Depth:	4-30 feet
Main Catch:	rainbow trout
Best Methods:	fly fishing
Season:	April through October
Best Time:	spring, fall
Tips:	Plan on fishing subsurface for the best action. These are big fish. Use a 4x fluorocarbon leader and keep your hooks sharp.

Flora Lake is one of six private fishing lakes at Antone. Photo by Gary Lewis
INSET: Fish average 16 to 18 inches here, but lunkers available. Photo courtesy flyandfield.com

High in the Ochocos, on the historic 40,000-acre Antone Ranch, you'll find six private fly fishing-only lakes in a variety of settings. Gold mining brought the first white men into the country. The old Dalles Canyon Wagon Road runs through the ranch and the original stagecoach stop is still standing. Eight soldiers, killed by Indians are buried in an old military cemetery that can be found on the ranch. The Antone Ranch is famous for its big trout to 14 pounds and its elk, deer and antelope herds. Watch for cinnamon teal, mallards and geese on the lakes.

Fort Lake is the first lake you come to after you leave the highway. It is a desert-type lake set in the sagebrush that fishes well with subsurface patterns like the Prince Nymph, Zug Bug, Tellico and water boatman patterns.

Six miles into mountains lies Fred's Lake, a pretty pond surrounded by tall pines and junipers. Two guest cabins sit on a knoll overlooking the water. One of the oldest lakes on the ranch, it has great trout habitat with shallows and weedbeds for growing insects, reeds, an island and deep pockets for escape cover. It is well-known for producing large rainbows. Bank fishing is possible, but a boat provides access to the best water.

Flora Lake was built about the same time as Fred's, about 40 years ago. The second largest lake, it is one of the prettiest of the six lakes on the ranch. Islands, shallows, willows and reeds provide ideal trout habi-

tat. It has deeper water, big fish, good weed structure and lots of insect activity. Fish near the island or along the willows near the dam. A good weedbed near the dam is known for booting out big, reel-burning rainbows. Midges, callibaetis, and damsel flies are good bets.

Clint's Lake is a small, long, skinny pond that runs about eight feet deep. The lake is fed by a small stream that enters at the end nearest the parking area. It is best fished from the shore. Fish average 12 to 14 inches, but bigger fish are available. Cast a red, purple, or black leech on an intermediate line and vary the retrieve until you find the right action.

Rock Lake is the biggest and highest in elevation. Fed by Rock Creek, it is a productive lake. Because of its size, Rock gets the least pressure of all the waters on the ranch. Target the weedbeds, shallows, rocky points and transitions to deeper water with leeches, callibaetis nymphs and chironomids.

High Lake is a smaller lake that is best fished from a float tube or pontoon boat. It has prime weed structure and riprap that provides good insect production. The water is deepest by the dam. Fish average 16 to 18 inches, but trout to 30 inches can be seen cruising along the banks.

If you'd like to try something different, try Rock Creek for native rainbows that average six to ten inches. Fish attractor dry flies like the Royal Wulff, Humpy and Irresistible.

Go for the day or reserve the ranch for several days. Picnic tables, grills on fire pits, and outhouses are available at some of the lakes. If you'll be staying overnight, you'll have the use of one of the cabins overlooking Fred's Lake. Each two-story cabin sleeps six. They have kitchens, running water, and showers. Solar panels collect the energy that provides the electricity feeding the cabins. A large propane tank provides the fuel for cooking and heating.

Contact Information: Go West Outfitters (541) 447-4082; Fly and Field Outfitters (541) 318-1616.

From Prineville, drive east on Highway 26 past the town of Mitchell. Turn right at mile marker 80 on the well-graveled and graded Antone Road. In 1.5 miles, you'll see Fort Lake on the right. 7 miles from the highway, turn right at a dirt road. You'll see Fred's Lake and the cabins in just over one mile. Because this ranch is high in the mountains, a sudden rainstorm or snowfall could happen any month of the year. Bring a four-wheel drive vehicle to negotiate the dirt roads.

BARNES BUTTE LAKE

Size: 45 acres
Depth: 30 feet
Main Catch: rainbow trout,
   largemouth bass, bluegill
Best Methods: fly fishing
Season: April through October
Best Time: spring for rainbows;
   summer for warmwater
   fish
Tips: For rainbows, troll a red or
   black leech pattern along
   edge of channel. Twitch
   the fly to give it action.

A few miles north of Prineville, in the shadow of Barnes Butte, lies a 45-acre fly fishing-only lake surrounded by sagebrush and interesting volcanic rock formations. Barnes Butte Lake is home to four different strains of rainbows, and some nice largemouth bass.

Shallow flats, a deep channel, shoreside reeds, submerged sagebrush and standing timber combine to create a diverse habitat. Fish for trout in the shallows in the early morning and then search the channel later in the day. Then move into the shadows of the standing trees and cast poppers or mouserats to big bucketmouths. The rainbows average 18 inches and can get a lot bigger. Largemouth bass average one to three pounds and run to six pounds.

To access the best fishing, bring a float tube, canoe, or a pontoon boat. Fish the shallow shelf on the east side of the lake first thing in the morning. Using an intermediate sinking line, troll leech patterns like the Woolly Bugger, Lake Bugger and Mohair Leech or pull a soft hackle wet fly like the Carey Special. Other effective patterns include the Hares Ear, Zug Bug and Prince Nymph.

As the sun comes up, the fish move to deeper water. Target the transitions to deeper water. An old creek bed runs the length of the reservoir.

Chironomids will produce fish any time of year. Use a floating line, strike indicator and a long leader to fish No. 14-18 midge larvae and pupa patterns. Set the indicator to hold the fly above the top of the weeds. Cast downwind, keep your line tight. Occasional one-inch twitches may bring the strikes.

Largemouth bass fishing heats up when the water warms in late April or early May and the females claim their nests in the shallows along the shore. Fish from the bank in either arm on the north end of the lake or from your float tube. Bring polarized glasses to help you see through the glare on the water. Cast big poppers or streamer patterns to provoke a big female guarding her nest.

After the spawn, use minnow-imitating streamers like the Zonker, or weighted Muddler Minnow. The six-inch Bunny Leech streamer and the Mouserat are other effective patterns for Barnes Butte bass. Cast to the shore and to submerged timber. Vary the retrieve until you find the action that sparks the bass bite.

Contact Central Oregon fly shops for more information.

From Prineville, head north on Main Street. Turn right and drive a mile west on NE Barnes Butte Road, you'll see the lake on your right.

FAR LEFT AND BELOW: To access big rainbows like this one, bring a float tube, canoe, or a pontoon boat. Gary Lewis (below) with a beautiful rainbow, reeled in from his float tube.

ABOVE AND LEFT: This 45-acre private lake is fly fishing only. Barnes Butte dominates the horizon.

Gary Lewis photos

BEAR CREEK RESERVOIR

Size: 36 acres
Depth: 85 feet at deepest
Main Catch: rainbow & redband trout
Best Methods: fly fishing
Season: entire year
Best Time: spring, fall
Tips: Troll and twitch an olive leech pattern on a diagonal between dock and rocky point

This private fly fishing-only mountain reservoir grows some nice size rainbows. For the best fishing, bring a float tube or a pontoon boat.
Photos by Gary Lewis

In the foothills of the Maury Mountains, east of Alfalfa and southeast of Prineville Reservoir is a small, deep reservoir that grows big rainbows. Bear Creek Reservoir is a private mountain lake surrounded by ranchland and good deer and elk habitat. Pines and junipers cloak the hills around the water. An old windmill stands silent sentinel, testament to early efforts to tame the land.

Bear Creek was dammed in the mid-1980s to form the irrigation impoundment. Native redband rainbows quickly adapted to the new conditions and continue to spawn in the inlet creek. Fed by Deer Creek and Bear Creek, the reservoir is fishable throughout the summer in some years, but may be closed during times of drought to protect the fishery.

Big rainbows are stocked in the lake from time to time to augment the existing fishery. The hard-fighting trout average 13 to 17 inches and quickly take to the air to throw the hook. Biggest Bear Creek fish run to 26 inches and eight pounds. Fishing is limited to fly tackle and catch and release.

Crayfish were added to the lake a few years ago, but it is unclear whether they were successful in establishing a colony. Midge and caddis hatches are strong on this lake. Bring damselfly and dragonfly nymphs. Fish a crayfish pattern close to the bottom. Try a dry bumblebee pattern if you make it there during the summer or in the early fall.

For the best fishing, bring a float tube or a pontoon boat. Using an intermediate sinking line, troll leech patterns like the Lake Bugger and Mohair Leech or pull a soft hackle wet fly like the Carey Special. Other effective patterns include the Tellico, Zug Bug and Prince Nymph.

Chironomids will produce fish at any time of year. Use a floating line, strike indicator and a long leader to fish No. 14-18 midge larvae and pupa patterns. Set the indicator to hold the fly above the top of the weeds. Cast downwind, keep your line tight and twitch the fly occasionally.

The east end of the lake is shallow with some grass in the water. Fishing can be good here early in the spring and then later in the summer as trout seek the cooler water of the inlet streams. A rocky point on the north side of the lake is another good spot. Try trolling between the dock and the rocky point.

Action Outfitters manages the lake. Exclusive memberships are available that include access to the cabin. Cabin sleeps six comfortably and is equipped with cooking appliances and running water. Battle Creek Outfitters leases the hunting rights on the surrounding property. Other activities available include hunting and sporting clays. You'll see pronghorn antelope, elk, mule deer, ground squirrels and coyotes. Contact Action Outfitters and Guide Service (541-536-5893) and Central Oregon fly shops for reservations.

A high-clearance vehicle is recommended but not necessary for negotiating the last 200 yards to the cabin.

ALDER CREEK RANCH

Size:	13 acres
Depth:	7 feet avg; max. depth 20´
Main Catch:	rainbow trout
Best Methods:	fly fishing
Season:	March through October
Best Time:	spring, fall
Tips:	Bring polarized glasses and stalk trout from the shore before launching tube or pontoon boat.

East of Sisters, nestled in a grove of junipers and pine trees is a pretty little lake fed by a creek. Supplemented by well water the lake stays cold throughout the summer. When you go, expect to see geese and ducks resting on the lake. If you arrive early enough in the morning, you'll see a herd of mule deer feeding in the fields. Coyotes, bobcats and hawks hunt pheasants, chukar and quail in the nearby rimrock and sage.

Trout grow fast in this nutrient-rich water. Rainbows average 16 to 18 inches, but you'll see and hook plenty of bigger fish. Every year, several trout over ten pounds are caught and released. Fish from a float tube or stalk the bank and sight-fish to trout feeding in the shallows.

Fishing from shore, bring small wet flies such as the Tellico, Brown Hackle, Woolly Worm, San Juan Worm, and Flashback Nymphs. Don polaroid glasses to cut the glare and approach the water cautiously. Conceal yourself behind willows and shore-side brush and cast to fish feeding or resting near the shore. Let the fly hit the water, three to four feet away. Let it begin to sink then twitch it. Often the fish will start toward deeper water, then make a hard right or left turn and grab your fly, going airborne when it feels the steel.

If you bring a float tube or a pontoon boat, trolling a leech pattern is an effective way to put fish in the net. If you have an intermediate sinking line, this is the place to use it. Pull your fly along the weed beds in the transition zones from the shallows to deeper water. Or anchor and cast a floating line downwind with a strike indicator above a chironomid imitation.

The lake at Alder Creek Ranch is a terrific place to spend a half-day or a full day chasing trout in Central Oregon. Views of Broken Top and South Sister provide scenic beauty. Grassy banks, a picnic table and a dock are in a nice setting for a shore lunch.

Contact Information: Alder Creek Ranch (541) 549-3019; Central Oregon fly shops.

CLOCKWISE: Views of Broken Top and South Sister provide scenic beauty at the lake at Alder Creek Ranch. (above) This angler, a touring musician, has "big" success. (left) Gary Lewis has success as well! Top photo and photo above courtesy Alder Creek Ranch; Photo left Gary Lewis photo.

LAKE IN THE DUNES

Size: 5 lakes
Depth: easily waded
Main Catch: rainbow & brown trout
Best Methods: catch-and-release
fly fishing only
Season: March 1–Oct. 15
Best Time: consistent throughout
fishing season; best
in morning
Tips: private trout fishing
operation only, pay-to-fish

Imagine the amazing experience of standing at 4,000 feet elevation in the middle of a remote alkali and sagebrush desert, a harsh

RIGHT: Peter Bowers shows off a thick bodied rainbow from Lake in the Dunes.
Peter Bowers photo

BELOW: Catching trophy fish is what makes these manmade lakes so special.
Photo by Loren Irving

environment of extreme temperatures and landscape and having at your feet five lakes filled not merely with your average trout but with leviathans of two trout species. Lake in the Dunes is a unique venture for those rare souls willing to drive to the middle of nowhere and pay to catch lunker salmonids, only to gently release them.

Lake in the Dunes is one of the finest private trout fishing operations in the state, offering pay-to-fish, catch-and-release fly fishing with barbless hooks. The operation is not a profit-making venture; fees just cover expenses. These small, fertile, manmade desert lakes are located near Summer Lake off State Highway 31, about 107 miles south-southeast of Bend.

Formed by a series of dikes, the lakes are fed by springs providing more than 2 million gallons of water daily at a constant 56°F temperature, ideal trout growing conditions. The pure, crystal clear water and the shallow nature of the lakes make catching these trophy fish a real challenge. Combined, the lakes cover approximately 40 acres on the 480-acre ranch. The bulk of the ranch is managed as wetlands for wildlife. Bird watchers and photographers often rent the ranch solely for these opportunities, particularly in the spring.

Naturally reproducing rainbow trout dominate the lakes and average 12 to 16 inches, with some from 16 to 20 inches and a few up to 10 pounds. Fewer in number, brown trout average 12 to 15 inches, with the largest over 20 inches in length.

Presentation and fly size are the most important factors to consider while angling here. These fish are wary; you can see them, and they can see you. You must be stealthy.

Fly selection will depend on the time of year. The lakes support a large variety of insects, so productive patterns will change as the day progresses. Mayflies predominate, and there is an abundance of damselflies.

The rainbow trout can usually be caught on small dries, often callibaetis, baetis, and midge imitations. Be prepared to fish both dries and nymphs. The browns will take pretty much the same flies as the rainbow, with a possible preference for small emergers and small mayfly dries. Midge imitations to size 20 or smaller may be necessary. Adams, Comparadun, Elk Hair Caddis, Olive Dun, callibaetis, and Deer Hair Spider patterns would complete an adequate selection of dry flies. Prince Nymphs, damsel and chironomid imitations, Hare's Ears, Montana and black AP Nymphs, Pheasant Tails, and Woolly Buggers round out a generous nymph assortment. Fishing success is pretty consistent throughout the March 1 through October 15 season.

Fishing is often best in the morning, due to periodically heavy afternoon winds. Since most of the lakes are shallow enough to be easily waded, floating devices are not needed. Grasses and cattails line the banks, and the bottoms are mostly smooth sand with some aquatic weeds. Additional structures, including manmade islands, are being added as time goes by.

A rustic log cabin is available on the property which will accommodate up to five people. There is a loft; a small, fully equipped kitchen; electricity, and an indoor bathroom with shower. It is possible to camp on the property with permission. The town of Summer Lake, 7 miles away, has a motel, gas, a restaurant, and

Fisherman, Jeff Rose, is proud of his beautiful Lake in the Dunes rainbow.
Photo by Loren Irving

a store. Nearby BLM land provides an opportunity for primitive camping.

Reservations for Lake in the Dunes are exclusively for your party. The booking contact is The Patient Angler Fly Shop in Bend. Prices for the 2005 season are as follows: weekends: 1–5 persons, $350 a day; weekdays: 1–5 persons, $300 a day. Cabin rental is included in the daily rates. Guides are available through the booking agent for an extra fee, but are really not necessary. Directions to Lake in the Dunes are given when you make your reservation.

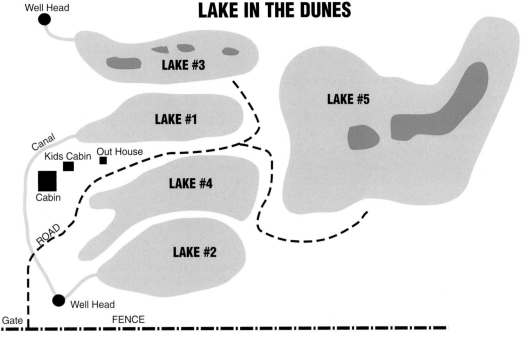

LAKE IN THE DUNES

GRINDSTONE LAKES

Size:	200 surface acres in 5 lakes
Depth:	varies
Main Catch:	rainbow trout
Best Methods:	fly fishing
Season:	entire year
Best Time:	spring, fall
Tips:	Fish two chironomid patterns in tandem under a strike indicator.

Deep inside Oregon's historic GI Ranch, situated on the flanks of the Ochoco Mountains, you'll find a collection of five private reservoirs called Grindstone Lakes. These fly fishing-only waters are famous for producing rainbow trout measured in pounds, not inches.

Several old homesteads remain on the ranch. Deer, elk and pronghorn antelope can be seen browsing in meadows or resting in the shade of a juniper. Expect to see ground squirrels, cottontails and maybe a coyote or a badger. Bird life includes killdeer, ruddy ducks, scaup and osprey.

Supporting abundant aquatic insect life, Grindstone's lakes grow fish fast. Important trout foods include: chironomids, callibaetis, damselflies, caddis, leeches, freshwater shrimp, dragonflies, snails and waterboatmen.

Williams Lake, the largest on the property, is the most frequently fished water. Here, the trout average 19 inches and run to ten pounds. A few remnant brook trout are in the lake and can be caught near the dam. Fish it from a float tube or pontoon boat or stalk trout along the bank.

Named for the dead junipers left in the lake when the dam was built, Black Snag has some of the best big fish potential. Norcross Reservoir is also well-known for producing trophy fish. Leave your little trout net at home. These fish can tip the scales in the low 'teens. If you're fishing lighter than a 3X tippet, you're asking for trouble.

Grindstone Lake has good shoreside weed growth that pulls the big rainbows close to the banks to feed. Before you put your tube in the water, ease along the bank and try to hook a big one feeding the weeds.

Bueker is the smallest of the five reservoirs. Its dam was repaired in 2003 and the lake is anticipated to fish well after restocking in 2004.

To start, tie on an olive, black or red leech pattern with a Damselfly Nymph or Pheasant Tail for a dropper. Twitch your flies as you troll and retrieve with four- to six-inch strips.

To fish chironomids, use a floating line, strike indicator and a long leader to fish the No. 14-18 midge larvae and pupa patterns. Set the indicator to hold the fly above the top of the weeds. Cast downwind, keep your line

tight and keep your eye on the indicator. Fishing pressure is restricted and lakes are rested after a day's fishing, assuring that Grindstone's trout don't become leader-shy.

Book your Grindstone trip for an overnight stay, or better yet, stay for three nights, fishing a different lake each day. Each angler must bring their own gear, including float tube or pontoon boat. Some rental equipment is available upon request. Buy your fishing license in advance.

Lodge accommodations are comfortable and clean. All meals are provided and the food is good. Bring your own sleeping bag, pillow and towels.

A four-wheel drive vehicle with high ground clearance is recommended for negotiating the ranch roads.

Call (541) 416-9191 for reservations.

To reach Grindstone Lakes from Prineville (start with a full fuel tank), head east on Highway 26 and turn right on Combs Flat Road at the edge of town. In 1-1/2 miles, the road forks. Stay left and travel 55 miles to Paulina. Continue past mile marker 65 and turn right on Grindstone Road. In 1-1/2 miles the road forks, stay to the right and continue traveling on a well-groomed dirt and gravel road for 10 miles. You'll reach an intersection. Turn left and travel for one more mile to reach a locked gate where your guide will meet you at the appointed time.

BUCKHORN LAKE

Size:	15 acres
Depth:	25 feet
Main Catch:	rainbow and largemouth bass
Best Methods:	fly fishing
Season:	spring, fall
Best Time:	spring, late fall
Tips:	Fish a chironomid beneath a strike indicator.

Buckhorn Lake is a pretty reservoir fed by water from Three Sisters Irrigation, with views of the Three Sisters and Broken Top to the south. Mule deer, Rocky Mountain elk and coyotes make their living on the surrounding ranchland. Bald eagles and osprey hunt from the top of a nearby snag.

A fly fishing-only lake, Buckhorn produces rainbows from three to 12 pounds and largemouth bass to six pounds. Rainbows must be released, but bass may be retained.

Kamloops rainbows and Summer Lake triploids can be found in the lake. Largemouth bass prowl the shallows from late spring through the fall. Buckhorn Lake was formed when the dam was built, flooding a

Five private reservoirs make up Grindstone Lakes, situated on the flanks of the Ochocos. Gary Lewis Photo

canyon. For cover, the fish hide beneath lava ledges and under downed timber. Old ponderosa pine stumps and dead junipers provide fantastic habitat along the west shore.

Substantial weedbeds and shoreside reeds provide insect growth. Baby bass, frogs, dragonflies, damselflies, chironomids, and snails are some of the primary trout foods.

To reach the best fishing, bring a float tube or pontoon boat, but good bank access allows the angler to fish from shore.

A clear, intermediate, slow-sinking line will allow the fisherman to reach more trout when trolling flies. Use at least nine feet of fluorocarbon leader and don't go too light. These fish are big. Tie on an olive or black Woolly Bugger with a Damselfly Nymph for a dropper. Twitch your flies as you troll and retrieve with four- to six-inch strips.

Chironomids make up the bulk of a trout's diet in most stillwaters. Buckhorn is no exception. To fish chironomids in three to 15 feet of water, use a floating line, strike indicator and a long leader to drop the No. 14-18 midge larvae and pupa patterns into a big trout's dining room. Set the indicator to hold the fly above the top of the weeds. Cast downwind, keep your line tight and your eye on the indicator.

Barbless hooks are recommended. Crimp your barbs before you fish. When you bring your trout to hand, keep it in the water as you slide the hook out. If you need a picture, lift it out when the cameraman gives you the word, then put the fish back in when the shutter snaps. Cradle the fish as it regains its strength, gently rocking it, until it kicks away under its own power.

Central Oregon is home to huge resident goose populations. In the fall, when waterfowl migrations are under way, duck and goose hunting is available at Buckhorn Ranch in combination with a fishing trip.

For more information, contact Marc Thalacker (541-390-5453).

To reach Buckhorn from Bend, drive north on Highway 97 through Terrebonne. Head west on Lower Bridge Road and drive past mile marker 9 and turn right at the mailbox marked 70625 NW Lower Bridge Way.

WILD BILLY LAKE

Size: 200 acres
Depth: 21´
Main Catch: rainbow trout
Best Method: wet flies
Season: ice-off to ice-up (typically mid-Feb. to mid-Dec.)
Best Times: spring, fall
Tips: private fee lake

LEFT: Outdoor writer Steve Probasco with a Kamloop trout. Photo by Ron Meek

BELOW: A big rainbow for Daren Henderson. Photo by Butch Price

Wild Billy Lake gets its name from two men named Bill; both got in fights in early pioneer times that resulted in deaths. Nowadays most of the fighting at Wild Billy Lake is between anglers and trout with casualties ranging from sore fish lips to wrist exhaustion. The rest is verbal disagreements over who caught the biggest fish. A pay-to-fish operation since 1996, Wild Billy is gaining a reputation as one of Oregon's premier private fly fishing lakes.

A natural lake in the Sprague River valley east of Chiloquin, Wild Billy is planted with four strains of rapidly growing rainbow trout: Lassen, Kamloop, steelhead hybrid and triploid. All regularly attain sizes over 10 pounds. Lake operators are excited about recently introduced triploids, which are sterilized female trout. The theory is sterile fish won't waste energy spawning, just live long lives eating and growing to obscene sizes, possibly as large as 18 pounds. The current lake record is estimated at 15 pounds (13 inches long, with a girth of 17 inches) with the average trout running 18 inches, weighing about 3 lbs.

The best action is with minnow imitating wet flies on sinking lines cast toward shore and stripped back to the boat. Large trout hit minnow patterns hard, frequently breaking 6- and 8-pound tippet if they happen to strike while an angler is stripping. If trout aren't visibly chasing minnows in the shallows, try fishing deeper with Woolly Buggers and leeches toward the middle of the lake. A creek inlet in the northwest corner, rocky bank along the southeast shoreline, and underwater ridges toward the middle of the lake are prime places to begin searching for submarine size trout.

There are damselfly, dragonfly, mayfly and midge hatches in warm weather, but the fish display only fleeting interest in them with the higher energy minnow food source so available. Most Wild Billy anglers forget about dry flies once they've experienced what minnow patterns can do. Eighty is the record for most fish caught in one day. One butterfingered angler lost three rods in a day to the hard-charging trout.

At least 5- or 6-weight rods are recommended with type II, III and IV uniform sinking lines. 4X-6X tippets are necessary to give anglers a fighting chance on the bigger fish. Leader length doesn't seem to matter. It would be silly to fish without a lot backing. A quality reel with smooth drag system certainly helps. Size 6 minnow/leech/streamer pattern flies in black, green, white and tan do a good job imitating the minnows. Best times are February through June, sometimes into July depending on algae blooms, and in October and November.

Operators maintain the quality of the fishery by limiting use to three days a week by a maximum of 24 people per week. All fish must be released. Only small gap barbless hooks are allowed. Even at the rate of $150 per day per angler (in 2005) the lake is booked months in advance. Cabins can be rented for an additional $60 per night. Camping is allowed at two sites. Driftboats are included in the fee, giving anglers a mobility advantage over float tubes, which work well for those who aren't in a rush to get around this medium size private lake. Fishing from shore can be effective.

Wild Billy Lake is about 45 miles east of Chiloquin via the Sprague River Road. Chiloquin is 115 miles south of Bend on U.S. Highway 97; 26 miles north of Klamath Falls on Highway 97. Contact Wild Billy Lake (541) 747-5595 for information, reservations and directions. Lodging and restau-

BELOW: Randy Rosin with another beautiful Kamloop trout. Photo by Ron Thienes

BACK COUNTRY LAKES

For anglers wishing to explore an area with more remote fish-filled lakes than can be experienced in a lifetime, Central Oregon is a dream-come-true. Magnificent scenery, old growth forests, sparkling clear, uncrowded water, and no motor vehicles, the hike-in lakes offer all this and fish. Most of the following lakes are in roadless wilderness areas; there are a few to which anglers can drive.

All angling techniques will work on these lakes. The fish have little fishing pressure and are not "educated in the ways of anglers," but they are wary of predators and can be spooked. Still-fishing bait, casting and trolling small lures, such as Rooster Tails or Thomas lures, are effective methods. Early in the season, the fish are aggressive and hungry (and so are the mosquitoes). Bait is popular early in the season, and flies are often best late in the season, especially for brookies, but any of these techniques can work year-round. Anglers should try wind drifting bait along the bottom, especially in mid-summer when fish are deep. Grasshoppers, worms, and Power Bait are all good choices. Fly fishing can, at times, be outstanding, either by matching the hatch or using old standbys, such as ant imitations, damsel nymph imitations, Woolly Buggers, Hare's Ears, and Tied-down Caddis. For brook trout, bucktail streamers are excellent. Ultra-light spinning gear with a bubble and fly is also effective. Light equipment is best for both packing in and catching small fish. Anglers should use small hooks, small lures, and light leaders.

Most, but certainly not all, of the back country lakes are similar in nature: shallow, snow-fed, with fairly stable water levels, short growing season, and very long winters. Fish in these lakes tend to be small; it takes a lot longer for them to get big. Excellent water quality contributes to both the beauty of the lakes and lower productivity. Most of the lakes are short on cover for the fish, and many are prone to winterkill. The natural beauty of these areas is, without a doubt, their most outstanding characteristic.

Northwest Forest Passes and wilderness permits are required in selected National Forests and wilderness areas including many trails in the Deschutes National Forest as well as the Mt. Jefferson Wilderness (MJW), Three Sisters Wilderness (TSW), and the Mt. Washington Wilderness (MWW). The trailpark permits are sold at ranger stations, Forest Service offices, and many local sports shops. Contact the local ranger district for further information. The wilderness permits are self-issued at the trailhead.

Some areas of the wilderness are "being loved to death," and use of these areas is discouraged. Of the lakes described in this section of the book, Green Lakes and Matthieu Lakes have been identified by the Forest Service as high-use areas. Better experiences of solitude exist at other locations. Use no-trace techniques while in the wilderness; pamphlets on the subject are available free from the Forest Service. Wilderness and National Forest maps can be purchased at Forest Service offices. The most recent MJW map was published in 1991, the

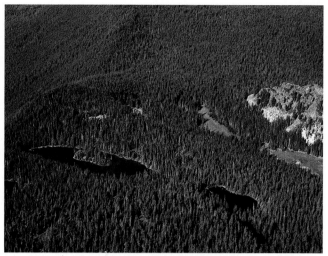

Back Country lakes offer exercise, solitude, scenic beauty, and often, good fishing. Photo by Geoff Hill

TSW map in 1994. Forest policy currently is to show only destination names on signs in the wilderness, without distances and trail numbers. Therefore, hikers and anglers should carry maps.

Forest Service campgrounds listed with descriptions of the lakes have campsites and outhouses, most have tables, and some have drinking water. Nearly all of the lakes have primitive campsites on their banks, and camping is always allowed on Forest Service land not otherwise posted. Stay limit outside of campgrounds is 30 days and within Forest Service Recreation Sites, 14 days.

Most of these lakes have, in the past, been stocked annually; however, due to lack of funding, helicopter stocking is now done during odd years only. The Confederated Tribes of Warm Springs stock sporadically. Lakes outside of wilderness areas are stocked by truck. Limited planting of pack-in lakes is accomplished using llama and human backs, mainly at lakes within 1 or 2 miles of roads. The more remote lakes have to depend on natural reproduction and weather conditions conducive to survival.

In the following descriptions, the species normally stocked in each lake are designated as follows: **BT** = brook trout; **CT** = cutthroat trout; **RB** = rainbow trout. Small numbers of other species left over from discontinued plantings may also be present in the lakes. Check with local ODFW offices for information on fish survival in unstocked and unlisted lakes. Also, check to be sure the lake is "fishable." Some may be too brushy to fish without a float tube or raft.

Locations of each lake are indicated by notations similar to 25/6/9, an abbreviation of the legal nomenclature for Township 25/Range 6/Section 9. Water depths listed are the maximum for each lake.

Be sure to check the current Oregon Sport Fishing Regulations before fishing.

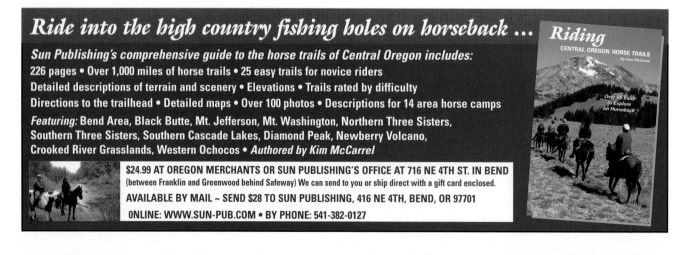

CRESCENT LAKE AREA

Crescent Lake lies 75 miles southeast of Eugene just off State Highway 58 about 10 miles east of Willamette Pass. At the small community of Crescent Lake Junction, Forest Route 60 heads south and reaches the lake in 2 miles then runs along the west and south shores for about 5 miles to its junction with Forest Route 6015. Forest Route 6015 then follows the eastern shore back to Highway 58 just east of the lake.

Coming from Chemult, Crescent Lake is 18 miles northwest of the junction of Highway 58 and U.S. Highway 97. A shortcut from Bend is available by turning west onto County Route 61 from Highway 97 at the town of Crescent and following Route 61 to its junction with Highway 58 in 12 miles. It is then 3 miles west to Crescent Lake Junction on Highway 58.

Developed Forest Service campgrounds with various facilities are situated around Crescent Lake as well as a resort, store, and other services (see Crescent Lake on pages 94 and 95 for more details). The Oregon Cascades Recreation Area (OCRA) is not a wilderness but is an area designated for non-motorized, mechanized use, which allows the operation of mountain bikes (unlike in the wilderness areas). The remainder of the lakes in the Crescent Lake area are within the Diamond Peak Wilderness (DPW). Permits are required for entry and are self-issued at trailheads. A Northwest Forest Pass may also be required.

Darlene Lake - BT, 5,950 feet elevation, 11 acres, 47 feet deep. Location 25/6/7, OCRA.

Take Forest Route 60 along Crescent Lake's west shore and park at the Windy Lakes Trailhead about .75 mile south of Tandy Bay Campground. Take Windy Lakes Trail 50 for 4 miles to the junction with Trail 46, then take Trail 46 1 mile east to Suzanne Lake. Darlene is 1 mile east of Suzanne on the south side of the trail.

Farrell Lake - BT, 5,580 feet elevation, 4 acres, 11 feet deep. Location 24//5 1/2//23, DPW.

From Forest Route 60 along the west shore of Crescent Lake turn onto Forest Route 6010, .25 mile south of Tandy Bay Campground, and drive west toward Summit Lake. Park at the Meek Lake/Snell Lake Trailhead in 4 miles and take Trail 43 north toward Snell Lake. Farrell Lake is about .5 mile in and about .1 mile bushwhack east of the trail. A small Forest Service campground with few amenities is available at Summit Lake, another 3 miles west of the Meek Lake/ Snell Lake Trailhead on Forest Route 6010.

Fawn Lake - BT, 5,680 feet elevation, 43 acres, 27 feet deep. Location 24/6/4, DPW.

The trail to Fawn Lake originates at the boat trailer parking lot in Crescent Lake Campground on the northernmost point of Crescent Lake, just off Forest Route 60. It's 2.7 miles northwest on Trail 44A to Fawn Lake.

Meek Lake - BT, CT, 5,580 feet elevation, 11 acres, 38 feet deep. Location 24/5/26, OCRA.

Follow directions to Farrell Lake, parking at the Meek Lake/Snell Lake Trailhead. Meek Lake is less than .5 mile to the south along Trail 43.1.

Oldenberg Lake - BT, 5,200 feet elevation, 28 acres, 29 feet deep. Location 25/6/10, OCRA.

From Forest Route 60 along the west shore of Crescent Lake continue on around to the south shore past the entrance to Spring Campground. About .25 mile past Spring park at the Oldenberg Lake Trailhead. Oldenberg is about a 4-mile hike to the south along Trail 45.

Snell Lake - BT, 5,555 feet elevation, 9 acres, 17 feet deep. Location 24//5 1/2//23, DPW.

See directions to Farrell Lake. Snell is a short distance north of Farrell on the east side of Trail 43.

Summit Lake - Stocked BT, RB, and kokanee (as food) for the self-sustaining mackinaw, 5,550 feet elevation, 470 acres, 63 feet deep. Location 24//5 1/2//28, OCRA.

A large drive-in lake along Forest Route 6010 west of Crescent Lake and bordered on the west shore by spur road 700. From Route 60 along the west shore of Crescent Lake take Forest Route 6010, .25 mile south of Tandy Bay Campground, west about 5 miles to Summit Lake. Route 6010 continues along the west bank of Summit Lake. In addition to road access, Trail 46 runs for a short distance along the east shore, and the Pacific Crest Trail (PCT) touches the south shore. The trailhead for 46 is on the northeast point of Summit Lake on Route 6010. Summit Lake Campground is on the northwest corner of the lake.

Summit Lake and Diamond Peak.
Photo courtesy Franklin Carson

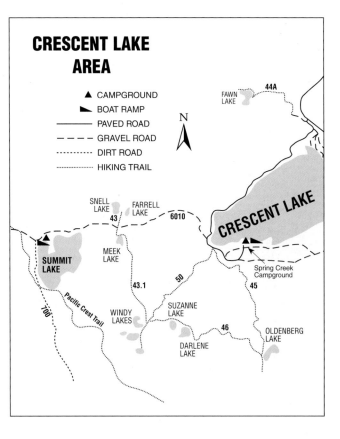

Suzanne Lake - BT, 6,000 feet elevation, 10 acres, 47 feet deep. Location 25/6/7, OCRA.

Take route 60 along Crescent Lake's west shore and park at the Windy Lakes Trailhead about .75 mile south of Tandy Bay Campground. Take Windy Lakes Trail 50 for 4 miles to the junction with Trail 46, then hike Trail 46 1 mile east to Suzanne Lake.

Windy Lake, East - BT, 6,190 feet, 14 acres, 14 feet deep. Location 25//5 1/2//12, OCRA.

Windy Lake, North - BT, 6,190 feet, 5 acres, 27 feet deep. Location 25// 5 1/2//12, OCRA.

Windy Lake, South - BT, CT, 6,000 feet, 11 acres, 28 feet deep. Location 25//5 1/2//12, OCRA.

Windy Lake, West - BT, 6,000 feet, 16 acres, 18 feet deep. Location 25//5 1/2//12, OCRA.

The Windy Lakes are a group of four lakes at the end of the trail. The South lake usually has the best fishing. Two access routes exist, one approach is to continue on past Meek Lake (described previously) 4.5 miles on Trail 43.1.

The second possibility is to park at the Windy Lakes Trailhead about .75 mile south of Tandy Bay Campground on the west shore of Crescent Lake and take Windy Lakes Trail 50 for 4 miles to the northernmost of the group of lakes. The south lake is nearly 1 mile south of North Windy Lake.

WILLAMETTE PASS

Willamette Pass is on State Highway 58 about 70 miles southeast of Eugene, just west of Odell Lake. From Chemult, Willamette Pass is 21 miles northwest of the junction of Highway 58 and U.S. Highway 97. A shortcut from Bend is available by turning west off Highway 97 onto County Route 61 at Crescent and following Route 61 to its junction with Highway 58 in 12 miles. It is then about 8 miles west to the Pass.

Developed Forest Service campgrounds in this area are available at Odell Lake, Gold Lake, Waldo Lake, and Crescent Lake. (See detailed information for these areas on pages 94-100 and 216-217.)

Gold Lake - All natural reproduction, BT, RB, 4,800 feet elevation, 104 acres, 25 feet deep. Location 22/6/30, Willamette National Forest.

A drive-in lake with excellent camping and open to fly angling only. No motors are allowed. Three miles west of Willamette Pass on State Highway 58, take Forest Service spur road 500 north off Highway 58. It's about 2 miles into Gold Lake. See page 100.

Brook trout are the most common species found in the high, back country lakes. Photo by Gary Lewis

Maiden Lake - BT, 6,360 feet elevation, 6 acres, 23 feet deep. Location 23/6/1, Crescent Ranger District (CRD), Deschutes National Forest.

The most popular route into Maiden Lake is from the Pacific Crest Trail (PCT) north of Willamette Pass. Park at the PCT trailhead on the north side of Willamette Pass. Travel 2.5 miles into Rosary Lakes then continue on to the junction with Trail 41. A 2-mile hike to the east on Trail 41 brings you to Maiden Lake.

It's a shorter hike to Maiden Lake from the Davis Lake area. From the Eugene area Davis Lake is reached by taking Highway 58 east over Willamette Pass. About 3 miles past Crescent Lake Junction turn left onto County Route 61. In another 3 miles turn left onto Forest Route 46 toward Davis Lake. The turn toward West Davis Campground is in another 3 miles onto Forest Route 4660. Continue on Route 4660 past the turn toward the campground, following signs to the Maiden Lake Trail for another 2 miles. At the junction with Forest Route 4664 turn right. In a very short distance on 4664, spur road 100 heads west (left). The trailhead is at the end of this spur road in a little over 1 mile, and it's about a 3-mile hike into the lake.

From Bend take U.S. Highway 97 south about 18 miles to the turn to Fall River on County Route 42. Follow 42 west to its junction with County Route 46, about 26 miles. A left onto 46 will bring you to the turn toward West Davis Lake Campground and the Maiden Lake Trailhead in about 14 miles. Continue on Forest Route 4660 following signs to Maiden Lake Trail for a total of about 5 miles to the junction with 4664, turning right. In a very short distance on 4664, spur road 100 heads west (left). The trailhead is at the end of this spur road in a little over 1 mile. From this vantage point Maiden Lake is a 3-mile hike to the west on Trail 41.

Rosary Lake, Lower - BT, RB, CT, 5,710 feet elevation, 42 acres, 50 feet deep. Location 23/6/3, CRD, Deschutes National Forest.

Rosary Lake, Middle - BT, 5,830 feet elevation, 9 acres, 31 feet deep. Location 23/6/3, CRD, Deschutes National Forest.

Rosary Lake, Upper - BT, 5,835 feet elevation, 8 acres, 21 feet deep. Location 23/6/3, CRD, Deschutes National Forest.

From Willamette Pass on State Highway 58, take the PCT northeast reaching Lower Rosary Lakes in 2.5 miles. See directions to Maiden Lake for more details.

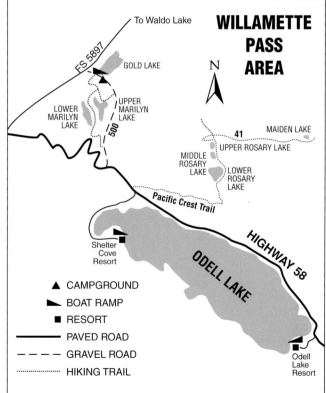

WALDO LAKE AREA

Developed Forest Service campgrounds are available at Waldo Lake.

Bobby Lake - BT, RB, 5,420 feet elevation, 86 acres, 71 feet deep. Location 22/6/14, Crescent Ranger District, Deschutes National Forest.

The shortest hike in is from the west. Turn off State Highway 58, 3.5 miles west of Willamette Pass Summit onto Forest Route 5897 toward Waldo Lake. A 5.5 mile drive brings you to Trail 3663 and a small parking area on the right hand side of the road. The trailhead to Bobby is right across the road from Betty Lake Trailhead which has a very large parking area. Bobby is 2 miles east on Trail 3663.

Bobby can also be reached from the east by taking Forest Route 4652 west off Route 46, the Cascade Lakes Highway. The turn is just across the highway from the entrance to North Davis Creek Campground. About 3.5 miles down 4652 take spur road 400 which ends at the trailhead in about .5 mile. It is then a 4.5 mile hike into the lake.

Charlton Lake - BT, 5,700 feet elevation, 100 acres, 74 feet deep. Location 21/6/14, Bend Ranger District (BRD), Deschutes National Forest.

Charlton is a short hike along the Pacific Crest Trail (PCT) from off Forest Route 4290. Turn off State Highway 58, 3.5 miles west of Willamette Pass Summit onto Forest Route 5897 toward Waldo Lake. Continue north on Route 5897 about 12 miles to the junction with Route 4290. The PCT trailhead is 1 mile east on 4290. Charlton is .25 mile to the south on the PCT. Charlton can also be accessed from the east by taking the turn onto Forest Route 4290 from the Cascade Lakes Highway (Route 46) just 3 miles south of Rock Creek Campground on Crane Prairie Reservoir. From the east the PCT is a 10-mile drive on 4290.

Hidden Lake - BT, 6,200 feet elevation, 13 acres, 35 feet. Location 21/6/26, BRD, Deschutes National Forest.

Off the beaten path, Hidden Lake is 1.5 miles due south of Charlton Lake, on the west slope of Gerdine Butte. See directions to Charlton Lake. From Charlton, either continue on the PCT to its junction with Trail 21 west of Hidden Lake and about 1 mile south of Charlton or take Trail 19 for 1 mile south of Charlton Lake to connect with Trail 21 east of Hidden Lake. Hidden Lake is between these two trail junctions, approximately .5 mile south of Trail 21. No official trial leads to the lake, and it is difficult to find; most people end up at Found Lake instead. Take a good topo map of the area and a compass.

Johnny Lake - BT, 5,400 feet elevation, 20 acres, 21 feet deep. Location 21/7/29, BRD, Deschutes National Forest.

Five air miles due east of Waldo Lake, Johnny can be reached either from the east off Forest Route 46 (the Cascade Lakes Highway) or from Waldo Lake. From the east, take Forest Route 4290 west at the junction of Route 46 and Route 42, 2 miles south of Crane Prairie Reservoir. In about 4 miles, turn south onto spur road 200 which dead-ends in about 1 mile at the trailhead to Johnny Lake. Trail 99 reaches Johnny in about .5 mile. From the Waldo Lake area, turn east on Route 4290 near the north end of Waldo and drive about 7 miles east to spur road 200.

Charlton Lake (front), a short hike along the Pacific Crest Trail, lies a short distance east of Waldo Lake. Photo by Geoff Hill

Lily Lake - BT, 5,700 feet elevation, 13 acres, 44 feet. Location 21/6/12, BRD, Deschutes National Forest.

Lily Lake is easily reached from the PCT east of Waldo Lake. Turn off State Highway 58, 3.5 miles west of Willamette Pass Summit onto Forest Route 5897 toward Waldo Lake. Continue north on Route 5897 about 12 miles to the junction with Route 4290. The PCT trailhead is 1 mile east on 4290. Lily Lake can also be accessed from the east by taking the turn onto Forest Route 4290 from the Cascade Lakes Highway (Route 46) just 3 miles south of Rock Creek Campground on Crane Prairie Reservoir. From the east, the PCT is a 10-mile drive on 4290. Hike the PCT north for 1.5 miles to the junction with Trail 19. Lily Lake is less than .5 mile east on the north side of Trail 19.

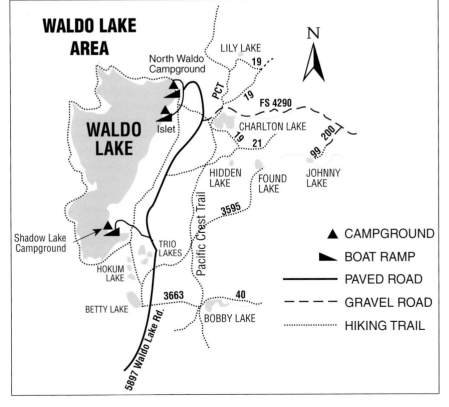

CULTUS LAKE AREA

Most of the following lakes are in the Three Sisters Wilderness (TSW). Developed Forest Service campgrounds are located on Cultus Lake and Little Cultus Lake.

To reach Cultus Lake take the turn to Sunriver (County/Forest Route 40) off U.S. Highway 97, 15 miles south of Bend and 15 miles north of LaPine. Twenty-two miles west of Sunriver, Route 40 reaches a junction with Route 46. Turn left (south) here and in a little over 1 mile turn right onto Forest Route 4635 toward Cultus Lake Resort and Cultus Lake. It's about 3 miles into Cultus Lake.

For access from the Eugene area take State Highway 58 over Willamette Pass continuing on to Crescent Lake Junction. Three miles past Crescent Lake Junction turn left toward Crescent on County Route 61. In approximately 4 miles turn left (north) onto Forest Route 46 toward Davis Lake. It's about 32 miles up the Cascade Lakes Highway (Route 46) to the turn into Cultus Lake.

To find Little Cultus Lake, about 1.5 miles in toward Cultus Lake on Route 4635, turn left onto Route 4630, following signs to Little Cultus Lake and Irish and Taylor Lakes. The east end of Little Cultus Lake is reached in about 3 miles at the junction with spur road 640 to Deer Lake. Turn left at this junction to reach Little Cultus Campground in less than .5 mile.

Big Finger Lake - BT, 5,400 feet elevation, 5 acres, 15 feet deep. Location 19/7/33, TSW, 3 air miles north of Cultus Lake.

Take the turn to Deer Lake on spur 640 off Forest Route 4630 into Little Cultus Lake. Drive in as far as you can to a dead-end and the beginning of Trail 6 to West Cultus Lake Campground. Trail 6 reaches to West Cultus Lake Campground, which has a boat dock and outhouses, in 1.4 miles. From the campground take Trail 6 northeast for about .5 mile to the junction with Trail 16 to Winopee Lake. In .4 mile toward Winopee Lake, Trail 9 heads to Teddy Lakes, Trail 16 continues to Winopee Lake. At the junction with Trail 33 in 4.1 miles, just past Winopee Lake, take Trail 33 east to Snowshoe Lake. Big Finger is .25 mile east of Snowshoe, with no official trail leading to it. It may be a smart idea to bring a good topo map and your bushwhacking gear.

Blowdown Lake - BT, 5,500 feet elevation, 4 acres, 8 feet deep. Location 20/7/31//36, Bend Ranger District (BRD), Deschutes National Forest.

From Little Cultus Lake Campground continue on spur road 600 past the lake about 4 miles. There is no sign and no maintained trail into Blowdown. The primitive trail is exactly 1 mile east of the Pacific Crest Trail (PCT) trailhead. The lake is accessed by a brief adventure through the brush, .25 mile south of the road. Good campsites are available at Irish and Taylor Lakes 1 mile west on spur 600.

Brahma Lake - BT, 5,500 feet elevation, 12 acres, 12 feet deep. Location 20/6/13, TSW, 3 air miles due west of Cultus Lake.

From Little Cultus Lake Campground continue on spur road 600 past the lake about 5 miles to the trailhead for the PCT. Brahma Lake is 2 miles north on the west side of the PCT.

Deer Lake - CT, 4,900 feet elevation, 70 acres, 20 feet deep. Location 20/7/21, BRD, Deschutes National Forest.

You can drive right to Deer Lake from the road into Little Cultus Lake. Where Forest Route 4630 touches the east end of Little Cultus Lake take spur road 640 north about 2 miles to Deer Lake. There are a few primitive campsites on the lake.

Dennis Lake - BT, 6,100 feet elevation, 12 acres, 42 feet deep. Location 20/6/12, TSW.

From Little Cultus Lake Campground continue on spur road 600 past Little Cultus about 5 miles to the trailhead for the PCT. Hike north along the PCT 4.2 miles to Blaze Lake. One-quarter mile beyond Blaze you cross a spring creek. At this point Dennis Lake is

.25 mile to the northwest and a steep 400 feet above the PCT. There is no official trail to the lake so take a good USGS topo map. Dennis has good bank fishing.

Hanks Lake, East - CT, 5,500 feet elevation, 10 acres, 27 feet deep. Location 20/7/30, TSW.

Hanks Lake, Middle - RB, 5,500 feet elevation, 15 acres, 30 feet deep. Location 20/7/30, TSW.

Hanks Lake, West - BT, 5,500 feet elevation, 15 acres, 13 feet deep.

The Many Lakes Trailhead to Hanks Lakes is 1.5 miles east of the PCT, about 3.5 miles west of Little Cultus Lake on spur road 600. Trail 15 heads north from the trailhead and reaches the west shore of Middle Hanks Lake in less than .5 mile. West Hanks is just to the west of Middle Hanks, and East Hanks is southeast of Middle Hanks.

Irish Lake - BT, 5,550 feet elevation, 28 acres, 16 feet deep. Location 20/6/25, TSW.

Irish Lake is a drive-in lake located along spur road 600 about 5 miles west of Little Cultus Lake and just east of the PCT trailhead. Irish Lake is on the north side of the road, the PCT follows the west shore of the lake. Taylor Lake is on the south side of the road just before Irish. Motors are prohibited on both lakes.

Kershaw Lake - BT, 5,500 feet elevation, 4 acres, 13 feet deep. Location 20/7/30, TSW.

The Many Lakes Trailhead, 1.5 miles east of the PCT and about 3.5 miles west of Little Cultus Lake on spur road 600, leads to Kershaw Lake. Many Lakes Trail 15 heads north and reaches the west shore of Middle Hanks Lake in less than .5 mile. To find Kershaw Lake continue on about another .5 mile north until you cross a depression with a small creek connecting a series of ponds. Kershaw Lake is east of the trail, a short bushwack just past this creek. Total distance from the road is not more than 1 mile.

Lemish Lake - BT, 5,200 feet elevation, 14 acres, 13 feet deep. Location 21/7/5, BRD, Deschutes National Forest.

The trailhead to Lemish Lake is about 1 mile west of Little Cultus Lake on spur road 600 on the south side of the road. It's about a .5-mile hike in.

Raft Lake - BT, 4,900 feet elevation, 10 acres, 27 feet deep. Location 20/7/29, TSW.

You'll need the USGS topo map for this one. About .5 mile west of the Lemish Lake Trailhead on spur 600, about 1.5 miles west of Little Cultus Lake, Raft Lake is .5 mile cross-country to the north. There is no official trail, and there are many other small lakes in the same area that you may find instead of Raft Lake.

Redslide Lake - RB, 5,500 feet elevation, 2 acres, 18 feet deep. Location 20/6/24, TSW. This can be a tough one to find; bring the topo maps.

From Little Cultus Lake Campground continue on spur road 600 past the lake about 5 miles to the trailhead for the PCT. Brahma Lake is 2 miles north on the west side of the PCT, and Red Slide is about .25 mile south of Brahma. There is no official trail in to Red Slide and you may find any of the numerous other lakes instead.

Snowshoe Lake, Lower - BT, 5,100 feet elevation, 18 acres, 15 feet deep. Location 19/7/33, TSW.

Snowshoe Lake, Middle - BT, 5,150 feet elevation, 3 acres, 13 feet deep. Location 19/7/33, TSW.

Snowshoe Lake, Upper - BT, 5,150 feet elevation, 30 acres, 8 feet deep. Location 19/7/29, TSW.

Off Forest Route 4630 into Little Cultus Lake take the turn to Deer Lake on spur 640. Drive in as far as you can to a dead-end and the beginning of Trail 6 to West Cultus Lake Campground. Trail 6 reaches to West Cultus Lake Campground, which has a boat dock and outhouses, in 1.4 miles. From the campground take Trail 6 northeast for about .5 mile to the junction with Trail 16 to Winopee Lake. In .4 mile toward Winopee Lake, Trail 9 heads to Teddy Lakes, and Trail 16 continues to Winopee Lake. At the junction with Trail 33 in 4.1 miles, just past Winopee Lake, take Trail 33 east to Snowshoe Lake. Lower Snowshoe Lake is on the east side of Trail 33. Middle Snowshoe is .25 mile west of the northern end of Lower Snowshoe. Continuing north on Trail 33 from Middle Snowshoe will bring you to Upper Snowshoe in .5 mile.

Strider Lake - RB, 5,000 feet elevation, 3 acres, 22 feet deep. Location 20/7/29, TSW.

Strider Lake is in the same ballpark as Raft Lake on the north side of the 600 spur road west of Little Cultus Lake. About .75 mile past the Lemish Lake Trailhead, Strider is a .5 mile bush-pusher north.

Teddy Lake, North - BT, RB, 4,900 feet elevation, 30 acres, 28 feet deep. Located in 20/7/10, TSW.

Teddy Lake, South - BT, RB, 4,900 feet elevation, 17 acres, 10 feet deep. Location 20/7/10, TSW.

On the way to Little Cultus Lake take the turn to Deer Lake on spur 640 off Forest Route 4630. Drive in as far as you can to a dead-end and the beginning of Trail 6 to West Cultus Lake. Trail 6 reaches West Cultus Lake Campground in 1.4 miles. From the campground take Trail 6 northeast for about .5 mile to the junction

with Trail 16 to Winopee Lake. In .4 mile toward Winopee Lake, Trail 9 heads to Teddy Lakes, Trail 16 continues to Winopee Lake. South Teddy Lake is not much more than 1 mile north of West Cultus Campground on the west side of Trail 9. North Teddy is .25 mile northeast of South Teddy.

Timmy Lake - RB, 5,500 feet elevation, 3 acres, 15 feet deep. Location 20/6/24, TSW.

Continue past Little Cultus Lake about 4 miles on spur road 600 to the PCT trailhead on the west side of Irish Lake. Timmy Lake is about 2 miles north on the PCT and about .25 mile east of the trail, just south of Red Slide Lake. There is no maintained trail in and the lake is difficult to spot because of its location on the top of a rise. Timmy is easy to fish from shore.

Winopee Lake - BT, RB, 4,950 feet elevation, 40 acres, 43 feet deep. Location 19/7/33, TSW.

From the east end of Little Cultus Lake take the turn to Deer Lake on spur 640 off Forest Route 4630. Drive in as far as you can to a dead-end and the beginning of Trail 6 to West Cultus Lake. Trail 6 reaches West Cultus Lake Campground, which has a boat dock and outhouses, in 1.4 miles. From the campground take Trail 6 northeast about a .5 mile to the junction with Trail 16 to Winopee Lake. Winopee is about 3 miles north.

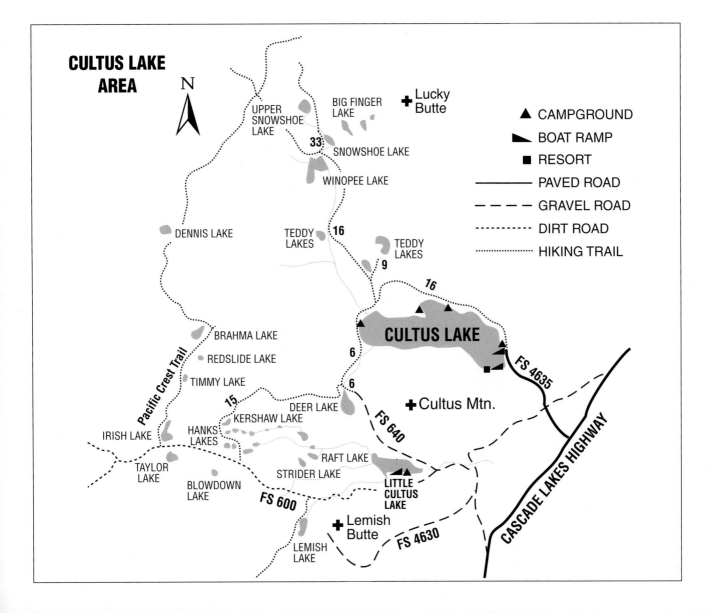

CULTUS LAKE AREA

N

UPPER SNOWSHOE LAKE
BIG FINGER LAKE
Lucky Butte
33
SNOWSHOE LAKE
WINOPEE LAKE
DENNIS LAKE
TEDDY LAKES
16
TEDDY LAKES
9
16
CULTUS LAKE
BRAHMA LAKE
REDSLIDE LAKE
6
TIMMY LAKE
FS 4635
6
15
DEER LAKE
Cultus Mtn.
KERSHAW LAKE
FS 640
IRISH LAKE
HANKS LAKES
RAFT LAKE
TAYLOR LAKE
STRIDER LAKE
BLOWDOWN LAKE
LITTLE CULTUS LAKE
FS 600
Lemish Butte
LEMISH LAKE
FS 4630
CASCADE LAKES HIGHWAY

Pacific Crest Trail

▲ CAMPGROUND
◤ BOAT RAMP
■ RESORT
—— PAVED ROAD
– – – GRAVEL ROAD
········ DIRT ROAD
·········· HIKING TRAIL

SISTERS AREA

Most of the following lakes are within the Mt. Jefferson Wilderness (MJW), but several have road access.

Booth Lake - BT, 5,050 feet elevation, 8 acres, 34 feet deep. Location 13/8/7, MJW.

To reach Booth Lake take U.S. Highway 20 to the Santiam Pass Summit either from Bend to the east or from the Albany area in the Willamette Valley to the west. The Santiam Pass/Pacific Crest Trail (PCT) parking lot is on the north side of the highway about .5 mile east of Hoodoo Ski Bowl. There is ample parking space, including room for horse trailers. Booth Lake is easily reached by first hiking a short distance from the parking area on the PCT, then continuing about 2 miles on Trail 4014 to Square Lake. Continue another 1.4 miles to Booth Lake on the Old Summit Trail. Booth is on the west side of the trail. The nearest developed campgrounds are at Lost Lake to the west or Suttle Lake to the east on Highway 20.

Cabot Lake - CT, 4,550 feet elevation, 6 acres, 22 feet deep. Location 1/8/34, MJW.

Take U.S. Highway 20 either from Bend to the east or from the Albany area in the Willamette Valley to the west. Seven miles east of the Santiam Pass Summit, 1 mile east of Suttle Lake, and about 13 miles west of Sisters, turn north onto Forest Route 12 from U.S. Highway 20. Drive north 5 miles on Route 12 then take Forest Route 1230 for 9 miles to its end at the trailhead. A 2-mile hike on Trail 4003 gets you to Cabot Lake. The nearest developed Forest Service Recreation Site is Abbot Creek Campground just off Forest Route 12.

Cache Lake - BT, CT, 4,350 feet elevation, 8 acres, 9 feet deep. Location 13/8/33, Sisters Ranger District (SRD), Deschutes National Forest.

The namesake of the Cache Lake Basin collection of lakes,

Cache Lake, itself, is a drive-in experience. Take U.S. Highway 20 either from Bend to the east or from the Albany area in the Willamette Valley to the west. Seven miles east of the Santiam Pass Summit, 1.5 miles east of Suttle Lake, and about 13 miles west of Sisters, turn south onto Forest Route 2066 off U.S. Highway 20. Stay on 2066 for about 2 miles then take Forest Route 2068 another 3 miles to the junction with spur road 600. Cache Lake is a short distance down the spur on the south side of the road. Primitive campsites are located on the lake. Motors are not allowed. The closest developed campground is at Scout Lake. To reach Scout Lake, take the Suttle Lake turn-off Highway 20 at the east end of Suttle Lake. Continue on this road about 1 mile to a fork, then take the left fork to reach Scout Lake in less than 1 mile.

Carl Lake - CT, 5,450 feet elevation, 30 acres, 51 feet deep. Location 11/8/28, MJW.

Take U.S. Highway 20 either from Bend to the east or from the Albany area in the Willamette Valley to the west. Seven miles east of the Santiam Pass Summit, 1 mile east of Suttle Lake, and about 13 miles west of Sisters, turn north onto Forest Route 12 from U.S. Highway 20. Drive north 5 miles on Route 12 then take Forest Route 1230 for 9 miles to its end at the trailhead. A 2-mile hike on Trail 4003 gets you to Cabot Lake, another 2.6 miles and the trail reaches Carl Lake. The nearest developed Forest Service Recreation Site is Abbot Creek Campground just off Forest Route 12.

Link Lake - CT, 4,350 feet elevation, 13 acres, 20 feet deep. Location 13/8/32, SRD, Deschutes National Forest.

One of several good lakes in the Cache Lake Basin, Link Lake is reached from Highway 20, 2 miles west of Suttle Lake, by turning south onto Forest Route 2076 at Corbett Sno-Park. Link Lake is about .1 mile off the west side of the road in 2 miles. A fire road leads into the lake. The nearest developed campgrounds are at Suttle Lake. No motors are allowed on Link Lake.

LEFT: This view of Island Lake includes the top of Three Fingered Jack. MIDDLE: Island Lake is a picturesque lake along the trail to Link Lake. Its shallow waters are subject to winterkill. RIGHT: The shoreline of Link Lake. Photos by Don Burgderfer

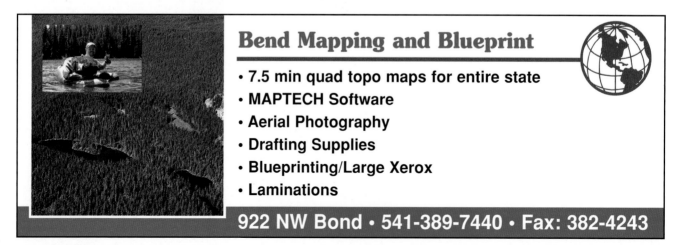

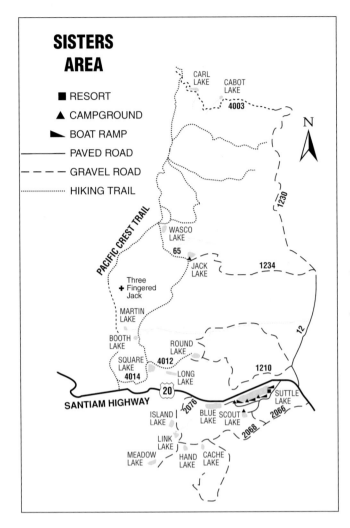

SISTERS AREA

■ RESORT

▲ CAMPGROUND

► BOAT RAMP

—— PAVED ROAD

– – – GRAVEL ROAD

········· HIKING TRAIL

also be reached from U.S. Highway 20 at the Santiam Pass/PCT trailhead. From Highway 20, Square Lake is 1.1 miles off the highway on Trail 4014.

Wasco Lake - CT, 5,150 feet elevation, 20 acres, 25 feet deep. Location 12/8/20, MJW.

Travel one mile east of Suttle Lake on U.S. Highway 20, then take Forest Route 12 north for 5 miles, then Route 1230 for 2 miles west, then Route 1234 for about 5 miles to its end. Jack Lake Campground and Trail 65 are at the end of the road. Wasco Lake is 2.3 miles up the trail.

Fishing back country lakes has its rewards.
Photo by Ed Park

MCKENZIE PASS AREA

A primitive Forest Service campground (no drinking water) is located at Lava Camp Lake. Both of the following lakes are in the Three Sisters Wilderness (TSW). The Matthieu Lakes are designated as a high use area. From Central Oregon, drive to Sisters via U.S. Highway 20 then take State Highway 242 toward McKenzie Pass from the west end of the town of Sisters. It's about 16 miles west to the top of the pass. From the Eugene area travel State Highway 126 east to its junction with Highway 242 to McKenzie Pass then about 21 miles to the pass summit.

Matthieu Lake, South - BT, 5,850 feet elevation, 6 acres, 15 feet deep. Location 15/8/28, TSW.

From Sisters, head toward McKenzie Pass on State Highway 242. About 15 miles west of Sisters, .5 mile east of Dee Wright Observatory, take the turn toward Lava Camp Lake and the Pacific Crest Trail (PCT) trailhead. It's about 3 miles to South Matthieu Lake.

Yapoah Lake - RB, 5,520 feet elevation, 10 acres, 25 feet deep. Location 15/8/34, TSW.

Follow directions to Matthieu Lake. A short distance southeast of South Matthieu take Trail 4068 east for a little less than 1 mile. You'll need radar (or more likely, good eyes) to find the unmarked and unmaintained trail that goes into Yapoah. Look for a flat area after a short downhill section 1 mile in. The lake is .25 mile south of the trail. Yapoah is easy to fish from shore.

Martin Lake - RB, 5,150 feet elevation, 8 acres, 20 feet deep. Location 13//7 1/2//12, MJW.

A bit of a bushwhack, the route to Martin Lake begins at the Square Lake Trail, north of Highway 20 at the Santiam Pass/PCT parking lot, .5 mile east of Hoodoo Ski Bowl. Continue past Square Lake on Trail 4014 to Booth Lake, about 3.3 miles. In another .25 mile, follow a small creek due west and uphill about .5 mile and 400 vertical feet to Martin Lake. Developed campgrounds are at Lost Lake to the west and Suttle Lake to the east on Highway 20.

Meadow Lake - BT, 4,550 feet elevation, 16 acres, 20 feet deep. Location 4/8/5, SRD, Deschutes National Forest.

One of several good lakes in the Cache Lake Basin. Follow directions to Link Lake then continue 1 mile farther on Forest Route 2076. Meadow Lake is .25 mile west of the road. A fire road gives foot access to the lake. Only electric motors are allowed on the lake.

Round Lake - CT, 4,250 feet elevation, 22 acres, 41 feet deep. Location 13/8/16, SRD, Deschutes National Forest.

You can drive to this one. Take Forest Route 12 north off U.S. Highway 20, 1.5 miles east of Suttle Lake. Turn left onto Route 1210 in 1 mile, reaching Round Lake Campground in 4 miles. A church camp is located on the west shore. Motors are prohibited. Round Lake can also be reached by foot from the west by following directions to Square Lake and then continuing on Trail 4012, 2 miles farther east to Round Lake.

Square Lake - BT, 4,750 feet elevation, 55 acres, 43 feet deep. Location 13/8/19, MJW.

Follow directions to Round Lake, continuing on past Round Lake on spur road 600 about .5 mile to its end at a trailhead. Square Lake is then 2 miles west on Trail 4012. Square Lake can

WARM SPRINGS RESERVATION

Only lakes mentioned here are open to the public. Regulations for public use of the Warm Springs Reservation are outlined in "The Confederated Tribes of the Warm Springs Reservation of Oregon Fishing Permits and Regulations" brochure. A Warm Springs Permit is required to fish Area 1.

Area 1 - High Cascade Mountain Lakes

The High Cascade Mountain Lakes angling area of the reservation consists of seven lakes along the western border of the reservation. Among these is a chain of five high lakes with Trout Lake the farthest east and Island, Dark, Long, and Olallie lakes in a row along an unmaintained trail to the south. The other two lakes listed below are nearby. Only Olallie and Trout lake have road access. Tribal fishing permits are required of all anglers. Only anglers are allowed to camp overnight on the reservation and only at Trout Lake Campground.

Regulations on the reservation are as follows:
  Fishing season is open from the last Saturday of April
    weekend through October 31.
  Daily Bag Limit, 15 trout, no minimum size.
  No motor propelled craft allowed.
  All motorbike, ATV, and snowmobile riding are prohibited.
  No woodcutting or gathering allowed.
  Dogs must be kept on leash.
  No horses allowed.
  Overnight camping at Trout Lake only.

Boulder Lake - BT, RB, 4,780 feet elevation, 50 acres, 29 feet deep.
  Boulder Lake is .5 mile southeast of Trout Lake on the western edge of the reservation. The trail begins about .25 mile east of Trout Lake Campground. Boulder Lake has about 2 miles of brushy shoreline with very large boulders covering most of the lake's bottom.

Dark Lake - BT, RB, 4,690 feet elevation, 22 acres, 52 feet deep.
  Dark Lake is accessible only by trail from Olallie or Trout Lake. Dark Lake is 1.5 miles west of Trout Lake Campground and is the middle lake in the chain, just west of Island Lake. Dark Lake is the deepest lake in the chain, surrounded by steep, high talus slopes on the west and south shores. There is little shoal area to fish.

Harvey Lake - BT, 5,400 feet elevation, 27 acres, 40 feet deep.
  Harvey Lake is a lightly fished hike-in lake in a gorgeous setting accessible by trail only. Harvey is reached by a 1.5-mile hike south from Breitenbush Campground on Breitenbush Lake. High, steep talus slopes surround this beautiful lake. An inlet waterfall from Lake Hilda and outlet waterfall into Shitike Creek frosts the cake. There is limited shoal area.
  From the Salem area, take State Highway 22 about 50 miles east to Detroit. From Detroit, follow Forest Route 46 up the North Fork of the Breitenbush River about 20 miles to Forest Route 42, following signs to Breitenbush Lake for about another 9 miles.
  From Central Oregon, take U.S. Highway 97 to U.S. Highway 20 toward Sisters and Santiam Pass. Continue on 20 to its junction with Highway 22 at the Santiam Pass Summit. It is then 31 miles to Detroit.

Island Lake - BT, 4,650 feet elevation, 26 acres, 10 feet deep.
  With most of its acreage covered by 3 feet or less water, Island Lake is the shallowest lake in the chain. A 1-acre island located in the center of the lake gives it its name.
  Island Lake is accessible only by unimproved trail from Olallie or Trout Lake. Island Lake is the next lake west of Trout Lake, a 1-mile hike by trail. Island can also be reached from Olallie Lake, as can all the lakes in the chain, but the shortest hike is from Trout Lake. Island Lake is best to fish from a floating device. Motors are prohibited.

Long Lake - BT, 4,850 feet elevation, 40 acres, 34 feet deep.
  The fourth lake west from Trout Lake, Long Lake is just .4 mile east of Olallie Lake. The shortest hiking distance is from Peninsula Campground on Olallie Lake. A trail around the south end of Olallie connects with Trail 730 to Long Lake in .6 mile. It is then .4 mile on Trail 730 to Long Lake.

Trout Lake - RB, BT, 4,600 feet elevation, 23 acres, 28 feet deep.
  Some natural reproduction occurs among the species in Trout Lake. Farthest east in the chain of five lakes, Trout Lake is a drive-in site with a primitive campground. To reach Trout Lake, take U.S. Highway 26 from Portland heading southeast, or from Madras driving northwest. From Highway 26, 6.5 miles north of Warm Springs on Highway 26, take Road p-600 west. Drive 4.5 miles west on this good gravel road to road b-210. It is then a 13-mile drive on b-210 to Trout Lake.

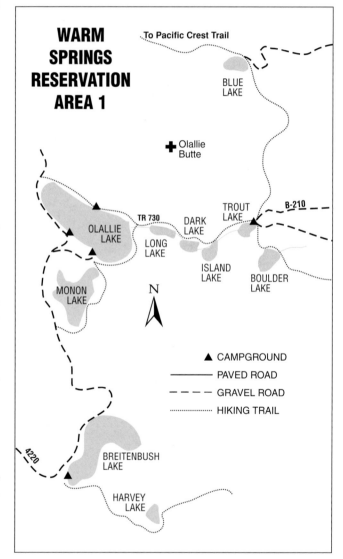

WARM SPRINGS RESERVATION AREA 1

To Pacific Crest Trail

BLUE LAKE

Olallie Butte

TROUT LAKE   B-210

TR 730   DARK LAKE

OLALLIE LAKE   LONG LAKE

ISLAND LAKE   BOULDER LAKE

MONON LAKE

N

4220

BREITENBUSH LAKE

HARVEY LAKE

▲ CAMPGROUND
—— PAVED ROAD
– – – GRAVEL ROAD
········· HIKING TRAIL

PROTECT CULTURAL RESOURCES
Cultural resources include anything over 50 years old that shows evidence of having been made, used, or altered by humans. Cultural resources are non-renewable, limited in number, and important to tribal cultures and their national heritage.

Area 6 - McQuinn Strip

No Tribal Permit is required to fish these lakes. Forest Service campgrounds are available at Breitenbush Lake, Monon Lake, and Ollalie Lake.

Breitenbush Lake - BT, 5,500 feet elevation, 60 acres, 30 feet deep.

Breitenbush is a drive-in lake 105 miles southeast of Portland. Take Highway 26 southeast from Portland to the cutoff onto Forest Route 42 about 10 miles south of the junction of Highway 35 and 26. Stay on Route 42 for about 30 miles to its junction with Forest Route 4220, following signs to Olallie Lake. Olallie Lake is roughly 45 miles from Highway 26. Continue on past Olallie to Breitenbush Lake, another 4 miles south. Breitenbush has good shoal areas. A Forest Service campground is located on the lake. Motors are prohibited.

From the Salem area, take State Highway 22 about 50 miles east to Detroit. From Detroit, follow Forest Route 46 up the North Fork of the Breitenbush River about 20 miles to Forest Route 42, following signs to Breitenbush Lake for about another 9 miles.

From Central Oregon, take U.S. Highway 97 to U.S. Highway 20 toward Sisters and Santiam Pass. Continue on 20 to its junction with Highway 22 at the Santiam Pass Summit. It is then 31 miles to Detroit.

Brook Lake - BT, 4,700 feet elevation, 4 acres, 8 feet deep.

Brook Lake is located 3 miles north of Olallie Lake. See Breitenbush Lake for directions to Olallie Lake. Drive to Olallie Meadow Campground, 4 miles north of Olallie Lake on Forest Route 4220. A trail leads from the campground to a series of three lakes, of which Brook Lake is the first, the farthest west of the group. Brook Lake is .5 mile southeast of Olallie Meadow Campground. The lake's brushy shoreline is best fished from a floating device.

Gibson Lake - BT, 5,800 feet elevation, 6 acres, 14 feet deep.

A hike-in lake where overnight camping is allowed, Gibson Lake is .5 mile north of Breitenbush Lake. The trail to the lake starts across from the entrance to the Breitenbush Lake Campground. See directions to Breitenbush Lake.

Jude Lake - BT, 4,550 feet elevation, 2 acres, 14 feet deep.

Jude Lake is just east of Brook Lake and is the middle lake in the row of three. Jude Lake also has very brushy shores. See directions to Brook Lake.

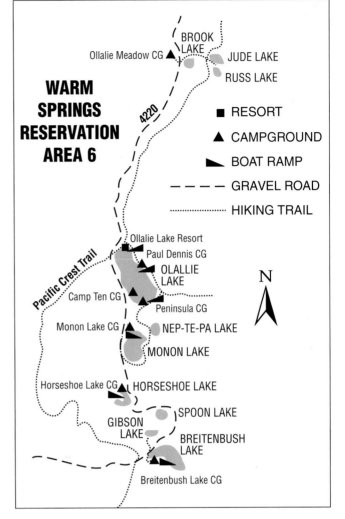

The experience and solitude of the wilderness lakes make them worth the hike in. Ed Park photo

Monon Lake - CT, BT, 5,000 feet elevation, 91 acres, 39 feet deep.

Monon is a drive-in lake .25 mile south of Olallie Lake on the same road, Forest Route 4220. Monon Lake Campground, a developed Forest Service facility, has a boat ramp.

Nep-te-pa Lake - BT, 5,000 feet elevation, 2 acres, 25 feet deep.

Located between the south end of Olallie Lake and the north end of Monon Lake, Nep-te-pa Lake is reached by a .5-mile hike south from Peninsula Campground on Olallie Lake.

Olallie Lake - BT, RB, 4,900 feet elevation, 240 acres, 48 feet deep.

Olallie Lake is the most popular and the farthest west of a chain of five lakes, which ends with Trout Lake to the east. See directions to Breitenbush Lake. Motors are prohibited on the lake. There are four Forest Service campgrounds on the lake, plus Olallie Lake Resort.

Russ Lake - BT, 4,700 feet elevation, 5 acres, 8 feet deep.

Russ Lake is the farthest east of the three lakes east of Olallie Meadows Campground and is considered to have the best fishing of the three. It is about .75 mile east of the campground. See directions to Brook Lake.

Spoon Lake - BT, 5,800 feet, 2 acres, shallow.

Spoon Lake is no longer stocked and is prone to winterkill. Spoon Lake is located along the west side of Skyline Road (Forest Route 4220) just north of Gibson Lake. A small population of brook trout struggles to survive here.

North and Northeast Central Oregon

Many fine fishing opportunities exist in the northern and northeastern areas of Oregon.
The next several pages cover popular waters north to the Columbia River,
south to the John Day River, east to Cold Springs Reservoir, and west to Hood River.

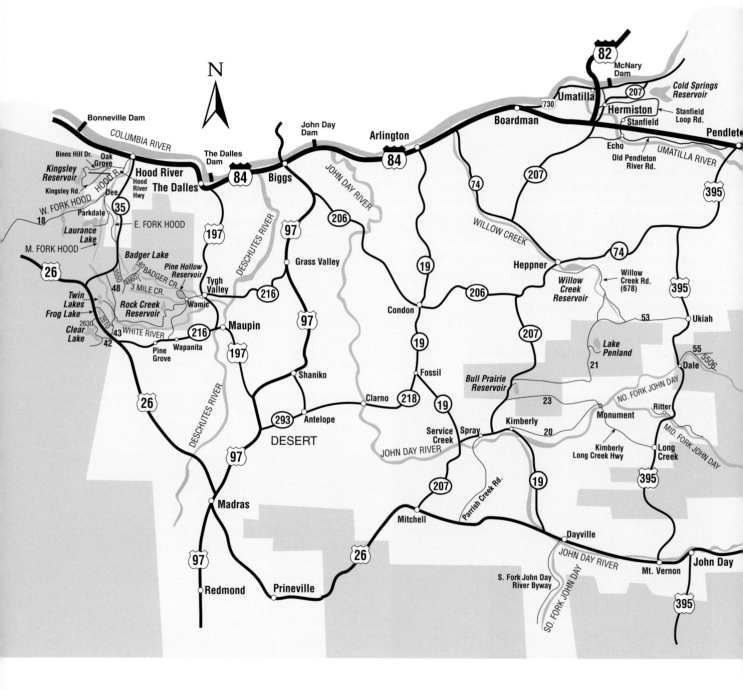

CLEAR LAKE (WASCO COUNTY)

Size: approx. 600 acres
Depth: fluctuates due to irrigation
Main Catch: rainbow & brook trout
Best Methods: spin fishing, trolling, bait fishing, fly fishing
Season: check OSFR
Best Time: May through October
Tips: Fish small crayfish imitations or trap crayfish and use tail to catch rainbow and brook trout.

Surrounded by fir trees, rhododendrons and mountain hemlock, Clear Lake is a 600-acre irrigation reservoir in the White River watershed. Heavily stocked with rainbow trout, the lake is popular with Portland area anglers and Central Oregon residents. Hatchery rainbows and resident brook trout average between eight and 18 inches, though bigger fish are present. Clear Lake is one of the places where the ODFW plants excess brood stock.

Dependent on the time of year, the lake is by turns whipped by mountain winds or calm and quiet. Trolling is one of the most popular methods on this lake. A 10-mph speed limit is in effect. The boat launch is on the east bank, near the campground. Later in the summer, when irrigation drawdowns have lowered the water level, the ramp is only accessible to smaller boats.

Bank anglers should try the area near the dam. Bait fishermen should use Power Bait, salmon eggs, and nightcrawlers. Spin fishermen should cast Rooster Tails and small spoons.

Bigger rainbows and brook trout feed on Clear Lake's abundant crayfish. Fly fishermen can duplicate them with fur and feathers, while spin fishermen should employ plastics or large orange spinners. Fish close to the bottom and duplicate the crayfish' slow-fast-slow, erratic escape tactics.

Boat anglers will do well along the east shore. Look at the topography of the shoreline for an indication of where to concentrate your efforts. Rocky points or steep shoulders give indication that the ridge will continue below the surface. This type of structure will hold feeding rainbows in the morning and evening.

Go slow. When using trolling blades, troll just fast enough to keep the blades turning. The slower speed is tantalizing to fish, but speed up the retrieve from time to time. Make sudden direction changes, accelerate and then slow down.

Don't troll in a straight line. Make S-turns along your course, to make your lure change directions suddenly, diving and climbing in the water column, just like a baitfish being pursued by a predator. Such direction changes trigger strikes from predatory fish.

The Clear Lake campground has 28 basic sites with no hookups. Tables, cooking grills, drinking water, and vault toilets are provided.

The road to Clear Lake can be found less than ten miles east of Government Camp on Highway 26. Drive south one mile on Forest Road 2630 to the lake.

ABOVE: Boat anglers will do well along the east shore. Hatchery rainbows and resident brook trout average between eight and 18 inches.

RIGHT: Clear Lake is surrounded by fir trees, rhododendrons and mountain hemlock.

Photos by Gary Lewis

FROG LAKE

Size:	approx. 11 acres
Depth:	3 to 6 feet
Main Catch:	rainbow trout
Best Methods:	spin fishing, bait fishing, fly fishing
Season:	check OSFR
Best Time:	April through October
Tips:	Use a fly and bubble on a spinning rod. Best patterns are Beadhead Prince Nymph, Woolly Bugger and weighted baitfish patterns.

Frog Lake is an 11-acre body of water surrounded by firs and hemlocks, high in the White River watershed. Heavily stocked with rainbow trout, the lake is popular with traveling anglers and is a good place to bring children or beginners. Hatchery rainbows average between 8 and 11 inches, though bigger fish are present. ODFW also stocks surplus brood stock in Frog Lake.

Many fishermen fish from the bank, but a small boat or a float tube can be used. Motors are not allowed.

All methods work well at Frog Lake, but fly fishing can be very productive. One effective technique incorporates the spinning rod, a casting bubble and flies.

The casting bubble is the key to making this technique effective. It must be the type that can be filled with water, which provides the weight necessary for long-distance casting. Whether fishing on the surface or below the surface, the best choice is the medium size, clear plastic bubble that is the approximate size of a chicken egg.

Slide the bubble over your main line and tie on a No. 12 or 14 black barrel swivel. Knot a three-foot, four-pound test leader to your barrel swivel, then tie on the fly. For starters, use a wet fly such as a No. 8 Woolly Bugger, or No. 10 Woolly Worm. Good nymph patterns are flies like the beadhead Pheasant Tail, or Prince Nymph. When fishing for bigger fish, try minnow patterns.

Cast, tighten up the line, and begin to reel — slowly. Vary the depth and retrieve until you find the fish. A slow retrieve is usually the most effective.

Spoons that imitate baitfish work well at Frog Lake. Little Cleos, Triple Teasers, and Kastmasters are some of the more popular models. Smaller is better when targeting hatchery trout. Add a snap swivel, then tie the spoon directly to your main line and add a little weight if needed. Cast, let it sink, and retrieve just fast enough to keep your lure wobbling, not spinning.

The best plugs for catching these trout are minnow imitations. Try small Rapalas and FlatFish. You may need to add a little weight for casting. Vary your retrieve and depth until you start hooking rainbows.

The Frog Lake Campground opens in June each year. Thirty-three basic sites provide tables, cooking grills, toilets and drinking water.

The road to Frog Lake can be found less than 8 miles southeast of Government Camp on Highway 26. Watch for the sign at Forest Road 2610. The lake is a short drive east of the highway.

ABOVE: Anglers have success fishing from the bank or from a small boat. Motors are not allowed on Frog Lake.

LEFT: Views of Mt. Hood can be seen from the lake.
Photos by Gary Lewis

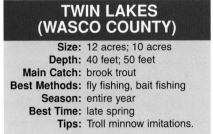

TWIN LAKES (WASCO COUNTY)

Size: 12 acres; 10 acres
Depth: 40 feet; 50 feet
Main Catch: brook trout
Best Methods: fly fishing, bait fishing
Season: entire year
Best Time: late spring
Tips: Troll minnow imitations.

Lying high along the crest of the Cascade Mountains, on the south slope of Mt. Hood are Wasco County's Twin Lakes. An easy 1.5-mile hike through a forest of tall fir trees, vine maple, ferns, Indian paintbrush, and Oregon grape will lead you first to lower Twin.

Popular with hikers, swimmers, and fishermen, you may not find solitude at Twin Lakes, but you might find some good fishing. Stocked every other year with brook trout, these waters can produce some memorable angling after the snows recede and the trail is accessible.

Deep lakes (lower Twin is 40 feet deep and upper Twin is 50 feet deep), insect growth is limited to the shoreside shallows. Thus, the best trout fishing is found along the ledges adjacent to deeper water.

Here, the brook trout average seven to ten inches, but holdover trout can stretch the tape to 15 inches or more. Probe the deeper water for the biggest fish.

The Twin Lakes are best fished from a float tube or rubber raft, but shore access is very good. Bait fishing will produce fish throughout the season. Use rainbow or chartreuse Power Bait in the spring. Use a sliding sinker and 28 inches of leader. Rig the bait on a No. 14 or 16 treble hook. Cast, let the bait sink to the bottom. Leave your bail open and let the fish take the bait.

Where you find the best still fishing, for fast action, switch to spinners, spoons or plugs. Tie on a 1/16-ounce Rooster Tail spinner, Thomas spoon, or Rapala and add a little split shot to aid in dropping the lure to the proper depth. Cast and retrieve, experimenting with depth, until you get the first strike.

Troll flies from a float tube along the ledges that transition to deeper water or prospect around rocky points and submerged timber. Minnow imitations, Woolly Buggers, and soft hackle wet flies like the Carey Special, Brown Hackle, and the Soft Hackle Hare's Ear, are good bets. Use an intermediate sinking line to keep your fly in the strike zone. In the late-summer and fall, watch the shallows along the shoreline for trout rising to ants that have blown in the water.

Car campers will find good camping at nearby Frog Lake (See Frog Lake chapter). For the best chance at finding an open campsite, go during the week. There are several primitive sites at lower Twin.

Drive west on Highway 26 almost to the junction with Highway 35. Watch for the Frog Lake sign. Park at the Snow Park/Rest Area and take the Pacific Crest Trail west for one mile and watch for the trail leading to the right. After another half mile, you'll see the lower lake through the trees. The upper lake is another half mile beyond.

Reached with an easy 1.5-mile hike, the Twin Lakes are best fished from a float tube or rubber raft, but shore access is very good. Photo by Gary Lewis

WHITE RIVER

Size:	approx. 50 miles
Depth:	wadeable
Main Catch:	rainbow trout, steelhead
Best Method:	flies & lures only; nymphing most effective
Season:	check OSFR
Best Time:	spring
Tips:	limited access due to private land; glacial water color limits visibility

Heading in a glacier, high on the slopes of Mt. Hood, the White River flows approximately 50 miles to the east where it feeds the Deschutes, north of Maupin. Its name comes

from the color of the glacial water and it is often ignored by anglers who are used to water they can see into.

Other factors that limit angler attention are the distance of the stream from population centers, a high percentage of private land ownership along the lower river and the rugged terrain.

The river runs through a deep canyon after leaving the Mt. Hood National Forest. Groves of oak and pine give shade to the deer, elk, bear, wild turkeys and gray squirrels that take their water from the stream. On the slopes above the river, you can sometimes hear the "chuk-chuk-chuk" of the chukar call.

Rapids, pools and tailouts are characteristic of this stream that loses so much elevation in 50 miles. Almost every year, in August or September, a piece of the glacier that feeds the river breaks off, and the river will run high and muddy for up to three weeks.

Fish can be found throughout most of the river, from the point where it is crossed by Highway 35 down to its confluence with the Deschutes. Rainbow trout are the predominant species. In the upper river, as in the upper reaches of most mountain streams, fish are small. Catch a 12-incher and you've landed a trophy. With more food at the lower elevation, the rainbows average to 15 inches in the middle river. Three falls in the last three miles of river divide the trout population. Below the falls, the angler can find the biggest fish.

Steelhead can be found in the lower river, and all rainbows over 20 inches in length are considered steelhead. All non-finclipped

steelhead must be released unharmed.

Fishermen are restricted to angling with artificial lures and flies throughout the river. Downstream from the lowest falls, the fishing is regulated by Deschutes River section one rules. Fish early and late in the day for the best success. During the day, try the shaded, deeper water. Look for the biggest fish in the slower water where trout have to expend less energy to survive.

With a gravel bottom and some silting in the lower river, the White River is wadeable throughout most of its length. Cast brown, black and orange Rooster Tail or Bangtail spinners in the lower and middle river. Use flies from the headwaters to the mouth.

Visibility in the water is low throughout the year, but dry flies do bring fish to the surface. One of the most effective techniques for the White River is nymphing with bead head flies like the Prince, Hare's Ear, Zug Bug and Brassie. Use a strike indicator positioned on the leader to keep the fly drifting at the proper depth.

Weighted crayfish imitations and baitfish patterns are also effective. Fish them on a shorter leader with a tight line, making them swim and scoot along the bottom.

To fish the upper White River from Bend take Highway 26 towards Mt. Hood; head north on Highway 35 to the river. Take Forest Road 48 south to the Barlow Road Crossing. From Barlow Crossing, Forest Road 3530 follows the west side of the river for approximately 4 miles. To find the lower river, take Highway 216 then turn left between Wapinitia and Pine Grove. Or, take Highway 197 to the bridge east of Tygh Valley where it crosses the river.

FAR LEFT:
Gary Lewis shows off a nice White River rainbow that took a black Woolly Bugger. Photo by Jennifer Lewis

LEFT: The White River as seen from Tygh Valley State Wayside. Photo by Jon Gnass

INSET: Jennifer Lewis with a White River rainbow that fell for a Prince Nymph. Photo by Gary Lewis

PINE HOLLOW RESERVOIR

Size: 240 acres
Depth: 15 feet average
Main Catch: rainbow trout, largemouth bass, bluegill, bullhead
Best Methods: bait fishing, trolling
Season: entire year
Best Time: spring
Tips: Troll through buoy line.

Pine Hollow Reservoir is a pretty, popular irrigation reservoir set in a forest of mixed pines and oaks, west of Tygh Valley. Less than two hours drive from Portland or Bend and less than an hour away from The Dalles, it attracts plenty of attention on spring and summer weekends. For good reason. The Department of Fish and Wildlife makes sure that there are plenty of trout in the water, including a number of big brood stock rainbows. Trout average 10 inches with holdovers running to 16 inches. The lake has produced rainbows that have stretched the tape to 32 inches.

Largemouth bass grow big here, as well. Five-pounders are not uncommon. From June through September, the reservoir's bluegills and catfish provide good sport for warmwater fisherman.

Many of the biggest fish are taken on Power Bait. Use a sliding sinker to a barrel swivel and 28 inches of leader terminating at a No. 14 treble hook. Mold a Power Bait nugget around the hook. The bait will float off the bottom. Leave a little slack in the line and set the hook when the line starts to move.

Trolling accounts for a lot of the rainbows that are taken every year. Anglers have success with Thomas Buoyant spoons and Kwikfish in rainbow, tiger and silver/blue color schemes. Try a zigzag trolling pattern through the buoy line. Another good trolling area is in the northwest corner near Camp Morrow.

Best fishing from the bank is on either side of the east shore boat ramp. At the south shore boat ramp, bank access can be found west of the ramp. Use Rooster Tail spinners or plunk Power Bait. When the water is calm, use a bobber and worm or Pautzke's Balls-O-Fire salmon eggs. Experiment with leader length until you find the proper depth.

Two boat ramps are available, one on the east side and the other on the south shore. A 10-mph speed limit is enforced for most of the year. Waterskiing is permitted on the west half of the lake from July 1 through Labor Day. Motorboats, pontoon boats, paddleboats and jet skis are available for rental from the resort. If you bring your own boat, you can rent a spot at the dock.

Lakeside Resort and RV Park, on the east shore, is your best bet for camping at Pine Hollow. Campsites are rented by the day or the week. Toilets, showers, and water are pro-vided. RV sites have water, electric and sewer hookups. Cabins and A-frames are available by the day or week. At the general store, you'll find snacks, fuel, fishing tackle and propane. Next door is Lexie's Restaurant with a view of the water.

Lakeside Resort hosts a fishing derby during the last week in April and a kid's derby on Free Fishing Weekend in June. Contact the resort for details.

From Highway 216, head west on Tygh Valley Road. Proceed into Wamic and turn left on Wamic Market Road (between storage building and tavern). Drive for 4 miles, then turn right on Ross Road. Proceed 3.5 miles and turn left at the intersection.

ABOVE: Trout average 10 inches with holdovers running to 16 inches … with some larger.

BELOW: Two boat ramps are available, one on the east side and the other on the south shore. Photos by Gary Lewis

ROCK CREEK RESERVOIR

Size:	100 acres
Depth:	10 feet average
Main Catch:	rainbow trout, largemouth bass, bluegill, bullhead
Best Methods:	bait fishing, fly fishing
Season:	entire year
Best Time:	June, October
Tips:	Fish along the edge of the weedbeds.

Rock Creek Reservoir is an irrigation reservoir in the foothills about 13 miles west of Tygh Valley. Oak trees and ponderosa pines surround the basin and provide shade for weary fishermen. Silver gray squirrels skitter in the leaves and mule deer come out to feed at the edge of small clearings.

The Department of Fish and Wildlife stocks catchable rainbow trout throughout the spring and summer and fishing can be very good for rainbows, largemouth bass, bluegills, and brown bullhead catfish.

All methods work well at this lake. Trout average ten to twelve inches, but holdover fish grow to 18 inches and beyond. Rainbows can be found by fishing in the shallows early and late in the day. Fish deeper water when the sun is higher in the sky. To target trout, use spinners, spoons, plugs or Power Bait. Troll rainbow Rapalas or frog pattern FlatFish along the transitions from shallow to deeper water and parallel to the dam.

Look for bass near tall grass and shoreside willows and around rocky points. For bass, use a plastic worm and a sliding bullet sinker. Cast, let it sink then retrieve it very slow along the bottom. In the evening, try using a popper for bass. Cast it to the shoreside willows, let it hit the water and rest, then make it twitch.

Bluegill can be found in the shallows where they take cover around the grass and submerged trees. Look for bluegill also around the weedbeds. Bluegill are best caught on grasshoppers, small bits of worm under a bobber. Bluegill are fun on a fly rod. Find the fish feeding on the surface and cast small dry flies or unweighted nymphs. Watch for the swirl, then set the hook.

Catfish are best fished for when they come into the shallows at dark. Nightcrawlers, chicken livers and blood baits are a good choice. In any case, put your bait on the bottom to catch a cat.

Best bank access is on the north shore. Fish from the dam for trout or explore the shallows east of the dam for warmwater fish.

A small ramp on the south end of the lake is suitable for small boats. Gas motors are not permitted on the lake.

Within the campground you will find 33 basic sites with no hookups. Maximum length is 18 feet. Managed by the Forest Service, you can call 1-800-280-CAMP for reservations. Picnic tables, grills, pit toilets, and drinking water are provided.

Overflow camping is available in the forest surrounding the reservoir. Use established campsites and fire rings.

From Tygh Valley, head west on Tygh Valley and Wamic Market Roads for six miles. From Wamic, head west on Rock Creek Dam Road for 6.5 miles. Turn right (west) on Forest Road 4820, then turn right on Forest Road 120 and follow signs to campground and boat launch.

An irrigation reservoir in the foothills about 13 miles west of Tygh Valley, Rock Creek Reservoir is surrounded by oak trees and ponderosa pines which provide shade for weary fishermen. The best bank access is the north shore. A small boat ramp is available on the south shore. Photos by Gary Lewis

BADGER LAKE

Size: 30 acres
Depth: 45 feet
Main Catch: rainbow trout, brook trout
Best Methods: fly fishing, bait fishing
Season: entire year
Best Time: when road opens
Tips: Use crayfish and crayfish imitations.

Deep in the head of a canyon between two high ridges on the southeast slope of Mt. Hood, you'll find Badger Lake. Known for its aggressive rainbows and its brook trout, the lake is popular on summer weekends, despite the long, rough roads. Mountain snows limit access for most of the year, but the road is generally open by the first of July.

By mid-summer, Badger's holdover rainbows run between 13 and 15 inches, with some fish measuring up to 17. Bulking up on the lake's abundant crayfish, they are in fine shape when the snows begin to fall in October. Though you'll catch more rainbows, there is a good population of brook trout to keep things interesting.

Spin fishermen should start with a silver Blue Fox or Panther Martin spinner. Fish it deep for best

Known for its aggressive rainbows and its brook trout, Badger Lake is popular despite the long, rough roads to reach the lake. The rainbows bulk up on the lake's abundant crayfish, another popular catch here. Photos by Gary Lewis

effect. Trolling accounts for a lot of the rainbows that are taken every year. Anglers have success with Thomas Buoyant spoons in silver/blue color schemes. Try a zigzag trolling pattern.

Many fish are taken on Power Bait. Use a sliding sinker to a barrel swivel and 28 inches of leader terminating at a No. 14 treble hook. Mold a Power Bait nugget around the hook. The bait will float off the bottom. Leave a little slack in the line and set the hook when the line starts to move.

Fly fishing is most productive in the fall, use minnow imitations and crayfish patterns to hook the biggest fish. When the wind blows, watch for trout feeding near the shore on flying ants.

If you plan to camp, leave the RV at home and bring a tent. Vault toilets, picnic tables and fire pits are provided. There are sites with views of the lake and down in the canyon, beside the creek.

Several roads lead to Badger, but none of them are easy. There's a boat ramp at the lake, but don't plan on launching anything that comes on a trailer. Trailers are prohibited on this single-lane, rutted track. The best approach seems to be from the 48 Road. Take Forest Route 4860 north. The first 3.5 miles are paved, then the road turns to gravel. After a long, uphill climb through manzanita, pines, cedars and vine maple, you'll start on a downhill slope, which leads to an intersection, follow the sign and turn right on NFD 140 which rounds a mountain and leads into the Badger Creek canyon. If you're traveling before July, bring a winch and a shovel.

If you like treacherous traveling on rutted, one-lane roads, carved out of knife-edge ridges, take the 3550 road in from Bennett Pass. You'll see stunning mountain views that those who travel the paved roads will never know. Wildflowers grow on the steepest slopes and gnarled hemlocks cling to a tenuous existence on the rocky outcroppings. For wildlife, you'll glimpse hawks riding the mountain thermals and, if you're lucky, a pika, sunning on the shale.

BADGER CREEK

Size: 25 miles
Depth: varies
Main Catch: rainbow trout, brook trout
Best Methods: fly fishing
Season: entire year
Best Time: when road opens
Tips: Use attractor flies on the surface

Badger Creek, a tributary of Tygh Creek in the White River drainage, flows out of Badger Lake on the southeast side of Mt. Hood. Upstream, it is fished from the trail that follows along its bank. Roads cross the stream at Bonney Crossing and just below Badger Lake. Downstream, the creek is crossed by several smaller roads and Forest Road 47 and again at Tygh Valley, by Highway 197. Leave your bait box at home and bring an ultralight spinning rod equipped with four-pound test line. Cast small black Rooster Tail spinners or tiny pink Berkeley Power Worms. Spinning gear works best when the water is running cold with snowmelt.

Later in the season, bring your fly tackle. In riffled water, use small attractor flies like the Humpy, Royal Wulff, and Irresistible. In longer, slower runs, switch to soft-hackle wet flies, leech patterns and streamers. Fish beadhead nymphs beneath a strike indicator in deeper sections.

If you plan on spending the night nearby, there are good campgrounds at Badger Lake and Bonney Crossing.

Badger Creek flows out of Badger Lake on the southeast side of Mt. Hood. Upstream, it is fished from the trail that follows along its bank. Photo by Gary Lewis

LAURANCE LAKE

Size: 104 acres
Depth: 15 feet average
Main Catch: rainbow trout, cutthroat trout, bull trout
Best Methods: flies, lures
Season: April - October
Best Time: June, October
Tips: Troll flies in the shallows on the south shore.

For good fishing in a peaceful, pretty setting, head to Laurance Lake on the east slope of Mt. Hood. A small, serene campground sits on the south shore, looking across at a steep forested ridge. Blacktail deer feed out of the openings and the high-pitched cry of the pika can be heard from the hillside rocks they call home.

Hatchery rainbow trout, native cutthroat trout, and bull trout are the main catch in the Laurance. Smallmouth bass are available also. Only finclipped trout and bass may be kept.

To protect bull trout, bait fishing is not permitted at the reservoir. This keeps many anglers away and guarantees a measure of peace not found at nearby lakes.

Most anglers fish along the south shore, close to camp. Best bank access is near the new bridge spanning Pinnacle Creek and east to the dam. Anglers do well in this section, casting Rooster Tail or Bangtail spinners or a fly beneath a float. To find the most fish, pay

Rooster Tails
Courtesy Yakima Bait Co.

attention to stream inlets and rocky points adjacent to deeper water. Use a 1/8-ounce Rooster Tail. Try black, brown or rainbow patterns. Cast, let it sink, then retrieve. To fish a fly, use a casting bubble. It must be the type that can be filled with water, which provides the weight necessary for long-distance casting. Whether fishing on the surface or below the surface, the best choice is the medium size, clear plastic bubble that is the approximate size of a chicken egg.

Slide the bubble over your main line and tie on a No. 12 black barrel swivel. Knot a three- to four-foot, four-pound test leader to your barrel swivel, then tie on the fly. For starters, use a wet fly such as a No. 10 Prince Nymph or black Woolly Bugger.

Cast, tighten up the line, and begin to reel — slowly. Vary the depth and retrieve until you find the fish. A slow retrieve is usually the most effective.

For boaters, trolling along the north shore or dam can produce fast action. Fly fishermen should employ a clear intermediate sinking line and a nine-foot leader. Good patterns for the lake include the Prince Nymph, Woolly Bugger and Pheasant Tail nymph. To go deeper, try using a beadhead pattern.

Spin fishermen can troll spinners, plugs or spoons. Another effective technique is to pull flashers trailed by a single Prince Nymph on a three-foot leader.

Two small boat ramps are provided on the south shore. Gas motors are not permitted on the lake.

At Kinnikinnick Campground on the south shore of Laurance Lake, you'll find 20 basic sites with no hookups. Maximum length is 16 feet. Tables, grills, and vault toilets are provided. Bring your own drinking water.

From Highway 35, head west on Cooper Spur Road at Mt. Hood Corner. Drive 4.5 miles and take a right onto Evans Creek Road. Proceed along a paved road reaching the lake in five miles.

ABOVE: A floating device is helpful to reach many of the deeper areas.

RIGHT: A small, serene campground sits on the south shore, looking across at a steep forested ridge.

Photos by Gary Lewis

KINGSLEY RESERVOIR
(also called Green Point Reservoir)

Size: 60 acres
Depth: 20 feet
Main Catch: rainbow trout
Best Methods: bait
Season: entire year
Best Time: spring
Tips: Cast Rooster Tails from the dam.

If you like to combine motorsports with your fishing, then Kingsley Reservoir is the place for you. On any weekend during the spring, you'll find motorcyclists and four-wheelers climbing the hill and going over jumps and roaring around on various trails through the brush. And most of them are fishermen. After they run out of gas, they head down to the water.

Though the environment is noisy, the fishing can be good. The Department of Fish and Wildlife stocks Kingsley (also known as Green Point Reservoir) on a regular basis with legal rainbows. This is one of those lakes you can fish well from the bank. The best access is at the dam where the water averages about 20 feet deep. To get away from the crowd, walk across the dam around to the west side of the lake.

Bait fishing is popular here and trolling accounts for a lot of fish. In the deep water by the dam, where most of the bait fishing takes place, you can catch fish on brown Rooster Tails or Bangtails. Cast, let it sink, give it a twitch and retrieve. Keep the spinner moving fast enough to keep the blade revolving, but don't reel so fast that you spook the trout. There are a few snags out there, but that's the price you pay for hard strikes and fast limits. Fish average 10 inches and holdovers can run to 15 inches.

Power Bait is popular on Kingsley, but bait fishing with nightcrawlers and Pautzke's is just as productive. Use a No. 10 single bait hook and about three feet of leader beneath your float or bobber.

If you've got a small boat, there's a launch

Nice rainbows are the main catch at this lake where bank fishing can be very productive.
Photo by Gary Lewis

near the dam that you can use. There is no dock and the parking area is not paved, nor is it marked. Motors are permitted on the lake. Try slow-trolling a nightcrawler or pulling a small wobbling plug in a rainbow, frog, or crayfish pattern.

Lower Green Point Reservoir can be found downhill, north of the lake. A road follows the eastern shore.

Mixed age stands of firs, and maples surround Kingsley Reservoir. Ferns and huckleberries grow in the openings. The campground is open and primitive with about 20 unmarked spots. There are no

hookups. Some groups arrange their RVs in a circle to protect against wind and weather. The campsites are suitable for smaller RVs and tents. A few tables and a toilet are provided. Use existing fire rings. There is no drinking water.

Drive from Hood River to Oak Grove. From Oak Grove's Reed Road, proceed west on Binns Hill Drive. Turn left on Kingsley Road and follow for six miles to the reservoir. The road goes up, up, up, through a tree farm that has been clearcut and selectively harvested. Be cautious, the road is a single lane with turnouts.

HOOD RIVER

Size:	approx. 50 miles long
Depth:	2 feet to 6 feet
Main Catch:	rainbow trout, steelhead, coho & chinook salmon
Best Methods:	fly fishing, spin fishing
Season:	check OSFR
Best Time:	June through October
Tips:	Fish small sculpin imitations in the riffles and along the seams to catch the biggest rainbow trout.

The Hood River displays a variety of personalities. Long rapids and fast-flowing pools are characteristic of this stream.
Photos by Gary Lewis

Fed by glaciers and snowmelt on the east-side of Mt. Hood, the Hood River flows almost 40 miles east and north to the Columbia. The Hood and its tributaries drain some of the most beautiful country east of the Cascades, from the mountains to the pastoral apple orchards and croplands surrounding the communities of Parkdale, Dee, Odell, and the town of Hood River.

Long rapids and fast-flowing pools are characteristic of this stream. Native rainbow trout can be found throughout most of the river. Steelhead, coho and chinook can be caught from the mouth upstream to Powerdale Dam at river mile four.

Fishermen are restricted to angling with artificial lures and flies upstream from Powerdale Dam. Steelhead fishing is not allowed above the dam. The season runs from Memorial Day weekend through the end of October. All trout must be released. Check OSFR before fishing as changing regulations may differ.

When fishing the upper reaches for native trout, ply the seams adjacent to the riffles where trout have to expend less energy to survive. Ledges and rock overhangs offer cover to the bigger trout. Fish these spots for a chance at catching a predator waiting for the river to bring him insects and unwary baitfish.

Small spinners and spoons in brass, black, and brown are effective. Fly fishermen should drift small stonefly and caddis patterns or try attractor dry flies like the Royal Wulff, the Irresistible and the various Humpy patterns.

Baitfish patterns are also effective. Try the Muddler Minnow and the Zonker. Fish them on a five- to six-foot leader with a tight line, making them swim and scoot along the bottom.

In the last four river miles, from the dam to the mouth, fishing with bait is legal. Hike in to some of the best fishing, or park near the dam or at the mouth where public access is good. Bank access near the dam is in the PP&L parking lot. Here, the river is open to fishing for coho salmon, and fin-clipped steelhead the entire year. Fish early and late in the day for the best success. During the day, try the shaded, deeper water.

Find the East Fork by following Highway 35 north from Highway 26. You will cross the White River first and then the East Fork of the Hood. In a few miles, you will cross the river again and follow it for approximately 12 more miles. Try Robinhood Campground or Sherwood Campground in this stretch.

To fish the lower river, access it from Highway 84 at the town of Hood River. Highway 35 runs parallel to the lower river for the first four miles. Take the Hood River Highway to follow the mainstem Hood as far upstream as the town of Trout Creek.

The West Fork of the Hood River and its tributaries and the Clear Branch and Pinnacle Creek are closed to angling to protect spawning trout, salmon, and steelhead.

COLUMBIA RIVER

Size: approx. 160 miles between Bonneville and McNary Dams
Depth: 2 feet to 100 feet
Main Catch: sturgeon, steelhead, coho salmon, chinook salmon, walleye, bass
Best Methods: casting, spin fishing
Season: check OSFR
Best Time: March through October
Tips: Fish buoyancy-neutral spinners baited with nightcrawler to catch walleye, bass, perch, pikeminnow and catfish.

The Bonneville Dam spans the Columbia above Hood River. Photo by Gary Lewis

Flowing down out of British Columbia on its 1,210-mile journey, the Columbia River gathers water from Washington and Oregon before it reaches the sea. One of the world's great rivers, it also hosts the greatest fishery in the Pacific Northwest.

The Columbia system is home for millions of ocean-going salmon, steelhead, cutthroat trout, sturgeon, shad and smelt. Resident fish include walleye, largemouth and smallmouth bass, several species of catfish, crappie, yellow perch, sunfish and other species.

Central Oregon's section of the Columbia (from Umatilla downriver to Bonneville Dam) is one of the most productive sections of the river for warmwater fish. Ocean-going species move through this section as well, and provide great sport during certain parts of the year. To time your best fishing for salmon, steelhead and shad, watch the counts on the Columbia dams fish passage report at www.dfw.state.or.us/.

Salmon

Chinook, silver, and sockeye salmon migrate through this section of the river on their way to their native streams. Hatchery-reared or wild-born, the salmon makes an epic journey. Some salmon log up to 3500 miles on their round-trip journey. From ocean to native stream, a fish may travel hundreds of miles on energy stored over three or four years at sea. In general, salmon spawn in late summer and fall and hatch in the spring. Species differ in timing of the runs but may share the same river for weeks leading up to the spawn.

For sportsmen they are a particularly interesting quarry as the timing of the run, proper gear and bait selection, water reading skill, presentation, and strength are all required to subdue a salmon.

Chinook will average 15 pounds but 20- and 30-pound fish are common. And every year a few lucky fishermen boat 40- and 50-pound fish. But chinook salmon do grow bigger.

Salmon may be found in eight to 45 feet of water with the bulk of the fish holding in ten to 16 feet. Fish closer to the shore when the water is cold.

One effective technique for hooking salmon employs a lightweight Bob Toman or a Tee Spinner. Find the slots where upriver kings travel, then ambush them with a well-positioned spinner. Employ a two- to eight-ounce sinker on a dropper to hold the lure in place.

Or back-troll salmon plugs such as the Worden's FlatFish or Luhr-Jensen's Kwikfish. This technique works well on holding fish. Back the boat downstream while bouncing your lead and plug rig through fish-holding water. Lift the rod, and give line as needed to keep the lead bouncing and the lure working back to waiting fish. Set the hook when the line goes limp or breaks from the flow of the current.

When back-trolling, tie the line directly to the eye snap for best action. Also, use lighter line if you want the lure to dive deeper. Heavy line creates more drag, preventing the lure from diving as deep. The technique is

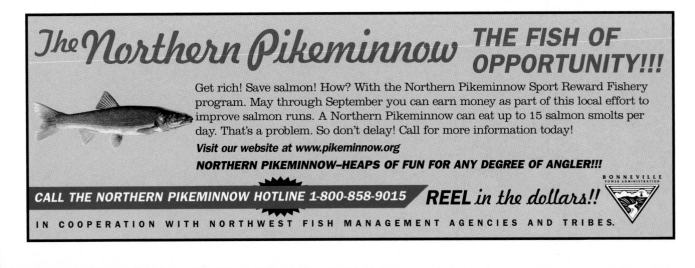

effective because the lure backs fish down, daring them to strike or get out of the way.

Steelhead

The ocean-going rainbows we call steelhead average 24 to 30 inches in length, between four and ten pounds. Any fish that breaks the 20-pound mark is considered a trophy. Catching a steelhead of any size is a thrill. They use reel-burning runs, high twisting leaps and dogged determination to throw the hook. Often, the fish will take to shoreside brush in an effort to escape, wrapping the line around every tree root, branch and

BELOW: Anglers caught these nice steelhead on the Columbia below the John Day Dam. Photos by Shawn Sellard

sharp rock in its path.

Steelhead follow the path of least resistance upstream. That might be the center of the river, but just as often it is an underwater path along a bank or high cliff. Look for seams in the water, and foam lines, indicating the transitions of swift and slow water. Such places allow steelhead to travel with fewer obstacles.

Holding water consists of any place where a school of fish can take refuge. It might be a deep pool downstream from a riffle. It might be the pillow of water in front of a boulder. It might be the calm in the downstream shadow of a boulder. It might be a pool below a fallen tree. It will be a place where the fish can feel reasonably comfortable, and secure from predators.

Steelhead water can be 18 inches deep or 18 feet deep. It moves at walking speed with a ripple on the surface. The fish could be lying under the grass at your feet or out in the center of the river. Here the river bottom is gravel or smooth stones. Larger boulders or downed trees provide resting places on the upstream migration.

One effective technique for taking steelhead in the Columbia employs a WiggleFin Chuckle Head or similar squid bait. Find the slots where the steelhead travel, then ambush them. Employ a two- to eight-ounce sinker on a dropper to hold the bait in place.

Sturgeon

The meat of the white sturgeon is highly-prized and that has contributed to its decline in the Northwest. Over-harvest in the late

1800s and early 1900s reduced the number of fish in Oregon and Washington. Still, Columbia River sturgeon provide great sport for many anglers every year.

Sturgeon can live for more than 100 years and may reach lengths exceeding 15 feet. One fish, taken by gill net, tipped the scales at 1,285 pounds. A Fraser River sturgeon weighed 1,800 pounds. As with many other species of fish, the largest ones are females. These large females are valued spawners and, when hooked, should be played and released quickly. One large female that was caught and killed was said to have carried 250 pounds of eggs.

Sturgeon are opportunistic bottom feeders that follow the feed, rooting with their snouts and detecting morsels with their sensitive barbels. Find the feed and you will find the fish. Contrary to common belief, a sturgeon's eyesight is sharp, though it relies mainly on its excellent sense of smell to find a meal.

Freshwater clams, decaying flesh, lamprey larva, eggs, worms, crayfish, snails, and anything else that lives, grows, and dies on the bottom can be food for sturgeon. Columbia River fish travel up and down the river to find the best concentrations of food.

Little depressions in the river bottom concentrate the food as the current sweeps it downstream. A depth finder helps the fisherman find these hidden sturgeon kitchens. Look for places where the depth changes, little depressions ten to twenty feet deeper than the surrounding bottom. The exception is when sturgeon are feeding on clams which

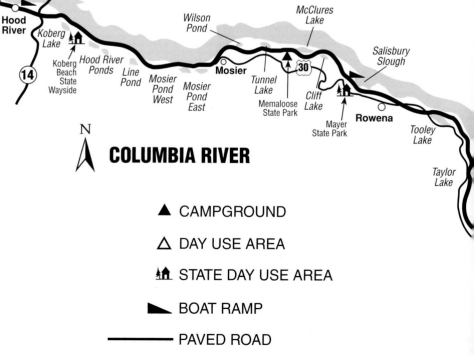

Gary Lewis with a nice Columbia sturgeon! Gary Lewis photo

are usually found in flat beds.

When your depth finder locates the kitchen, look for the fish, then set up upstream to run your lines back to them. Often the fish finder will show other fish higher in the water column. Because of their smaller air bladders, sturgeon are harder to spot. Look for blips along the bottom. Use the 'zoom' feature on your depth finder to magnify the bottom.

The most important part of your tackle is the hook. Fishing regulations on the Columbia River require a barbless hook to facilitate a quick release. Use a 5/0-9/0 barbless single hook, tied on Dacron leaders. Tie up leaders in advance for quick replacement on the river. Leave the leader long until it is rigged with bait. When rigged, best leader lengths for sturgeon are six to fourteen inches, unless you're using whole shad for bait. When fishing with whole shad, use a longer leader. Leader length depends on the type and size of bait being used as well as how it is rigged. Use a longer leader if you half-hitch the bait and shorter if you thread the bait.

Use a sliding sinker rig to allow the fish to take the bait without feeling much resistance from the weight, but heavy enough to keep your bait on the bottom. This will change based on current and tidal influence. Sinkers should be rigged to slide freely on the line using plastic tubing to protect your main line. Keep a selection of sinkers from 4- to 48-ounce.

The main line for fishing for "keeper" fish should be between 30 and 40 pound test. Most anglers use a non-stretch braided line. Bank anglers often choose monofilament because it offers better abrasion resistance. Braided line is a good choice for the boat angler because it doesn't stretch and allows a quick hook set. Go to heavier line when fishing for oversize fish.

A final word: Sturgeon fishing regulations are in a constant state of evolution as scientists, fisheries managers, and fishermen learn more about these great fish. Take the time to read the current regulations before you fish.

Walleye

The first two weeks of April give anglers a chance at catching pre-spawn walleyes in the Columbia. The water is beginning to warm and the fish are healthy. Serious fishermen start fishing in early spring for the best chance at landing a big female, full of eggs. After the walleye spawn in May, good fishing will continue through the month of October.

Walleye average four to eight pounds in the Columbia. They feed heavily on perch, northern pikeminnow (squawfish), bass, and shad. The biggest fish are females. Anglers come from all over the United States for a chance at catching big fish, running from ten pounds up to the current state record of 19 pounds, 15.3 ounces.

In general, walleye prefer a stone, gravel, or sandy bottom. For the best walleye water look for a section of river with shallow spawning runs, located close to deep pools or channels. Watch for places where small fry might congregate, and do your walleye hunting there. Jetties where riprap can hold minnows, drop-offs, ledges, rocky points, and gravel bars are some examples.

One effective rig that will take walleye throughout the season employs a three-foot leader, a light spinner blade, fluorescent green beads, and double hook setup baited with a whole nightcrawler. The nightcrawler is rigged to hang straight down on the two hooks. Five inches of hollow core lead on a slider rig keeps the bait bouncing along the bottom.

Whenever possible, the baits should be presented on a long line or off to the side of

Walleye average four to eight pounds in the Columbia.
Photo by Gary Lewis

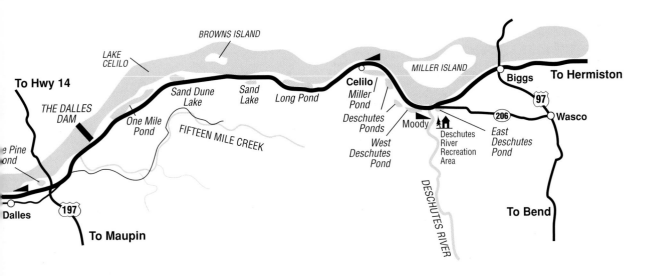

the boat's path of travel. When you feel the strike, drop the rod and count to three before lifting the tip, gently setting the hook.

Smallmouth Bass

Smallmouth bass prefer warm, flowing water and can be found in great numbers around weed beds, grassy banks, along the seams of riffles, deep along rock walls, and in gravel flats. On clear summer days when the sun is high, the biggest fish will be found in deeper water. On overcast days or when the sun is low on the horizon, smallmouth can be caught on or closer to the surface.

They are aggressive predators, feeding on smaller fish, insects, leeches, snails, and crayfish. Since big bass eat little bass, the smaller bass tend to stay in schools away from larger fish. If you are catching little bass, move to deeper water to target the larger fish.

Crankbaits and minnow imitations work very well in smallmouth water, especially along ledges or around submerged structure. Use patterns to imitate local baitfish. Chub, perch and rainbow patterns work well for minnow imitations. Orange and olive crayfish patterns are good crankbait options.

Another good tactic is to dead-drift a plastic worm, allowing it to tumble through the best bass-holding water. Rig the worm weedless (with hook point buried in the worm) to minimize hooking up on the bottom.

Shad

Shad, imported by homesick easterners, were introduced into Oregon and Washington in the mid-1880s. The spawning run begins when river waters warm in the spring. Mature adults average three to four pounds in size, and may return to the river to spawn as many as four times.

For shad, light gear is preferable. Six- to ten-pound test line and a slow-action rod makes a good combination for the angler who favors spinning or casting gear. Small jig heads baited with a small rubber grub are employed and allowed to hang in the current. Best colors include red, yellow, white, pink, blue, gold, and silver. Flash and color are important. Depth is crucial and enough weight should be used in fast water to take the lure close to the bottom.

Feeding on microscopic creatures, shad strain their food through gill-rakers. Running upriver, they strike mainly out of frustration, instead of feeding impulses. Small spoons, spinners, and yarn flies will bring fish to the net, but jigs are used far more than any other tackle.

Rig a sliding sinker on the main line to a barrel swivel and 30 inches of leader to the jig. Plain lead jigs with no color will catch fish. When the bite slows, add a little color.

Timing the shad run is the most important thing. When 10,000 fish a day are going over Bonneville Dam, throw your tackle in the car and head for the water.

Timing the shad run going over the Bonneville Dam is important for the best catch. Gary Lewis photo

A nice Columbia smallmouth bass! Gary Lewis photo

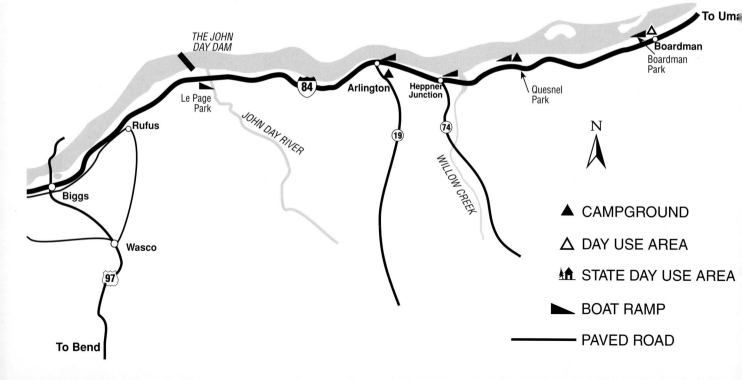

THE JOHN DAY DAM

To Uma

Boardman
Boardman
Park

84 Arlington   Heppner
Junction   Quesnel
                 Park

Le Page
Park

JOHN DAY RIVER

Rufus

19   74

Biggs   WILLOW CREEK

Wasco

97

N

To Bend

▲ CAMPGROUND

△ DAY USE AREA

🏕 STATE DAY USE AREA

◣ BOAT RAMP

—— PAVED ROAD

Other Species

Largemouth bass, yellow perch and crappie can be found in the Columbia's slower water. Fish protected areas where the current is slowed. Target bass and crappie near piers, bridge abutments, rocky points and other structure. Several species of carp and catfish are available throughout the river.

A nice Columbia largemouth bass!
Gary Lewis photo

Boat Launches

In the area immediately below Bonneville Dam, there are three good launches on the Oregon side.

The Fishery is accessible from eastbound and westbound I-84. There are two ramps: the lower ramp is large r and most used. It has two launch lanes (best bet is to use the downriver lane on this ramp) and ample dock space. Four-wheel drive is recommended for upper ramp. It can be windy in this section of the river and strong currents are possible.

Dalton Point is accessible from eastbound I-84. There is one ramp with two lanes and no dock.

Rooster Rock is accessible from eastbound and westbound I-84. There is one ramp with four lanes and a small dock. This launch is wheelchair accessible and is sheltered from wind and currents. But don't use this ramp when the river is low.

Above the dam, there is a marina at Cascade Locks Marine Park. Good launches are available at Hood River, Mayer State Park, The Dalles, Celilo, Moody and Rufus.

In the John Day area, Le Page Park is a good place to put in at the mouth of the John Day River. Launches can be found upstream at Arlington, Heppner Junction, and Boardman. A good launch and park is available at the State Park in Irrigon. Upstream, below the McNary Dam at Umatilla, there are great facilities for the boater.

Camping

There are several options for camping in the Bonneville area. Ainsworth State Park (503-695-2301) provides tables, grills, toilets, water, showers, dump station. For RVs,

water, electric and sewer hook-ups are available. Max length for RVs is 60 feet.

At Cascade Locks Marine Park (503-374-8619), there are tables, toilets, water, showers, dump station, telephone, playground, gift shop, boat ramp, and a marina. No hook-ups are provided for RVs. The maximum length is 35 feet.

At Wyeth (503-386-2333), there are tables, grills, toilets and water. There are no hook-ups. Maximum length is 32 feet.

Upstream, find good camping at Viento State Park with 75 total sites, some with hookups. Find open camping at Celilo Park with no hookups. The Deschutes River State Recreation Area has 89 total sites with a max RV length of 30 feet. Across the river from Biggs, a private RV park at Peach Beach near Maryhill Museum offers good camping with hookups and showers.

At Arlington, the Arlington Marina and RV Park has 32 total campsites, 12 with hookups. Maximum length is 40 feet. Boardman RV Park has 63 total sites with hookups and a max length of 80 feet. The Umatilla Marina and RV Park has 36 sites (some hookups) and a maximum length of 60 feet.

Be Careful Out There

The Columbia River has been tamed, turned into a highway for heavy commercial traffic. It is controlled by dams, used to generate electricity, and provide food. It is also a playground for water skiers, hunters, fishermen and pleasure boaters. But beneath its benign exterior beats the heart of a beast. This river can kill you. Deep, strong currents called undertows can pull you down and keep you down. High winds can whip up whitecaps that can swamp a small boat or beat your craft to pieces on a jetty. Sandbars that can destroy your outboard prop lurk beneath the surface in the middle of the river. Drifting debris can eviscerate your boat or destroy your motor. And a tugboat pushing a barge can crush your boat beneath its prow. Those

ABOVE: In the area immediately below Bonneville Dam, there are three good launches on the Oregon side.

LEFT: There are numerous areas for camping along the Columbia.

Photos by Gary Lewis

are just a few of the ways that the river can kill. Don't help it by operating a boat under the influence of alcohol.

Learn where the navigable channel is so you don't run aground in shallow water. Learn to recognize navigational aids such as red and green buoys, range markers and the five-blast danger signal from a vessel bearing down on you. See the Oregon Boater's Handbook for more information.

Setting anchor and pulling anchor are operations fraught with danger in a river as powerful and prone to change as is the Columbia. Old pilings, submerged cars, floating timber, old fishnets and many other hazards lurk beneath the surface. Commercial traffic, changing tides and varying water levels are all factors you must deal with, each time you boat on the Columbia. When at anchor, be on the lookout for floating debris that may come down on your anchor line. Be alert, be safe.

COLUMBIA PONDS

Size:	5-50 acres
Depth:	15 feet average
Main Catch:	Columbia warmwater species
Best Methods:	bait
Season:	entire year
Best Time:	summer
Tips:	Target bass with nightcrawlers or plastic worms.

From its headwaters to the mouth, the Columbia feeds numerous backwaters, ponds, and lakes on both sides of the river. In periods of high water, fish travel back and forth between the river and the ponds.

Sheltered from the current and largely ignored by anglers, these waters are a haven for the Columbia's warmwater species. Largemouth bass, smallmouth bass, crappie, bluegill, yellow perch, walleye, carp and catfish are among the species that can be found in these backwaters.

One characteristic constant among these waters is weed growth. Many ponds have steep banks reinforced with riprap. If you think this sounds like good habitat for bass, you'd be right. From Bonneville Dam upstream to the Umatilla, largemouth bass and smallmouths flourish in the Columbia River ponds.

A boat isn't necessary. Nor is it convenient in most places. Instead, fish from the bank. If you fish plastics or spinner baits, move along the shore, casting to likely holding places along the weed beds or in the shadow of the willows.

When bass can be seen in shallow water, cast an unweighted plastic worm (try purple or motor oil) and retrieve it slowly along the bottom. In deeper water, use a sliding bullet sinker. At the strike, drop your rod tip to give the fish time to swallow the worm, then set the hook.

Weedless spinnerbaits are another good bet. Cast and retrieve at a fast rate of speed. Vary the depth until you get a strike. Sometimes, with the lure bulging just under the surface, you'll get strikes on every cast.

If you angle with bait, pick a likely place and take a seat. Because of the weeds, fishing a nightcrawler under a float is a good choice. Time your trip to coincide with warmer weather. June through September will provide the best fishing.

In the evening, when bass move close to the surface, try fly fishing with a popper. Cast to the bank. Let the popper rest after it hits the water, then give it a twitch and a chug.

Look for bluegill in the shallows where they take cover around grass and submerged trees. Look for bluegill also around the weedbeds. Bluegill are best caught on grasshoppers and small bits of worm under a bobber. To catch bluegill on a fly rod. Find the fish feeding on the surface, then cast small dry flies or unweighted nymphs.

Fish for catfish when they come into the shallows at dark. Nightcrawlers, chicken livers and blood baits are a good choice. Put your bait on the bottom to catch a channel cat or brown bullhead.

Try Viento Pond at mile 56 near Viento on the north side of the highway. Kolberg Lake is past mile 65. McClures Lake, at 50 surface acres, is at mile 74 (best access is from the westbound lanes). Long Pond, with 27 surface acres, is at mile 94. There's a frontage road from Exit 97.

Most of the Columbia ponds are surrounded by public land, but some are private. If the water is posted 'No Trespassing,' keep moving. There's another pond around the next bend.

To fish the Columbia ponds, drive I-84 in either direction. Find a wide spot on the shoulder and pull over or take a frontage road for better access. Camping is available in State parks along the river.

Sheltered from the current and largely ignored by anglers, these Columbia Pond waters are a haven for the Columbia's warmwater species.
Photo by Gary Lewis

BULL PRAIRIE RESERVOIR

Size: 27 acres
Depth: 10 feet
Main Catch: rainbow & brook trout
Best Methods: bait fishing, fly fishing
Season: entire year
Best Time: September
Tips: Fish along the edge of the weedbeds.

Between Heppner and Spray, high in the Umatilla National Forest is a pretty little reservoir surrounded by pines and fir trees. The 27-acre manmade lake is quiet water that holds hatchery rainbows and brook trout. Cattails ring the lake and provide habitat for red-winged blackbirds, ducks, and fish feeding in the shallows. Several fishing docks make reaching the fish an easy prospect from the trail that runs the perimeter of the lake. Bull Prairie Reservoir is a good place to bring a young angler or the family.

The short growing season doesn't allow the fish to reach great proportion in this lake, but the season is open year-round. Some anglers fish it through the ice in the dead of winter.

Still fishermen should try a bit of nightcrawler or Pautzke's salmon eggs beneath a float or bobber. To fish Power Bait, use a sliding sinker, 28 inches of line and a No. 16 treble hook.

Another effective method for taking trout employs a spinning rod and fly tackle. The casting bubble is the key to this technique. It must be the type that can be filled with water, which provides the weight necessary for long-distance casting. Whether fishing on the surface or below the surface, the best choice is the medium size, clear plastic bubble that is the approximate size of a chicken egg.

Slide the bubble over your main line and tie on a No. 12 black barrel swivel. Knot a three-foot, four-pound test leader to your barrel swivel, then tie on the fly. For starters, use a wet fly such as a No. 10 Prince Nymph or black Woolly Worm with red tail.

Cast, tighten up the line, and begin to reel — slowly. Vary the depth and retrieve until you find the fish. A slow retrieve is usually the most effective.

A boat launch, suitable for small craft, is provided. Motorized boats are not allowed on the lake. North of the boat launch, you'll find a wheelchair-accessible fishing platform and trail.

Bull Prairie Recreation Area, managed by the Forest Service, has 21 basic sites and no RV hookups. The maximum length is 40 feet. Tables, grills, toilets, drinking water, and a dump station are provided.

From Spray, drive 17 miles north on Highway 207. From Heppner, drive 38 miles south on Highway 207. Drive three miles east on Forest Road 2039. Head left to the day use area or right to the campground.

The 27-acre manmade lake at the Bull Prairie Recreation Area is quiet water that holds hatchery rainbows and brook trout. The area is managed by the Forest Service and has 21 basic sites, a boat launch, and fishing platforms.
Photos by Gary Lewis

JOHN DAY RIVER

Length: 280 miles
Depth: fluctuates seasonally
Main Catch: smallmouth bass,
steelhead, trout
Best Methods: bank, boat, & fly fishing
Season: check OSFR
Best Time: April-Sept. for bass,
Oct.-Mar. for steelhead
Tips: many sections
accessible only by boat

The John Day River is a world class small-mouth bass fishery, a fine steelhead river, a decent trout fishery in its upper reaches, and a wonderfully scenic area to boat. Flowing nearly 300 miles from its sources in the Strawberry and Blue mountains to its confluence with the Columbia River, the John Day offers towering canyons, colorful rock formations, challenging boating, funky little towns, good visitor and camping facilities, and outstanding fishing. Catches of more than 100 bass a day have been documented, and the fishing is improving with habitat restoration and a growing catch-and-release ethic. Intriguing names, such as "Hoogie Doogie Mountain," "Picture Gorge," "Spray," and "Twickenham," add to the allure of the area.

Eighty smallmouth bass were planted in the John Day River at Service Creek in 1971. Later that year smallmouth fry were scattered over a 50-mile stretch. Today, smallmouth dominate the lower 200 miles of river, in numbers estimated up to 1,000 per mile. Bass average 12 inches, about 1 pound apiece, but get much larger. Contributing author, Brooke Snavely, caught and released a 6-pound, 20-1/2-inch smallmouth his first day on the river while researching this section. The John Day appears capable of producing the next state record smallmouth bass. Medium diving crankbaits are best March-May for big spawners that feed before the more numerous, smaller bass wake up. Crawdad imitating plastic lures fished slowly along the bottom work well in backwaters as the water warms. Non-stop

action is likely late summer when low water levels concentrate bass in pools, eddies and riffles where they compete for anything thrown their way. When bass are very aggressive, try removing the front hooks from crankbaits to limit physical damage and to expedite release. Live bait is also good but tends to make the fish difficult to release. Fly fishing with streamers can produce outstanding results. Bass limits are 5 fish per day, no more than 1 over 16 inches. Smallmouth bass between 12 and 16 inches must be released un-harmed. Bass fishing is permitted year-round in the mainstem from the mouth to the North Fork at Kimberly. Upstream, the bass season coincides with trout and steelhead seasons. Check the OSFR.

The John Day has one of the strongest wild inland steelhead runs in the state, varying from as few as 5,000 fish in poor years up to 40,000 in good years. John Day steelhead average 5-7 pounds with a few larger, multiple salt fish. Biologists theorize the John Day's shallow spawning habitat favors smaller, one salt steelhead. Like the Deschutes, the John Day gets its share of

ABOVE: Steelhead from the John Day River.
Photo by Brian O'Keefe
BELOW: The scenic canyons of the John Day country are enjoyed while floating through them.
Photo by Scott Staats

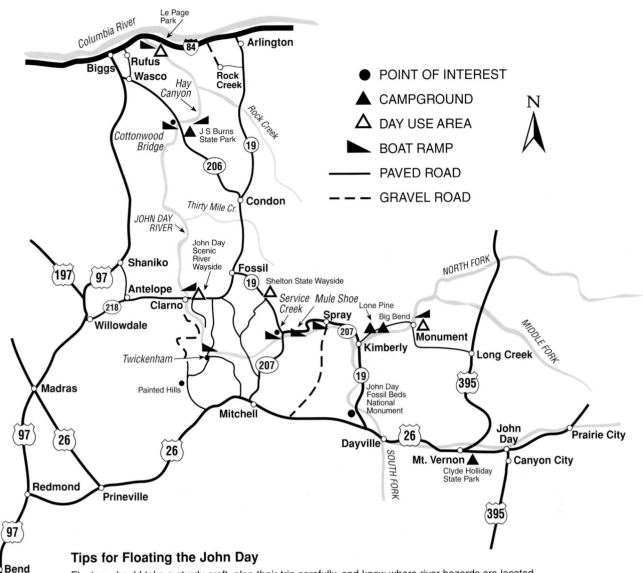

Tips for Floating the John Day

Floaters should take a sturdy craft, plan their trip carefully, and know where river hazards are located.
Guided trips for fishing on the John Day are readily available for anglers who don't have the proper boats and gear or the skills to negotiate this wilderness waterway. Bear in mind that water levels can fluctuate wildly between flood stage and drought, and that early season waters are cold enough to cause hypothermia after an accidental dunking.

Canoe, Driftboat, or Raft? The upper stretch is more suited to canoes and driftboats, while the lower section is most commonly floated in rubber rafts. Remember that open canoes, johnboats, and similar craft may swamp (fill with water) even in small rapids. Scout all whitewater from shore if you are uncertain about how to make the run correctly and line or portage if you are unsure of your ability to get through safely. It's a good idea to always wear your life jacket while floating or lining, just in case. Also be aware that motors are not permitted from Clarno downstream (and may be impractical upstream during periods of low water).

stray wild and hatchery fish, primarily near the confluence with the Columbia up to Tumwater Falls. About 25% of steelhead caught are fin-clipped. The majority of keepable hatchery steelhead are caught below Clarno, all others must be released, but that doesn't spoil the fun of trying for the turbo charged trout. Steelhead generally show at the mouth in late August or early September. The fish push up the river in October and November with cooler temperatures and higher flows at the end of irrigation season. They move through the basin all winter, spawning in the upper reaches of the mainstem, north and middle forks January through March.

Techniques to try include drifting worms with pencil lead sinkers, corkies and slinkies, spoons, spinners and plugs in the deep holes. Jig fishing with bobbers is still untried here but could be the next great method. Fishing for steelhead is permitted Jan. 1-March 31 and June 16-Dec. 31 from the mouth up to Tumwater Falls. Steelheading is legal all year from Tumwater Falls to the North Fork. Above North Fork check the OSFR for varying seasons and restrictions on steelhead fishing in the mainstem, north and middle forks. The limit is 2 steelhead per day, 20 per season. Non-adipose clipped steelhead must be released unharmed.

Native redside and planted rainbow trout are available in the upper mainstem, espe-

Brooke Snavely with a 5-pound smallmouth caught while researching this editorial ... what a job!
Photo courtesy Mah-Hah Outfitters
BELOW: Gorgeous 5 lb. summer steelie on the North Fork of the John Day.
Photo by Kevin Borst

cially in shaded, brushy areas with in-stream structure, such as downed trees and current breaking boulders. Hunters often encounter the best trout fishing of the year in October on the south, middle and north forks. Hatchery trout are planted in parts of the north, middle and south forks. Worms, salmon eggs and roe are legal and effective in most forks during high flows. Check to be sure. As water levels drop, flies and spinners are better. Most forks have midge, caddis and mayfly hatches. Trout season is the Saturday of the Memorial Day weekend to October 31. Limit is 2 trout per day. Trout over 20 inches are considered steelhead. There is no limit on the number or size of brook trout that may be kept. Bull trout are present in the headwaters and must be released unharmed.

The John Day River has a run of spring chinook salmon averaging 15-25 pounds, but it is closed to sport fishing at this time. The run averages 3,000 fish per year. The salmon arrive in spring, hold through sum-

mer and spawn in September in the upper reaches. They are rarely caught but if so, must be released. Fisheries managers hope that habitat improvement projects increase salmon numbers.

MAINSTEM

From the mouth up to impassable Tumwater Falls the lower 9 miles is slack water, primarily a plug trolling fishery for steelhead when they are present; bass, crappie and catfish year-round on lures and bait. Le Page Park is a complete boating/camping facility just off I-84 with additional camping and restrooms at Philippi Park accessible by boat a few miles upstream. Motorized boats are prohibited above Tumwater Falls to Clarno from May 1-October 31.

From Tumwater Falls upstream to Twickenham shore access is limited to bridge crossings, boat ramps and widely scattered parcels of public land. Floating in drift boats, canoes, kayaks and rafts is by far the most effective and enjoyable method to fish the lower river.

Rafting skills are required to maneuver through class 2 - 4 rapids, which change difficulty at different flows. Adequate supplies must be carried for long drifts, weather extremes and primitive camping conditions. Popular fishing drifts are from Service Creek to Twickenham (12 miles), Twickenham to Clarno Rapids (35 miles), and from Cottonwood Bridge on Highway 206 to Rock Creek (18 miles). Longer, multiple night float trips are common.

Recommended flow lev-

els for white-water thrill seekers is 2,000 to 6,000 CFS, with peak flows occurring April through June. Minimum flows for rafts are 1,500 CFS. Canoes, drift boats and smaller craft can get by in 500 CFS flows. Bass fishing is best when flows are stable or falling.

Steelhead require higher water levels to migrate but won't bite in turbid conditions. The John Day is unregulated by dams but subject to irrigation withdrawals and responds rapidly to precipitation or snowmelt. For river flow information call the U.S. Dept. of Commerce, River Service Center at (503) 261-9246. Their website can be found online at http://www.oregon.wr.usgs.gov. Shuttle information may be obtained from Wheeler County Visitor Information: P.O. Box 122, Fossil, OR 97830, (541) 763-2355.

The BLM requires no trace camping in all boat-in campsites along the river. This includes packing out all trash, human waste and no campfires during fire season. Use elevated fire pans, propane or white gas stoves. Keep flames away from dry grass and vegetation. The river canyon is extremely susceptible to fast moving range fires. Burn only wood from home, driftwood or charcoal. Do not cut live or dead vegetation. Pack out ash. Leave no fire rings. Smoking is permitted only while in a boat on the river. Group size is limited to 16 people to reduce impacts to campgrounds. It's okay to urinate on the ground away from the river but solid human waste must be carried out in porta-potty style containers and dumped at disposal stations at Clarno and Cottonwood take-outs. Check with the BLM in Prineville (541) 416-6700 for additional boating, camping and river use information.

There is good bank access to bass and steelhead water above Service Creek along Highway 19 through Spray, Picture Gorge, the John Day Fossil Beds National Monument, Kimberly and Dayville. Boat ramps are available at the North Fork confluence in Kimberly; at Bologna Creek; at milepost 99; at the ODOT gravel pile above Balm Creek; in Spray and at Muleshoe Creek BLM campground above Service Creek. Bass are present a short distance above Dayville. Highway 26 parallels the river through Mt. Vernon, John Day to Prairie City.

INSET: Bass poppers.
Photo by Brian O'Keefe

LEFT: Rapids add to the excitement on the John Day. Photo by Jon Gnass

County and forest roads follow the mainstem to its source near Lookout Mountain. Steelhead are available during winter up to Indian Creek. Wild trout are present from Mt. Vernon upstream to the headwaters. Much of the upper mainstem above Dayville is bordered by private ranch land. Ask permission first or try Clyde Holiday State Park east of Mt. Vernon. There is an RV Park in John Day, campgrounds south of Prairie City on county road 62, and forest camps in the nearby Malhuer and Whitman National Forests. Hotels, gas, services and supplies are available in Spray, Kimberly, Dayville, Mt. Vernon, John Day and Prairie City.

NORTH FORK

The North Fork heads in the Elkhorn Mountains west of Baker, flowing about 115 miles WSW to the mainstem at Kimberly. Bass are present up to Wall Creek, small stretches are stocked with rainbow trout, otherwise it's primarily a steelhead stream with bull trout in the headwaters. The best steelheading is November through April from Kimberly to the Highway 395 bridge. Paved then gravel roads follow the river upstream from Kimberly through Monument to Birch Creek. River miles 28 to 39 are roadless, best accessed by boats drifted from Camas Creek near Dale. A gravel road runs downstream from Dale to Potamus Creek.

Paved and gravel forest roads 55 and 5506 follow the North Fork about 11 miles above Dale. Above that, trail 5506 follows the river to its headwaters in the John Day Wilderness. Fishing is discouraged in the headwaters, as it is primarily salmon and steelhead rearing habitat with bull trout in deep holes. All must be released. Legal rainbow trout are stocked in the North Fork from Dale upstream 5 miles to Texas Bar Creek, and in Camas Creek. Campgrounds are available east of Dale at Tollbridge, Trough Creek, Gold Dredge and Oriental Creek. Primitive camping is allowed along the river downstream from Dale to Potamus Creek. Lone Pine campground is 1.5 miles NE of Kimberly toward the town of Monument.

MIDDLE FORK

The Middle Fork flows 75 miles west from Austin Junction, joining the North Fork at river mile 31 above Monument. More riffle than pool on its run through a shallow rimrock canyon, it offers good steelhead and rainbow trout fishing and road access for all but the lower 9 miles. Trout are planted as fingerlings, growing to 9-14 inches. Steelheading is best February-March up to the Highway 395 steelhead deadline east of Ritter. Developed camping is available at the Middle Fork Campground, about 6 miles NW of Highway 26 and at Dixie Campground, about 12 miles east of Prairie City.

SOUTH FORK

The South Fork flows about 60 miles north from Snow Mountain through Izee to join the mainstem at Dayville. The river plunges and pools in the upper reaches but meanders slowly the majority of its run. It has smallmouth in the lower reaches, planted and wild trout higher up. Occasionally unimproved roads follow almost its entire length. There is a lot of private property. Some of the best access and fishing is in the Murderer's Creek Wildlife Management Unit about 15 miles south of Dayville. The ODFW recently brought more land in the area into public ownership and is busy improving riparian habitat which should improve the fishing. Black Canyon Creek flowing in from a wilderness area by the same name can also be productive. Primitive camping is allowed in the Black Canyon Wilderness and Ochoco National Forest to the west and Malheur National Forests to the east and south.

Vehicle access is available at the John Day Pool where the river enters the Columbia River 30 miles east of The Dalles. Upstream access is drastically limited by private land. Road access is available at Rock Creek off State Route 19, at Cottonwood Bridge on State Route 206, at Clarno on State Highway 218, at Bridge Creek off U.S. Highway 26, and at Twickenham off State Highway 207.

State Highway 19 parallels the river from Service Creek all the way upstream past Kimberly to the junction with U.S. Highway 26 west of Dayville. At Kimberly, the North Fork comes in from the northeast, its headwaters in the Umatilla Forest.

East of Kimberly, County Route 20 parallels much of the Middle Fork into the Malheur National Forest. From its junction with Highway 19, Highway 26 runs along the mainstem upstream through Dayville to the junction with Forest Route 14 at Prairie City.

At Dayville the South Fork comes in and is paralleled by roads its entire length into the Ochoco National Forest south of Izee. Forest Routes follow the mainstem from Prairie City to its headwaters in the Ochoco National Forest.

BELOW: A John Day River winter steelhead. Photo by Kevin Borst

INSET: Channel catfish are present in the lower river. Photo by Brian O'Keefe

BOTTOM: John Day River and Cathedral Rock. Photo by George W. Linn

LAKE PENLAND

Size:	67 acres
Depth:	shallow
Main Catch:	rainbow trout, bluegill
Best Methods:	bait, flies
Season:	entire year
Best Time:	summer and fall
Tips:	Troll a Prince Nymph.

A little lake surrounded by tall pine trees in the Umatilla National Forest, Penland is remote, but worth the trip. Early in the morning, you'll see mule deer come down to the water or hear a Rocky Mountain elk bugle his challenge on a September morning.

Regularly stocked by the Department of Fish and Wildlife, Penland Lake is full of trout. The shallow water grows lots of weeds which provide cover and habitat. The insect growth is fantastic and the trout put on weight over the summer. Holdover rainbows can grow to 15 inches in their second year and bigger fish are available. The lake is also home to a population of bluegill.

Still fishermen should try nightcrawlers or Pautzke's salmon eggs beneath a float or bobber. Spinners and spoons can catch fish here, but the weeds you pull in tend to discourage casting.

Bait fishing works well here, but flyfishing is a better bet. For the best angling, bring a canoe or rowboat. Leave your float tube at home, the weed growth makes motivation challenging.

Match the hatch and cast dry flies to rising trout, or troll unweighted nymphs and wet flies like the Hare's Ear, Zug Bug, Prince Nymph, Woolly Bugger, Spruce and Brown Hackle.

One effective technique for taking trout and bluegill combines the simplicity of the spinning rod with the subtleties of fly fishing. The casting bubble is the key to making this technique effective. It must be the type that can be filled with water, which provides the weight necessary for long-distance casting. Whether fishing on the surface or below the surface, the best choice

BELOW: A young angler gets fishing instructions at Lake Penland.
Photo courtesy Russ Morgan, ODFW

is the medium size, clear plastic bubble that is the approximate size of a chicken egg.

Slide the bubble over your main line and tie on a No. 12 or 14 black barrel swivel. Knot a three-foot, four-pound test leader to your barrel swivel, then tie on the fly. For starters, use a wet fly such as a No. 8 Woolly Bugger, or No. 10 Woolly Worm.

Cast, tighten up the line, and begin to reel — slowly. Vary the depth and retrieve until you find the fish. A slow retrieve is usually the most effective.

A boat ramp on the south end of the lake is suitable for launching smaller craft. No motors are allowed on the lake.

Picnic tables and restrooms are available, but camping spaces are limited. Best to arrive during the week to find an open site. Options include camping in primitive sites in the forest or at Cutsforth County Park.

Penland fishes well spring, summer and fall and indeed is open year-round. Snow will block the road. Before you plan a spring trip call ahead to the office of the Heppner Ranger District (541-676-9187) to find out if the road is open.

From Heppner, head southeast on Willow Creek Road (County Rd. 678) into the Umatilla National Forest. Continue past Cutsforth Park onto Forest Road 21. After 2.5 miles, make a left turn on Forest Road 2105 leading to the lake.

WILLOW CREEK RESERVOIR

Size:	110 acres
Depth:	deep
Main Catch:	rainbow trout, crappie, smallmouth bass, largemouth bass, bullhead pumpkinseed sunfish
Best Methods:	lures, bait
Season:	entire year
Best Time:	spring
Tips:	For trout, troll small spoons or spinners along the south shore.

In uplands, one mile south of the town of Heppner, surrounded by gentle grassy hills, you'll find Willow Creek Reservoir. The 110-acre irrigation impoundment is fed by water from Willow Creek and the Balm Fork of Willow Creek. It usually reaches full pool by late May and can be drawn down in October.

Rainbow trout make up the main catch on this lake until late spring when anglers set their sights on white crappie, bass, pumpkinseed sunfish and brown bullhead catfish.

Good bank fishing access makes this reservoir a safe bet for anglers without a boat. Drive past the boat launch along the south shore and take a gravel road down to a parking lot above a riprap bank. Walk down to the water or fish from the car. A trail along an old roadbed provides plenty of room for fishermen to spread out.

Rainbow trout are stocked annually. Best catches can be made in deep water along the south shore. Paddle a float tube or a small boat to troll or cast Thomas spoons, minnow plugs, or 1/8 ounce Rooster Tails or Bangtails. Fly fishermen should troll small spinners or flies such as the No. 8 Woolly Bugger or Spruce. Use minnow imitations like the Zonker to spark the predatory instinct in the bigger brook trout and rainbows. While trolling baitfish imitations, change direction,

speed and depth to simulate the escape tactics of a worried minnow.

For crappie, look for a road that parallels the Balm Fork arm and fish the shallows near the inlet. Use rubber-skirted red and white or yellow jigs beneath a float. Cast and reel in with a slow, erratic retrieve.

Target bass near ledges and points along the south and north shore. Look for submerged timber along the north bank. Cast plastic worms or tubes or use crankbaits tuned to run at the depth of the water.

Best baits for catfish include nightcrawler, grasshoppers, shrimp, crayfish, meat, cheese, liver and fish. Rig a sliding sinker on your main line. Tie on a swivel and 18 inches of leader. The bait should be fished on the bottom. Catfish take the bait with a hesistant tap-tap-tap, tasting, spitting it out and mouthing it again. Wait until the line begins to pull away, then set the hook.

A paved ramp and a nice dock make launching your boat easy. Ample parking and restrooms are available at the ramp.

Willow Creek Campground is located

high on the western shore, overlooking the dam and the lake. Managed by the City of Heppner (541-676-9618), the camp is open from March 1 into November. It has 24 hook-up sites, offering water, electric and sewer. Maximum length is 40 feet. Covered tables, barbecues, flush toilets, drinking water, showers and telephone are available.

From I-84, turn right at Exit 147 and follow State Route 74 south to Heppner. Proceed through town and follow the signs uphill to the reservoir.

TOP: Some nice rainbows for dinner.

MIDDLE: Surrounded by gentle grassy hills, Willow Creek Reservoir is a 110-acre irrigation impoundment fed by water from Willow Creek. Rainbows make up the main catch, but other species are available.

BOTTOM: Tiffany Lewis battles a fighting rainbow.

Photos by Gary Lewis

COLD SPRINGS RESERVOIR

Size: 1,500 acres
Depth: 70 feet
Main Catch: crappie, largemouth bass, yellow perch, bullhead, carp
Best Methods: bait
Season: March 1 - September 30
Best Time: late spring
Tips: For crappie, fish rubber-skirted jigs near submerged willows.

Six miles east of Hermiston, surrounded by farms and small ranches, you'll find the 3,112-acre Cold Springs National Wildlife Refuge. Established by Theodore Roosevelt in 1909, the refuge is a preserve and breeding ground for many species of birds. Around the lake, watch for bald eagles, red-tailed hawks, mourning doves, white-crowned sparrows, killdeer, American avocet, downy woodpecker, dark-eyed juncoes, California quail, pheasants, owls and red-winged blackbirds, as well as many species of waterfowl.

Cold Springs Reservoir is a 1,500-acre irrigation impoundment that is fed by seasonal run-off and year-round springs. Cottonwood trees and abundant willows provide the shoreline habitat that protects wildlife and fish. The lake is home to a good variety of warmwater fish, which include black crappie, white crappie, largemouth bass, yellow perch, brown bullhead catfish, and carp.

Limited bank fishing is available near the inlet by Lot B. A small boat, canoe or float tube is necessary to reach the best fishing.

Crappie are the main catch at Cold Springs and can be found throughout the lake, dependent on season and weather. Early in the season, focus your efforts near the inlets

Cottonwood trees and abundant willows provide the shoreline habitat that protects wildlife and fish at the Cold Springs Reservoir. The lake is home to a good variety of warmwater fish, including crappie, bass, perch, bullhead, and carp. Photos by Gary Lewis

and dense stands of willows. As the water warms, look for crappie in shallow, timbered coves. In early summer, you may find crappie in the main lake, but continue to prospect near points, channels, brush, standing timber and the riprap dam face.

Crappies will move deeper during the day and can be found in shallower water in morning and evening. Lure choice depends on the depth of the fish. Use jigs, grubs and small baits in water deeper than 10 feet. When probing the shallows, tie on a small spinner, minnow plugs, spoons, or streamer flies. Red, white and yellow are good colors for crappie lures. A slow, erratic retrieve produces the most consistent action. Often, the fish will strike as the lure sinks.

Evening is the best time to catch the brown bullhead catfish when they move into the shallows to feed.

Best bullhead baits include nightcrawler, grasshoppers, shrimp, crayfish, meat, cheese, liver and fish. Rig a sliding sinker on your main line. Tie on a swivel and 18 inches of leader. The bait should be fished on the bottom. Catfish take the bait with a hesistant tap-tap-tap, tasting, spitting it out and mouthing it again. Wait until the line begins to pull away, then set the hook.

Submerged vegetation provides good habitat for the largemouth bass. Fish close to submerged trees and near the dam where the fish hide in the riprap structure. Employ weedless plastic worms, fished slowly along the bottom for best results on bass.

Two primitive boat launches, suitable for nothing bigger than a car-topper or canoe are available on the south side of the lake. The best launch is located in Lot B on the southwest end. From the East Loop Road, turn left and proceed for 1.3 miles to the end of the road. The other launch is found in Lot D along the south shore. For latest information on federal refuge regulations, call 509-545-8588.

From I-84, take Exit 188 at Stanfield. From Stanfield, follow the Stanfield Loop Road north until you see the signs for the lake. No camping or overnight parking is permitted on the refuge. Closest campgrounds are north along the Columbia. Nearby Hermiston offers all services.

Boat launches are primitive and only suitable for small boats or canoes.
Photo by Gary Lewis

UMATILLA RIVER

Size: 95 miles
Depth: shallow
Main Catch: salmon, steelhead, rainbow trout, smallmouth bass
Best Methods: float and jig, spinners
Season: check OSFR
Best Time: spring, fall
Tips: For trout in the upper river, use small attractor dry flies, such as the Irresistible & Royal Wulff.

Gathering its water on the west slope of the Blue Mountains, the Umatilla River, fed by its north and south forks, flows west through Pendleton then heads north to the Columbia at Umatilla. Shaded by willows and cottonwoods, it meanders through farmland and rolling countryside. It is a good salmon, steelhead and trout stream that flows mostly through private land and the Umatilla Indian Reservation, but has good public access in the lower river and in the upper reaches.

Paved roads follow the river from Pendleton all the way to the mouth. Upstream, paved and gravel roads can lead you to the river through Indian Reservation lands. The upper Umatilla and its south and north forks are in the Umatilla National Forest.

Salmon fishing is supported by hatchery runs of spring and fall chinook and fall coho. In years when good runs of salmon are expected, spring chinook angling is open from mid-April through the end of June. Fishing for adult coho and fall chinook jacks is open from September through November. Check OSFR for exact season dates.

The Umatilla hosts runs of both winter and summer steelhead. Angling is open from January through mid-April and from September through December for adipose fin-clipped steelhead. Always check OSFR before fishing.

You can find good fishing for salmon and steelhead right in downtown Umatilla. Look for pull-outs along the road that give access to the river. One popular spot is just south of the Highway 730 Bridge. A narrow beach stretches for 150 yards and affords room for anglers to spread out, casting Blue Fox spinners, spoons and floats and jigs.

Pendleton has several good salmon and steelhead holes located below the Highway 11 Bridge.

One of the easier steelheading methods to master is the jig and float technique. All you need are a spinning rod and reel with a feathered jig and a balsa wood float.

Start with a 1/8-ounce jig tied to the main line with a balsa float positioned above it. Adjust the float so the jig runs at or above the level of the fish. If you don't know how deep the fish are, set the jig to run 18- to 24-inches off the bottom. Cast across and upstream, keep your rod high, and let the current take the lure through the run. The float keeps the jig suspended. When the fish takes the lure, the drifting float stops, sinks, or runs upstream. Set the hook and hold on.

Color and size make a difference to the fish. Keep an assortment of 1/8 and 1/4-ounce jigs in black, red, fluorescent green, hot pink, and pink/white.

Best trout fishing on the Umatilla River is in the upper reaches and in the South Fork of the Umatilla River. Fishing is catch and release for wild rainbows and bull trout.

Small Rooster Tail spinners are effective. Flyfishermen should use small attractor dry flies in the river. Patterns like the Irresistible, Humpy and Royal Wulff are good choices.

Smallmouth bass, crappie, carp and other warmwater fish are caught in the lower river. Fish for bass with rubber grubs and shallow-running crankbaits near rocky points and riprap. Catch crappie with small minnow imitations and red or yellow rubber-skirted jigs.

Warmwater fishing is open year-round below the footbridge in the city of Umatilla. Warmwater fishing is open upstream as well with the exception of a closure from mid-April through mid-May. Check the Oregon Sport Fishing Regulations for details.

A tribal permit is required to fish on the portion of the river that flows through the Indian Reservation. Permits may be purchased in Mission, east of Pendleton.

The river's shallow waters and diversion dams make boating tricky. A driftboat or raft is appropriate. You'll find dams at Threemile, Westland, Cold Springs and Stanfield. Minor dams are present elsewhere in the river. Scout the river prior to floating it. When the river is low, leave the boat on the trailer.

Camping is available at private and public campgrounds in and around Umatilla and Pendleton. To the east, in the Umatilla National Forest, Umatilla Forks, Elk, South and Langdon Lake Campgrounds offer rest for the traveling fisherman.

One popular spot is just south of the Highway 730 Bridge where a narrow beach stretches for 150 yards and affords room for anglers to spread out. Photo by Gary Lewis

East and Southeast Central Oregon

Many fine fishing opportunities exist in the east and southeast areas of Oregon. The next several pages cover popular waters from Chickahominy Reservoir east to Beulah and Malheur reservoirs and southeast to Mann Lake and the Donner Und Blitzen River.

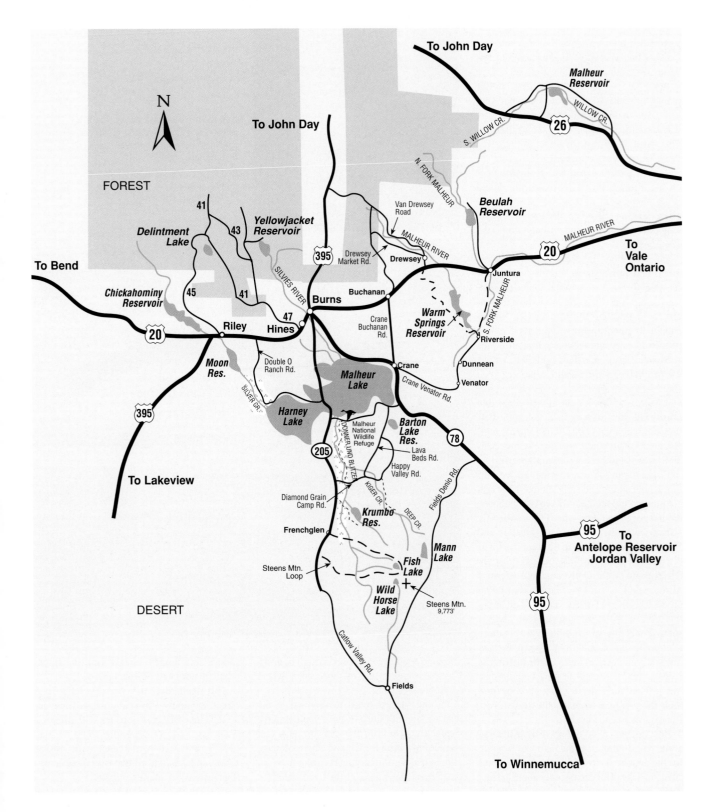

CHICKAHOMINY RESERVOIR

Size: 491 acres
Depth: 10´ average; 28´ max.
Main Catch: rainbow trout
Best Method: flies, bait, lures
Season: entire year; check OSFR
Best Time: early spring at ice-out
Tips: Ice fishing can be good.

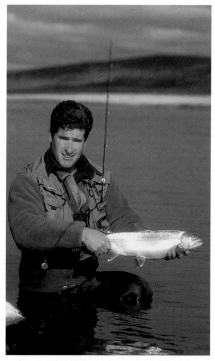

LEFT: This beautiful rainbow is the reason anglers travel the distance to Chickahominy Reservoir.
Brian O'Keefe photo

BELOW: A wind/shade shelter is useful at this wide open reservoir.
Photo by Brooke Snavely

Chickahominy isn't much for scenery — surrounded by miles of rolling sage and few trees — but what most anglers come to this desert reservoir for is under the water: fast-growing rainbow trout, lots of them. ODFW plants 100,000 3-inch fingerlings per year here. Dining on a rich diet of scuds, midges, water boatmen and leeches, Chickahominy trout grow an average of 8 inches their first year. Carryovers reach an average of 16 inches their second year and push 20 inches by the third. A few will stretch the tape a little longer. Add to that consistently good catch rates, and here is a place anglers travel long distances to fish and willingly forgo the scenery.

Chickahominy is open to fishing year round and produces well three of the four seasons, the heat of summer being slowest. Ice fishing is popular and productive in winters cold enough to produce ice strong enough to support people. Typically that happens in January and February, if at all.

Most ice fishing is done with bait such as worms, Velveeta cheese and salmon eggs on size 14-18 hooks. Also try small crappie jigs and Swedish Pimples on 2- and 4-lb. line tipped with bait. Start by fishing near the bottom and reel up in two foot increments until fish are located. If nothing happens, move 25-50 feet, drill another hole and start over.

Fishing can be very good at ice-out, throughout spring and early summer. The fish are hungry and on the prowl in the shallows, around edges and drop-offs. This is when fly fishers casting red and black leeches and Prince Nymphs on sink tip lines catch a lot of big trout from shore. Slow, bottom-creeping retrieves are best. Lightly weighted offerings of roe, nightcrawlers and Power Bait begin producing for bait fishers. Bays and inlets are the favored spots; the theory being there is some gravel amidst the bottom muck where the trout try unsuccessfully to spawn. Beware of truck-sucking mud holes on the dirt access roads around the reservoir in wet conditions. Many four wheel drives have sunk beyond their axles only to be rescued by tow trucks from Burns. Big towing bill.

Boat anglers avoid the mess by launching at the paved ramp near the dam and heading for the popular "narrows" where power lines cross the lake. This area is only about 10 feet deep, but frequently produces on trolled Thomas spoons, by casting Rooster Tail spinners, bait fishing with worms, or by fast

stripping Muddler minnows. When it's good, Chickahominy is one of those lakes where all techniques work.

Fishing success tends to drop off in the heat of summer (July-August temperatures frequently near 100°F), due to increased recreational boat traffic and algae blooms, although determined anglers should try in the deepest water near the dam and watch for evening rises to abundant midge hatches in the coves. Fishing revives in late September, October and November with trout going on

fall feeding binges. Locals from the Burns area tell stories of 50 fish days.

The standard 5 fish per day limit is in effect, with only 1 over 20 inches. There are 28 developed BLM campsites with drinking water and restrooms costing $6.00 per day (2005), a no-fee picnic area with shaded tables, and lots of primitive lake shore camping accessed by marginal roads.

Chickahominy is located 100 miles east of Bend and 30 miles west of Burns on U.S. Highway 20.

DELINTMENT LAKE

Size: 50 acres
Depth: 15 feet maximum
Main Catch: rainbow trout
Best Method: bank fishing
Season: entire year
Best Time: spring
Tips: Lake becomes weedy by mid-summer.

Delintment Lake is one of several popular reservoirs in the southern part of the Ochoco National Forest. Delintment covers 50 acres when full and has a maximum depth of 15 feet. The lake is surrounded by ponderosa pine forest and has an attractive Forest Service campground.

Stocked annually with fingerling rainbow trout, this rich reservoir grows them fast, but is prone to winterkills. The reservoir becomes very weedy by mid-summer. Average fish are 8 to 14 inches with the rare holdovers to 3 and 4 pounds. There is good opportunity for bank fishing, a gravel boat ramp, and a 5-mph boat speed limit. Delintment also has a universally accessible fishing dock.

There are three major access routes; one from Hines, just west of Burns: another through Paulina, if coming from the west; and along Silver Creek, just west of Riley on U.S. Highway 20. See Ochoco National Forest maps for details.

YELLOWJACKET LAKE

Size: 35 acres
Depth: 10 feet
Main Catch: rainbows
Best Methods: fly fishing, bait
Season: entire year
Best Time: spring, fall
Tips: Fish the deepest water in the center of the lake and by the dam

High in the Malheur National Forest, 30 miles north of Hines, you'll find Yellowjacket, a pretty, shallow lake nestled in the pines below Sugarloaf Mountain. It is a narrow lake beneath a low ridge. An earthen dam contains the water and willows provide cover for shore birds, coots, ducks and fish. The deepest water is in the center of the lake and close to the dam. Marsh claims the shallows at the north and south ends of the lake. Expect to catch rainbow trout that average eight to 12 inches.

Early in the spring, when the ice comes off the water, fish the shallows with bait or flies. Later in the spring, when the water warms, cast or troll small Thomas spoons or Rooster Tail spinners in deeper water. Fly fishermen should troll black or red leech patterns in the evening and fish chironomid patterns during the middle of the day.

For bait, suspend a No. 14 hook baited with a Pautzke's Balls O' Fire salmon egg or a chunk of nightcrawler beneath a bobber. In the winter, when ice covers the lake, bore your hole in the center and fish salmon eggs or worms. Start by fishing close to the bottom, then reel up in two foot increments until the fish start biting.

The campground is located on a gentle slope on the west shore. 20 basic sites are available with a maximum length of 30 feet. Tables, grills, pit toilets and drinking water are provided. A primitive boat launch will accommodate smaller boats.

Just inside the city limits of Hines, watch for the Hines Logging Road. Turn left and head north for 30 miles on a paved road. Turn right on FS 37 and then on FS 3745, you'll see the lake ahead of you through the pines.

TOP: It's Kid's Derby Day at Delintment Lake. Photo courtesy Mark L. Armstrong

LEFT: Yellowjacket is a pretty, shallow lake nestled in the pines below Sugarloaf Mountain. Photo by Gary Lewis

MOON RESERVOIR

Size:	600 acres
Depth:	varies
Main Catch:	rainbow trout, largemouth bass, crappie, bluegill
Best Methods:	bait and lures
Season:	entire year
Best Time:	spring, fall
Tips:	Target rocky points and submerged structure

Out in the desert, in a rugged canyon nine miles southeast of Riley, you'll find Moon Reservoir, a fertile irrigation impoundment that is home to largemouth, crappie, bluegill and rainbow trout. Fed by Silver Creek, in periods of drought, the reservoir can go dry. Following a dry spell, the fishery takes a few years to rebuild.

Moon Reservoir is open to fishing throughout the year and produces decent trout fishing in spring, fall and winter. After a few years of ample water, this lake is capable of growing big rainbows that feed on a diet of scuds, leeches, water boatmen, chironomids and minnows. Your best bet is to bring a boat. Prospect for trout in the channel and in the deeper water near the dam. Troll Thomas spoons tipped with a salmon egg or Rooster Tail spinners, changing direction often. Fly fishermen should troll black or purple leeches on an intermediate line or submerge a chironomid pattern under a strike indicator.

To tempt trout with bait, use Berkley Power Bait rigged on a No. 14 treble hook, a 30-inch leader and a sliding sinker. Mix it up by adding a section of nightcrawler.

Largemouth bass are another attraction. Fish near structure, targeting submerged junipers and sagebrush or lava rock. The fish will be deeper at midday and closer to the surface at morning and evening. Cast and crank Luhr-Jensen or Yakima crankbaits tuned to run at the depths where you expect to find the fish. With plastic worms and grubs, a slow, bottom-crawling retrieve works well.

To catch crappies, fish along the canyon walls. Crappie like to chase their food and minnows are at the top of the menu. Use red and yellow rubber-skirted jigs and Berkley minnow imitations to tempt hungry crappie.

Fly-rodders can catch crappie on mylar minnows fished deep and stripped fast to imitate a frightened baitfish.

From the rim above the lake, you can see all the way to the Cascades across a sea of sagebrush. Wild horses, jack rabbits and pronghorn antelope can be seen on the plains above the water.

For camping, head back to Chickahominy Reservoir, six miles west of Riley, or pitch your tent in the brush along the lakeshore.

Take Highway 20 east to Riley and watch for the S Ranch Road and turn south. If the first road is closed, find access a couple miles to the east on OO Road (Double O Road). A boat ramp on the north end is suitable for smaller craft. Turn right and travel for 9 miles then take a right turn across a cattle guard. You'll find the lake in 3-1/2 miles. There is good access by the dam, where you'll find a primitive boat launch and a restroom. Take the road north to find Powerline Point, an overlook with access to the lake. Bring a 4x4 or a vehicle with enough ground-clearance to negotiate a few ruts and boulders.

Although your best bet is to bring a boat, some bank fishing is available at Moon Reservoir. This fertile irrigation impoundment is home to largemouth bass, crappie, bluegill and rainbow trout and after a few good water years … big rainbows. Photos by Gary Lewis

BEULAH RESERVOIR

Size: 2,000 acres
Depth: 10-80 feet
Main Catch: rainbow trout, bull trout, whitefish
Best Methods: fly fishing, lures
Season: entire year
Best Time: spring, fall
Tips: Target willows and rocky points.

Fifteen miles south of Juntura, you'll find Beulah Reservoir (a.k.a. Agency Valley Reservoir), a 2,000-acre irrigation impoundment in a valley surrounded by juniper-studded ranchland.

Fed by the North Fork Malheur River, Warm Springs Creek and several smaller tributaries, Beulah can be very low in summer and fall. Willows line the banks of the lake and the trill of the red-winged blackbird can be heard throughout the day. Stocked rainbow trout, bull trout and whitefish grow fast in the fertile waters of Beulah Reservoir.

Fish for rainbows in the upper end of the lake, targeting the willows and shallow flats. Troll leech patterns in black, red and purple or cast dry flies to rising fish. Chironomids (midges), make up a large part of the rainbow's diet. Chironomid pupae range from under 1/8-inch to over an inch in length. Fish

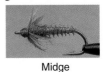
Midge
Courtesy Umpqua.com

these small flies on a floating line with a long leader under a strike indicator.

Gear fishermen should troll Thomas or Little Cleo spoons or similar lures. Try tipping your hook with a single salmon egg or a bit of nightcrawler. Later in the season, fish the deeper water nearer the dam and cast

Rooster Tails
Courtesy Yakima Bait Co.

spoons or Rooster Tails. For bigger fish, use a minnow imitation like a Rapala in a rainbow or whitefish finish. To tempt rainbows with bait, use Berkley Power Bait rigged on a No. 14 treble hook, a 30-inch leader and a sliding sinker. Or, employ a marshmallow and half a nightcrawler threaded on a No. 10 bait hook.

Predatory bull trout can reach ten pounds or more in Beulah Reservoir. In trouble across much of their territory, bull trout should be released unharmed. It is a colorful fish with olive or brown flanks, speckled with red, orange, pink or yellow spots. Its belly is white and its tail forks. Its head is long and broad. Big bull trout feed on whitefish and rainbows up to one-third their size. Large minnow imitations, such as Rapalas and swim baits, are extremely productive. Troll in deeper water near the dam or cast to rocky points.

TOP: Also known as Agency Valley Reservoir, Beulah is a 2,000-acre irrigation impoundment where stocked rainbow trout, bull trout, and whitefish grow fast in the fertile waters.

CENTER: Bull trout, which may reach ten pounds, must be released unharmed (photo taken prior to ESA listing).

BOTTOM: Colorful wildflowers dot the dry desert terrain.
Photos by Gary Lewis

Whitefish, feeding primarily on snails, freshwater shrimp, stonefly larvae, caddis and chironomids, grow to an average of 10 to 14 inches. Bait fishermen can catch whitefish on small bits of worm, salmon eggs, mealworms, crickets and grasshoppers. Fly fishermen will hook whitefish on small nymphs and wet flies.

Since the water level can fluctuate during the winter, ice fishing is discouraged. If you plan to camp (and you should if you make the trip), bring your own drinking water. Camping will be primitive, as facilities are limited. The boat ramp and dock are on the south side of the reservoir next to the dam.

Drive Highway 20 to Juntura and look for a left turn on the west side of town. Turn left on the well-graveled Beulah Road and follow it south through chukar and cattle country for 15 miles along the Malheur River until you reach the reservoir.

WARM SPRINGS RESERVOIR

Size: 4,500 acres
Depth: fluctuates
Main Catch: rainbow trout, smallmouth bass, channel cats, brown bullhead
Best Methods: bait, lures
Season: entire year
Best Time: spring
Tips: Bring a depth finder to find the rocky structure that holds the best fishing.

In the desert, southwest of Juntura, you'll find Warm Springs Reservoir, an irrigation impoundment. Fed by the South Fork of the Malheur River, this lake holds rainbow trout, smallmouth bass, channel catfish, brown bullhead and yellow perch. The fertile water grows big fish, but in periods of drought, the reservoir can go almost dry and the fishery may take a few years to rebound.

For trout, fish near the dam or troll along the channel. Bring a depth finder to identify the best structure. Trolling is an effective technique for taking trout in this lake. Multiple in-line spinner blades create action and vibration in the water. The flash of several revolving blades simulates a school of baitfish and draws your quarry's attention to your bait. A similar effect can be achieved with artificial bait that leaves a trail of sparkles, which suggest tiny fish scales and can trigger strikes. Don't troll in a straight line, make S-turns along your course and change speeds to suggest that your bait is taking evasive action.

Later in the spring and throughout the summer, fish bait closer to the bottom. Use Berkley Power Bait rigged on a No. 14 treble hook, a 30-inch leader and a sliding sinker. Or, employ a marshmallow and half a nightcrawler threaded on a No. 10 bait hook.

Target submerged trees, grasses and ledges to catch smallmouth bass. In the shallows, fish a four-inch purple plastic worm. On the initial strike, drop your rod tip and let the fish take the bait before you set the hook. Minnow imitations work very well for smallmouth, especially around grass or rocky ledges. Use yellow perch or rainbow trout patterns. Cast and retrieve, holding the rod tip at the surface of the water. Waggle the rod tip to give it the action smallmouth love.

When fishing for yellow perch, use a bobber and a No. 6-10 hook baited with half a nightcrawler, a grasshopper or yellow corn. Perch will mouth the bait before they take it. Be patient.

To catch a catfish, use bait. Good baits include nightcrawlers, grasshoppers, shrimp, crayfish, meat, cheese, liver or a commercial blood or meat bait. Rig with a sliding sinker on the main line. Tie on a swivel, 18 inches of leader and a sharp hook. Fish late in the evening for your best opportunity.

Two boat launches provide access to the water. The North ramp may be high and dry during low-water years. Your best bet is the South ramp, where you'll find a restroom and ample parking.

The nearest campground is a long way away, but you can find good dry-land, primitive camping along the west shore. You'll see cattle, geese, ducks and pronghorn antelope and hear chukar in the hilltops.

Take Highway 20 east toward Juntura. At milepost 171, turn right on Warm Springs Road, follow a well-graded, graveled road south for 14 miles.

RIGHT: These lucky anglers show off two nice 20-inch rainbows and a large bass.
Photo courtesy Dale Putman, Kevin Borst, Roy Geiger

BELOW: The fertile water of Warm Springs Reservoir grows big fish, but in periods of drought, the reservoir can go almost dry and the fishery may take a few years to rebound. Photo by Fred McDonald

MALHEUR RESERVOIR

Size: 2,000 acres
Depth: fluctuates
Main Catch: rainbow trout
Best Methods: fly fishing
Season: entire year
Best Time: spring
Tips: Troll flies along rocky points.

In cattle country, northeast of Ironside, you'll find Malheur Reservoir, a long, 2,000-acre irrigation impoundment in a sea of sagebrush. The fertile water grows big desert rainbows on a diet of leeches, snails, chironomids and water boatmen.

After several years of drought, the lake can go dry. When the reservoir refills, it may take a few seasons for the fishery to come back. Check on the fishing forecast with the regional office of the Oregon Department of Fish and Wildlife before you plan your trip.

As with many other desert reservoirs, Malheur's trout fishing is best in spring and fall. Bring a boat or a float tube. A depth finder can help you spot underwater structure. Early

in the spring, fish the shallows. As the water warms, target the rocky points and narrows.

Troll weighted leech patterns in black, red and purple on an intermediate line or cast dry flies to rising fish. For bigger trout, use big streamers that imitate baitfish.

Chironomids (midges), make up a large part of the rainbow's diet. Chironomid pupae range from under 1/8 of an inch to over an inch in length. Fish these small flies on a floating line with a long leader under a strike indicator.

Gear fishermen should troll Thomas or Little Cleo spoons and similar lures. Try tipping your hook with a single salmon egg or a bit of nightcrawler. For bigger fish, use a minnow imitation like a Rapala in a rainbow finish.

To tempt rainbows with bait, use Berkley Power Bait rigged on a No. 14 treble hook, a 30-inch leader and a sliding sinker. Or, employ a marshmallow and half a nightcrawler threaded on a No. 10 bait hook.

Boat launches with parking and restrooms can be found on the north side of the lake. It is

possible to launch smaller boats at several places along the shore. For camping, pick a spot somewhere on the north shore. If you want shade, bring your own tree. You'll see geese on the water and hear coyotes at night. If you want a good look at the stars, you'll get it here. You can't see a light for miles.

Malheur Reservoir is privately owned, but open to public use. Be careful with fire during the dry season and pack out your trash.

Head east on Highway 26 past the towns of Unity and Ironsides. Between Brogan and Ironsides, look for Indian Gulch Road. Turn left on a well-graveled road and follow the signs to the reservoir.

TOP: A healthy looking rainbow.
Photo courtesy Garrison's Guide Service

LEFT: The Malheur Reservoir is a long, 2,000-acre irrigation impoundment in a sea of sagebrush whose fertile water grows big desert rainbows.
Photo by Gary Lewis

MALHEUR RIVER

Size: 130 miles
Depth: 5 feet
Main Catch: rainbow trout
Best Methods: fly fishing, bait fishing
Season: entire year
Best Time: April, May, June
Tips: Match the hatch and cast to visibly feeding fish.

Much of the snow and rain that falls on the desert and mountains west of Burns, north of the Steens and south of the Strawberry Mountains ends up in the Malheur River system. Drawn down by irrigation requirements the river runs at its fullest from April through June when the snow is melting on the mountains. From July through October, some parts of the river are still floatable. During the fall and winter months, water is held in the reservoirs and the river becomes a trickling shadow of its former self.

The Malheur and its forks are open to fishing throughout the year. Bait fishing is allowed, with a daily limit of five trout, only one of which may be over 20 inches. Check the regulations for exact details as the rules are subject to change from year to year. Few trees provide shade, and in shallow reaches, the trout feed mainly at low light. When the water is low, trout can be found in the deepest holes.

Redband rainbows make up the bulk of the Malheur fishery. Hatchery rainbows to five pounds can be found downstream from Beulah and Warm Springs reservoirs. The Middle Fork has redbands and smallmouth bass. Above Beulah, you may find whitefish and bull trout (which must be released) in the river.

Water clarity is seldom very good in any section of the river, but the fish are used to it. Freshwater shrimp, stoneflies, mayflies, leeches, damselfly nymphs and midges are some of the main trout foods. Minnows and crayfish feed the larger trout. In the summer, grasshoppers and crickets provide even more variety.

In April, fish a floating line with a strike indicator above a weighted Orange Scud and a beadhead Pheasant Tail in tandem. In late May, fish the same rig but switch out the scud for a stonefly nymph. Late in the afternoon and evening, watch for a mayfly hatch. Use emerger patterns such as the Baetis Soft Hackle or Hare's Ear Wet until you see fish taking naturals on the surface. For bigger fish, explore the deeper runs and pools with small streamers or crayfish imitations, fished close to the bottom. In August and September, drift a grasshopper or an imitation close to the bank.

Spinfishermen, targeting rainbows will do well employing small plugs and Rooster Tail spinners in the deepest water. For smallmouths, probe fast, rocky water with lures or plastic worms.

CLOCKWISE: Open year-round for fishing, the Malheur River runs at its fullest in the spring when the snow is melting on the mountains. Bank fishing the deepest holes can be very productive. Photos by Gary Lewis

Lady angler has big success. Photo by Brian O'Keefe

Campers will find a place to rest (and some public fishing access) in beautiful Chukar Park on the North Fork. The campground, managed by the Bureau of Land Management, is located six miles north of Juntura on the Beulah Road. It has 18 basic sites with no hookups. The maximum length is 28 feet. Tables, grills, toilets and drinking water are provided.

To reach the Malheur, drive east on Highway 20. The road crosses the river near Drewsey a few miles after you cross the Stinking Water Mountains. You'll find the best access and good fishing from the tail-race below Warm Springs Reservoir, downstream to a few miles above Namorf. To explore up the North Fork that runs out of Beulah Reservoir, drive north on the Beulah Road. You'll find access to the river, directly downstream from the Beulah dam and again at Chukar Park.

KRUMBO RESERVOIR

Size: 150 acres
Depth: 10-16 feet
Main Catch: rainbow trout, largemouth bass
Best Methods: fly fishing
Season: check OSFR
Best Time: spring, fall
Tips: To catch a summer largemouth bass, wait till late evening and cast poppers in the shoreside rushes.

Anglers often have Krumbo all to themselves. Photo by Brian O'Keefe

Krumbo Reservoir is a shallow desert lake on the west side of the Steens, capable of producing big trout and largemouth bass. Along the shore, you can watch pronghorn antelope and shorebirds. Chukar and quail can be heard in the rimrock and glimpsed coming down for water at midday.

Most people come to Krumbo for the trout. The Department of Fish and Wildlife stocks Krumbo throughout the season to provide action for legal-size rainbows. Trout that winter-over grow to 16 inches in their second year. Every season the lake produces a number of 20-inch and bigger rainbows.

Flyfishing is the most popular method. Float tubers launch at the ramp and fish out from the cove to 15 yards from the rocky point on the south. A long weedbed stretches from there, north across the lake. Rainbows stack along the weeds, feeding on insects and minnows.

Callibaetis and chironomids are some of the important food sources. Fish a No. 12 callibaetis pattern or a gray No. 16 midge larva under an indicator. The lake averages ten feet deep.

Most flyfishermen pull nymphs such as the Prince Nymph, Tellico and Callibaetis patterns. Use a clear intermediate sinking line and troll parallel to the weedbed. Effective streamer patterns include the Woolly Bugger and beadhead mohair leeches. Try black or red. As you troll, twitch the fly to entice strikes from following trout.

There is some bank access. Anglers can walk from the ramp to one of two rocky points that look out over some of the lake's deeper water. Fish a sliding sinker and 28 inches of leader terminating at a No. 14-16 treble hook. Mold rainbow Power Bait over the hook and get it in the water.

Krumbo is capable of producing some very big largemouth, though they are often ignored by anglers. In early morning or late evening, cast flyrod poppers to the shoreside bulrushes. Bass come into the shallows to feed in low light. Spin fisherman can put a liplock on a big bass by cranking four-inch floating minnow imitations like the Rapala or shallow running crankbaits. During the day, go deep for bass, prospecting near rocky points where largemouth wait to ambush their feed. Try plastic worms, deep-running crankbaits, or nightcrawlers.

At the end of the road, the parking area is paved. Covered tables are provided in the lee of a high bank that protects picnickers from the wind. A restroom can be found near the dam and at the boat ramp. A handicap-accessible fishing platform is near the boat ramp. The launch is a one-lane paved ramp with a nice dock. Only boats without gas motors are allowed. Electric motors are permitted.

Bring your binoculars and leave some time in your schedule to go birding on the refuge. Or try the nearby Donner und Blitzen River for native redband trout.

If you'll be spending the night, Page Springs campground can be found a few miles down the road. There is RV camping available in private campgrounds on both sides of the Malheur National Wildlife Refuge. For more luxurious accommodations, try the historic Frenchglen Hotel, the Steens Mountain Inn or Steens Mountain Resort.

Head east to Burns on Highway 20. At the corner of Broadway and Monroe, head east on Highway 78. Proceed for 1.7 miles and turn right on Highway 205, heading south. Drive 45 miles south and turn left on Krumbo Res. Road. You'll reach the lake in 3.7 miles on a well-graveled road. Krumbo is open for day-use only from the opening of trout season through October 31. No camping is allowed. There is an automatic gate that opens 1/2 hour before sunrise and closes 1/2 hour after sunset. The road follows the south side of the lake and ends at the ramp.

A happy angler nets a big rainbow.
Photo by Brian O'Keefe

DONNER UND BLITZEN RIVER

Size:	Main stem: 65 miles
Depth:	5 feet average; 10 feet max.
Main Catch:	native redband rainbow trout
Best Method:	flies, lures
Season:	entire year; check OSFR
Best Time:	summer & fall
Tips:	The fish go nuts for grasshoppers in September & October.

Fishing on the Donner Und Blitzen River is a bush-wacking, rock-hopping, snake-dodging, native-trout-catching experience. Named for dramatic thunderstorms, the Donner Und Blitzen (German for thunder and lightning) is a Designated Wild and Scenic River that drains the west slope of Steens Mountain, flows north through the Malheur Wildlife Refuge, emptying into Malheur Lake. Only the upper half of the river above Bridge Creek is open to fishing, and most anglers concentrate on the upper third above Page Springs. This is rugged, remote, but surprisingly lush high desert country that requires a lot of walking to reach the best fishing areas.

Native redband rainbow trout are the main attraction. Mature redbands have striking red

TOP RIGHT: Brian O'Keefe with a native redband rainbow before releasing it.

BOTTOM LEFT AND RIGHT: The Donner Und Blitzen River is a beautiful place to fish.
Brian O'Keefe photos

slashes; juveniles strings of ruby-colored par marks along their lateral lines. Tolerant of desert temperatures and fluctuating water flows, redbands feed hard in the short summer and fall growing season, fueling consistent action bordering on fantastic when conditions are right. The average Blitzen redband trout is 8 to 12 inches, with good numbers of 16- to 18-inchers and enough 24-30-inch trophies to keep anglers coming back year after year. Considered for special protection, the future of Blitzen redband rainbow is bright. In some reaches, fish populations have doubled where livestock grazing has been restricted, allowing streamside vegetation to regenerate. Fish passage issues around water diversion projects that block spawning migrations are also being addressed. A 2-fish harvest limit, only 1 over 20 inches, no bait and flies and lures only, catch-and-release fishing only from November 1 through late May. Anglers are encouraged to release all trout in this river system which is managed as a trophy trout fishery.

In spring and early summer, the Blitzen and its five major tributaries: Bridge, Fish, Indian and Mud Creeks and the Little Blitzen River flow high, cloudy and cold with snowmelt from Steens Mountain. The best early season fishing is with spinners and streamers in the lower, warmer sections in the Malheur Wildlife Refuge. Fishing is permitted in the refuge downstream from Page Springs to the confluence of the Blitzen and Bridge Creek, including East Canal and Mud

Rugged and remote, this river often requires a lot of walking to reach the best fishing areas. Above, a fly fisherman works the overhanging brush. Photo by Brooke Snavely

Creek. the Little Blitzen is catch-and-release only, and no bait is allowed. Anglers can only fish the aforementioned waters and walk designated access routes. Some areas are closed to protect sensitive birds, plants and mammals. No boats or floating devices of any kind are allowed on the refuge except on Krumbo Reservoir, a few miles north. Back casting space is limited, due to thick vegetation, favoring casting with spinners or roll and arrow casting with flies. Long rods to poke through brush and a willingness to bush-wack are mandatory in the refuge; big fish are the reward.

The river above Page Springs to Blitzen Crossing becomes fishable as runoff slows and temperatures rise in July and August, spurring a variety of insect hatches and good fly fishing. Here the river bounces, riffles and pools through undercut banks, lined with junipers and cottonwood trees, bushes, tall grass and rimrock basalt. Watch for rat-

tlesnakes in the tall grass. Beating the grass with a stick or rod and staying in the water are ways to avoid fanged encounters. Wading is easy in shorts, old tennis shoes or wading boots and a welcome relief from summer heat. A #14 Royal Wulff is a good dry searching pattern. Adams, Comparadun, Elk Hair Caddis, Hopper, Humpy and Renegade are other effective dry flies. If no surface takers, probe in the shade of overhanging trees and undercut banks with Prince, Pheasant Tail or Hare's Ear nymphs and Woolly Worm, Muddler, Sculpin and Rainbow pattern streamers. There is enough pressure from Page Springs upstream two miles to the second dam to make the fish selective. Anglers willing to travel farther up the canyon and into the tributaries will find uneducated fish. Some anglers camp overnight on long hikes up the canyons. Afternoon and evening are usually best but fish bite periodically throughout the day.

The fish go nuts for grasshoppers in September and October. Plus, there is a noticeable upstream movement of large fish in search of springs and cool tributaries. Some of the creeks are so small that a person can step across them, and often there is no room to cast. The fish actually seem to like skated flies that drag on the water or swim upstream on the retrieve. 1/16- and 1/32-ounce chartreuse spinners work well in the small tributaries. There is a good fall feeding frenzy before winter's chill puts an end to sizeable insects. There is probably good midge fishing during winter but few people try.

Excellent camping facilities await those who make the 63-mile trek south of Burns on Highway 205. Page Springs and South Steens BLM campgrounds feature large, shaded sites with pit toilets and drinking water for $8.00 per night (in 2005). RV hookups, trailer rentals and some camping and fishing supplies are available at Steens Mountain Resort near Page Springs.

The nearby town of Frenchglen has two restaurants, a hotel, gas and groceries. Steens Mountain Backcountry Byway, Malheur Wildlife Refuge, and numerous pioneer settlements offer fascinating history, wildlife and sight-seeing opportunities.

ABOVE: Excellent camping facilities can be found at the Page Springs Recreation Site.
Photo by Brooke Snavely

RIGHT: The scenery changes season to season.
Photo by Brian O'Keefe

BOTTOM: Designated as a Wild and Scenic River, the Donner Und Blitzen River drains the west slope of Steens Mountain and flows north, emptying into Malheur Lake.
Photo by Brooke Snavely

FISH LAKE
(Harney County)

Size:	16 acres
Depth:	15 feet average; 30 feet max.
Main Catch:	rainbow trout, brook trout
Best Methods:	bait, lures, flies
Season:	access limited by snow
Best Time:	summer, fall
Tips:	no motors allowed

Located 7,371 feet up the western flank of Steens Mountain, this is the highest of a dozen "Fish Lakes" in Oregon and quite possibly the prettiest. This 16-acre alpine gem is surrounded by stands of aspens and grassy meadows filled with wildflowers. It offers productive fishing for 8-12-inch stocked rainbow trout and a self-sustaining population of wild brook trout averaging 9-13-inches with trophies to 3 lbs.

No motors are allowed, making it ideal for rubber rafts, canoes and float tubes. Lacking motorized propulsion, wind drifting bait from boats is the most popular fishing technique. Many anglers bounce offerings of worms, salmon eggs and Power Bait off the bottom as they drift in whatever direction the wind takes them. Canoeists and row boaters do well casting and trolling Mepps and Panther-Martin spinners and Thomas spoons. Float tubers encounter success fishing dry flies in the shallows mornings and evenings, and with deeper sinking lines and streamer/leech patterns during bright daylight hours. Fly fishing is often excellent in the fall. Bank fishing is most effective from the north and south shorelines.

The deepest spot, 31 feet, is basically dead center of the lake. Underwater springs on the east end near the campground and the outlet to Lake Creek on the west end can attract fish at times.

Catch limits are 5 fish per day, minimum 8 inches, 1 over 20 inches. The water is fairly cold most of the year, limiting all but the bravest swimmers to wading in the shallows. There is an attractive 23-space BLM campground and picnic area on the east end of the lake with drinking water and restrooms. Camping fees are $8.00 per night (in 2005) up to 14 days with sites available on a first-come, first-serve basis. Overflow camping is available at Jackman Park 2 miles up the road.

Check with the BLM before making the 80-mile drive south of Burns. Snow usually blocks the road to the lake through the first of June, sometimes later after heavy winters. Also be aware that the lake is exposed to strong winds that can last for days, as well as sudden, dangerous but spectacular thunderstorms.

Other nearby activities include hiking, wildlife watching, sight seeing from the 9,773-foot summit of Steens Mountain.

From Burns, take State Highway 205 for 60 miles to Frenchglen; travel 20 miles east on Steens Mountain Back Country Byway to Fish Lake.

ABOVE: Grassy meadows and stands of aspens surround this high alpine, 16-acre lake. Fall is often the best time for fly fishing from the bank or with a floating device such as a canoe or float tube. Motors are not allowed. Photos by Brooke Snavely

INSET: A real pretty Eastern brook trout. Photo by Brian O'Keefe

LEFT: Fresh brook trout for dinner tonight! Photo by Brian O'Keefe

MANN LAKE

Size:	276 acres
Depth:	6 feet average; 14 feet max.
Main Catch:	Lahontan cutthroat trout
Best Method:	flies, lures
Season:	entire year; check OSFR
Best Time:	spring, fall
Tips:	Fly fishing may be difficult due to high winds. Boats, canoes, & float tubes are useful.

For anglers who like challenges, Mann Lake is a must. Literally in the middle of nowhere, with spectacular scenery, primitive camping facilities, extreme weather and terrific fishing, this lake has a lot to offer, but is not for everyone.

Mann Lake is home to Lahontan cutthroat trout, a threatened species on both federal and state ESA lists. Lahontans are highly evolved desert trout that survive temperature and water quality extremes that preclude most other fish. With characteristic red slashes under their jaws and the same healthy appetite as west slope cutthroat, Lahontans are easy to fool and sporting to catch. They may also be fished for in Wild Horse Lake and Willow Creek.

Mann Lake is open year-round. Because of its remote location, it gets very little pressure during the winter, though ice fishing can be good with crappie jigs, bead headed flies and small spoons, jigged straight up and down. No bait is permitted. The fish feed ravenously at ice-out (March-April) by rooting around in the shallows for scuds, leeches and aquatic insects.

Casting with flies and lures from shore or wading produces excellent results. The lake is basically oval shaped with fish holding water within casting distance of almost all 2.6 miles of shoreline. Fly fishers do best with black and green Woolly Worms, Woolly Buggers, Damselflies and small black or grey Midges. Fishing two or three different dropper flies under a strike indicator is common when fish are shallow. Spin fishers catch plenty casting chartreuse-colored Mepps, brown Panther Martin spinners, and two-tone Thomas spoons. Hint #1: bring a spinning rod. Strong wind often makes fly fishing impossible, but spin fishers can make tremendous down wind casts that cover a lot of water. Hint #2: Green is the best color.

Mann is an excellent float tube, canoe, rubber raft and small boat lake. Motors are allowed. Flat-line trolling is good early in the year. Boat anglers merely add split shot or use heavier flies or lures when fish move into deep water, all of 14 feet. There are two improved gravel ramps and easy launching for car-toppers and tubes anywhere along the gradual shoreline.

FROM THE TOP:

Mann Lake produces some good size Lahontan cutthroat; this one fills the net.
Photo by Brian O'Keefe

Dressing warmly during early season fishing is essential at Mann Lake, as a chilly wind often blows.

This Lahontan cutthroat caught with a green-bodied Rooster Tail spinner displays the characteristic red slashes under the jaw.

There is an amazing variety of bird, animal, and plant life in this remote setting.
Photos by Brooke Snavely

Aside from good fishing, this remote high desert lake offers remarkable scenery during any season of the year. Photo by Brian O'Keefe
INSET: Another nice Lahontan cutthroat. Photo by Gary Weber

Fishing stalls in the heat of summer with thick algae blooms, courtesy of the many cattle that fertilize the watershed. But it comes back strong by late summer and fall, fueled by terrestrial insects, such as grasshoppers and ants, that fall or get blown into the lake, producing the best dry fly fishing of the year. The same spinners and spoons continue producing.

Catch-and-release is encouraged at Mann Lake. Barbless flies and lures are a good idea although not required. The limit is 2 fish per day, minimum 16 inches. The fish are muddy tasting. Most anglers release their fish.

As far as human comforts are concerned, there are none. The no-fee campgrounds are primitive with no developed sites. There are vault toilets and newly graveled access roads but not much else. No trees, no wind breaks, no drinking water. If you want it, you bring it. The closest store, restaurant and services are 50 miles south in Fields. They do a booming flat repair business there, as the gravel roads in this area are vicious on tires. Mann Lake veterans frequently carry two spares. Campers should use tents designed to withstand strong wind and dust and be prepared for noisy nights. Many people bring ear plugs to deaden the sound of the wind. It is almost easier to camp in a car, truck or RV.

The rewards for roughing it at Mann Lake are sublime. Besides the great fishing, the scenery is staggering. A 9,773-foot Steens Mountain towers over the wide-open landscape. While mostly dry and hot, there is an amazing variety of bird, animal and plant life near water. Crumbling homesteads hint at rich pioneer and Native American history.

With nothing to do other than fish, watch wildlife and the weather, most Mann Lake visitors quickly fall into the patterns of the old west. Retire at dusk, wake up at dawn, fish all day and look forward to bathing when they get back home.

Mann Lake is located 87 miles southeast of Burns. From Burns take State Highway 78 southeast approximately 65 miles. Turn south on the Field/Denio Road (Harney County #201) and travel 22 miles to the lake.

WILD HORSE LAKE

Size:	20 acres
Depth:	10-15 feet
Main Catch:	Lahontan cutthroat trout
Best Methods:	fly fishing
Season:	entire year
Best Time:	September
Tips:	Fish small dark nymphs and wet flies.

Wild Horse Lake is a pretty, 20-acre alpine lake at the top of 9,773-foot Steens Mountain. A shallow lake that is generally not accessible until August, it is home to wild Lahontan cutthroat trout that average eight to ten inches and can be caught on spinners, spoons, and trout flies.

When you go, plan on an easy mile hike downhill and a hard pull coming out. If you bring a boat, you'll have to carry it on your back, but the fishing is worth it.

Cutthroat are strong fighters that don't jump as much as the average rainbow. Instead, they run, or thrash or dive, seeking the safety of submerged cover.

The Lahontan is a rare strain of cutthroat that is found in some desert lakes. Cutthroats don't compete well with other species. Due to their tendency to hybridize with rainbows, they are not as well represented in northwest waters as they used to be. Even where the law doesn't require you to release wild fish, care should be taken to release most, if not all of your wild cutthroat.

One of the most effective lures for cutthroat trout is a 1/8-ounce black Rooster Tail fished on four-pound test line. Seek out deeper water where the fish can rest, secure in the shadows. Cast, let the lure sink, twitch it and start to reel, keeping a slow retrieve yet forcing the blade to turn.

Fly anglers have good success employing wet flies and streamers in black, olive, yellow, orange, or red. In many cases, it is good to let the fly sink for a few seconds before beginning the slow retrieve.

Cutthroat will take dry flies on the surface, but they are not as prone to coming to the top to eat as is a rainbow.

Camping is available at nearby Fish Lake Recreation Site through October 1. Tables, grills, vault toilets and drinking water are available at Fish Lake. For primitive camping at Wild Horse, bring a warm sleeping bag. A nice meadow near the lake provides a few campsites.

Head east to Burns on Highway 20. In Burns, at the corner of Broadway and Monroe, head east on Highway 78. Proceed for 1.7 miles and turn right on Highway 205, heading south. Drive 59 miles south to Frenchglen and take the Steens Mountain Loop Road to the East Rim Viewpoint on Steens Mountain, where you'll see the sign to Wildhorse Lake. Turn south, drive to the end of the road, then lace up your boots for the mile hike downhill to the lake.

CLOCKWISE:
Fishers usually find a solitary setting while at the lake.
Looking down at Wild Horse from near the road.
Another view of Wild Horse Lake.
Photos by Mark L. Armstrong USDI BLM/Burns

South Central Oregon

Many fine fishing opportunities exist in the south and southeastern areas of Oregon.
The next several pages cover popular waters from Lemolo and Miller lakes
in the north of this section to the Klamath River in the south,
east to the Chewaucan River and west to Hyatt Reservoir.

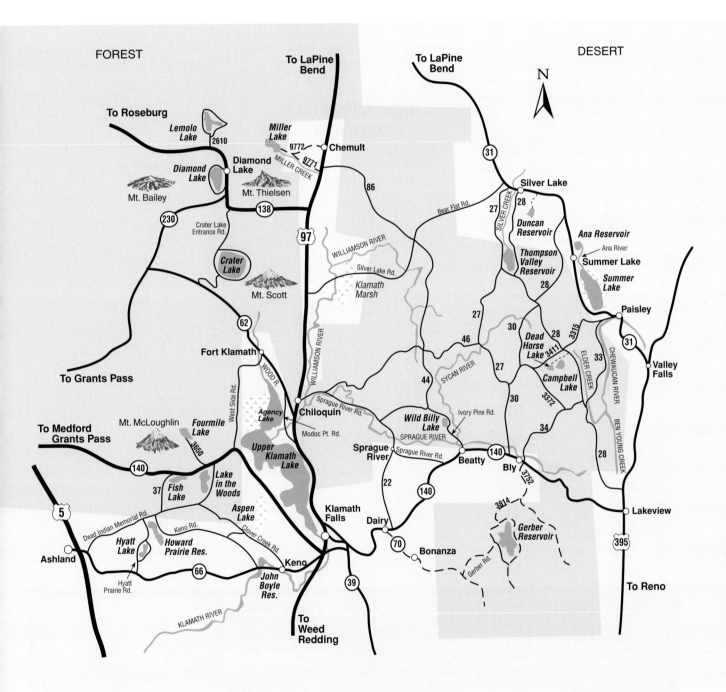

THOMPSON VALLEY RESERVOIR

Size: 2,500 acres at full pool
Depth: 30 feet
Main Catch: rainbow, largemouth bass
Best Methods: trolling
Season: check OSFR
Best Time: spring, summer, fall
Tips: Early in the season, fly fish the shallows for best results. Target largemouth bass near submerged trees.

Located 14 miles south of State Highway 31 and the town of Silver Lake, Thompson Valley Reservoir holds planted rainbow trout, cutthroat trout, largemouth bass, and hybrid white bass. The reservoir's surface acreage varies from 2,550 acres to a low of 210 acres, due to irrigation drawdowns. Maximum water depths range from 34 feet down to seven feet.

Wildlife abounds at Thompson Reservoir. Bald eagles and osprey nest in nearby trees. Excellent habitat for grebes and migratory shorebirds is found around the reservoir along with habitat for white pelicans, sandhill cranes, and migratory waterfowl. Mule deer and antelope are often seen as well.

Thompson Valley is open to fishing year-round. Spring and fall offer the best fishing for rainbow or cutthroat trout. Rainbows are stocked and holdover fish can reach 24 inches. Early in the spring, fly fish the shallows

for the best results. Troll spinners or small minnow imitations as the water warms. Summer offers the best fishing for large-mouth, target wooden structure and rocky points to connect with a bass. In the middle of winter, when ice covers the lake, bore a hole over the deepest water and keep your bait close to the bottom. There is no length or bag limit on largemouth bass. You may keep one 16-inch or larger hybrid bass per 24 hours.

Two Forest Service campgrounds are available at the lake: one on the east shore and one on the north shore. Boat launches are found at each campground. A 10-mph

speed limit is in effect. Tables, grills, pit toilets and drinking water are available. For RV parking, the maximum length is 35 feet. No hookups are provided.

From Highway 97, south of LaPine, take County Route 31 and head southeast toward the community of Silver Lake. To reach the north shore campground: turn right on Forest Route 27 one mile west of Silver Lake. Proceed for almost 14 miles and turn left on Forest Road 021. You'll find Thompson Valley Reservoir one mile down the paved road.

To reach the east shore campground: Take Forest Route 28 (East Bay Road) and follow signs to the reservoir.

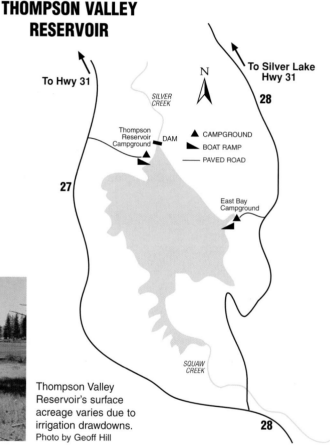

THOMPSON VALLEY RESERVOIR

Thompson Valley Reservoir's surface acreage varies due to irrigation drawdowns.
Photo by Geoff Hill

SILVER CREEK

Size: 10 feet across; approx. 15 miles long
Depth: 2 feet
Main Catch: rainbow trout
Best Methods: fly fishing
Season: check OSFR
Best Time: June through October
Tips: Use small dry flies to match the hatch. Approach carefully, use long leaders, keep your shadow off the water.

DUNCAN RESERVOIR

Size: 35 acres
Depth: 15 feet
Main Catch: rainbow trout, brown bullhead
Best Methods: bait fishing
Season: check OSFR
Best Time: June, July
Tips: Stinky baits work best for catfish. Use a sliding sinker to keep the fish from feeling resistance when they mouth the bait.

Silver Creek flows north out of Thompson Valley Reservoir past the town of Silver Lake to the Paulina Marsh. Silver Creek and its tributary, the West Fork of Silver Creek are good trout streams that are home to hatchery rainbows and native desert redbands averaging five to ten inches.

Deer, beaver, cottontails and quail can be seen in the Silver Creek canyon. Their tracks are found winding in and out of the abundant willows and grasses that shade the water. Mosquitoes also make their home in and around Silver Creek. In the summer, bring repellent.

Open to fishing year-round, late spring is the best time to fish Silver Creek. The limit is two trout, eight inches or longer. Stretches of the stream have been dammed by beavers, and silt buildup has destroyed some trout habitat. Fish the deep pools and free-flowing stretches with deeper runs and rapids.

Fly fishing is the best method for hooking Silver Creek rainbows. Small dry flies, like the Adams, Mosquito and Royal Wulff, are the best bet, but small wet flies like the Brown Hackle and black Woolly Worm can be productive. Prospect for rainbows in the pocket water and cast to rising fish in the larger beaver ponds.

Campers can find a place to pitch a tent on the West Fork of Silver Creek. From County Route 31, head south on Silver Creek Road (Route 27) for approximately 10 miles. The campground is surrounded by a stand of big ponderosa pines. Sites are graveled. Tables, grills, vault toilets, drinking water, corrals and hitching posts are provided. Camping is also available at nearby Thompson Valley Reservoir.

From Highway 97, south of LaPine, take County Route 31 and head southeast toward the community of Silver Lake. You'll cross Silver Creek right before you reach the city limits. To find the upper stretch of Silver Creek and West Fork Silver Creek, take County Route 31 southeast and turn right at Silver Creek Road. Upstream, logging roads provide access to the creek.

Silver Creek is home to hatchery rainbows and native redbands. Photo by Geoff Hill

FAR RIGHT: Fish the deep pools on Silver Creek from the bank. Photo by Gary Lewis

For catfish, some large trout, and unbeatable star-gazing, head to 35-acre Duncan Reservoir on the rim above Silver Lake. The lake is set in a shallow basin, surrounded by arid, rocky flats populated with juniper trees, sagebrush, and bunchgrass. Duncan has a good boat ramp that is serviceable for small boats even when the water is low.

Brown bullhead catfish provide some of the best fishing in this reservoir. Evening is the best time to catch them when they move into the shallows to feed, but catfish can be caught all day long.

Best baits for catfish include nightcrawler, grasshoppers, shrimp, crayfish, meat, cheese, liver and fish. Look for commercial meat and blood baits at sporting goods stores. Rig a sliding sinker on your main line. Tie on a swivel and 18 inches of leader. The bait should be fished on the bottom. Catfish take the bait with a hesitant tap-tap-tap, tasting, spitting it out and mouthing it again. Wait until the line begins to pull away, then set the hook.

Many anglers troll for Duncan's rainbows. Spoons, spinners and streamer flies are effective. Look at the topography of the shoreline for an indication where to concentrate your efforts. Rocky points or steep shoulders give indication that a ridge continues below the surface. This type of structure will hold feeding rainbows in the morning and evening.

Troll slow, but speed up from time to time and make sudden direction changes. Make S-turns along your course, to make your lure change directions suddenly, diving and climbing in the water column, just like a baitfish being pursued by a predator. Such direction changes trigger strikes from predatory fish.

Duncan Creek, which flows out of the reservoir, dries up in the summer, but fish that escape the reservoir can sometimes be found downstream. Fishing Duncan is open year-round.

Camping at Duncan Reservoir is courtesy

Small boats can launch from the boat ramp at Duncan Reservoir even when the water is low. Photo by Geoff Hill

of the Bureau of Land Management. As of 2005, there is no fee for camping. Seven basic sites with picnic tables, fire rings and vault toilets are available. Bring your own drinking water.

From Highway 97, south of LaPine, take County Route 31 and head southeast toward Summer Lake. Past mile marker 52, turn right on well-graveled Duncan Road. Watch for the sign marking the road to Duncan Reservoir. Turn right and follow a good dirt road uphill four miles to the reservoir.

ANA RESERVOIR

Size:	approx. 60 acres
Depth:	20 feet, deeper by dam
Main Catch:	hybrid bass, largemouth bass, rainbow trout
Best Methods:	spin fishing, bait fishing
Season:	check OSFR
Best Time:	January through October
Tips:	For hybrids, fish the northwest corner of the lake in the winter. When using bait, wear rubber gloves to keep the human odor from tainting the bait.

Ana Reservoir is a 60-acre reservoir hidden in the sagebrush near Summer Lake in south Central Oregon. Spring-fed, it is ice-free and fishable year-round due to the constant influx of 58°F water. Since the water is warm, some of the best fishing can be had in the wintertime, but bring warm clothes to protect yourself from the constant wind. Hybrid bass, a sterile mixture of striped and white bass, are the main catch in the reservoir. Largemouth bass and rainbow trout round out the fishery.

Hybrids have been stocked in the lake since 1982 with additional stockings every other year. The fish average four to ten pounds, and dedicated hybrid bass anglers think the current eighteen-pound, eight-ounce record will be replaced soon.

Most fishermen employ bait, fishing from the bank. Favorite baits are frozen anchovies, herring, prawns, and chicken liver. Hybrids, like stripers, travel in packs, searching out schools of prey. At such times, any bait or lure seems to work. Some people fish jigs or troll plugs. Rainbow or chub pattern minnowbaits and crankbaits are productive.

Solitary fish cruise the edges of underwater shelves, searching for minnows, leeches and other bits of food. Plunking with bait is an effective way to catch these fish which can sometimes be observed through polarized glasses from high on the bank.

In the winter and spring, look for deeper water that stays at a constant temperature. As warmer weather raises the water temperature, hybrids will leave the deep holes and roam the lake on the hunt.

In the summer, target largemouth bass with crankbaits and plastic worms worked near rocky points and structure. Use a chub pattern crankbait and fish it right along the bottom, bouncing it off pilings and rip-rap. Work plastic worms and crayfish slowly along the bottom. There is no minimum length or bag limit for largemouth bass.

From March through June, fish for trout in the deeper water near the dam. Troll flies near the surface or cast to rising fish in the evening. Spin fishermen can fish bait along the ledges and troll or cast Rooster Tail spinners and minnow imitations.

Because of the big hybrids and largemouth and a healthy population of rainbow trout, fishing Ana Reservoir can be exciting at any time of the year.

From Highway 97, south of LaPine, take County Route 31 and head southeast toward the community of Summer Lake. Watch for the sign to Ana Reservoir about five miles north of Summer Lake. You'll find the reservoir less than two miles to the east down a well-graveled road.

ABOVE: A private RV Park with full hookups, showers, and laundry facility is located within a short distance to the reservoir.

FAR LEFT: Hybrid bass, a sterile mixture of striped and white bass, are the main catch in the reservoir. This beauty was mounted and hangs in the Paisley Mercantile.

LEFT: The spring-fed Ana Reservoir is surrounded by sagebrush and is open for fishing year-round.

Photos by Geoff Hill

ANA RIVER

Size: approx. 10-15 feet across, approx. 12 miles long
Depth: 3 feet
Main Catch: rainbow
Best Methods: fly fishing
Season: check OSFR
Best Time: spring, fall
Tips: Approach carefully, use long casts, keep your shadow off the water.

Ana River is a challenging trout stream that meanders generally south out of Ana Reservoir and flows into Summer Lake. Carving a canyon through the desert, the river is bordered by sagebrush, head-high grasses and willows. Deer, ducks and quail come to water in the canyon and, many days, anglers are hard to find on this little stream.

Stream flows are reliable and the water temperature is constant in winter, keeping insect hatches productive. Regular planting of hatchery rainbows keeps the fishery interesting. Hatchery trout average six inches to five pounds. Bait fishing is allowed and the bag limit is five trout per day.

Pocket water is the key to Ana's rainbows. Runs and riffles bring the food to feeding trout, but at the first hint of danger, fish flee to the banks. Ana's rainbows seek refuge beneath undercut banks and in the shadow of the high grass and willows.

Approach the river with caution. Heavy footsteps can betray the angler 50 feet from the water's edge. When casting, keep your rod tip low and your shadow off the water.

In the winter, time your arrival for early afternoon to coincide with hatches of midges and blue-winged olives. Spring brings more insects to life and fly fishing turns on when the water warms.

Use small dry flies and emerger patterns to take the most fish. In late summer and early fall, try grasshopper patterns. Tie on a small streamer fly such as the Muddler Minnow or a Zonker to catch larger trout.

Camping is available at the reservoir, the RV park at the reservoir, or in the nearby Summer Lake Wildlife Area.

From Highway 97, south of LaPine, take County Route 31 and head southeast toward the community of Summer Lake. Watch for the sign to Ana Reservoir about five miles north of Summer Lake. You'll find the reservoir less than two miles to the east down a well-graveled road. Drive past the boat launch, across the dam and proceed a quarter mile to the parking area. Be careful on the dirt road after you leave the dam. In wet weather, the soil turns to gumbo and you might have to go looking for someone to pull your car out of the ruts.

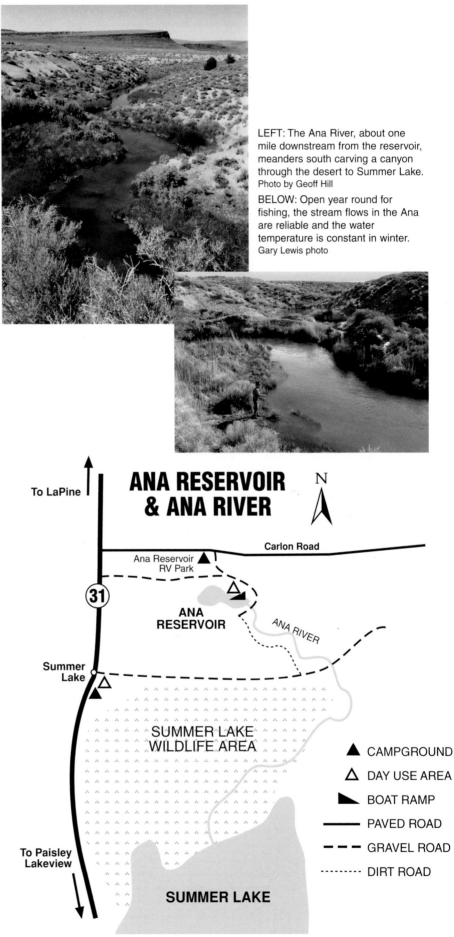

LEFT: The Ana River, about one mile downstream from the reservoir, meanders south carving a canyon through the desert to Summer Lake. Photo by Geoff Hill

BELOW: Open year round for fishing, the stream flows in the Ana are reliable and the water temperature is constant in winter. Gary Lewis photo

ANA RESERVOIR & ANA RIVER

N

To LaPine
Carlon Road
Ana Reservoir RV Park
31
ANA RESERVOIR
ANA RIVER
Summer Lake
SUMMER LAKE WILDLIFE AREA
To Paisley Lakeview
SUMMER LAKE

▲ CAMPGROUND
△ DAY USE AREA
◣ BOAT RAMP
— PAVED ROAD
--- GRAVEL ROAD
······ DIRT ROAD

CHEWAUCAN RIVER

Size: 50 miles
Depth: varies
Main Catch: rainbow trout
Best Methods: fly fishing
Season: check regulations
Best Time: spring, late fall
Tips: Fish small attractor dry flies in fast, deeper water.

Heading high in the Fremont National Forest, the Chewaucan is the largest and one of the most productive trout streams in Southeast Oregon. Gathering its water from a number of tributaries, the river flows northwest out of the mountains to the town of Paisley and then southeast into the Chewaucan Marsh and Abert Lake.

It is a clear running, high desert forest stream punctuated by slow, shallow pools, swift runs and small waterfalls. Good streamside habitat protects trout and provides insect production. Anglers will find dead junipers cabled into the bank at strategic places to control erosion and provide consistent cover. Because of the rocky outcroppings you'll negotiate on the way to the best holes, a pair of hiking boots is a better choice than waders.

Once stocked by the Department of Fish and Wildlife, the Chewaucan is now managed for its native redband rainbows. Most fish average six to ten inches, but there are a surprising number of trout in the 20-inch range. Late in the year, some of the larger trout run downstream and winter over in a large private lake near Abert Lake. In the spring, many of those same fish will make their way back up toward Paisley.

Three weirs are in place on the river that in the past have formed a barrier to upstream fish passage. The weirs are for the purpose of diverting water for the use of Paisley residents and two large ranches. These weirs have recently been revamped with fish ladders that now allow fish passage. The Forest Service is also replacing several culverts to allow easier migration. It is hoped that, in the future, trout will be able to migrate from the river to the headwaters and back.

Cooperative projects with area ranchers have resulted in stream fencing on private lands to keep cattle out of the water and to allow for willows and aspens to grow again along the banks.

Early in the year, the blue-winged olive mayflies make their appearance, providing food for trout and a hatch for fly fishermen to match. Later in the spring, watch for the March Brown's emergence, and carry a few soft-hackled Gold-Ribbed Hare's Ears and March Brown Sparkle Duns.

In late spring, you'll see a stonefly hatch. Keep a few small Girdle Bugs and Montana Stones in your arsenal. Caddis flies are another important trout food on this river. You may see hatches of caddis from June through October. Caddis larva and pupa patterns are important, as well as No. 12-16 Elk Hair Caddis dries. In late summer, make sure your box is well-stocked with grasshopper patterns.

When approaching the stream, keep from throwing your shadow over the water. Keep your profile low and throw your casts from a distance to minimize the risk of spooking wary trout. A pair of polarized glasses will help you cut the glare on the water and might allow you to spot a trout, resting along a grassy bank.

From Highway 31 at Paisley upstream, the Chewaucan is open to trout fishing all year long. Use artificial flies and lures only. Two trout may be kept, with not more than one over 20 inches.

Downstream from Highway 31 at Paisley, the river opens on the last Saturday in May and runs through the end of October. A two trout per day bag limit is in place and bait fishing is allowed. Check the current regulations before you fish.

Between May and October, you can find good camping at Marsters Spring Campground, eight miles upstream from Paisley. Shaded by pine, cottonwood, willow and alder trees, this camp sits right on the banks of the Chewaucan. There are 11 basic sites with no hookups and a maximum length of 30 feet. Tables, grills, vault toilets, and drinking water are provided.

A few more miles upstream, you'll come to Jones Crossing Forest Camp. Sheltered by pines, junipers, and aspens, this is a relaxing spot when you need a place to kick back after a day of walking the river.

When headed to the upper Chewaucan early in the spring, call the Forest Service office in Paisley (541-943-3114) to check on the opening of the road.

From LaPine, drive south on Highway 31 to Paisley. To follow the river downstream,

TOP: The two personalities of the Chewaucan River are seen here.

BOTTOM: There are excellent shady sites on the bank of the river at Marsters Spring Campground and others just upstream.

Top & Bottom photos by Geoff Hill
Center photo by Gary Lewis

take Forest Road 330. To reach the upper river, turn right on Mill Street (Forest Road 33) and drive upstream until you began to see access to the river. Respect private property, there is plenty of public access.

CAMPBELL LAKE

Size: 20 acres
Depth: 20 feet maximum
Main Catch: rainbow trout, brook trout
Best Methods: fly fishing, bait fishing
Season: entire year
Best Time: when road opens in spring; fall
Tips: Troll a leech with a small nymph on a dropper.

Campbell Lake is a pretty, quiet lake nestled in the lodgepole pines in the Chewaucan River watershed. With 20 surface acres and a maximum depth of 20 feet, Campbell is shallow enough to promote good insect growth. Rainbow trout make up most of the catch, but brook trout are available. Fish average 8 to 12 inches, but trophy trout, up to 5 pounds prowl the depths.

High in the Fremont National Forest, Campbell, and nearby Dead Horse, are accessible, in most years, from July through October. Call the Forest Service office in Paisley (541-943-3114) to check on the opening of the road.

Bring a small boat, raft, or float tube. In the day-use area, you'll find a single-lane graveled boat launch, suitable for launching smaller boats. There is a small dock. Motors are prohibited on this lake. Shallow, sloping sides make the bank fishing less productive. The lake has a muddy bottom.

The north end of the lake is a good bet for still-fishing and trolling. Try still-fishing on the south end as well. Use Power Bait on a sliding-sinker rig or fish Pautzke's Balls-O-Fire under a bobber. Try slow-trolling a bit of nightcrawler.

Gear fishermen will do well trolling small rainbow Rapalas or Thomas Buoyant spoons. Or anchor, and cast a brown Rooster Tail.

This is a good place to bring the fly rod. Try nymphs (Pheasant Tail, Hare's Ear, Bird's Nest) and wet flies (Water Boatman, Brown Hackle, Carey Special) and probe the water at different depths.

Explore the transitions from shallows to deeper water and watch for other fish-holding cover such as downed trees and points.

Tall pine trees surround the lake and provide great shade for camping. Tables, grills, pit toilets, and drinking water are provided. There are 15 large, basic sites with no hookups. Maximum length is 25 feet. Campsites are first-come, first-served.

From LaPine, drive south on Highway 31 to Paisley. Turn right on Mill Street (Forest Road 33). Drive 19 miles and turn right on Forest Road 28. After 9 miles, turn left onto the one lane graveled Forest Road 28-033. You'll come to the lake in 2 miles.

DEAD HORSE LAKE

Size: 29 acres
Depth: 30 feet maximum
Main Catch: rainbow & brook trout, kokanee
Best Methods: fly fishing, bait fishing
Season: entire year
Best Time: when road opens in spring; fall
Tips: Fish weighted minnow imitations in deep water.

It's hard to imagine a more pleasant place to fish than Dead Horse Lake in the Fremont National Forest. Small enough to keep the fishing intimate, it is still large enough, at 29 acres, to let the few anglers spread out.

With ample shallows, a muddy bottom, submerged grass, and fallen timber in the water, insect production is good which translates to a healthy fish population.

Rainbow trout, which average 8 to 12 inches, provide the most action. Brook trout and kokanee are also available. Fingerlings, and legals are stocked on a regular basis. Trophy trout, hatchery-grown and holdovers provide a little more excitement.

Many fish are taken on nightcrawlers. Use a small sliding sinker to a barrel swivel and 28 inches of leader terminating at a No. 12 single hook. Put a section of worm on the hook and cast. Leave a little slack in the line and set the hook when the line starts to move.

For the best fly action, fish wet flies and small streamers. Some good choices include leech patterns, water boatman imitations, and mayflies. Dry fly action can be good on warm summer evenings. When the wind blows in September, watch for trout feeding near the shore on flying ants.

Good bank access is available and fallen trees provide a path to put the shore angler closer to the best fishing. But a boat is a good idea. Gas motors are prohibited on this lake, but electric motors are allowed. The one-lane boat ramp is suitable for launching smaller craft. There is a small dock. One of the best spots to fish is on the south end of the lake, off the end of the boat ramp.

With tall trees providing shade, this is a pleasant place to camp. Tables, grills, pit toilets, and drinking water are provided. There are 9 basic sites with no hookups. Maximum length is 16 feet. Group campsites are available on top of the hill. Campsites are first-come, first-served.

Dead Horse and nearby Campbell, are accessible from July through October. Call the Forest Service office in Paisley (541-943-3114) to check on the opening of the road.

From LaPine, drive south on Highway 31 to Paisley. Turn right on Mill Street (Forest Road 33). Drive 19 miles and turn right on Forest Road 28. After 9 miles, turn left onto the one-lane graveled Forest Road 28-033. You'll pass Campbell Lake and reach Dead Horse in 3 miles.

MILLER LAKE

Size: 565 acres
Depth: 148´ max.
Main Catch: brown trout, kokanee
Best Methods: trolling, still-fishing,
fly fishing near shore
Season: entire year; check OSFR
Best Time: just after ice-out; fall
Tips: kokanee deep
in mid-summer

Miller Lake, eight miles west of Chemult as the raven flies, offers year-round fishing for kokanee, rainbow and brown trout. Even though there is nothing striking (except the fish) about the area, the outdoor experience is exceptionally pleasant. Miller Lake's wooded shoreline and 565 acres of inviting water is accessible yet secluded, 12 miles off U.S. Highway 97, Central Oregon's "freeway." Miller Lake lies at 5,616 feet elevation.

Overly successful natural reproduction of kokanee has caused size to decrease in recent years, the average fish currently about 8 inches in length, but they are abundant. Kokanee are caught by trolling, still-fishing with bait, or jigging a small lure. Since the lake's maximum depth is 148 feet, the kokanee can be quite deep by mid-summer.

Brown trout are stocked annually, and there are some good-sized ones prowling in here. Brown trout average from 20 inches in length up to 30-inch lunkers. Rainbow trout are no longer stocked, but some are still present in the lake. Both species of trout are angled for by trolling lures and flies. Troll slowly with a long line for brown trout. Fly fishing near shore and stream inlets in the evenings can be good. Brown trout are often more easily caught in the fall or very early or late in the day.

The east end of the lake is the most frequently fished section. Fishing from shore is not common, since most banks have a fairly

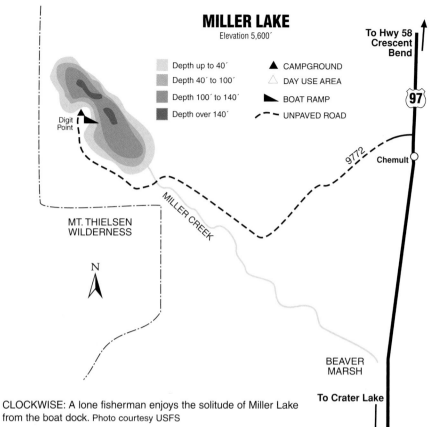

MILLER LAKE
Elevation 5,600´

Depth up to 40´
Depth 40´ to 100´
Depth 100´ to 140´
Depth over 140´

▲ CAMPGROUND
△ DAY USE AREA
◣ BOAT RAMP
— ─ UNPAVED ROAD

Digit Point

To Hwy 58
Crescent
Bend

97

9772

Chemult

MT. THIELSEN
WILDERNESS

MILLER CREEK

N

BEAVER
MARSH

To Crater Lake

CLOCKWISE: A lone fisherman enjoys the solitude of Miller Lake from the boat dock. Photo courtesy USFS

The publisher's son-in-law Dave Hogue *(of Host Campers)* shows off a nice brown trout.

Dave Hogue and kids enjoy a family outing near the swimming area of Miller Lake. Photos by Kim Hogue

steep drop off. The more shallow east end is one of the few spots fished from shore. The east end also supports most of the weedbeds. Many anglers fish from the boat dock near the campground. Water levels are quite stable. Cover for fish is mainly in the form of logs lying along the shoreline.

Winema National Forest's Digit Point Campground on the northwest shore of the lake offers excellent camping facilities: a boat ramp and dock, picnic area, a pressurized drinking water system, flush and vault toilets, trailer dump sites, a swimming area, a waterskiing area, and trailheads. A fee is charged to camp. Be ready for hoards of mosquitoes in this area.

The catch limit is 25 kokanee per day with no size restrictions, in addition to the trout limit of 5 per day with a 8-inch minimum, and of these no more than 1 over 20 inches. Boats are limited to a speed of 10 mph throughout most of the lake. Miller Lake is now open to angling 24 hours per day to take advantage of the abundant brown trout.

Trailheads from Digit Point lead into the Mount Thielsen Wilderness and around the lake. Another trail leading into the Wilderness takes off from Forest Route 9772, 1 mile from the campground. Many high lakes accessible from these trails offer decent fishing. During the winter, this is a popular recreation area for cross-country skiers and snowmobilers. A sno-park is located just off Highway 97 on Route 9772 into the lake. Ice fishermen are uncommon. The nearest services are in Chemult.

Miller Lake is 12 miles west of U.S. Highway 97 just north of Chemult. From the Eugene area take State Highway 58 over Willamette Pass all the way to it's junction with Highway 97. Turn south on Highway 97 and drive 8 miles to the turn onto Forest Route 9772 (a rough gravel road) one mile north of Chemult. Miller Lake is at the end of Route 9772, in 12 miles. From Bend drive south on Highway 97 about 74 miles to the turn onto Route 9772.

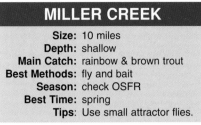

MILLER CREEK

Size: 10 miles
Depth: shallow
Main Catch: rainbow & brown trout
Best Methods: fly and bait
Season: check OSFR
Best Time: spring
Tips: Use small attractor flies.

Miller Creek is ten miles of trout fishing delight, set in sub-alpine pine forest. The outlet for Miller Lake, it runs south and east to its terminus in a marsh where it seeps away into the ground.

Easily stepped across in some places, the creek widens into big, shallow pools, then breaks and runs over small waterfalls. Green grass and algae provide good insect production. Cut banks and fallen logs span the creek in many places, allowing for quick access by foot to the opposite bank.

The creek is not stocked, but it has a good population of rainbow and brown trout. Regulations allow the angler to use bait and keep fish for dinner. For bait, use a small nightcrawler or Pautzke's salmon eggs. Flyfishermen should try small attractor dry flies or beadhead nymphs dead-drifted into holding habitat.

To reach the upper creek, take Forest Road 9772, about one mile north of Chemult. Forest Road 9771 follows the creek downstream. Expect to do some hiking to reach the best water.

Easily stepped across in some places, Miller Creek widens into big, shallow pools. Cut banks and fallen logs span the creek in many places. Green grass and algae provide good insect production. Photo by Gary Lewis

DIAMOND LAKE

Size: 3,000 acres
Depth: max. depth 48´
Main Catch: hatchery rainbow trout
Best Methods: still fishing from a boat, fly fishing
Season: last Saturday in April to Oct. 31; check OSFR
Best Time: early spring to mid-July
Tips: Fish rainbow with Power Bait on a long leader with a sliding sinker.

Diamond Lake's setting in the Umpqua National Forest, surrounded by Mount Thielsen, Mount Bailey, and the remains of Mount Mazama (Crater Lake), is a fishing, camping, and hiking mecca. Diamond Lake lies at an elevation of 5,182 feet, covers approximately 3,000 acres, and has a maximum depth of 48 feet. This rich body of water normally grows large fish fast, but has suffered problems with illegally introduced tui chubs over the last decade.

If all goes according to plan, there are exciting times in store for Diamond Lake. The Umpqua National Forest has begun the process of restoring the water quality and recreational fishery.

Diamond Lake is 4 miles in length and 1.5 miles in width, with a total of 11.5 miles of gently sloped, tree-lined shore. Water levels fluctuate little, and there are many weedbeds. Silent Creek at the south end of the lake and Lake Creek at the northwest corner both form channels that extend about .25 mile into the body of the lake. Afternoon winds are common, as are afternoon thunderstorms in the summer.

The best time to catch trout on Diamond Lake is from very early spring through mid-July. Catching slows in July then picks up again in September. Fishing is improving and can still be good despite the chub. In years without chub competition, the autumn provides good fishing for spring-planted rainbow fingerlings grown to 10 inches in length.

The most often used method of catching fish here is still-fishing from a boat with Power Bait. Some fishers troll surface lures, such as FlatFish or artificial flies in early morning and evening. Bank fishing is primarily along the north and northwest shores. A few fishers use float tubes or wade in from shore. Always check the current OSFR before fishing.

In order to restore Diamond Lake to its former glory, the Forest Service plans to treat the lake with rotenone in 2006. The chemical will kill the tui chub responsible for throwing off the lake's ecological balance. Plans are to construct a canal in the summer of 2005 to draw down the lake level through the winter of 2006.

For the summer of 2006, a temporary boat ramp and dock facilities will be built. Because trout will be concentrated in smaller areas, fishing is expected to be very good. As many fish as possible will be removed from the lake during this time. In the fall, ODFW will begin netting and trapping operations to remove tui chub. Rotenone treatment is scheduled for the fall of 2006. Diamond Lake will likely be closed to public access during the treatment process, 2 to 3 weeks.

In the winter and early spring of 2007, Diamond will be allowed to refill with natural stream flows, snow melt and rain. Water quality will be monitored. Pending

TOP: Spectacular Mt. Thielsen is viewed through a break in the trees from the west shore of Diamond Lake.
Photo by George W. Linn

CENTER: This lucky angler displays his batch of rainbows.

LEFT: Larry Wade of Roseburg shows the biggest trout caught at Diamond Lake since 1957, an 18 1/4-pound, 32-inch rainbow.

Photos courtesy Diamond Lake Resort

continued improvement of water quality and the ecosystem, ODFW will begin restocking the lake.

For 2007, stocking plans call for 50,000 to 100,000 fingerlings and 10,000 to 25,000 catchable size predacious trout. In 2008, ODFW plans to stock 100,000 to 200,000 fingerlings and 10,000 to 25,000 catchables. In 2009, ODFW will stock 100,000 to 300,000 fingerlings and 10,000 to 25,000 catchables. In 2010 and 2011, 200,000 to 300,000 fingerlings and up to 25,000 catchable size predacious trout will be stocked.

A 10-mph boat speed limit is in effect during fishing season except in the middle of the lake from 9:00 am to 6:00 pm where water-skiers may cool off. Paved boat ramps are available at South Shore Picnic area, Thielsen View Campground and Diamond Lake Campground.

Three large Forest Service campgrounds are located on the lake: Thielsen View Campground on the west shore, Diamond Lake Campground on the east shore, and Broken Arrow Campground set back in the woods on the southeast corner of the lake. All three charge a fee and have pressurized water systems and units for the disabled. There are many other facilities on the lake, including a full-service resort, restaurants, convention center, stables, and an RV park. Other recreational opportunities include hiking trails and a paved bike path around lake. In the winter, snow-cat skiing, snowmobiling, cross-country skiing, ice-skating, snow-shoeing, and a snow-play hill with ski tow are available.

Diamond Lake is located 90 miles southwest of Bend. From Bend, take U.S. Highway 97, to State Highway 138 toward Roseburg, then take State Highway 230 and Forest Road 6592 into the south shore. At the next junction, Forest Road 4795, Broken Arrow Campground, South Shore Picnic Area, and Thielsen View Campground are to the left, and Diamond Lake Campground and the resort are straight on 4795.

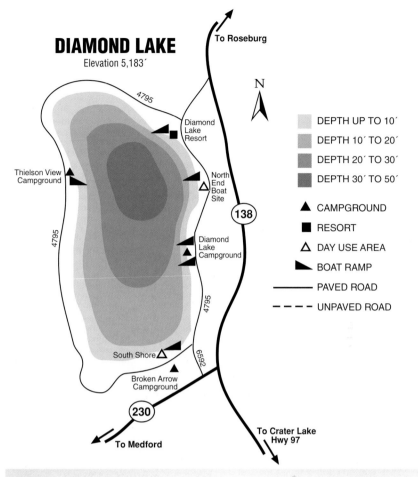

A view of Diamond Lake taken from the Pacific Crest Trail. Sun Publishing file photo

LEMOLO LAKE

Size:	420 acres total
Depth:	max. depth 110'
Main Catch:	brown trout & kokanee
Best Methods:	casting & trolling lures; drifting bait
Season:	last Saturday in April to October 31
Best Time:	very early in the season; fall for kokanee
Tips:	Stillfish with bait. Troll deep for larger browns.

Lemolo Lake is home to notoriously large, aggressive German brown trout, all of which are wild. The lake boasts good populations of rainbows and kokanee, along with the less abundant Eastern brook as well. It also has the outstanding characteristic of being fed by the beautiful and productive North Umpqua River. The reservoir covers approximately 420 acres and is 110 feet deep at the dam. Lemolo also has many shallower shoals and inlets that hold fish throughout the year.

The water level drops after Labor Day and is raised again in April, but levels remain very stable during fishing season. At low water, stumps can be hazardous to boaters in some areas. At high water, waterskiing and jet skiing are popular pastimes, and winds generally remain much calmer than at Diamond Lake.

The lake was formed when a dam was built in the late 50's impounding the North Umpqua and Lake Creek. Both form deep channels which connect and run clear to the dam. The channels are often trolled deep with large lures and spinners. Most anglers prefer to troll for the lakes large fish, but many do well still fishing bait or flies. Most fish caught are Browns ranging from 10-20 inches with some real lunkers thrown in to keep it exciting. Rainbows make up about 25 percent of the catch depending on tactics, and they range from 8-18 inches, along with many hold over trout weighing up to 5 pounds. The brookies run smaller at 8-12 inches, but their beauty more than makes up for their size.

Tackle is generally light, due to the clear water and wary trout, four pound test line is most common. Popular lures include, Bingo Bugs, Tasmanian Devils, Kwik Fish, floating and sinking Rapalas, and Triple Teazers. Baits used are generally night crawlers or meal worms. Popular flies are big Clouser minnows, rabbit strip leeches, Muddler minnows, and small caddis and mayfly imitations, ants are also very popular on the lake.

The best time of year to catch the wild browns is early spring when water temps are low, because they tend to stack up in the inlets and they get very aggressive. Late in the year, before the spawn, they head back to the inlets and fishing is excellent also. The rainbows tend to be more consistent, and they hold all over the lake, concentrating at the dam, and inlets.

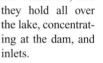

There are five campgrounds on the lake, Lemolo Lake Resort, Poole Creek, Bunker Hill, Inlet, and East Lemolo. Lemolo Lake Resort has full hook-ups in the RV Park, a Café, and a store, which includes a tackle shop. The resort also has cabins and boat rentals. Poole Creek is developed with outhouses, centralized water, paved roads, a boat ramp, group camp, and a swimming area. All other campgrounds are primitive with outhouses and picnic tables.

To Get to Lemolo Lake travel Highway 138 from either eastern or western Oregon take the turn onto Birds Point Road (2610) 6 miles north of Diamond lake and 73 miles east of Roseburg. Lemolo Lake Resort is 5 miles in from hwy 138. The turn offs are all well marked with recreational signs.

CLOCKWISE FROM TOP:
Rainbows make up about 25 percent of the catch at Lemolo Lake. Photo courtesy Lemolo Lake Resort

The North Umpqua River flows into Lemolo Lake. Photo by George W. Linn

Brown trout are the predominant catch at Lemolo Lake. Photo by Brian O'Keefe

Lemolo Lake from the resort area, Mt. Thielsen in background. Photo by George W. Linn

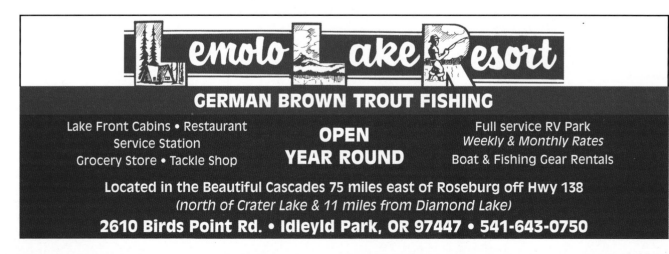

CRATER LAKE

Size:	5 miles in diameter
Depth:	2,000 feet
Main Catch:	kokanee, rainbow trout
Best Methods:	spinners
Season:	entire year
Best Time:	summer
Tips:	Cast weighted spinners for rainbow trout.

A large body of water in the crater left by the ancient eruption of Mt. Mazama, Crater Lake attracts thousands of visitors from around the world. Only a few of those people are fishermen. Thought by researchers to have contained no fish prior to stocking in the late 1800s and early 1900s, the Crater Lake now contains two species of fish: kokanee and rainbow trout.

Kokanee populations, which feed on zooplankton and average 8 to 18 inches, are thought to number in the hundreds of thousands. Though not as numerous, rainbow trout grow larger in Crater Lake. Rainbows average 10 to 14 inches, with the biggest on record tipping the scales at over 6 pounds.

Fishing is allowed at the end of the trail in Cleetwood Cove and at Wizard Island. No private boats are allowed on the lake, but regular boat trips to the island take place from 10 o'clock to 12 o'clock. At 4 o'clock, the boat returns to pick up passengers from Wizard Island. Fishing is allowed from the boat.

To get to Wizard Island, buy a ticket at the trailhead: $21 for adults, $13 for children, free for kids 12 and under. Boat tours end in mid-September.

To catch rainbows, cast Rooster Tail spinners and Thomas spoons. Some anglers bring a flyrod, but a better choice may be a float bubble with two small beadhead nymphs in tandem. For kokanee, try casting and jigging pink and orange kokanee jigs.

Angling is restricted to artificial fly and lure only. All fish must be retained. There is no limit, and no license is required. Pack out all trash and do not clean fish in or near the lake.

Backcountry streams are closed to angling to protect native bull trout. Angling in Crater Lake Park is regulated by the National Park Service, for information, call (541) 594-2211.

Two campgrounds offer rest for the fisherman. Lost Creek campground is suitable for tents only. It has 16 sites, with tables, grills, vault toilets and drinking water. Mazama has 200 basic sites with no hookups and a maximum length of 30 feet. Tables, grills, flush toilets, showers, drinking water, laundry, telephone, and food service are provided.

From Bend, drive south on Highway 97, then head west on Highway 138 to the junction with the Crater Lake Entrance Road. Turn south and follow the signs to the lake.

LEFT: Mt. Scott stands tall on the east rim.

ABOVE: Wizard Island protrudes into the wide expanse of Crater Lake. Mt. Thielsen peeks over the north rim. Photos by Geoff Hill

BELOW: Wizard Island as viewed from the northwest. Photo by Marv Binegar

WILLIAMSON RIVER

Size:	86 miles
Depth:	6´ average; 50´ max.
Main Catch:	wild rainbows, browns
Best Methods:	flies, lures
Season:	regulations complex; check OSFR
Best Time:	June-Oct.
Tips:	big fish generally from Klamath Lake upstream to Kent Canyon

The Williamson is probably the best river in Oregon for a chance at 5- to 15-pound rainbow and brown trout. The monster trout migrate from Upper Klamath Lake June through October in search of comfort and spawning habitat. Like steelhead, the big fish are wary and hard to catch. They come up out of the lake covered with cocopods, a kind of fresh water lice. Fresh fish announce their presence by jumping and rolling in an effort to shake the parasites. There are smaller resident and juvenile trout that would probably be considered big fish in other streams.

The best big fish opportunities are from Klamath Lake upstream about 15 miles to Kent Canyon. Within this stretch, most of the fishing is concentrated from the U.S. Highway 97 bridge to Chiloquin.

Below this reach the river turns to slack water and is better suited to trolling from boats motored up from the lake. Access is difficult with most of the riverbanks in private ownership. The minimal public land around Collier State Park is heavily fished, and the big migratory trout don't get that far upstream until September or October. There is a public park off the south Chiloquin access road where small trailered boats can launch, although the ramp is steep and four-wheel drives are advisable. Shore anglers can wade a short distance downstream from the Chiloquin put-in but constant pressure educates fish in the area. Beat the access and pressure problems by hiring a guide who has permission to fish private property, or stay at resorts with river frontage.

A drift downstream from Chiloquin takes a boat angler through shallow riffles that

ABOVE: Although many of the riverbanks are in private ownership, access by wading is still available, especially through guides with permission to fish private property or at a resort with river frontage.
Photo by Brian O'Keefe

RIGHT: There are so many good fishing spots it can take all day to float the Williamson.
Photo by Geoff Hill

spill over rock ledges into deep pools, along brushy banks and through deeply slotted channels. Good boat handling skills are required to prevent hanging up in shallow spots, let alone spotting fish-holding water before disturbing it. A driftboat with a fishing guide at the oars pointing out places to cast and flies to try is the best way to learn. Many do-it-yourselfers float the river in canoes, kayaks and float tubes, though tubers may have to stand up in places. There are so many good fishing spots it can take all day to float the 5 miles from Chiloquin to the Highway 97 bridge.

The Williamson offers a variety of hatches that fluctuates madly from day to day. The *Hexagenia limbata* (Yellow Mayfly) is noteworthy, eliciting surface strikes from even the most reluctant lunkers and presents good nymphing opportunities. Look for them in July in slower water where bank side vegetation allows adult mayflies to congregate. Other dry and emerger patterns to have on hand are Blue Wing Olive, caddis, stoneflies, Pale Morning Duns and Red Quill. Use leeches, Seal Buggers and streamers most of the time. The migratory trout are accustomed to feeding on big nymphs and baitfish in the lake, and that preference continues in the river. Big wet flies far and away produce the most fish. Fish them all on at least 14-foot leaders, 6X tippets for dries, 4X for wets when the light is low and be prepared to make 60-foot casts. Practice casting before hitting the river.

The upper Williamson begins as a spring roughly 25 miles northeast of Chiloquin in the Winema National Forest, flows north then west through mostly private land into the Klamath National Wildlife Refuge where access is closed during sensitive bird nesting seasons. Check with the refuge headquarters before trying this area. From the marsh, the river acquires a root beer brown color that is mostly strained out near Kirk, where the river flows underground before re-emerging a short distance downstream. Until Spring Creek joins it at Collier State Park, the upper

The Williamson River is known for its large trout, as evidenced by this nice 6-pound rainbow, as well as its scenic surroundings.
Photo by Geoff Hill; inset photo by Brian O'Keefe

Williamson is a small stream sporting mostly small brook and some decent rainbow trout. It can be good fishing in places, barren in others and difficult to access because of all the private land. A map of the Winema National Forest is a must, as is a copy of the Oregon fishing regulations.

From the mouth upstream to the Modoc Point Bridge Road, the Williamson is open to all angling methods late May through October 31 with a 1 fish limit. From Modoc Point Bridge upstream to Chiloquin Bridge, no fishing from boats under power, same season but catch-and-release is required for trout after August 1 and tackle is restricted to artificial flies and lures. From Chiloquin Bridge upstream to Kirk Bridge no fishing is allowed from floating devices in addition to the previous restrictions, essentially eliminating public access below Collier State Park. Finally, from Kirk Bridge upstream to the

headwaters the river is open to the harvest of 2 rainbows, and any number of brook trout late April through October 31. Designed to protect spawning runs, these progressively restrictive regulations are subject to change so check before going.

Services and accommodations are available around Chiloquin, where there are highway hotels, RV parks, cafes, fishing lodges, gas, groceries and supplies. Camping is available at Collier State Park and Williamson River Campground. A fair number of small planes land at the Chiloquin airstrip, disgorging passengers with rod cases.

The river is located 115 miles south of Bend or 25 miles north of Klamath Falls on U.S. Highway 97.

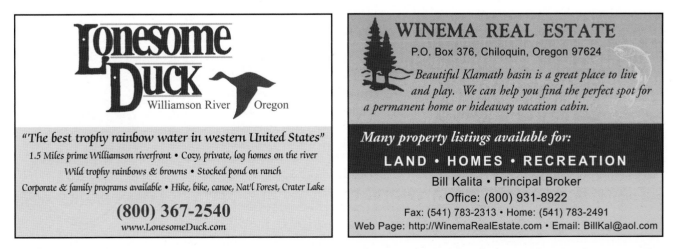

SPRAGUE RIVER

Size: 100 miles
Depth: 5´ average; 10´ max.
Main Catch: trout, bass, catfish
Best Methods: flies, lures, bait
Season: late April-Oct 31
Best Time: early summer, fall
Tips: remote fishing as area relatively unknown to tourists

The Sprague is a major tributary of the Williamson River originating in the Gearhart Mountain area about 100 miles east of Chiloquin, about 30 miles west of Lakeview. The upper Sprague and its tributaries offer good fishing for wild rainbow, brook and bull trout. The mainstem has brown trout, largemouth bass and catfish. Near its confluence, the Sprague shares

RIGHT: Erwin Miller of Chiloquin proudly displays the mount of his 16-lb. rainbow caught on his lunch break in late October, 1993.

BELOW: The scenic Sprague River is home to some large trout which migrate from the Upper Klamath Lake and Williamson River.

Photos by Geoff Hill

some of the Williamson's big rainbow trout that migrate from Upper Klamath Lake. The Sprague River is relatively unknown to tourists but lacks nothing in the way of scenery, fishing and camping opportunities. For those who enjoy outback style fishing experiences this area is well worth exploring.

The Sprague heads in the Gearhart Mountain Wilderness, an area of stunning vistas, dense forests, steep ridges and cold creeks that peaks out at 8,300 feet above sea level. The upper 10 miles of the North Fork are Designated Wild and Scenic and home to good populations of wild brook, rainbow and bull trout. Bull trout must be released unharmed. Anglers are allowed to keep 2 trout per day, minimum 8 inches, only 1 over 20 inches. There are no size restrictions or harvest limits on brook trout. In fact, harvest of brook trout probably helps the native bull trout, which are nearing threatened and endangered status.

All techniques, including bait in one section, are permitted. Bait works wonderfully well on brookies and can provide a positive experience for beginning anglers. Spinners, dry flies and nymphs are also effective. Forest roads 19, 3411 and 3372 parallel much of the Wild and Scenic section and cross it several places, affording easy access with short hikes getting anglers away from pressured areas. The South Fork is good for small brook up high and brown trout in the lower reaches and is accessible from State Highway 140 and Forest Highway 34. Always check OSFR.

The slower flowing mainstem is an under-utilized warm water fishery, offering miles of bass, catfish and brown trout habitat. Shore fishing is limited to sidings along highways 858 and 140, bridge crossings, the Sprague River Day Use area east of Bly and permission from property owners. Most anglers target catfish with worms. Bass will take spinnerbaits, plastic worms and floating crankbaits. Brown trout go for mouse, grasshopper and streamer pattern flies. Floating the river in a canoe, kayak or pram would be the best way to access unexplored waters. Get permission from property owners first.

Good populations of wild brook, rainbow and bull trout are found on the North Fork of the Sprague River. Photo by Todd Ostenson

There are scads of rough fish in this section, some of which are protected (short-nosed and Klamath suckers, blue and tui chubs) and must be released.

Access improves and springs cool the river just above Chiloquin where rainbow and brown trout to 3 lbs. share the water with bass and catfish. Bait, lures and flies will all work in this section. Access is via Chiloquin Ridge Road off Sprague River Road. Downstream from the dam near Chiloquin High School to the Williamson River, angling is restricted to artificial flies and lures and limited to 1 trout per day. Large trout migrate into the lower Sprague from Klamath Lake. They are catchable in late summer and fall on leeches, Woolly Buggers and spinners. Upstream from Chiloquin Dam, the Sprague River is open to fishing the last Saturday in April through October 31. Below the dam the season is from late May through October 31. Check the OSFR.

Other than small hotels in Chiloquin, it's all camping for overnight visitors to the Sprague River. Near the headwaters, Sandhill Crossing, Lee Thomas and Campbell Lake forest camps offer toilets, picnic tables and fire rings. None charge fees. If they are full, camping is permitted anywhere on National Forest land for up to 14 days. S'Ocholis private campground is 12 miles east of Chiloquin on Hwy. 858.

Points of interest include the Mitchell Monument, site of the only deaths on the continental United States during WWII. In May 1945, six people on a Sunday school picnic were killed when a Japanese balloon bomb exploded. Weyerhaeuser Co. maintains a picnic area and monument about 10 miles northeast of Bly on Hwy 34.

The Sprague River is accessible from Chiloquin from the west and Lakeview from the east. State highways 858 and 140 are the primary routes with numerous side roads. Winema and Fremont National Forest maps provide details.

WOOD RIVER

Size:	30 miles
Depth:	15´ average; 5´ max.
Main Catch:	rainbow & brown trout
Best Methods:	flies, lures
Season:	last Saturday in April to Oct. 31
Best Time:	Aug.-Oct.
Tips:	catch-and-release only; boat required to fish effectively

The Wood River is a wide, meandering meadow stream full of twists and turns with undercut banks and cold, clear water. Photo by Brooke Snavely

The Wood River is often lumped together with the Williamson in conversations about fishing in the Klamath basin. They are similar but do not fish the same. Trout migrate up the Wood like they do the Williamson to escape warm lake conditions and to spawn. The migrations occur about the same times (June-October), the fish can be very large (5+ pounds) and access is difficult due to extensive private property holdings. But there the similarities end. The Wood is a 30-foot wide meandering meadow stream with undercut banks, downed trees, and breathtakingly cold, crystal clear waters. It has a grasshopper season, which makes fools of the biggest fish. And it is strictly catch-and-release throughout the season, the last Saturday in April through October 31.

From its source at Jackson F. Kimball State Park, the Wood River flows south through pastureland about 15 miles as the crow flies to Agency Lake. Actual river length is closer to 20 or 30 miles factoring in all the river's sinuous twists and turns. A boat is required to fish it effectively. Most drifts are from bridge to bridge or from the lower most bridge crossing (Weed Road) to the mouth, the most popular drift. Some bridges have very low clearance, requiring a short portage, favoring small boats like canoes, kayaks, float tubes and personal pontoon boats. Weed Road features a steep dirt ramp where driftboats can launch. Except for the bridge crossings, anglers must stay in their boats, as virtually all the shorelines are private property. The Wood River has no whitewater but flows deceptively fast through an irregular channel with occasional snags and twisting currents.

There is limited shore fishing access at the headwaters at Jackson F. Kimball State Park, though the fish are small and the mosquitoes ravenous. A few miles downstream, the Wood River Day Use Area off Sun Mountain Road features a quarter-mile of bank access with two handicap fishing platforms and nice trails. It is possible to launch car toppers and tubes here, but there is no ramp. The next shore access is many miles downstream at the Weed Road Bridge. The lower 1.5 miles were recently brought into public ownership. This area is accessible on foot or bike from the Modoc Point Highway. Most anglers launch at Petric Park on Agency Lake, then motor or paddle 1.5 miles to the mouth of the Wood.

Most fishing on the Wood occurs at the mouth where it flows into Agency Lake and the lower 3 miles along Wood River Ranch which is now managed by the BLM. Large green, black and brown leech pattern flies with the tails trimmed to discourage short strikes fished just below the surface will fool rainbows. Upstream there's a better chance at brown trout with mouse pattern flies cast onto the far shore, pulled into the water with a splash, then fast stripped back to the boat, especially after sunset. Rainbows and browns rise willingly to grasshopper imitations drifted along undercut banks in late summer. There are other insect hatches but few rival the grasshopper surface action in August and September. Leeches and streamers are the best all around patterns for fly fishers. Spin fishers can present flies with plastic bubbles or cast and retrieve spinners, spoons and crankbaits through likely holding areas.

Lodging is available in Fort Klamath, at fishing lodges on the Wood River and in Chiloquin. Nearby campgrounds include Jackson F. Kimball State Park, Fort Klamath RV Park, and Agency Lake Resort on Agency Lake. Nearby points of interest include Crater Lake National Park, historic Fort Klamath, and the Klamath State Fish Hatchery.

From Bend, travel 115 miles south on U.S. Highway 97 to Chiloquin then west 15 miles to Fort Klamath. From Klamath Falls, travel 25 miles north to Chiloquin, then west 15 miles to Fort Klamath.

SYCAN RIVER

Length:	50 miles
Depth:	varies seasonally
Main Catch:	brook, brown, & rainbow trout
Best Methods:	flies & lures only
Season:	late April-Oct. 31;
Best Time:	spring, fall check OSFR
Tips:	light use due to rough roads

Flowing through a basalt canyon over large water carved boulders, the Sycan River is reminiscent of the Crooked River, only more forested and much more remote. A medium size tributary of the Sprague River, the Sycan heads in the northeastern corner of Klamath County, flows about 20 miles northwest into the Sycan Marsh, then 30 miles southwest before joining with the Sprague near Beatty. Divided by the marsh, the entire upper and much of the lower river are Designated Wild and Scenic. Most of the river flows through National Forest and private timberland that is open to the public. Rough roads explain the Sycan's light use, mostly by anglers in summer, hunters in fall and a brief shot of rafters during spring runoff.

The upper Sycan and its tributaries, such as Long and Coyote creeks, harbor mostly small brook trout that willingly rise to flies and chase lures. There are native redband rainbow trout to 14 inches and occasionally larger bull trout. Bull trout must be released unharmed. The trout limit is 2, one over 20 inches per day, but feel free to keep all brook trout regardless of size. ODFW wants brook trout eradicated, and what better way than to cook them over a campfire. Access the upper Sycan via Forest roads 28, 30 and 3239, which parallel and cross the river in several places. Developed campsites are available at Pike's Crossing and Rock Creek. There are nice dispersed campsites along the river

available to those willing to hike, drift or drive unimproved roads. A word of caution to streamside campers: the drainage is actively logged and subject to flash flooding. Camp above the high water mark and keep an eye on the weather. Thunderstorms are common in summer. Rising river levels cause turbidity which can hurt the fishing.

Downstream from the privately owned Sycan Marsh, 10-to 18-inch brown trout are available to anglers willing to travel. The lower Sycan is warmer and by late summer shallow and weedy. Focus fishing efforts near springs where cool water concentrates game fish. Or try earlier in the year during higher flows for spawners migrating up from the Sprague. Undesirable and in some cases

protected chubs, dace, suckers and sculpin are also present. Streamer pattern flies can be effective for browns. Traditional caddis, mayfly and midge patterns will take rainbow. There are no developed campsites along the lower river, but plenty of suitable areas accessible by secondary roads, foot, and horseback. Forest roads 44, 46 and 27 are primary routes. Don't go without maps of the Fremont and Winema National Forests.

From Klamath Falls travel about 40 miles northeast on State Highway 140 to Beatty. From Chiloquin, travel about 40 miles east on State Highways 858 and 140. From Lakeview, travel 45 miles west on State Highway 140. From Silver Lake, travel 35 miles south on Forest Road 28.

CLOCKWISE:

Another nice rainbow … nice smile too!

A nice Sycan rainbow.

The Sycan is a picturesque stream.
Photos by Brian O'Keefe

The remote Sycan River flows through a basalt canyon over large water carved boulders and is surrounded by National Forest and private timberland that is open to the public.
Photo by Brooke Snavely

UPPER KLAMATH LAKE

Size:	96 sq. miles
Depth:	7´ average; 50´ max.
Main Catch:	rainbow, brown trout
Best Methods:	flies, trolling, bait
Season:	entire year; check OSFR
Best Time:	summer & fall
Tips:	Fishing is best at mouths of creeks; around springs & weedbeds; in deep water; & along steep, rocky shorelines.

Upper Klamath Lake's shallow, weedy, bug-infested, wind-swept water does not fit the trout lake stereotype. But appearances are deceiving. This is trophy trout water, challenging to fish, a pleasure to visit.

Upper Klamath is home to Klamath strain rainbow trout, arguably the fastest growing, largest rainbow trout in North America. The average size fish here is 5-7 pounds. Ten-pounders are common. A few fish over 20 pounds are taken every year. Their amazing size can be attributed to ample feed and the species' penchant for eating minnows, a behavior long credited to the big brown trout with whom they share the lake.

Locating these monsters in nearly 100 square miles of water is no easy feat, but can be done by breaking the lake down into sections, seasons and methods.

Fishing is best at the mouths of creeks, around springs and weedbeds, in deep water, near the outflow, and along steep, rocky shorelines. By concentrating on these areas, anglers eliminate 95% of the lake. The primary techniques are trolling with lures, still fishing with bait and fly fishing. When the water is cold in winter and spring, trolling the shorelines is the best way to find widely scattered fish. Long-line, weightless trolling is effective with minnow imitating lures like Freaks, F-S-T's, Little Cleos, Rebels and Rapalas. Depth is not nearly as important as distance behind the boat. Most fish are caught within 10 feet of the surface, regardless of season or tactics. Dead minnows are also trolled with and without attractor blades. Shore anglers occasionally score with night-crawler and marshmallow combinations fished with slip sinkers on slack line. Trolled and still-fished dead chubs attract bigger fish. Do not catch and kill chubs or suckers from the lake, as they are protected. Dead bait is available at bait shops throughout the area. Minnow imitating streamers and black, brown and olive Seal Buggers and leech patterns are best for fly fishing.

As the water warms in late spring and early summer, the fish gravitate to deeper holes and cooler water. This is the time to focus trolling, bait and fly fishing efforts in deep water, of which there isn't much, also near springs and creek channels. The deepest water in the lake is at the tip of Eagle Ridge, also between the ridge and Bare Island south to Squaw Point. The mouth of Wocus Bay and the tip of Ball Point also have some deep spots. Fish also begin showing at the mouth of the Williamson River, Agency Lake strait, Thomas Creek, Pelican Bay and an area known as "Fish Banks" where the wildlife refuge projects into the main body of the lake. A lake map showing bottom contours and depthfinder is helpful. A boat and a willingness to move are essential to finding feeding fish. Lure, bait and fly patterns remain the same.

Fishing really gets good in summer as fish seek relief from the heat in cool water of creek mouths, around springs at Rocky Point, in deep channels and begin swimming up the creeks themselves. Big spawners migrate out of the lake in September and October. Pelican Bay is one of the best areas this time of year,

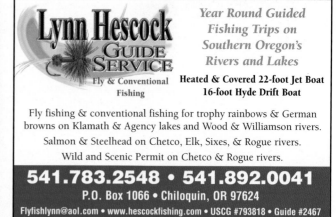

TOP: View of Mt. McLoughlin from the lake. Photo by Jon Gnass

ABOVE: A fisherman hooks one as another swims by the boat in the Rocky Point area of the lake. Photo by Brian O'Keefe

RIGHT: A happy angler with a good rainbow. Photo by Gary Lewis

with easy access to Crystal, Harriman, and Recreation creeks. All methods remain effective, though fly fishing may have an advantage with fish paying more attention to bug hatches. Midges are the most common insect, with large caddis, mayfly, damsel and dragonflies offering seasonal variety. Wet or dry, fish all patterns on long leaders, at least 12 feet. Big fish are instinctively cautious. Tippet material should be 4-6-pound test, strong enough to land large fish, supple enough to let the fly move realistically.   Use tapered leaders to keep suspended algae from hanging up on the line and ruining the presentation. Don't be thrown off by the lake's heavy algae growth. The fish use it for cover.

The limit is 1 trout per day, minimum 8 inches. Brown bullhead and perch are also available with no size restrictions or catch limits.

Upper Klamath is a spectacular bird watching, sight-seeing, boating, and camping area. At any time, upwards of 40 species of birds are present. Designated canoe trails give paddlers close-up views of water lilies, beavers and birds in the Klamath Wildlife Refuge. Regular afternoon winds make for great sailing. Numerous trails lead to many fine hike-in fishing lakes in the Sky Lakes and Mountain Lakes Wilderness areas. Picnicking, camping, and boat launches are available at public and private parks, marinas, campgrounds and resorts all around the lake. Moore Park on the lake's south shore in Klamath Falls is one of the prettiest waterfront parks anywhere. And be sure to watch the sunsets, especially when there are clouds to reflect the evening glow.

From Bend, travel 100 miles south on U.S. Highway 97 to Chiloquin, then west 20 miles to Fort Klamath to west shore or continue south along east shore to Klamath Falls for 26 miles.

From Medford: Travel 46 miles east on State Highway 140 to Rocky Point Jct., or continue south 24 miles along west shore to Klamath Falls.

From Ashland: Travel 64 miles east on State Highway 66 to Klamath Falls.

The scenery surrounding Klamath Lake is spectacular. Dominating the skyline is Mt. McLoughlin.

LEFT: The fishing can be as spectacular as the scenery. This angler is about to release a beautiful rainbow back into the water. Photos by Brian O'Keefe

BELOW: Todd Ostenson proudly displays his 25-inch Klamath rainbow. Photo by Derek Mouw

AGENCY LAKE

Size:	14 sq. mi. (8,960 acres)
Depth:	10' max.
Main Catch:	rainbow & brown trout, yellow perch
Best Methods:	shallow trolling with lures, flies, bait
Season:	entire year; check OSFR
Best Time:	May-Oct.
Tips:	Probe the side channels.

Agency Lake, named for the nearby Klamath Indian Agency, is basically part of the larger Upper Klamath Lake and fishes much the same. A broad, shallow, silty lake exposed to the wind and subject to dense algae blooms, water clarity is rarely more than 3 feet. None of this seems to bother the 5- to 15- pound brown and rainbow trout that migrate through on their way to and from spawning tributaries such as the Wood River and Seven Mile Canal. The lake's organically rich water grows trout fingerlings into 20-inchers in three years. Massive schools of yellow perch thrive in weedy, shallow areas, becoming available to anglers in mid-summer.

A boat is required to fish Agency Lake, as it is almost entirely surrounded by private lands. The 25-mile long shoreline consists mostly of man-made levies laced with canals and pumps designed to drain farmland. The steep sloped dirt levies are the dominant structure in the lake with outflow from canals and pumps creating fish attracting currents. In spring when farmers drain their fields, it's a good idea to cast lures and flies around the pumps where fish may feed.

The inlet of the Wood River and the straits draining the lake are two more hot spots. Long line surface trolling around the mouth of the Wood can be effective with Canadian Wonder spoons, shallow running

LEFT: Trophy-size rainbows from Agency and Upper Klamath lakes migrate up local rivers to spawn. Dale Luoma poses with a dandy. Photo courtesy Dale Luoma

BELOW: The organically rich water in this broad, shallow lake produces large fish. Photo by Geoff Hill

crankbaits, dead minnows or nightcrawlers. Still fishing can be good along levies and weed lines where submerged brush or overhanging trees may hold fish. Fly fishers favor leech and minnow type flies, both trolled and cast on floating and intermediate sinking lines, then stripped back with long, slow pulls. Beware of a deadline at the mouth of the Wood River denoting a change to catch and release, no-bait regulations and restricted seasons in the river itself.

Trout congregate in the mile-long narrow strait connecting Agency Lake to Upper Klamath as they pass through in search of comfortable water temperature, food and spawning habitat. Here again, shallow trolling with flies and lures is the best way to connect with roaming trout, though still fishing and casting can also produce. Be sure to probe the side channel created by dredging to build levies paralleling the natural strait. The side channel, also known as the inside channel, is deeper and frequently more productive.

Perch fishing is productive in July and August when schools congregate in Four Mile Canal. This 10-foot deep, tule-lined waterway is best fished with small jigs, worms without bobbers and perch meat. Agency perch average 10-12 inches and are considered very good eating. The perch fishery attracts many out-of-state anglers.

Free launch ramps are available at Petric and Henzel parks, county parks with restrooms. Agency Lake Resort charges a launch fee. All three ramps are accessible from the Modoc Point Road. Both lakes can whip up in a hurry in windy conditions, so keep an eye on the weather.

Regulations: 1 trout per day. No size limit or catch restrictions on perch.

From Bend travel 100 miles south on U.S. Highway 97 to Chiloquin, then west 5 miles on the South Chiloquin Road; turn north on the Modoc Point Road which fronts Agency Lake.

From Klamath Falls travel 30 miles north to Chiloquin on U.S. 97; from there follow the same directions to the lake.

ABOVE: The yellow perch fishery attracts many out-of-state anglers. Gary Lewis Photo

GERBER RESERVOIR

Size: 4,047 acres
Depth: 27' avg.; 65' max.
Main Catch: crappie, perch, bass, trout
Best Methods: small lures, bait
Season: entire year
Best Time: spring, fall
Tips: hard to reach so very
low fishing pressure.

Gerber Reservoir is probably the best publicly accessible panfish water in the Klamath basin. Gerber Reservoir produced the state record white crappie, a 4-lb., 12-oz., 18.5-inch beauty in 1967. The state record 4-lb., 18-inch black crappie came out of the Lost River downstream from Gerber in 1978. Yellow perch are available in abundance, along with largemouth bass and a few rainbow trout, remainders of a discontinued stocking program. Built for irrigation and flood control, Gerber features a variety of flooded timber, brush, inlets, coves, rocky shorelines, shoals and deep holding water. The habitat is so good and the reservoir large enough that most anglers haven't figured out where the fish go some of the year. A hard 50-mile drive east of Klamath Falls on narrow, bumpy roads, Gerber doesn't get much fishing pressure and has the potential to grow more state records.

The crappie bite starts in April or May when water temperatures reach 62° to 65°F, motivating the fish to spawn in shallow water with sand or gravel bottoms. 1/16 and 1/32 ounce maribou crappie jigs, small plastic grubs, worms and green peas catch mostly male crappies guarding the nests. The key is to approach quietly, not anchor on top of the nesting areas, drop the bait in with a long pole or cast from a distance and fish below a sensitive bobber. Creek inlets and shallow points around the island are perennial spawning areas. By mid-June, crappie move deeper, hanging around submerged trees close to the dam and near the eagle's nest on the Barnes Creek arm. Use light wire hooks that will bend if snagged or easily broken leader material.

In July and August when anglers complain the crappie disappear and switch to perch, crappie are probably suspended in open water off points and drop-offs, sometimes 15-30 feet deep. To locate them, try trolling soft bodied jigs and Beetle Spins, switching to vertical bait presentations when found. If fluctuating water levels permit, crappie move back into flooded brush and standing timber in the fall for another round of good fishing.

Perch follow similar patterns, but don't move as deep as crappie and prefer weeds over brush. Perch fishing is good most of the summer in 5- to 10-foot deep water with worms, leeches, perch meat, small jigs and lures. In areas where only small perch are caught, try a bit farther out and deeper for larger fish. Bigger plastic worms and spinner baits will catch bass in the same areas, especially around cover. Before trout stocking stopped, anglers used to troll the creek channels with good results. Now most trout fishing is limited to bank fishing in the narrows of Ben Hall Creek around the point to the dam. Miller Creek below the dam offers good stream trout fishing. Watch for rattlesnakes.

The BLM operates two nice day-use areas and campgrounds with restrooms, fish cleaning stations and gravel boat ramps on the west side of the lake. There is an improved boat ramp at Barnes Valley Creek on the east shore with fewer amenities.

From Klamath Falls, go 19 miles east on State Highway 140, then take County Road 70 about 17 miles to Bonanza and Lorella, then 8 miles NE up Gerber Reservoir Road.

From Lakeview, take Highway 140 west to Bly, follow Forest Route 375 and Forest Route 381 south for 10 miles to the lake.

From the dam, the wide expanse of this remote reservoir can be seen. Photo by Brooke Snavely

LAKE OF THE WOODS

Size: 1,146 acres
Depth: 55´ avg.
Main Catch: rainbow & brown trout, kokanee, bass
Best Methods: bait, trolling
Season: entire year; check OSFR
Best Time: spring, fall
Tips: Use big Rapalas to tempt biggest trout and bass.

A classic fish and ski lake in a beautiful wooded setting, Lake of the Woods sits on the east slope of the southern Oregon Cascades at 4,949 feet above sea level. A typical day finds anglers trolling at sunrise until about 10 a.m. when waterskiers take over. Then there's a raft and swimmer hatch in the shallows until about dinner time when the lake quiets down and anglers return to fish the evening bite. The timing works for all parties, including the fish.

Trolling with a set of flashers (Ford Fenders, Flashlights) and Wedding Ring spinner tipped with corn is the universal approach for kokanee, rainbow and brown trout. It is possible to catch fish without the heavy trolling blades, just a Dick Nite or Triple Teazer, with or without bait. Either way, the fish are available near the surface in the spring. Browns to 7 pounds are most likely this time of year, though they periodically surprise anglers expecting 9-to 12-inch kokanee and similarly sized rainbow trout throughout summer. The 11-lb., 4 oz. lake record rainbow was caught on a trolled Rapala in April of 1994, proving again that big trout like big baits. The lake record German brown trout was a brute that tipped the scales at over 15 pounds. Many big browns are caught each year.

Summer surface temperatures to 70°F push the trout down to the thermocline, typically 33 to 40 feet by late summer. Trollers add weight or fish with lead core line and concentrate on the deep water along the west shore, following the contours out into the north bay and back again. Good bait bank fishing and casting opportunities exist along all shores spring and fall, but mainly along the west shore in summer. Power Bait and worms are the best bait, with Rooster Tails and Panther-Martins the most effective lures for casting and retrieving. Perch, small catfish, and crappie are also caught on still-fished baits.

Look for largemouth bass near the west side docks, at the north and south end shallows and in the shadow of downed trees in Rainbow Bay. May and June offer good fishing for largemouth. Action picks up again in August and will continue through September. You'll catch some of the biggest bass on big baits. Target weed beds, docks and fallen trees. Cast Rat-L-Traps, Rapalas, and other minnow imitations in perch and

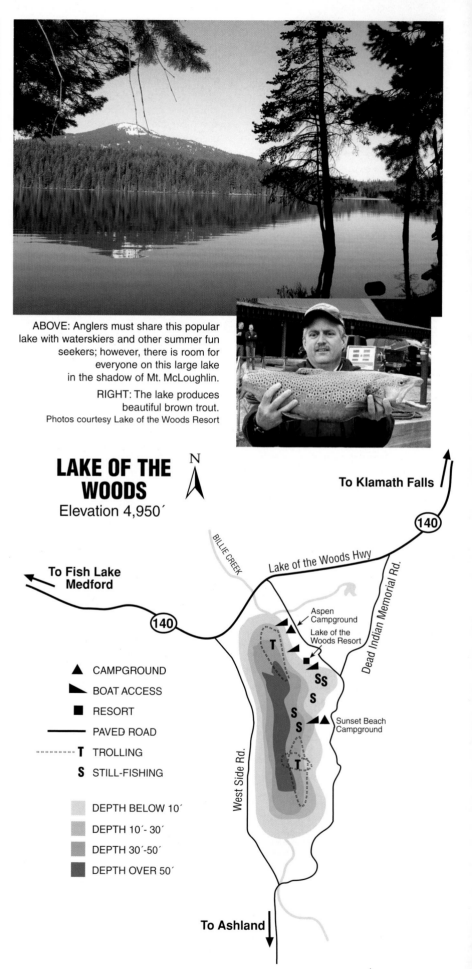

ABOVE: Anglers must share this popular lake with waterskiers and other summer fun seekers; however, there is room for everyone on this large lake in the shadow of Mt. McLoughlin.

RIGHT: The lake produces beautiful brown trout.
Photos courtesy Lake of the Woods Resort

LAKE OF THE WOODS
N
Elevation 4,950´

To Klamath Falls

To Fish Lake
Medford

140

140

BILLIE CREEK
Lake of the Woods Hwy
Dead Indian Memorial Rd.

Aspen Campground
Lake of the Woods Resort

Sunset Beach Campground

West Side Rd.

▲ CAMPGROUND
◣ BOAT ACCESS
■ RESORT
— PAVED ROAD
⋯⋯⋯ **T** TROLLING
S STILL-FISHING

DEPTH BELOW 10´
DEPTH 10´- 30´
DEPTH 30´-50´
DEPTH OVER 50´

To Ashland

rainbow patterns. Don't be afraid to use lures between 6 and 8 inches long. Divers have reported seeing very big bass under a few of the docks. The biggest largemouth caught on this lake weighed in at 12.9 pounds. Bass to 6 pounds can be caught on plastic worms and spinnerbaits during the day. Go deeper along bass-holding structure with long-billed Luhr-Jensen or Yakima crankbaits. After dark, create a disturbance on the surface with lures like the Berkley Power Pop Frog or a fly rod popper. A few smallmouth bass have been reported at Lake of the Woods, but not enough to warrant fishing for them.

Busy with school or work, most anglers miss the good fall bite when trout return to the surface to sip the last insects of the year with renewed vigor. Its about the only time fly-casters do well on dry flies. Trolled streamer pattern flies can be very good on fly rods or spinning rods on light monofilament. Kokanee spawn in the east shore gravel. By the time they get there they are too dark for eating but offer great sport. Target them before they turn color with jigged Buzz Bombs and trolled lures in 30-40 feet of water. Bass become very aggressive, chasing lures far from their usual haunts. Ice fishing is good in winter. Limits are 25 kokanee per day; 5 trout per day, 1 over 20 inches; 5 bass per day, 1 over 15 inches; there is no limit on bullheads, perch or crappie. Lake of the Woods is now open 24 hours a day to take advantage of the abundant brown trout.

There are three paved boat ramps, 130 Forest Service camp sites and the full service Lake of the Woods Resort, offering RV camping with hook ups, cabins, store, restaurant, marina and boat rentals. The resort remains open during the winter months for snowmobilers, cross country skiers and ice fishermen.

From Klamath Falls travel 35 miles west on State Highway 140; from Medford, take State Highway 62 north to Highway 140 then east 45 miles; from Ashland, travel 35 miles east on Dead Indian Memorial Road.

BELOW: There are paved boat ramps, cabins, campsites, a marina, and boat rentals at Lake of the Woods.
The fish are big here as well …
this angler holds a nice brown trout.
Photos courtesy Lake of the Woods Resort

FISH LAKE
(JACKSON COUNTY)

Size: 483 acres
Depth: 18´ avg.; 31´ max.
Main Catch: rainbow, brown & brook trout
Best Methods: trolling with bait & flies
Season: entire year; check OSFR
Best Time: spring, fall
Tips: Fish rainbow Power Bait on a sliding sinker.

For consistent trout fishing in a beautiful setting, head to Fish Lake in the southern Oregon Cascades. Located at 4,642´ elevation near the summit of Highway 140, surrounded by old growth forests, this is a clean, cool pleasant body of water to fish in or just hang around.

The lake is stocked annually with about 20,000 legal size rainbow trout. Those that carryover reach 15-16 inches in two years, and if they survive a third, attain 20 inches or more. Four pounds is considered the standard for big fish, and every year dozens that size and larger are caught. The lake record is a 9.75-lb. rainbow, on display at Fish Lake Lodge. ODFW also plants 5,000, 8- to 10-inch steelhead in the lake. The steelhead grow to 22 inches, tend to be slimmer than the rainbows, but are considered by some anglers more active when hooked. Brook trout are not stocked, but some are caught every year as they apparently spawn in the lake. A few brown trout are present, along with an illegally introduced population of chubs.

Trolling is the most popular method to catch fish in Fish Lake. Ford Fenders followed by a gold Needlefish with a red tip, a streamer fly or a Wedding Ring spinner tipped with a worm are the norm. The best trolling spots are near Doe Point and close to the dam. A 10-mile per hour speed limit keeps boat noise to a minimum.

Still-fishing is good from boats and shore with worms, salmon eggs and Power Bait. One of the best still-fishing spots is around a small island across from the lodge that sports a small cross. The cross memorializes a 1950s drowning victim. Also try suspending bait near the bottom off points in the main lake and near the dam. Good bank fishing is available next to the Doe Point boat ramp. The deepest water is right down the middle of the lake.

Where you find the best still-fishing, for fast action, switch to spinners, spoons or plugs. Tie on a 1/8-ounce Rooster Tail spinner, Thomas spoon, or rainbow Rapala and add a little split shot to aid in dropping the lure to the proper depth. Cast and retrieve, experimenting with depth, until you get the first strike.

Troll flies from a float tube along the ledges that transition to deeper water or prospect around rocky points and weed beds. Minnow imitations, beadhead wet flies and chironomid patterns are good bets. In the summer and fall, watch the shallows along the shoreline for trout rising to ants that have blown in the water. For brook trout, consider fishing Little Butte Creek below the dam. Beadhead nymphs, small streamers and attractor dry flies will pay off in fast action for stream trout.

Ice fishing is possible most winters,

LEFT: Fish Lake can produce trophy rainbows in the 6 to 8-pound class. Trolling is the most popular method, but spinner casting can produce fast action.
Photo by Gary Lewis

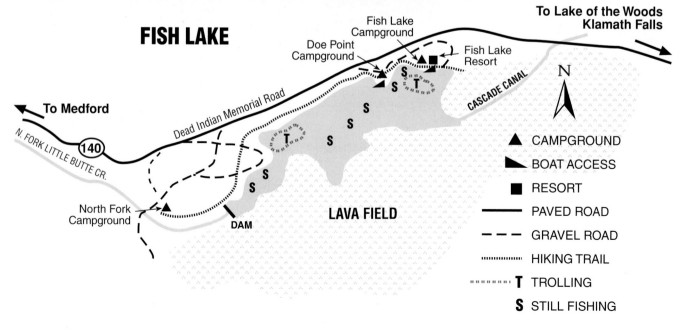

FISH LAKE

To Lake of the Woods
Klamath Falls

Fish Lake Campground

Doe Point Campground

Fish Lake Resort

CASCADE CANAL

N

To Medford

Dead Indian Memorial Road

N. FORK LITTLE BUTTE CR.

140

North Fork Campground

DAM

LAVA FIELD

▲ CAMPGROUND
◣ BOAT ACCESS
■ RESORT
— PAVED ROAD
- - - GRAVEL ROAD
·········· HIKING TRAIL
T TROLLING
S STILL FISHING

though not many people try, with worms and salmon eggs on small hooks and light line. Savage strikes are likely in spring on orange Rooster Tails cast to fish cruising the receding ice. Bait is good as soon as the water is open and throughout the year. Trolling gives more action and shows lures to more fish that get a little lazy in the summer months. There is terrific, uncrowded fall fishing September through mid-November. The limit is 5 fish per day, including steelhead, minimum 8 inches.

Boat ramps are available at Doe Point and Fish Lake campgrounds. Between the two campgrounds, there are 41 tent/trailer sites. Restrooms with flush toilets, ADA accessible sites, and fish cleaning stations are among the amenities. Fish Lake Resort offers an RV park with full hookups and lake views. The resort also offers ten cabins, boat rentals and a lodge (currently being updated) with restaurant and store. Check out the resort's photo albums full of proud anglers displaying their catches.

From Klamath Falls, drive 37 miles west on Highway 140 and watch for the Fish Lake sign.

From Medford, travel 30 miles east on State Highway 140. Fish Lake is on the south side of the highway

ABOVE: The lake is stocked annually with legal-size rainbows, with larger holdovers. Trolling can often be productive. Photo by Gary Lewis

RIGHT: A big rainbow gets a lot of attention from youngsters. Photo courtesy Fish Lake Resort

BELOW: Boat ramps and docks are available at this popular trolling lake. Photo by Geoff Hill

FOURMILE LAKE

Size: 763 acres
Depth: 75´ average; 155´ max.
Main Catch: kokanee, brown,
brook & rainbow trout
Best Methods: troll, still-fish, fly fishing
Season: late April-Oct. 31
Best Time: August
Tips: primarily boat fishing lake

Scenically located at the base of Mt. McLoughlin, Fourmile Lake is a large, deep, cold trout lake with nice camping and good access to many nearby hike-in lakes. At 5,744´ elevation on the crest of the Cascades, the lake is exposed to rapidly changing weather and can often whip into white caps in a hurry.

A natural lake artificially enlarged with a dam in 1922, the lake features submerged trees that provide good fish habitat but significant boating hazards. The lake is not four miles long as the name suggests (closer to 3 miles) but that doesn't diminish its popularity. The campgrounds are full most summer weekends.

Fourmile is primarily a boat fishing lake. The shorelines and shallows are littered with dead standing and fallen timber, making shore fishing difficult. Most anglers fish from boats along the edges of the submerged forests. It's kind of similar to Crane Prairie, except when boaters tie off to a tree, they may be in 50 or 60 feet of water. Effective trolling rigs for trout and kokanee consist of flashers; Wedding Ring spinners tipped with corn fished 20-40 feet deep. The best trolling area is off the trees along the north shoreline. Panther Martin and Rooster Tail spinners are also good trolling lures, and even better when cast to rising fish in and around the trees.

Fly fishers troll leech and crawdad pattern wet flies when nothing is rising, and switch to ants, dragonflies and damselflies when those hatches come off. The best still-fishing hole is on the southwest shore opposite the Swan Creek inlet. Here, anglers tie to trees and offer worms, salmon eggs and Power Bait close to the bottom. Anglers should be prepared with extra tackle, as snagging and losing equipment on the trees is likely. Four-pound test leaders are the norm in this very clear water.

Fourmile hosts an overabundance of small kokanee averaging 6-10 inches. The kokanee limit is 25. Ten- to 19-inch naturally reproducing brook trout are available in good numbers. Ten thousand rainbow trout are stocked annually. They run 10-22 inches. Browns average 10-14 inches, with larger specimens likely an experimental hybrid, unable to spawn, hopefully expending their energy eating the abundant kokanee.

Trout limits are 5 per day, 1 over 20 inches. ODFW is considering planting lake trout to control the kokanee and provide more variety for anglers. Motors are allowed. There is no boat speed limit though caution is advised with numerous deadheads.

Thirty developed campsites with hand pumps for water, handicap accessible vault toilets, gravel boat ramp and day use area are available on a first-come, first-serve basis on the lake's south end.

Other activities include climbing 9,495´ Mt. McLoughlin, a strenuous but rewarding 7-hour round trip, horseback riding, wildflower and wildlife watching.

From Medford travel 37 miles east on State Highway 140, then north 11 miles on Forest Service Road 3650 to Fourmile Lake. From Klamath Falls travel 37 miles west on State Highway 140, then 11 miles north on Forest Service Road 3650.

BELOW: Located at the base of Mt. McLoughlin, large, deep Fourmile Lake is primarily a boat fishing lake.
Photo by Brooke Snavely

HYATT LAKE

Size: 950 acres
Depth: 40 feet
Main Catch: rainbow trout, largemouth bass
Best Method: fly and bait
Season: check OSFR
Best Time: spring, fall
Tips: Use frog pattern lures and flies in spring.

Hyatt Lake is a big irrigation reservoir set in a flooded meadow in the mountains west of Klamath Falls. On a clear day, you'll enjoy views of the snow-capped peak of Mt McLoughlin. Fir trees and oaks timber the slopes to the east and west. Blacktail deer, Rocky Mountain elk, and black bear are glimpsed from time to time on the slopes above the lake. Take a hike away from the water and you'll see silver-gray squirrels, forest grouse and, possibly, a wild turkey.

But big fish are the main draw at Hyatt Lake. The shallow reservoir grows lots of insects and the rainbow trout and largemouth bass, grow fat feeding on them. The trout run from 14 to 20 inches, with a few caught every year that tip the scales to eight pounds. In 2003, a 13-pound largemouth was caught and released.

Access is easy and good bank fishing can be found at Hyatt Lake Resort and at several other places around the lake. Roads follow the shoreline all the way around.

Most anglers bring a boat or rent one at the resort. The trout and hatchery steelhead grow fast in this nutrient-rich water. Some of the biggest fish are caught by flyfishermen. Streamer and chironomids account for a lot of the fish.

Still-fishing is very productive. Use rainbow and chartreuse Power Bait in the spring. In the fall, pink, red, and jar baits are productive. Use a sliding sinker and 28 inches of leader. Rig the bait on a No. 14 or 16 treble hook. Cast, let the bait sink to the bottom. Leave your bail open and let the fish take the bait.

Trollers also do well at Hyatt Lake and account for many of the fish that are taken every season. A few big fish fall to the trollers, but the majority of the catch turn out to be the smaller size trout. In the spring, use lures with frog patterns. Hot Shots, FlatFish, Triple Teazers are good bets. With summer comes the algae bloom and most anglers drop anchor and soak baits to avoid pulling in all the green.

For bass, fish the perimeter of the lake. Target standing timber and flooded willows. The cove by Willow campground is one good spot for largemouth. Use a nightcrawler threaded on a wide-gap bass hook and fish it with no weight, casting toward the shallows. Plastic worms and weedless spinner baits are productive on this lake.

Boats can be launched at the Hyatt Lake Resort, for a small fee and also at the campground on the south end of the lake. There is a 10-mph speed limit.

Four campgrounds serve anglers at Hyatt Lake. Friendly advice and services are available at Campers Cove Resort and Hyatt Lake Resort.

To find Hyatt Lake, head west from Klamath Falls on the Green Springs Highway (Highway 66). About five miles past the town of Lincoln, turn right on Hyatt Prairie Road.

Alternatively, take Highway 140 west from Klamath Falls. Turn south on Dead Indian Memorial Road and then take a left on Hyatt Prairie Road and follow the signs to the lake.

TOP: Snags protrude from the north end of Hyatt Lake. Photo by Geoff Hill

CENTER: On a clear day, Mt. McLoughlin is visible from the reservoir. Photo by Gary Lewis

BOTTOM: Hyatt lake viewed through lakeside pines. Photo by Geoff Hill

HOWARD PRAIRIE LAKE

Size: 2,070 acres
Depth: 80´
Main Catch: rainbow trout, largemouth bass, catfish
Best Methods: trolling, bait & fly fishing
Season: late April-Oct. 31
Best Time: spring, fall
Tips: Fish near islands and rocky points.

For limits of rainbow trout and lunker largemouth, head to Howard Prairie Lake. This is Southwest Oregon's most popular fishery, for good reason. The lake is loaded with fish. Fishing is good here when it stinks everywhere else. And when fishing is good elsewhere, it's even better here. Limits are common. Add to that a beautiful location and excellent boating, camping and picnicking facilities and its obvious why Howard Prairie attracts more than one quarter million visitors annually.

An outstanding fishery since it was constructed as an irrigation reservoir in 1958, ODFW experimented with stocking rates for years, trying to produce a balance of quantity and quality size trout. They appear to have it dialed, stocking 350,000–400,000 3-inch fingerlings in May. By the following spring, the planters average 11-13 inches. Carryovers regularly stretch 15-22 inches. Bigger trout are possible. Abundant aquatic insect and minnow populations supply the food and give anglers plenty of things to imitate. The lake's three islands, varied shape and depth provide all kinds of fishing opportunities based on season and water levels.

Trout fishing is usually very good opening day (last Saturday in April) through midsummer, then again in the fall. The most popular techniques are trolling and still fishing with bait. Early and late in the season when the water is cold and fish are shallow, troll brass Needlefish or Triple Teazers on 4-pound test along the shorelines for quick limits. Add a piece of worm or corn to stimulate the bite. For larger trout, try small silver and gold Rapalas and dark colored F4 FlatFish to imitate the baitfish bigger trout feed on. As the water warms, add weight, flashers or use deeper diving lures to stay in touch with fish in the cooler depths. The most consistent trolling areas are the east and west shorelines south of Howard Prairie Resort toward the dam. Use a depth finder to find the old Beaver Creek channel that runs along the whole east side of the lake.

Still fishers do well with chartreuse and rainbow colored Power Bait, inflated worms, salmon eggs and marshmallows suspended 24 inches off the bottom on size 14 treble hooks. Red Rock Cove, Buck Island, the jetty at the resort and Doe and Fawn islands are perennial bait dunking hotspots. Start the

ABOVE: Howard Prairie Lake has been an outstanding fishery since it was constructed in 1958. Photo by Geoff Hill

RIGHT: A nice catch. Photo by Gary Lewis

HOWARD PRAIRIE LAKE
Elevation 4,526´

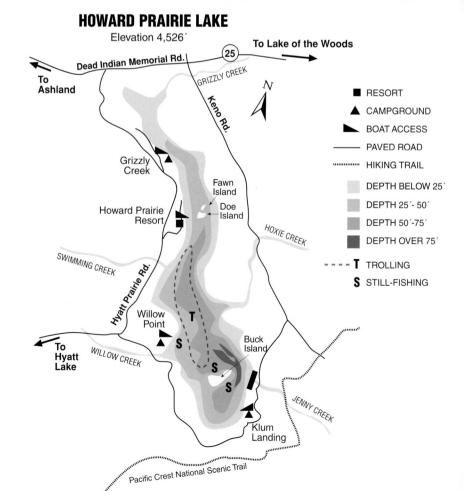

Legend:
- ■ RESORT
- ▲ CAMPGROUND
- ◄ BOAT ACCESS
- —— PAVED ROAD
- ·········· HIKING TRAIL
- DEPTH BELOW 25´
- DEPTH 25´- 50´
- DEPTH 50´-75´
- DEPTH OVER 75´
- - - - T TROLLING
- S STILL-FISHING

season in 15 feet of water, going deeper as conditions dictate.

Fly fishers do fine trolling and casting streamers, such as the Brown Bailey, towards shore and weed lines. Other popular patterns are the Brown Woolly Bugger and Pheasant Tail Nymph. Coves around the lake and the narrows up to Lily Glen are popular float tube areas.

Trout fishing slows in the heat of summer, because the fish have so much to eat, but is still worth the effort. Brown bullhead catfish feed in the shallows. Worms and chicken gizzards are popular baits.

Howard Prairie has a thriving warmwater population that includes both largemouth and smallmouth bass. For largemouth, fish the perimeter of the lake and concentrate on rocky points, standing timber, flooded willows and weedy shallows. In the spring, brown and purple plastic worms are effective. Later, crankbaits and spinnerbaits are productive lures. In morning and evening, fish topwater plugs for surface action.

Limits are five trout per day, only one over 20 inches. For bass, anglers are allowed five per day, no more than three over 15 inches. No limit on catfish. Always check OSFR.

Three Jackson County operated camp-

grounds (Klum Landing, Grizzly Creek and Willow Point) offer paved boat ramps, restrooms, picnicking and camping. Howard Prairie Resort on the west shore has boat rentals, moorage and stowage, cabins, RV

hook ups, 300 campsites, fishing supplies and advice. (For more information, see www.howardprairieresort.com) All facilities charge entry fees. Other activities include sailing, swimming, arrowhead hunting, bird and wildlife watching.

Take Highway 140 west from Klamath Falls. At Keno, turn on Clover Creek Road, then head west on Dead Indian Memorial Road. Take a left on Hyatt Prairie Road and follow the signs to the lake.

Alternatively, head west from Klamath Falls on the Green Springs Highway (Highway 66). About five miles past the town of Lincoln, turn right on Hyatt Prairie Road and follow the signs to Howard Prairie Lake.

TOP: Boat rentals, moorage, and paved boat ramps are available at the Howard Prairie Marina. Photo by Gary Lewis

LEFT: The large expanse of Howard Prairie is seen in this shot; Mt. McLoughlin rises in the background. Photo by Gary Lewis

INSET: Fishing is good all season. Photo by Brooke Snavely

KLAMATH RIVER

Length: 40 miles (in Oregon)
Depth: varies by stretch
Main Catch: rainbow trout, bass
Best Method: flies, lures, bait
Season: regulations are complex; check OSFR
Best Time: spring, fall

Only 18 of the Klamath River's 40 miles in Oregon are free flowing trout water. Dams back up the other 22 miles for power generation, irrigation and industrial uses. Most angling effort is focused on the free flowing sections, which are productive rainbow trout waters. Bass fishing is poor due to poor water quality.

The first mile of the river flowing out of Upper Klamath Lake into Lake Ewauna is known as the Link River, because it links the two lakes. A pretty little canyon just minutes west of downtown Klamath Falls, the Link River has resident rainbow averaging 10-16 inches and migratory trout to 5 lbs. Bait is best in spring, with lure and fly action in summer and fall. Access is via the Link River Trail from Lakeshore Boulevard to the north and Favell Museum on Main Street to the south. Veterans Park in downtown Klamath Falls offers good bank access and paved boat ramp at the upper end of Lake Ewauna. Fishing on the Link River and Lake Ewauna is open the entire year. Limits are 1 trout and 5 bass per day.

Lake Ewauna extends 16 miles downstream before Keno dam releases the highly productive 6-mile-long "Keno reach" which flows into J.C. Boyle Reservoir. This is deep pocket water flowing through a steep canyon. Off color water and irregular streambed make wading treacherous. Try boulder hopping instead. Weighted Woolly Buggers, Leeches, Zonker and minnow pattern streamers are best presented on sink tip lines. Heavier Rooster Tail spinners and sinking Rapalas are effective lures. No bait is

CLOCKWISE FROM TOP:
A peek at the river from Highway 66 with a zoom lens. Photo by Geoff Hill

Todd Ostenson with an 18-inch rainbow. Photo courtesy Trophy Waters Flyfishing Shop

Brian O'Keefe with a dandy rainbow. Brian O'Keefe photo

allowed. Trout average 13-17 inches in this stretch, with many over 20 inches. Access is from Highway 66. Park on the highway shoulder and hike down, or walk downstream from the Keno dam recreation area. This stretch is not boatable. The Keno reach is open Jan. 1-June 15 and Oct. 1-Dec 31. Warm water temperature and high fish mortality rates prompt the summer closure. Limit is 1 fish.

The Klamath runs cooler, clearer but shallower below J.C. Boyle Reservoir to the powerhouse. This 5-mile stretch is better dry fly water for trout averaging 8-12 inches. The Klamath River road provides good access throughout this reach. Make sure to take the lower of the two roads, otherwise access is cut off by a sluice carrying water to the Boyle powerhouse. Fishing from Boyle Dam to the California border is allowed the entire year. Tackle is restricted to artificial flies and lures. Limit is 1 fish. Catch-and-release is required June 16 to Sept. 30.

Below the generating station, the Klamath regains its size, as do the fish, averaging 12-15 inches. There are also more of them, making this the best quantity and quality stretch. Flows in the lower 9 miles fluctuate according to power demands. Call 1-800-547-1501 for flow reports. Fishing is best at low flows, usually morning and evening. But the fish are accustomed to changing water levels and usually resume feeding after flows stabilize. Try stoneflies in spring, caddisflies summer and fall and spinners throughout the season. Access to this area is by the Klamath River Road past the powerhouse. The road gets very rough beyond the whitewater boat launch.

Pacific Power & Light operates a comfortable campground with showers at Keno Recreation Area near Keno. BLM offers the Topsy Campground at J.C. Boyle Reservoir, a boat launch below the powerhouse and two primitive riverside camps on either side of the Oregon-California border.

Keno is located 12 miles west of Klamath Falls on State Highway 66; 45 miles east of Ashland on State Highway 66; 153 miles south of Bend on U.S. Highway 97 & State Highway 66.

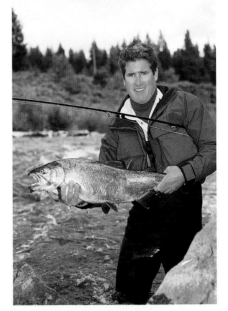

CLOCKWISE (from top):
Brian with a huge 11-pound native
Klamath River rainbow.
Brian O'Keefe photo
The Keno Dam, Klamath River.
The Keno reach of the Klamath River.
Photos by Brooke Snavely

Western Cascades Drainage

Many fine fishing opportunities exist along the highways crossing the Cascades.
The next several pages cover popular waters along highways 22, 20, 126, and 58.

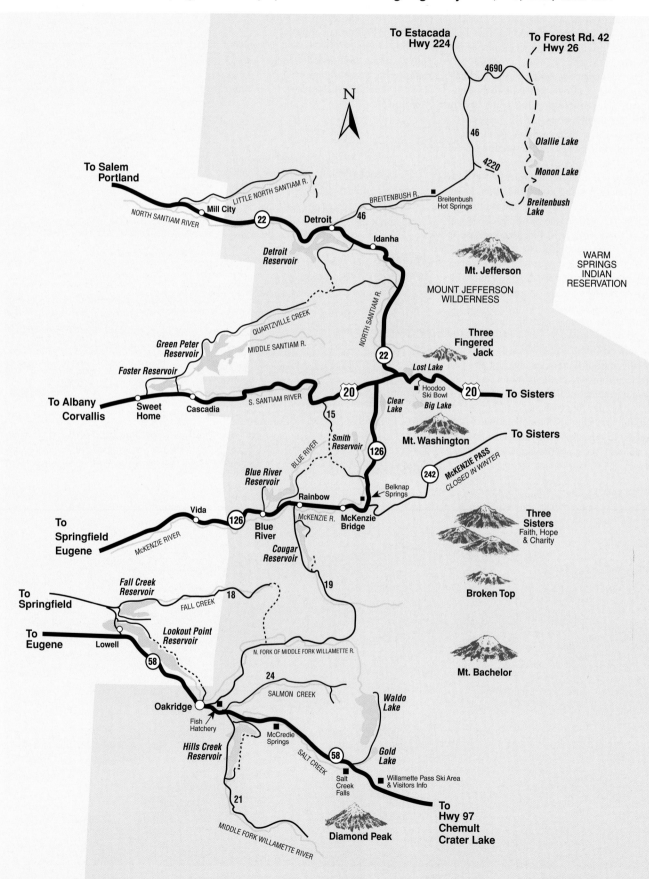

BREITENBUSH & OLALLIE LAKES

Breitenbush
Size: 60 acres
Depth: 30´
Main Catch: rainbow, brook trout
Best Methods: trolling flies, bait, lures
Season: entire year; check OSFR
Tips: fish feed on emerging insects mornings & evenings.

Olallie
Size: 240 acres
Depth: 48´
Main Catch: rainbow trout
Best Methods: flies, bait, lures
Season: entire year; check OSFR
Best Time: June-July
Tips: troll along the shoreline.

Breitenbush and Olallie are two of the largest lakes in the beautiful Olallie Lakes Scenic Area north of Mt. Jefferson. Of the two, Olallie is more developed and accessible, featuring a resort and four Forest Service fee campgrounds with very good fishing for planted trout. Breitenbush's remote setting lends itself to solitary camping and fishing for small wild brook and occasionally planted rainbow trout.

Olallie is stocked annually with about 15,000 legal-size rainbows and several hundred 4- to 10-pound brooders (640 in 1998), resulting in easy limits and an occasional whale before they are fished out or wise up. Power Bait and worms still fished from shore and boats catch lots of fish. Trolling along the shorelines from rowboats, rafts and float tubes with Spruce flies on a 2-lb. test leader can be very productive as the hatchery fish learn to

eat organic or starve. Casting or trolling Rooster Tails or Frog FlatFish work well, as does trolling worms behind Ford Fenders. No gas or electric motors are allowed. No swimming is permitted to protect the lake, which is a source of drinking water. Swimming is allowed in several nearby lakes.

Breitenbush Lake is four miles south over the rough Forest Service Road 4220 past Monon, Horseshoe, and Gibson lakes, all good camping and fishing spots.

Breitenbush has nice weed lines and shoal areas where fish feed on emerging insects mornings and evenings. In bright sunshine it may be necessary to fish deep with bait, lures and wet flies in the main body of the lake. Canoes, kayaks and float tubes allow anglers to keep up with cruising fish. A no-fee campground with picnic tables and a gravel boat

launch are the only amenities. Five fish limits, 1 over 20 inches, are in effect on all lakes in the Olallie Scenic Area.

Breitenbush Lake is in the McQuinn strip, a boundary area along the Warm Springs Indian Reservation. Any hiking or fishing expeditions to the east require a Warm Springs Tribal permit.

From Bend, Salem and Eugene go through Detroit, then north 24 miles on Forest Highway 46; east 7 miles on FS Road 4690; south 8 miles on 4220 to Olallie Lake. Turn off FS 46 at milepost 18 to reach Breitenbush Lake 8 miles up FS 4220.

From Portland take U.S. Highway 26 to FS Road 42, about 9 miles east of Government Camp. Ollalie is about 32 miles south on FS roads 42 and 4220. Breitenbush is 4 miles south on 4220.

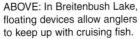

ABOVE: In Breitenbush Lake, floating devices allow anglers to keep up with cruising fish.

LEFT: A variety of methods from bank fishing to trolling work for anglers at Olallie Lake.

BELOW: Denise Martin (left) is happy with her 5-pound Olallie rainbow. Lynn Killon (right) shows off her 7-pound rainbow.
Photos by Brook Snavely

NORTH SANTIAM RIVER

Size: 60 miles in length
Depth: shallow above Detroit Reservoir; deeper below the dam
Main Catch: trout, steelhead, salmon
Best Methods: above reservoir: wade & bank fishing with flies, bait, & lures; below dam: boat & bank fishing
Season: check current OSFR
Best Time: winter steelhead: March–May; summer steelhead: April–Dec.; spring chinook: May–July
Tips: multiple recreational use area; many parks

The North Santiam River is the slightly larger of the north and south forks of the Santiam River, both very productive trout, steelhead and salmon streams. The North Santiam begins its journey high in the Cascade mountains at Santiam Lake in the Mount Jefferson Wilderness Area and runs for 60 miles to its confluence with the South Santiam near the town of Jefferson.

Above Detroit Reservoir, the crystalline, green-blue water of the North Santiam forms a wild rocky and shallow little river, with a steep gradient and water levels which fluctuate with the seasons. Below Cliff Dam, levels are fairly stable year-round; the river calms down a bit and is now nearly opaque and light green in color as a result of fine clay from the reservoir. This is a popular drift, although there are some nasty rapids. Boat ramps are available, starting 5 miles below the dam.

Salmon and steelhead are present in the river below Big Cliff Dam. Winter steelhead fishing is at its peak from March through May, summer steelhead are in the river from April through December, and spring chinook from May through July. Many fly fishers successfully fish for steelhead on the North Santiam, as do bait and lure anglers. Plugs, spinners and spoons, bobbers and jigs, and drift fishing with corkies and bait are all successfully used methods. Most of the

spring chinook fishing occurs between Stayton and Mill City. For salmon, most folks use bait, Kwikfish wrapped with a sardine, bobbers and bait, or floats and plugs. The best trout fishing is above Detroit Reservoir, especially with flies, although spinners, worms, and Power Bait are also effective. Trout in the North Santiam run up to 13 inches, steelhead 5 to 18 pounds with a few larger, and chinook 8 to 35 pounds.

For steelhead, the North Santiam is best fished from a boat. In January, fish the Stayton to Jefferson drift. Later in the run, try Mehama to Stayton and Packsaddle to Fisherman's Bend park. For bank access, try the Jefferson Boat Ramp, Green's Bridge, Stayton Bridge (north side of river), John Neal County Park, North Santiam State Park, and Fisherman's Bend.

Concentrate on fishing classic steelhead water between two and six feet deep that moves at the speed of a fast walk. Pay particular attention to soft inside seams and slow tailouts over pebble beds. Make sure you have felt on the bottoms of your wading boots. Winter wading on this river's smooth boulders can be tricky.

Pay attention to the fish counts over Willamette Falls (www.dfw.state.or.us), and focus on the lower river until mid-March. When large numbers of fish go over Willamette Falls, plan to meet them on the

The water below Detroit Reservoir (below) is distinctly different than the river water above the dam (left). Top photo by Raven Wing; Bottom photo by Geoff Hill

river 10 to 15 days later.

Wade and bank fishing is the rule above the reservoir. Boat and bank anglers have access to the river at the many parks below Big Cliff Dam. Various government agencies offer campgrounds along the North Santiam. Beginning farthest upstream and ending a few miles below Mill City they are: Marion Forks, Riverside, Whispering Falls, campgrounds on Detroit Reservoir (South Shore, Hoover, and Detroit Lake State Park), Niagra, Minto Park, Fisherman's Bend, and North Santiam. Several day-use areas with picnic sites and boat ramps are located below the reservoir.

Hiking, boating, and water sports on the reservoir, picnicking, drift trips, and, in the winter, snowmobiling and skiing round out the recreational opportunities along the North Santiam River.

State Highway 22 follows the North

Santiam from Stayton to within 8 miles of its headwaters. West of Stayton, a maze of county roads access the river at the Stayton-Scio Bridge, Hess Road, and the Jefferson-Scio Bridge.

From Salem take Highway 22 east to meet the North Santiam at Stayton. From Bend and Sisters, take U.S. Highway 20 west to the junction with Highway 22 at Santiam Junction. Highway 22 first crosses the river about 7 miles from Santiam Junction.

TOP: A spin fisherman displays a powerful steelhead from the North Santiam.
Photo by Brian O'Keefe

BELOW: Deep pools and rapids are characteristic of the North Santiam above Detroit. Photo by Geoff Hill

DETROIT LAKE

Size: 3,000 acres
Depth: varies according to downstream water & power needs
Main Catch: rainbow trout, kokanee, land-locked chinook salmon
Best Methods: still-fishing with bait, trolling
Season: entire year; check OSFR
Best Time: April–May for rainbow; fall for kokanee
Tips: most heavily stocked body of water in Oregon

Detroit Reservoir is the most heavily stocked body of water in Oregon. Sixty-five-thousand rainbow trout, kokanee, and land-locked chinook salmon are planted every year. Detroit offers year-round fishing, in addition to camping, waterskiing, sailing, picnicking, hiking, and mountain biking. At full pool, Detroit Reservoir covers over 3,000 acres. The reservoir's water level drops from Memorial Day in May on, but is most rapid from Labor Day in September through December. Boaters, beware of stumps at low water, and Piety Island becomes a peninsula.

Not much fishing is done here by wading; the shorelines are fairly steep. Fishing from shore is best in the Santiam, Breitenbush, and French Creek arms. Channels formed by the North Santiam and Breitenbush rivers come together on the south side of Piety Island to form the main Santiam channel. Winds can get very gusty in the afternoons; most boaters move to the arms to avoid whitecaps.

Rainbow trout here average 10 to 12 inches, and kokanee up to 14 inches. Chinook average 9 to 16 inches. Brown bullhead are also available in good numbers, mainly in the shallows near Detroit. Anglers may keep 5 trout per day over 8 inches, only 1 trout per day over 20 inches. From August 16 until October 31, trout 24 inches and longer must be released.

Most anglers still-fish with bait from boats or troll hardware. Fishing for rainbow is best

ABOVE: Piety Island is located at the eastern end of Detroit Reservoir and can become a peninsula at low water times in the fall.

BELOW: A roadside pull-off allows this view of Detroit Lake and Mount Jefferson.

Photos by Geoff Hill

Detroit Lake from near the dam.
Photo by Geoff Hill

in April and May, as is chinook fishing. Kokanee fishing begins around September 1. Anglers should try around Piety Island and in the Hoover Arm for trout. These hatchery trout will take about anything. A common trolling rig is flashers with a rubber snubber, followed by a wedding ring and half-worm and kernel of corn. Kokanee are caught on the same set-up, at the mouth of Blowout Arm and in the Santiam Arm. Many folks also still-fish for trout with a half-worm and a pinch of Power Bait. The chinook are mainly in deeper water on the highway side of the

reservoir. Catching the salmon will require a downrigger with flashers and a size 7 to 9 sinking Rapala. Check the current OSFR for season and catch limits.

Boat ramps are located at Mongold State Park (day-use only), Detroit Lake State Park, Kane's Marina, and Hoover and Southshore campgrounds. Campsites are available at Detroit Lake State Park, Upper Arm Campground, Hoover Campground, South Shore Campground, and on Piety Island. Additional accommodations are available at resorts on the lake and in the town of Detroit.

Detroit Reservoir is easily accessible from both the west and east from State Highway 22 which runs the length of its northern shore. Highway 22 extends from the Oregon coast highway (U.S. 101) and east to Salem, Detroit Reservoir, up along the North Santiam River, ending at its junction with U.S Highway 20 at Santiam Junction on the crest of the Cascade mountains.

From Bend and Sisters, take U.S. Highway 20 west to Santiam Junction then State Highway 22, continuing west to Detroit Reservoir.

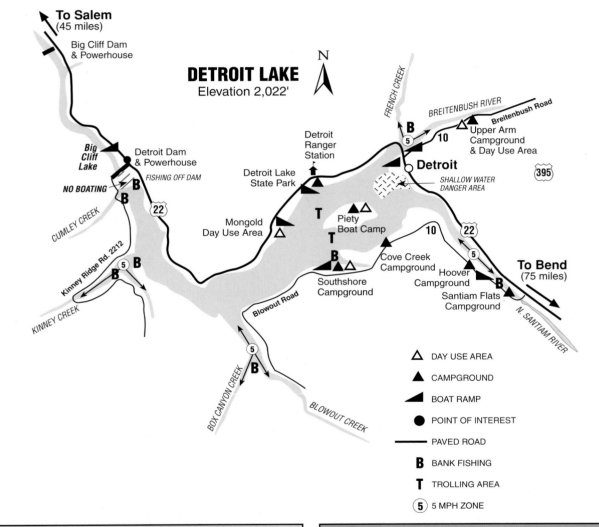

SOUTH SANTIAM RIVER

Size: 80 miles
Depth: seasonal fluctuations
Main Catch: summer steelhead, spring chinook
Best Methods: shore fishing with flies, bait & lures; drift fishing
Season: check current OSFR
Best Time: summer steelhead: April–Dec.; spring chinook: May–July
Tips: best trout fishing above Foster Dam

The South Santiam River begins high in the Willamette National Forest and flows about 80 miles to its confluence with the North Santiam near Jefferson. The South Santiam is the smaller of the north and south forks of the Santiam but is an equally productive stream for summer steelhead and spring chinook. Rushing through mixed conifer forests and dotted with forest service campgrounds in its upper stretches, the river's lower miles flow slowly through heavily populated areas.

Above Foster Dam, the South Santiam is a wild stream with associated seasonal fluctuations in water levels. It is lower and warmer than the North Santiam in mid-summer. Below the dam, water levels are stable from May to August. To Foster Dam, the South Fork is open to fishing for fin-clipped steelhead the entire year. From January 1 until August 15 and from November 1 until December 31, anglers may fish for fin-clipped chinook salmon. The use of bait is allowed. Check OSFR for details.

Fly fishers successfully fish for steelhead on the South Santiam, as do bait and lure anglers, although bait may soon be forbidden. Plugs, spinner and spoons, bobbers and jigs and drift fishing with corkies are all successfully used methods. Most steelhead angling takes place between Sweet Home and Foster Dam. Spring chinook fishing occurs below Foster Dam. Salmon anglers may soon be without their favorite methods: Kwikfish wrapped with sardines and bobbers and bait. Float fishing with unbaited jigs and casting plugs should continue to be legal. Trout fishing opportunities and techniques above Foster Dam are liable to change to catch and release with flies and lures to protect steelhead and salmon smolts, easily mistaken as trout. The south Santiam below Foster Reservoir is popular water for both driftboats and jet sleds. Boat ramps available at Wiley Creek Park, Sweet Home, Sanderson's Bridge, McDowell Creek and Lebanon Dam.

Campgrounds available on the South Santiam, beginning farthest upstream, include House Rock, Fernview, Yukwah, Trout Creek, Longbow, Cascadia State Park, those on Foster Reservoir, and at Gedney County Park.

U.S. Highway 20 follows the river closely from the confluence of the creeks that form the South Santiam, near House Rock Campground downstream to Foster Reservoir. Below Foster Reservoir, a tangle of county roads access the river in several spots, while the rest of the river is bordered by private property. Boat ramps are available at Foster Dam, Sweet Home, Gedney County Park, and Lebanon. U.S. Highway 20 is a slow, winding, two-lane mountain pass, not for those in a hurry. Many pullouts along the river and the wealth of campgrounds make access to the river easy.

From Albany, take U.S. Highway 20 east to Lebanon Park on the North Santiam. From Bend and Sisters, take U.S. Highway 20 west over Santiam Pass to the South Santiam just below House Rock Campground.

The South Santiam flows past Cascadia. Photo by Raven Wing

GREEN PETER RESERVOIR

Size: 3,720 acres; 10 mi. long
Depth: max. depth 327´
Main Catch: kokanee. rainbow trout
Best Methods: trolling flashers
Season: check current OSFR
Best Time: spring & early summer

Green Peter Reservoir is a flood control facility on the Middle Santiam River, just a few miles east of the town of Sweet Home. It is 10 miles long, covers 3,720 acres at full pool, and is 327 feet deep at the dam. Highest water levels occur in May and the lowest in December. The banks are heavily forested and fairly steep. The majority of angling here is for a self-sustaining population of kokanee, up to 12 inches in length. Most fishers troll flashers, such as Ford Fenders, while some use Buzz-Bombs or Nordic jigs from the bank on the southeast side of the dam or from the bridge on the Whitcomb Arm.

ODFW plants a few rainbow trout every April, and occasionally a native cutthroat or rainbow will be caught. Largemouth and smallmouth bass have been illegally introduced, and these might also turn up in the creel. Spring and early summer are the best times to fish for kokanee, and early spring for the stocked rainbow. Check the current Oregon Sport Fishing Regulations before fishing. Green Peter is also a popular water-skiing and jetskiing area.

Access to the reservoir is from a paved road that runs along the north side of the reservoir. Improved boat ramps are available at Thistle Creek Park and Whitcomb Creek Park, and small boats can be launched at a make-shift ramp on the southeast side of the dam. Thistle Creek Park is a day-use area with restrooms and a boat launch; Whitcomb Creek Park offers overnight camping, charges a fee, and has restrooms, drinking water, a picnic area and beach/swimming area, a boat launch, tent sites, and RV sites without hookups. Both are operated by Linn County Parks.

To get to Green Peter Reservoir, take the turn off U.S. Highway 20 toward Green Peter Reservoir, about 6 miles east of downtown Sweet Home. The dam is reached in 5 miles. Continue another 4.5 miles to Thistle Creek and an additional mile to Whitcomb Creek.

From the dam, Green Peter Reservoir stretches for 10 miles. Photo by Raven Wing

FOSTER RESERVOIR

Size: 1,220 acres
Depth: max. depth 126´
Main Catch: rainbow trout, kokanee
Best Methods: trolling lures. bank fishing along north shore
Season: check current OSFR
Best Time: April–June; October

Foster Reservoir lies directly below Green Peter Reservoir, covers 1,220 acres when full, and has a maximum depth of 126 feet. Its teal-blue water is surrounded by heavily forested banks, but they are less steep than at Green Peter, and bank fishing opportunities are much better. Foster is stocked heavily with rainbow trout; most caught will be 10 to 13 inches in length. Only kokanee and adipose fin-clipped trout may be taken. There is no limit on size or number of bass. Most rainbow are caught by trolling lures. Bank fishing opportunities are greatest along the north shore. Fishing is best from April through June and then again in October — check the current Oregon Sport Fishing Regulations for season and catch limits. Water levels at the reservoir are fairly stable, and this is a popular water-skiing and jet-skiing destination.

Several county recreation sites are located on Foster Reservoir: Shea Point, along U.S. Highway 20, is a rest stop and viewpoint; and Gedney Creek Park (boat launch) and Lewis Creek Park are both day-use areas located on

the north shore. Sunnyside Park, which offers a boat launch, camp sites with electricity, and RV sites with and without hookups, is located on the Middle Santiam Arm below Green Peter Dam.

Foster Reservoir lies along U.S. Highway 20 just east of the town of Sweet Home. Sunnyside Park is accessed from U.S. Highway 20 by taking the turn to Green Peter Reservoir. The north shore and Lewis Creek Park and Gedney Creek Park can then be reached by a left-hand turn past Sunnyside Park, or by continuing toward Sweet Home on Highway 20 and taking the turn to cross Foster Dam to the north shore.

RIGHT: Directly below Green Peter, Foster Reservoir is surrounded by heavily forested banks.
Photo by Raven Wing

McKENZIE RIVER

Size: 89 miles
Depth: varies
Main Catch: rainbow, bull & cutthroat trout
Best Methods: bait, lures, & fly fishing; drifting
Season: check OSFR
Best Time: June & July
Tips: well-known for whitewater; lower 50 miles accessed mainly by boat

The McKenzie River is well-known for its whitewater and the McKenzie driftboat, developed specifically for its rapids. This is a river of many personalities, beginning as a tiny mountain creek, emerging from Clear Lake and ending 89 miles later as a large, slow river near its junction with the Willamette River. Bait, lures, and fly fishing are all used successfully to catch fish on the McKenzie. Anglers should check the current Oregon Sport Fishing Regulations; the regulations for this river are complex.

The uppermost McKenzie, from Clear Lake to Trailbridge Reservoir, is fished little and mainly holds small, wild brook, cutthroat, and bull trout. This stretch is most appreciated for its rushing water punctuated by waterfalls and complicated by lava flows. From Trailbridge down to Paradise Campground, the river holds decent-size native rainbow, bull trout, and cutthroat trout, but in this fast water, good holes are few and far between. The best fishing is in June and July. Rafters and kayaks can frequently be seen running this stretch.

The most heavily fished miles of the McKenzie are between Paradise Campground and Hayden Bridge in Springfield. Much of this is also premier drift water. It is heavily stocked with rainbow trout which average 12 to 16 inches, with occasional catches between 18 and 20 inches. The bigger fish are generally downstream. There are also good numbers of native rainbow, cutthroat, and bull trout. The bulk of the steelhead and salmon fishing occurs below Hayden Bridge.

The lower 50 miles of the river are accessed mainly by boat — bank access is limited by private land. There are dozens of

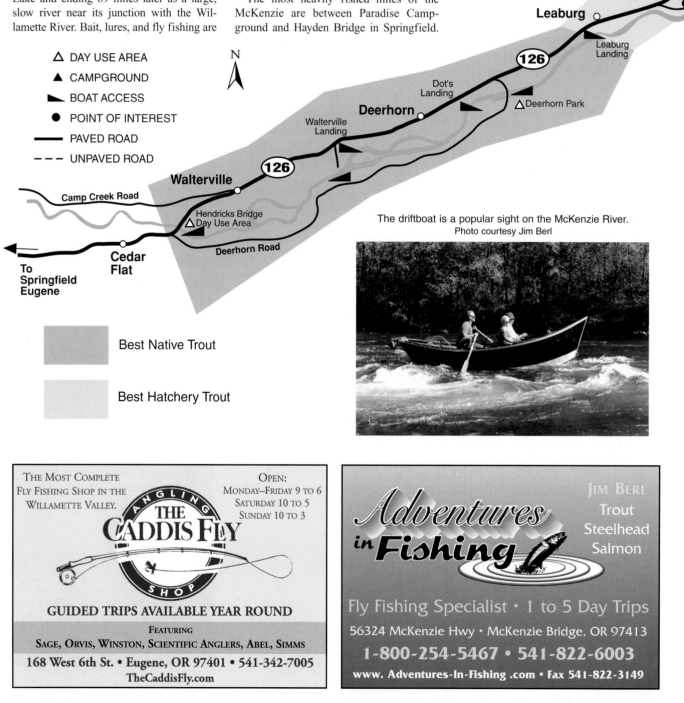

△ DAY USE AREA
▲ CAMPGROUND
◣ BOAT ACCESS
● POINT OF INTEREST
— PAVED ROAD
--- UNPAVED ROAD

N

Greenwood Landing
McKenzie Salmon Hatchery
Leaburg
Leaburg Landing
126
Dot's Landing
△ Deerhorn Park
Deerhorn
Walterville Landing
Walterville
126
Camp Creek Road
Hendricks Bridge
△ Day Use Area
Deerhorn Road
Cedar Flat
To Springfield Eugene

Best Native Trout

Best Hatchery Trout

The driftboat is a popular sight on the McKenzie River.
Photo courtesy Jim Berl

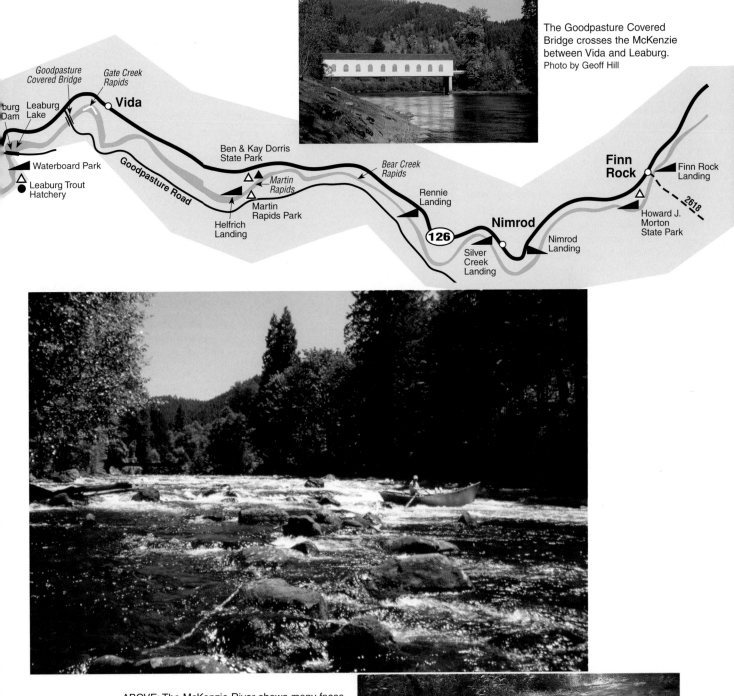

The Goodpasture Covered Bridge crosses the McKenzie between Vida and Leaburg. Photo by Geoff Hill

ABOVE: The McKenzie River shows many faces, starting as a small creek and ending as a wide, rambling river. Photo by carbonesflyfishing.com

RIGHT: There are numerous campgrounds along the McKenzie. Jim Berl, with trout in the pan, prepares dinner. Jim Berl photo

boat ramps on the McKenzie, the highest at Olallie Campground and the lowest at Armitage Park in Eugene. The most popular drift section is between Blue River and the Leaburg Dam. Notice to boaters: the Mc-Kenzie requires expert boating skills in several areas, and the 1996 flood created new obstacles near mile post 44, below Delta Campground and at Boulder Creek Rapids, .4 mile below the Frissel-Carpenter Bridge.

A variety of parks and waysides, but few camping opportunities, is available to visitors in the lower 50 miles of the river, although other accommodations are offered. Good Forest Service campgrounds are available from Blue River upstream, along with several small resorts.

Many hiking trails are within the National Forest, including the McKenzie River Trail. Winter offers skiing and snowmobiling. Farther downstream, civilization offers many pleasant distractions from fishing.

State Highway 126, the McKenzie Scenic Byway, follows the river from the town of Springfield upstream to its origin at Clear Lake 4 miles south of the junction of State Highway 126 with the South Santiam Highway, U.S. Highway 20. From Sweet Home or Sisters take U.S. Highway 20 to the junction with State Highway 126, 4 miles west of the Santiam Junction. The headwaters are 4 miles south on Highway 126. From Eugene/Springfield, follow State Highway 126 along the McKenzie for 89 miles to Clear Lake.

TOP: Anglers enjoy running the river and taking in the magnificent scenery, as well as the fishing.

LEFT: Summertime wading keeps fishers cool.
Brian O'Keefe photos

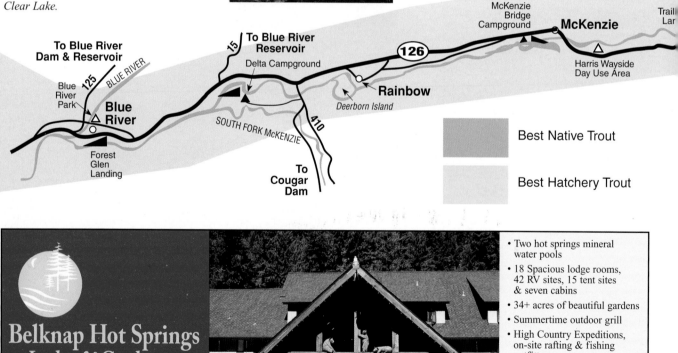

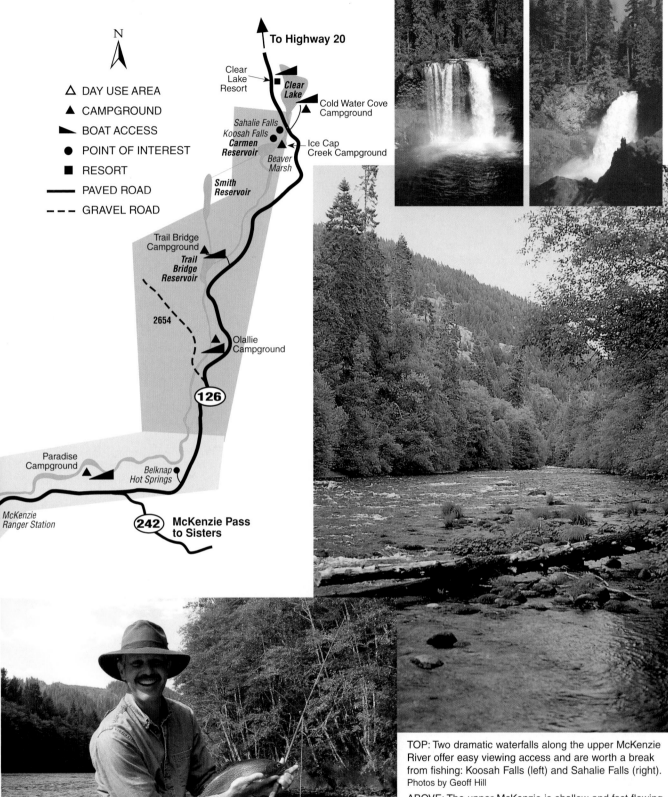

To Highway 20

△ DAY USE AREA
▲ CAMPGROUND
◣ BOAT ACCESS
● POINT OF INTEREST
■ RESORT
—— PAVED ROAD
--- GRAVEL ROAD

N

Clear Lake Resort
■ *Clear Lake*

Cold Water Cove Campground

Sahalie Falls
Koosah Falls
Carmen Reservoir

Beaver Marsh

Ice Cap Creek Campground

Smith Reservoir

Trail Bridge Campground
Trail Bridge Reservoir

2654

▲ Olallie Campground

126

Paradise Campground
▲

Belknap Hot Springs ●

McKenzie Ranger Station

242 **McKenzie Pass to Sisters**

TOP: Two dramatic waterfalls along the upper McKenzie River offer easy viewing access and are worth a break from fishing: Koosah Falls (left) and Sahalie Falls (right). Photos by Geoff Hill

ABOVE: The upper McKenzie is shallow and fast flowing near the Paradise Campground. Photo by Raven Wing

LEFT: A beautiful McKenzie rainbow! Photo by Jim Berl

LINTON LAKE

Size:	75 acres
Depth:	80 feet
Main Catch:	brown trout
Best Methods:	fly fishing, bait fishing
Season:	entire year
Best Time:	spring
Tips:	best fishing early in the season

Linton Lake is a good hike-in brown trout lake, hidden in a mountain valley, a mile south of the old McKenzie Pass Highway. With a reproducing population of brown trout and some brooks and rainbows available, this water is worth the walk.

A lava flow dammed Linton Creek to form this pretty lake. The trail leads through a forest of fern and firs. Rhododendrons, vine maples, and huckleberries grow in the openings between the taller timber. Look for pine golden-mantled squirrels and chipmunks along the way.

Expect Linton's brown trout to average 10 to 14 inches with a few tipping the scales near five pounds. Rainbows and brook trout average 8 to 12 inches.

Fish Linton from the shore or pack in a float tube or rubber raft. Bait fishing will produce fish throughout the season. Best bet is to rig up with a nightcrawler on a sliding sinker. Inject the nightcrawler with air or string a marshmallow on the line to lift the bait off the bottom. Then set your rod in a forked stick and leave the bail open. When the line starts moving, set the hook.

Since predatory browns are the main catch at Linton, small minnow-imitating Rapalas, Thomas spoons, and Rooster Tails are a good choice. Target transition areas where the shallows give way to deeper water and around the points of the lava islands. Also, try prospecting around the inlet of Linton Creek and the mouths of the other small streams feeding the lake.

For the fly fisherman, minnow imitations, and beadhead wet flies and are good bets. Use an intermediate slow-sinking line for the best results. In the summer and early fall, watch the shallows along the shoreline for trout rising to ants that have blown in the water.

Tiny Alder Springs Campground at the parking area has five tent sites, a day-use area and no hookups. Tables, grills and pit toilets are provided. Bring your own drinking water. If you'll be staying in the campground or tenting near the lake, keep your food strung in a tree at night to discourage the bears.

To find Linton Lake, drive 26 miles west from Sisters on the McKenzie Pass Highway. Past mile marker 66, you will see the parking area for the Alder Springs Campground. The trailhead is on the south side of the road. The lake is reached after a hike of just over a mile.

LEFT: A lava dam blocks Linton Lake at the lower end.

BELOW: Linton Creek empties into this good hike-in fishing lake hidden in a valley near the McKenzie Pass. Photos by Scott L. Staats

CLEAR LAKE
(Linn County)

Size: 148 acres
Depth: max. depth 175´
Main Catch: hatchery rainbow trout, cutthroat & brook trout
Best Methods: bait fishing from a boat or the bank
Season: entire year; check OSFR
Best Time: spring through July; fall for brook trout

The large expanse of the lake can be viewed looking south from the restaurant at Clear Lake Resort. This large, clear lake is fed by cold springs, thus the water temperature remains constant year-round. Photo by Geoff Hill

The source of the famous McKenzie River, Clear Lake was formed when the river was dammed by a lava flow about 3,000 years ago. The forest that was standing in the valley can still be seen through 100 feet of the lake's crystal-clear water. Fed by ice-cold springs, the lake stays between 34°F and 38°F year-round and, because of the huge volume of water coming from the springs, never freezes over. The lake covers 148 acres, has a maximum depth of 175 feet, and water levels are stable. It is surrounded by the thick forests of the Cascade Crest.

The major catch here is hatchery rainbow trout. Thirty-three thousand legal-size rainbow trout are stocked each year. The average catch will be 9 to 11 inches in length. There are also a few small native cutthroat, of which the largest are 11 inches, and introduced brook trout of mostly 6 to 8 inches, with a few in the 13- to 14-inch range.

Overall fishing is best when the lake is first accessed in the spring through July, although fishing for the brook trout is best in the fall. Bait is the most common fishing technique used — Power Bait and night crawlers still-fished from small boats. There is also much opportunity for bank fishing. Fish tend to stay scattered throughout the year-round fishing season. The catch limit is 5 trout per day, 8-inch minimum length, and of these no more than 1 over 20 inches, no limit or size restriction for brook trout. Always check the current OSFR before fishing. Motors are not permitted on the lake. Boat ramps are available at the resort and campground.

Coldwater Cove Campground, on the southeast shore of the lake, has 35 pay campsites, a hand pump for drinking water, a small boat launch, and it is completely paved. There is also a small beach, but swimming would be for Polar Bear Club members. Clear Lake Resort and picnic area, one mile north of the turn into the campground, is a plea-

sant area for relaxing. The resort is open year-round and offers accommodations, a restaurant, store, and boat rentals.

Other activities in the area include a variety of hiking trails, including the McKenzie River Trail, and trails around the lake, Koosah and Sahalie falls, additional fishing in the McKenzie River, Fish Lake and Carman, Smith and Trail Bridge reservoirs, photography, whitewater trips, mushrooming, and scenic drives.

Clear Lake is located on the McKenzie Scenic Byway, State Highway 126, 3 miles south of its junction with the South Santiam Highway, U.S. Highway 20. Clear Lake is 86 miles northeast of Eugene/Springfield, following Route 126. From Sweet Home or Sisters, take U.S. Highway 20 to the junction with State Highway 126, 4 miles west of Santiam Junction. The turn into Clear Lake Resort is 4 miles south on Highway 126, Coldwater Cove Campground is in 5 miles.

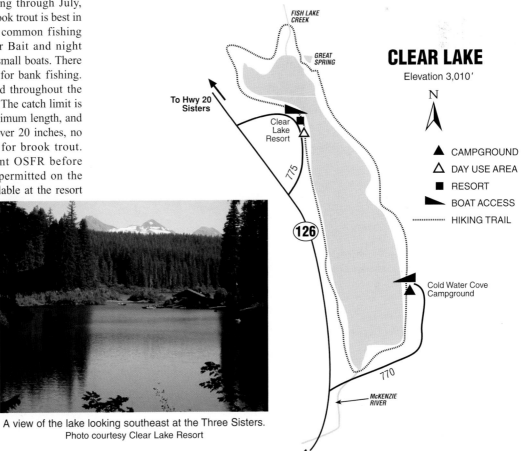

A view of the lake looking southeast at the Three Sisters. Photo courtesy Clear Lake Resort

CLEAR LAKE
Elevation 3,010´

N

▲ CAMPGROUND
△ DAY USE AREA
■ RESORT
◣ BOAT ACCESS
········ HIKING TRAIL

FISH LAKE CREEK

GREAT SPRING

To Hwy 20 Sisters

Clear Lake Resort

775

126

Cold Water Cove Campground

770

McKENZIE RIVER

To Eugene

CARMEN, SMITH, AND TRAIL BRIDGE RESERVOIRS

Carmen, Smith and Trail Bridge reservoirs are three easily accessible lakes along Highways 20 and 126 in the Santiam Pass area. These are small, surprisingly scenic waters for being so close to highways, offering productive fishing for planted trout. They are good "day trip" fishing holes, with many anglers stopping for a few hours on their way over the pass. Camping is popular at two of the three.

Carmen Diversion Reservoir is the smallest of three hydropower impoundments that generate electricity for Eugene. Located 72 miles east of Eugene on State Highway 126, Carmen covers 30 acres with a maximum depth of 25 feet. Stocked regularly with legal-size rainbow trout, it produces limits for those who know the secret of 2-pound leader, Power Bait, worms and salmon eggs. The best fishing areas are near the boat ramp, along the dam, off the bridge that crosses the McKenize River inflow and from anchored and rowed boats. The standard 5 fish, 1 over 20-inch limit applies here and on Smith Reservoir. No camping is permitted at Carmen, but there is a Forest Service campground a short walk upstream at Koosah Falls.

Water from Carmen is diverted to **Smith Reservoir**, the largest and perhaps most scenic of the power project reservoirs located a few miles west up a one-lane, switchback road. Long, narrow and deep, Smith favors boats, though shore fishers have access at the dam and from a metal floating log boom. Casting without weight, slowly sinking worms, salmon eggs and Power Bait produces eager strikes from frequently planted hatchery trout. Larger fish are taken with bait and lures around the mouths of inflowing streams. Camping is available at Lake's End Campground, accessible by boat on the upper end of the reservoir.

Trail Bridge is the lowest elevation, most visible, accessible and developed of the three hydro project waters. It offers the best camping, shore fishing and boat access to 30,000 rainbow trout stocked annually in this 120-acre reservoir. Fishing is catch-and release for trout, restricted to flies and lures only. Boat fishers should try the McKenzie River channel at the upper end of the reservoir.

Endangered bull trout are present in all of these three reservoirs and must be released unharmed. All three reservoirs are subject to water level fluctuations, according to power demands.

TOP: Scenic Carmen Reservoir covers 30 acres with a maximum depth of 25 feet.

MIDDLE: Shore fishers have access to Smith Reservoir via a metal floating log boom.

BOTTOM: A stringer of rainbows from Trail Bridge Reservoir. Looks like a fish fry tonight.

Photos by Brooke Snavely

COUGAR RESERVOIR

Size: 1,280 acres; 6 miles long
Depth: fluctuates
Main Catch: rainbow & bull trout
Best Methods: still-fishing, trolling
Best Time: early & late in season
Season: check current OSFR
Tips: best access with boats

Cougar Reservoir, filled by the South Fork of the McKenzie River, is 6 miles in length and covers 1,280 acres. It is heavily stocked with rainbow trout, and catches average 10 to 12 inches in length. Large bull trout also inhabit Cougar, and it is required to release them unharmed.

Shorelines are quite steep, and most fishing is done from boats, although bank fishing is possible around the reservoir. Water levels fluctuate from highest in mid-May to lowest after Labor Day in September.

Winds can be strong, usually in the afternoon during the summer. Fishing tends to be best early and late in the season, in March and April and then again in October and November.

Anglers have luck fishing the many coves for concentrations of trout and make sure to check the current Oregon Sport Fishing Regulations before fishing.

Still-fishing with bait and trolling Ford Fenders and gold or silver lures are the most used fishing methods on this water.

There are three U.S.F.S. campgrounds at the reservoir (Slide Creek, Sunnyside, and French Pete) and Echo Park day-use area. Slide Creek offers tent sits, trailer parking (without utility connections), piped water, picnic area, boat ramp, and waterskiing. Sunnyside has tent sites and a boat ramp, but no water. French Pete Campground, with tent sites and water, is located at the end of the reservoir.

In addition, Delta Camp ground, located below the reservoir between the McKenzie and South McKenzie rivers, offers trailer parking (without hook-ups) and has water. All areas have sanitary facilities. A new fee system is in effect.

To reach Cougar Reservoir take the McKenzie Scenic Byway, State Highway 126, to Forest Route 19, about halfway between the tiny towns of Blue River to the west and McKenzie Bridge to the east. It is 3 miles to the reservoir on Route 19. Turn to cross the dam on Forest Route 1993 to reach Echo Day-Use Area in another 3 miles, or continue another 8 miles past the dam on Route 19 to Slide Creek Campground. Boat ramps are available at both sites.

View was taken from the dam looking south. Photo by Geoff Hill

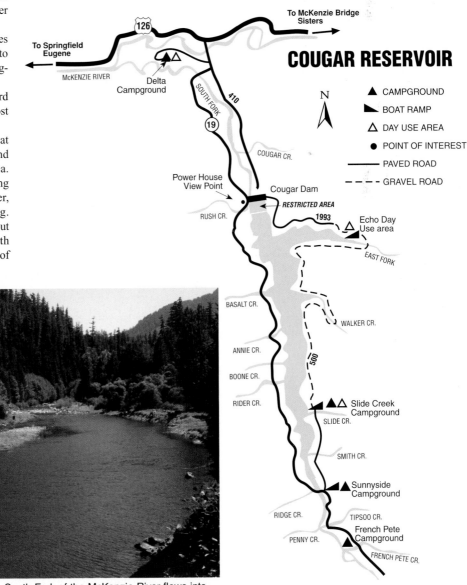

The South Fork of the McKenzie River flows into Cougar Reservoir. Photo by Geoff Hill

BLUE RIVER

Size: 11 miles long
Depth: varies; easily waded
Main Catch: rainbow trout, cutthroat
Best Methods: all methods
Season: check OSFR
Best Time: spring
Tips: hatchery trout not picky

A tiny, crystal-clear river with a tinge of turquoise, Blue River's entire existence is expended within 10 miles above Blue River Reservoir and a mile below. Little fishing is done below the reservoir due to private property. Above the reservoir, a gravel road follows the river for its entire length. At its largest point, the river is 10 to 20 feet in width, with varying depths, but never more than a few feet deep. It is lined with alder and surrounded by the timberland of the Willamette National Forest. There are many opportunities for primitive camping along the river. In addition, nearby Blue River Reservoir has a good Forest Service campground and other facilities, and accommodations are available in the small towns of Blue River and McKenzie Bridge.

Eight thousand rainbow trout are stocked in the river above the reservoir every June. Catches will max out at 10 to 12 inches, and fishing is best right after stocking. There is also a good population of native cutthroat of 5 to 12 inches in length. All methods work on this little stream — the hatchery trout are not picky. Bait, small lures, and artificial flies will all work. Water levels are highest during spring run-off and lowest in late summer. Check the current OSFR for season and catch limits.

Besides fishing this little river, visitors can go boating, fishing, or picnicking on the reservoir, visit the nearby towns of Blue River and McKenzie Bridge, or fish nearby Cougar Reservoir or the McKenzie River.

To get to Blue River above the reservoir, take State Highway 126, the McKenzie Scenic Byway, to the turn to Blue River Reservoir, about 3.5 miles east of the town of Blue River. Continue on Forest Route 15 past the reservoir and up along Blue River.

This crystal-clear river flows for just ten miles above Blue River Reservoir and one mile below. Photo by Geoff Hill

BLUE RIVER RESERVOIR

Size: 1,420 acres
Depth: varies; drops during summer
Main Catch: rainbow trout
Best Methods: all methods
Season: entire year; check OSFR
Best Time: April & May
Tips: best access with boats

Blue River Reservoir is a long, narrow body of water fed by Blue River. Its teal-blue waters cover 1,420 acres, and the shoreline is 6.5 miles long. Banks are quite steep and vegetation thick, so there is little access for bank fishing except down by the dam and at the inlets of Lookout Creek and Blue River. Water levels drop throughout the summer, and, at low pool, many stumps are exposed. This reservoir is more protected from wind than many, because it is so narrow.

Rainbow trout, mainly of catchable size, are stocked several times in the spring, and a few native rainbow and cutthroat trout enter Blue River Reservoir from the river above. The main catch is rainbow trout from 8 to 11 inches in length, with a few holdovers to 14 inches. Most fishing is done from boats, and the best catch rates are in April and May, immediately after the stocking. All methods will catch these hatchery trout: bait still-fished from shore and boats and small lures and flies cast or trolled. Always check the current OSFR before wetting that line.

There are two boat ramps on the reservoir: the one at Saddle Dam where the road first reaches the reservoir is better at low water. The other ramp is at a boating facility on Lookout Creek, 3 miles past Saddle Dam on Forest Route 15. Just past Lookout Creek, a road crosses the inlet to the reservoir (Blue River) which leads to Mona Campground, a nice facility with paved roads, group sites, drinking water, and fees. All campsites are right on the reservoir's shore.

Other forms of entertainment in the area include waterskiing when the water is warmest and highest, golf at nearby Tokatee, and fishing at a variety of nearby locations, including Blue River, the McKenzie River, and Cougar Reservoir *(see pages 214, 206-209, and 213 for information). To get to Blue River Reservoir, see page 214.*

Steep banks line Blue River Reservoir, a long, narrow body of water on the west side of the Cascades. Photo by Raven Wing

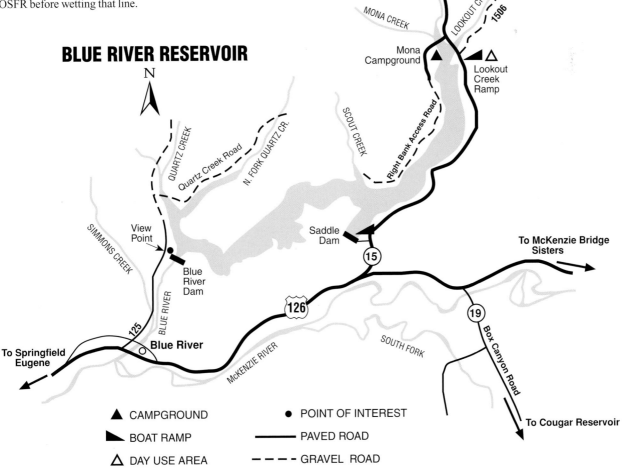

BLUE RIVER RESERVOIR

N

▲ CAMPGROUND
◣ BOAT RAMP
△ DAY USE AREA

● POINT OF INTEREST
—— PAVED ROAD
- - - GRAVEL ROAD

WALDO LAKE

Size: 10 sq. miles
Depth: 420′ max.
Main Catch: brook trout
Best Methods: trolling
Season: entire year; check OSFR
Best Time: June & October
Tips: fish very deep in summer; notorious for mosquitoes

A huge, crystalline, alpine gem, Waldo Lake contains some of the purest water in the world, chemically similar to manmade double-distilled. Small populations of brook trout, kokanee, and rainbow trout exist here, but in a lake this large it can be troublesome to find them. Waldo Lake covers 10 square miles and has a maximum depth of 420 feet. The cobalt blue water is so clear that the bottom can be seen through 100 feet of it. Waldo is the second largest and second deepest natural lake in Oregon, surpassed only by the Klamath/Agency Lake complex in size and Crater Lake in depth.

Waldo Lake is now managed for natural

RIGHT: Waldo Lake, the second largest natural lake in Oregon, as viewed from the south end.
Photo by Don Burgderfer

BELOW: The cobalt blue water in Waldo Lake is so clear that the bottom can be seen through 100 feet of it.
Photo by Geoff Hill

reproduction of all species. Brook trout are the most abundant, averaging 10 to 13 inches with the largest up to 18 inches. Most are caught by trolling lures, spoons, and spinners or fly fishing in the shallower areas of the lake. Shoal areas are at the north and south ends of the lake near Shadow Bay and North Waldo Campgrounds. Another popular fishing spot is at "the brookie slide" on the west side of the lake. Trolling is generally the most productive method unless surface feeding fish are found, then bait and fly fishing work well. Fishing is best in June when the lake is first barely accessible and then again in October after the mosquitoes are gone. In the summer, the fish are deep, making catching them even more difficult.

Stocking of rainbow trout ceased many

years ago. There is a small amount of natural reproduction in the lake outlet, but rainbow trout are probably on their way out. The story about kokanee in the lake is similar, with a small remnant population naturally reproducing in the lake. The kokanee range up to 14 inches in length but are seldom seen. Waldo is essentially a brook trout fishery.

Waldo Lake has primarily a rocky shore with only a few beach areas and is surrounded by thick hemlock forest. Even though there are steep drop-offs offering numerous spots from which to bank fish, most angling is done from a boat. Fishing near the campgrounds, from the bank or a boat, is liable to be as good as anywhere else on the lake. If the wind comes up, one should beware if in a small boat. Water levels fluctuate very little. The shoals on the north end are rocky. The only weedbeds are very short and occur in very deep water.

Reliable afternoon winds at Waldo Lake create a great spot for sailboats and windsurfers. Unfortunately, Waldo is notorious for mosquitoes that mob its shores through the month of August. Waldo has some of the least crowded campgrounds in Oregon. Getting far out on the lake sometimes offers respite from the ruthless bloodsuckers. In addition to angling and swatting, Waldo has sandy beaches for sunbathing, picnic areas, hiking and mountain bike trails, and is often used by canoeists and kayakers.

High lakes accessible by trail offer more fishing. The Pacific Crest Trail comes as close as a mile to the east shore. A spider web of other trails circle the lake, lead into many nearby high lakes, and head into the Waldo Lake Wilderness.

Waldo Lake has excellent camping and boating facilities. The Willamette National Forest maintains three Forest Service campgrounds on the eastern shore, reached by 13 miles of paved road. North Waldo Campground is farthest north, Islet Campground a mile south, and Shadow Bay Campground is at the south end of the lake. All have pressurized water systems, day-use and swimming areas, flush toilets, and boat ramps, and charge a fee to camp. Many primitive campsites are scattered around the lake. The west shore is only accessible by boat or trail. Rhododendron Campground, on an island on the west side of the lake, has an out-house and three tent sites.

Waldo Lake's 22 miles of shoreline is flanked by the Waldo Lake Wilderness on the north, west, and south. The crest of the Cascade Mountains is only a few miles east. At an elevation of 5,414 feet, the recreation season is brief. Campground facilities are usually open July 1 into September and can be snowed-in the rest of the year. The nearest year-round services are at the resorts on Odell Lake or at Crescent Lake Junction,

about 11 miles east on Highway 58.

Waldo Lake is open year-round but is not a popular ice fishing destination. The trout limit is 5 per day with an 8-inch minimum, and of these no more than 1 over 20 inches. Always check the current OSFR before fishing. There is a boat speed limit of 10 mph.

To get to Waldo Lake from the Eugene area take State Highway 58 about 50 miles east. The turn into Waldo on Forest Route 5897 is 3 miles west of Willamette Pass. From Bend follow directions to Odell Lake but continue approximately 3 miles past the west end to the turn onto Forest Route 5897.

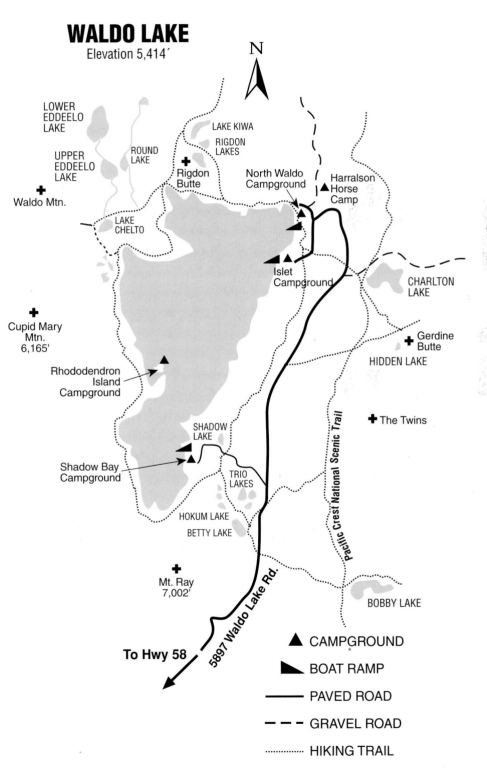

WALDO LAKE
Elevation 5,414´

N

LOWER EDDEELO LAKE

UPPER EDDEELO LAKE

✚ Waldo Mtn.

ROUND LAKE

LAKE CHELTO

LAKE KIWA

RIGDON LAKES

✚ Rigdon Butte

North Waldo Campground

Harralson ▲ Horse Camp

Islet Campground

CHARLTON LAKE

✚ Gerdine Butte

HIDDEN LAKE

✚ Cupid Mary Mtn. 6,165'

Rhododendron Island Campground

✚ The Twins

SHADOW LAKE

Shadow Bay Campground

TRIO LAKES

HOKUM LAKE

BETTY LAKE

Pacific Crest National Scenic Trail

✚ Mt. Ray 7,002'

BOBBY LAKE

To Hwy 58

5897 Waldo Lake Rd.

▲ CAMPGROUND

◣ BOAT RAMP

—— PAVED ROAD

--- GRAVEL ROAD

·········· HIKING TRAIL

WILLAMETTE RIVER
Middle Fork

Size:	40 mi. long
Depth:	varies
Main Catch:	hatchery rainbow trout
Best Methods:	bank fishing & drifting
Season:	check OSFR
Best Time:	throughout season
Tips:	easily accessible by car

The Middle Fork of the mighty Willamette River begins as a tiny mountain creek about 30 miles above Hills Creek Reservoir, south of Oakridge. The main catch above the reservoir is hatchery rainbow trout. Below Hills Creek Reservoir, the river flows for about 10 miles before being impounded in Lookout Point Reservoir. This stretch has wild rainbow and cutthroat trout and is a popular drift stretch, but has some nasty rapids. Boat ramps are available at Green Waters Park in

ABOVE:
The upper Middle Fork runs shallow in the Fall.
Photo courtesy Franklin Carson

LEFT:
The Middle Fork of the Willamette is a beautiful, freestone river, with good trout holding pocket water.

BOTTOM:
The mighty Willamette gains momentum as it nears the valley.

Photos by Brian O'Keefe

Oakridge and Black Canyon Campground downstream. Below Lookout Reservoir, the river is a hatchery salmon and steelhead game.

Both the Middle and North Forks are beautiful, aqua-colored freestone rivers, surrounded by maple, alder, and fir trees. Many Forest Service campgrounds are scattered along the Middle Fork. Both rivers are easily accessible by car in many, but not all, areas. There are a number of hiking and mountain biking trails in the area.

One can get to the headwaters of the Middle Fork from Lemolo Lake by back roads heading toward Timpanogas Lake. The Middle Fork is more commonly accessed from State Highway 58 between Springfield and Oakridge and from Forest Route 21 above Hills Creek Reservoir, a few miles southeast of Oakridge (see directions to reservoir on page 221). From the reservoir, one can continue toward the headwaters on Forest Route 21.

WILLAMETTE RIVER
North Fork

Size: 15 mi. long
Depth: varies
Main Catch: wild rainbow,
cutthroat & brook trout
Best Methods: fly angling with
barbless hooks only
Season: check OSFR
Best Time: summer
Tips: easily accessible by car
in lower reaches

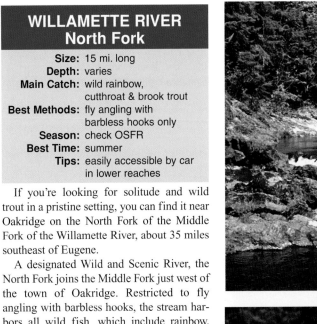

If you're looking for solitude and wild trout in a pristine setting, you can find it near Oakridge on the North Fork of the Middle Fork of the Willamette River, about 35 miles southeast of Eugene.

A designated Wild and Scenic River, the North Fork joins the Middle Fork just west of the town of Oakridge. Restricted to fly angling with barbless hooks, the stream harbors all wild fish, which include rainbow, cutthroat, and brook trout. At its mouth, the river is about 40 feet wide, but within 15 miles upstream has become creek-size. Much of the North Fork is pocket water. Anglers should look for fish-holding pools between the shallower sections.

Fed by Waldo Lake, the North Fork gathers water from numerous creeks in the Waldo Lake Wilderness and Willamette National Forest. Snowmelt and small spring-fed creeks keep the water cold in the springtime. Summer is the best time to carry a fly rod along the banks of this stream.

In riffled pocket water, use small attractor flies like the No. 14 Humpy, Royal Wulff, Irresistible and Goddard's Caddis. In small pools, switch to imitative patterns like the No. 14-16 Adams or Elk Hair Caddis. In longer, slower runs, use wet flies like the Soft Hackle Hare's Ear, leech patterns and streamers. Fish beadhead nymphs, especially caddis larva patterns beneath a strike indicator in deeper sections.

Rainbows, brooks and cutthroat trout average eight inches, but bigger fish can run from 12 to 17 inches. The river is open to fishing year-round. Anglers may keep two trout per day, from the fourth Saturday in April through October 31. There is no limit on the size or number of brook trout taken. Catch limits for other trout species do not apply to brook trout.

To reach the North Fork, just west of Oakridge, take the turn to Westfir and the North Fork of the Willamette River. Highway 19, a paved road, runs along the North Fork and is designated as the Aufderheide National Scenic Byway. Visitors may stop by the Oakridge Ranger Station for a tour brochure. The only Forest Service facility on the North Fork is Kiahanie Campground, 20 miles upriver, although unmarked camps are scattered along the length of the river.

The North Fork is a clear, fast moving stream tumbling out of the mountains. Flows vary significantly. Fish the pools and pocket water.
Top photo by Geoff Hill, Bottom photo courtesy Frank Carson

HILLS CREEK RESERVOIR

Size: 2,735 acres; 8 miles long
Depth: fluctuates; fullest mid-May
Main Catch: rainbow trout
Best Methods: bait fishing from boats
Season: entire year; check OSFR
Best Time: spring & fall
Tips: protected from afternoon summer winds

Hills Creek Reservoir is located on the Middle Fork of the Willamette River, a few miles from the town of Oakridge. The reservoir is 8 miles long and covers 2,735 acres. The 200,000 fingerling rainbow trout stocked here each spring reach 13 inches in one year, with the best catch rates in the spring and fall. Chinook salmon, cutthroat, bass, bluegill, and crappie also inhabit the reservoir in small numbers.

Bait fishing from boats is the most popular fishing method here, although some folks fish from the bridge at the south end of the reservoir and from the dam at the north end.

Shorelines are steep and rocky. Water levels drop about 90 feet each year between August and February, while the reservoir is at its fullest by mid-May. There is one channel that runs through the middle of the reservoir. This reservoir is somewhat protected from afternoon summer winds.

Three boat ramps are located on the reservoir. Packard Creek Campground is best when water is low. The other two are located at CT Beach, a day-use area with a grassy "beach" area on the Hills Creek Arm, and at

LEFT: The shorelines are steep at Hills Creek Reservoir. Best fishing from a boat.

BELOW: Hills Creek Reservoir is a large body of water, eight miles in length.
Photos by Frank L. Carson

the south end of the reservoir where Forest Route 21 crosses the reservoir.

The easiest path to the reservoir is to take State Highway 58 toward Oakridge. The turn to Hills Creek Reservoir is onto Forest Route 21, a couple of miles east of Oakridge. The dam is 2 miles up the road.

Cross the dam on Forest Route 23 to reach CT Beach in 3 miles. Stay on Route 21 instead of turning onto the dam to reach Cline Clark Picnic Area in about a mile, Packard Creek Campground in another 2.5 miles, and the south end of the reservoir in an additional 5.5 miles.

One of three boat ramps on the reservoir. Photos by Frank L. Carson

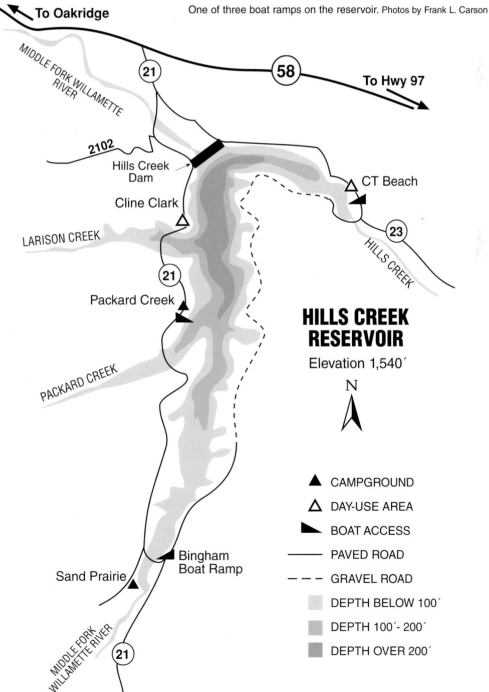

To Oakridge

MIDDLE FORK WILLAMETTE RIVER

21   58   To Hwy 97

2102

Hills Creek Dam

Cline Clark

CT Beach

LARISON CREEK

23

HILLS CREEK

21

Packard Creek

PACKARD CREEK

HILLS CREEK RESERVOIR

Elevation 1,540´

N

▲ CAMPGROUND

△ DAY-USE AREA

◤ BOAT ACCESS

—— PAVED ROAD

– – – GRAVEL ROAD

DEPTH BELOW 100´

DEPTH 100´- 200´

DEPTH OVER 200´

Sand Prairie

Bingham Boat Ramp

MIDDLE FORK WILLAMETTE RIVER

21

FLOAT TUBES AND PONTOON BOATS

The last few years have seen a dramatic increase in the use of float tubes. Newer technology provides a variety of shapes and sizes, and, for the most part, better quality than earlier models, which means safety afloat.

Float tubes allow fishers to reach water that cannot otherwise be fished from shore or to approach quietly an area without spooking the fish, which may not be possible by boat. Float tubes open up a lot of water that may not be fished effectively any other way.

Most users of float tubes are flyfishers fishing for trout, but various techniques can be used for both trout and other game fish. It is a relaxing, comfortable way to fish and can be very rewarding.

Besides the float tube, one must wear chest-high waders and a Coast Guard certified life jacket (some fishing vests have flotation and have been Coast Guard certified) with swim fins over the feet. The fins are used for propelling the float tube around the lake or pond. The movement of the float tube is backwards. Fishers raise their legs almost horizontally in front of them and use a slow, flutter kick.

Another advantage of float tubes is their compact size and portability. They can easily be packed-in to a back country lake and inflated with a foot pump. On the lake, fishers can move out from shoreline trees and bushes and have plenty of space to backcast. Some of these waters are only fishable by float tube and, thus, are seldom fished. A stealth approach to fish holding snags or vegetation can result in some exciting fishing.

When purchasing a float tube, it is wise to shop with someone who is knowledgeable of them or to ask the clerk many questions about the pros and cons of the various models; there is a wide price range from basic model to luxury model. A basic float tube that is built around an inner tube sells for approximately $100, a Urethane or PVC float tube with an open ended u-shape averages $100 to $300 (much easier to enter and exit tube), and the pontoon style ranges from $150 to $1,000. Some tubes offer an extra air chamber which doubles as a backrest and is well-worth the expense. Other options include storage compartments, small batteries and small electric motors, anchors, rod holders, beverage can holders, and brackets for electronic fish-finders.

The most popular type of fins are those that slip over stocking waders. They sell from $30 to $90. Fins are also available that strap over boot waders.

Float tubes allow anglers to reach water that cannot otherwise be fished. Photo by Gary Lewis

A beginning float tuber should start out with an experienced friend in shallow water with a gradual slope, until comfortable with the feel and maneuverability of the float tube.

There are several precautions that should be heeded. Do not use float tubes in rivers, tidal bays, or oceans and avoid large bodies of water where power boats are in use — float tubers are difficult to see, compared to other boats. It is not safe to inflate tubes at lower elevations then put in the car; they might over-inflate or burst while traveling to a higher elevation. And, do not attempt to make your own float tube — it could lead to an accident.

While float tubing on larger lakes or reservoirs, anglers should pack hiking boots in case the wind blows them across the lake. Whitecaps may give tubers a bumpy ride and mean more work with the fins, but they can usually be navigated safely.

Central Oregon offers many opportunities for float tubers. Hosmer Lake, Todd Lake, Sparks Lake, and North and South Twin lakes are popular, to name a few. Crane Prairie's shorelines, channels, and dead snag areas are also frequented by float tube fishers, with good results. And not to be over-looked are back country lakes.

Some anglers opt for the luxury of "rowing oars" on their inflatable pontoon boats. Photo by Rodger Carbone

FLY FISHING

Fly fishing is not nearly as difficult as it sometimes looks, but it does require some patience and practice. The rewards are immeasurable. Fool a fish with an artificial fly, which you may have tied, and you feel like the supreme fly angler. You'll get more pleasure fighting a fish on fly tackle than any other type of fishing gear. Fly fishing gear is, after all, the original ultra-light tackle.

Casting with any kind of fishing tackle requires some weight, otherwise the lure or fly goes nowhere. For instance, with spinning gear, you either pinch on splitshot or use a weighted lure to cast. With fly fishing gear, the line is the weight. Consequently, you have to repeatedly false cast (a back and forth action of the rod) until you have enough line out to reach the desired distance. You then complete the cast when you allow the fly to touch the water.

Timing and coordination are far more important in fly casting than brute strength, although some muscle is required. What you want to accomplish in fly casting is to create a bend in the rod on both the forward cast and back cast. This bend in the rod slings the fly line in the direction of the cast, almost like a bow catapults an arrow. You throw the line ahead of you in the forward cast. Watch to see and sense the line straightening. Just as the line fully extends, pull the rod back to begin the back cast. The line then extends behind you. Look back and see and feel the line reach full extension. Then, push forward to begin the forward cast. As you get accustomed to the back and forth motion, gradually release more line until you are ready to put the fly on the water.

It is during this back and forth motion of the false cast that a fly caster determines exactly where he or she wants to land the fly. Normally, it only takes a few false casts to get enough line out to make an average 30- to 40-foot cast. If you've witnessed someone false casting more often than that, you've either seen someone trying to make a longer cast or someone drying out a fly.

This matter of fly casting is really much easier done than said. Ask someone to show you or take a lesson, and you'll be on your way. Like a lot of sports, once you've actually done it and sensed how the system works, it will be much easier to keep at it. Such persistence is, for the most part, the mindset needed to master fly casting.

Now comes the fun part: determining what kind of fly to tie on the end of your leader. There are dry flies, wet flies, nymphs, streamers, and a host of variations thereof. The saying, "match the hatch," means

ANATOMY OF A FLY ROD

Leader (Tippet) Fly

Fly Line Tip Top Rod Tip

Leader to Line Knot

Ferrule

Guides

Rod Butt

Hook Keeper

Rod Grip

Reel Reel Seat

End Cap

Information and illustrations courtesy of
Central Oregon Flyfishers

CENTRAL OREGON FLY PATTERNS

LAKE FLIES

ALL AROUND COLLECTION

MIDGE & EMERGERS

NYMPHS

Having a variety of flies from which to choose is the key to fishing the waters of Central Oregon. The season, type of water, the hatch, and species of fish will dictate what fly to use.

Photos by Brian O'Keefe

STEELHEAD FLIES

putting on an insect that looks like the ones on which the fish are feeding. "Matching the hatch" also implies that you are watching trout grabbing insects off the surface. This is classic dry fly fishing, in which the fish come up to the surface to take your fly. A fish slashing at your fly never fails to get adrenaline pumping, as you try to react fast enough. Even if you don't hook a fish, being in an area where fish are feeding on the surface is exciting. Mayflies, caddisflies, and stoneflies represent the elite of Central Oregon's dry fly hatches, although there are dozens more.

Wet flies, appropriately, are flies fished under the surface. It's quite a hurdle for some anglers to comprehend trout eating flies underwater, but the fact is they do. Probably 90 percent of what fish eat is captured below the surface. What they are eating are immature forms of insects called nymphs.

Wet fly fishing is primarily done by feel, although watching the line at the point where it enters the water or watching a strike indicator, akin to watching a bobber, provides a lot of information as to what's happening down below. If the line or strike indicator should suddenly stop or move against the current (a dead giveaway), you can immediately suspect a fish has taken the nymph and set the hook. Often, you will see a fish flash or roll in the water near the area where you expect your nymph to be. This is another sign to set the hook.

Although fly fishing is traditionally associated with streams and rivers, it is just as effective in lakes. Trout in lakes tend to be larger than trout in streams, simply because they don't have to fight current all the time, and lakes often offer a more abundant food supply. Lake fishing typically involves nymphs and wet flies, although some surface feeding occurs, usually in early morning and late evening.

An 8.5- to 9.5-foot, 5- to 6-weight fly rod should handle most conditions you'll encounter in Central Oregon. Come prepared with a full complement of floating, sink-tip, and full-sinking lines, along with a variety of leader material, and you should be able to reach fish no matter where they're holding. On small creeks and high-altitude lakes, lighter gear may provide more sport for the pan-sized trout in those waters. By the same token, you might consider heavier rods for bigger fish, such as those in Crane Prairie Reservoir (up to 10 pounds) or to challenge steelhead in the fast-flowing, big water of the lower Deschutes River.

If you're buying fly fishing gear for the first time, take an experienced fly fisher with you or trust the professionals at your local fly shop. It's easy to spend hundreds, or even thousands, of dollars on fly fishing equipment. Good serviceable, pre-packaged fly fishing systems can be bought for under $200. Later, when you discover you like fly fishing, you'll be able to purchase a higher quality outfit with a much better idea of the type of gear you want.

If you come empty-handed when taking a class or guided trip, most instructors and guides will provide quality equipment at no additional cost. Further, you'll be getting advice on how to use the gear and how to select your own from from a seasoned professional.

MOST TROUT EAT aquatic invertebrates, some of which have complex life cycles. Mayflies, caddisflies, midges, and stoneflies have several stages of their life cycle that are available to the trout. The successful angler must try to imitate these stages with his flies.

Most aquatic insects have four stages in their life cycle: the egg, the larval or nymph stage, the pupal stage, and the adult stage. The first three stages are aquatic, while the last stage is terrestrial.

Below are two examples of such life cycles.

The Life Cycle of a Typical Mayfly

The mayfly stages that are most often imitated are the nymph, the emerging subadult, and the spent adult. Mayflies are common on both streams and lakes.

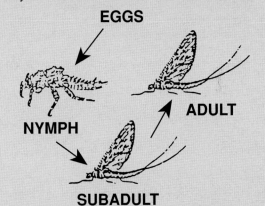

The Life Cycle of a Typical Stonefly

The life cycle of the stonefly is similar to that of the mayfly; however, they do not have a subadult stage. Cold western streams, such as the Deschutes, are well-known for their stonefly (salmonfly) hatches.

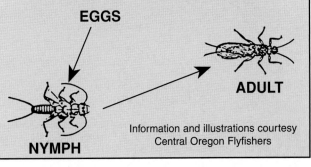

Information and illustrations courtesy
Central Oregon Flyfishers

TROLLING

Trolling is an excellent technique for fishing Central Oregon's lakes and reservoirs. Trolling allows you to cover a large area in a short time, pinpointing actively feeding fish. Once you catch a fish, turn around and troll repeatedly through that same area. If you've stumbled across a good concentration of fish, you may consider casting or still-fishing. And if you don't catch fish, trolling is a fine excuse for a leisurely boat ride through some wonderful scenery.

Depending on the season, trolling can be done on or near the surface (0 to10 feet), medium deep (10 to 30 feet), or really deep (40 feet plus.) In all instances, you should troll slowly but not steadily. Vary trolling speed by speeding up or slowing down the boat, by turning in a series of "S" curves, or by occasionally pulling the rod forward several feet then letting it fall back. Almost always, fish will strike when they think the lure is acting erratically or trying to get away from them.

Surface trolling is great, because it doesn't require any specialized equipment, and anyone can do it. Using either a small trolling lure, fly, or bait, strip off 50 or more feet of line and troll slowly behind whatever boat to which you have access.

Many anglers prefer a small rowboat, canoe, or kayak. The rower gets a little exercise while the means of propulsion – rowing – provides nearly perfect action to the lure. Hookups while surface trolling are great fun, because there is no weight to impede the fight of the fish. Surface trolling is best in the spring and fall when fish are near the surface and worth trying early in the morning and late in the evening throughout the summer.

In the summer when the water temperature warms, trout move deeper in search of the thermocline. This trout comfort zone can be anywhere from 20 to 80 feet deep, and if you're not fishing in it, you're wasting your time. Locate the thermocline with a depth finder or by asking other anglers who are catching fish, then fish in that depth of water. Also, plan on using gang trolls or flashers, as fish are spread out and need a reason to be attracted to your lure.

"Banana" weights ranging from .5 to 4 ounces can extend the effective trolling range of standard spinning gear down to about 40 feet. Many anglers go this route, but you can tell they struggle to feel anything with their overworked spinning rods bent double under the heavy weights. You'll feel more in control with lead-core line or a downrigger and beefier tackle.

Lead-core line is exactly that, line built around a core of lead which sinks, depending on the density of line, at a predictable rate. Lead-core line is usually colored in 20-foot increments. So when anglers talk about fishing "four-and-a-half colors," they suggest they were trolling 90 feet of line about 30 feet deep. Further, the depth is affected by the weight and drag of the rudder, flasher, and lure. Trolling with lead-core takes a little getting used to, but it works so well, and the equipment is so durable that it's usually worth the investment.

A typical lead-core trolling outfit consists of a large-capacity level wind reel and a stout 6- or 7-foot salmon-size rod and costs about $75. A recent trend toward lighter rods and smaller trolling blades has heightened the sporting aspect of lead-core gear. But there will be times when the largest blades and heaviest weights are necessary to reach and attract fish. Downriggers are state-of-the-art trolling tools, expensive, and awkward to handle. But once you understand their application, they are particularly useful for trolling. Their advantage is precise depth control. If the depth finder says fish are holding at 62 feet, a downrigger can put the lure at precisely that depth. This is a big advantage during the hottest weather when fish refuse to come up from the cool depths.

Downriggers are the way to go for mackinaw or lake trout and browns when they get in their bottom hugging mode. With a downrigger, you can physically drag the bottom of the deepest lake and literally stir the

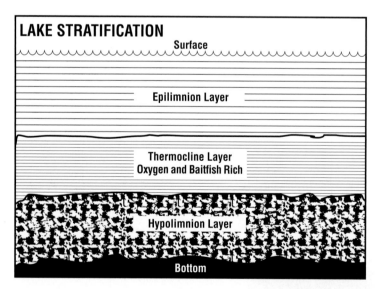

LAKE STRATIFICATION

Surface

Epilimnion Layer

Thermocline Layer
Oxygen and Baitfish Rich

Hypolimnion Layer

Bottom

Most lakes stratify into three layers during late spring and stay that way until late fall. The middle layer of water, the thermocline, contains both a large amount of dissolved oxygen and forage fish. Your trolling, to be most effective, should be concentrated close to or in the thermocline, which will be from 15 to 50 feet down in most lakes.
Illustrations courtesy Luhr Jensen & Sons

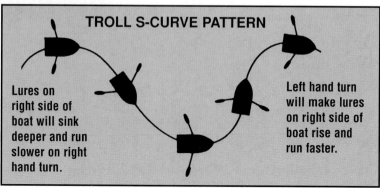

TROLL S-CURVE PATTERN

Lures on right side of boat will sink deeper and run slower on right hand turn.

Left hand turn will make lures on right side of boat rise and run faster.

fish up. Big dodgers and flasher blades, followed by plastic squids, hoochies, and FlatFish tipped with worms, will trigger these fish.

For novices, accompanying someone who knows how to use downriggers is a good way to see how they work. There are quite a few elements of their operation that are new to most casual anglers. Portable models that attach to any boat are available from $100. More expensive models include electric motors to lower and raise the weight, among other features. It's difficult to fish downriggers effectively without a good quality depth finder. Therefore, you're tied into two expensive purchases.

Leader strength and length are important considerations in trolling. If you're fishing with hard-digging flatfish, you'll need a strong leader just to withstand that kind of action, let alone land the big brown or mackinaw you're hoping to catch. Fluttering spoons require long, light leaders to work properly. Run the lure experimentally in the water where you can see it to ensure it works properly before sending it down. Trolling spoons, such as the Needlefish,

Triple-Teazer, and Dick Nite, is effective throughout Central Oregon. They are often combined with flashers and gang-trolls, such as the Beer Can, School-of-Minnows, and Ford Fender. When fishing for kokanee, it's a good idea to include a rubber snubber between the flasher and lure to absorb the strike of these soft-lipped fish, which often shake the hook.

Rudders and swivels are key to successful trolling, in that they prevent line twist and lure tangles. Nothing is worse than spending five minutes letting out enough line to reach the magic depth only to have a tangle somewhere between the reel and the lure. The time saved using rudders and swivels more than makes up for their minor cost.

Adding a kernel of white or yellow corn, a piece of worm, grub, or maggot can often make the difference between success and failure. No matter where you troll in Central Oregon, don't be afraid to consult with other anglers, especially those you see catching fish. The vast majority of people who fish in Central Oregon are more than willing to share their secrets.

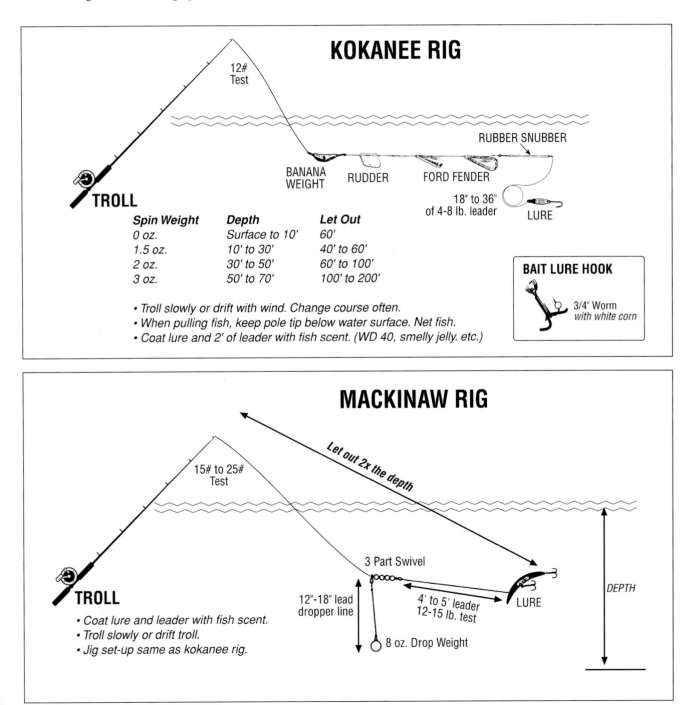

KOKANEE RIG

12# Test

RUBBER SNUBBER

BANANA WEIGHT

RUDDER

FORD FENDER

18" to 36" of 4-8 lb. leader

LURE

TROLL

Spin Weight	Depth	Let Out
0 oz.	Surface to 10'	60'
1.5 oz.	10' to 30'	40' to 60'
2 oz.	30' to 50'	60' to 100'
3 oz.	50' to 70'	100' to 200'

• Troll slowly or drift with wind. Change course often.
• When pulling fish, keep pole tip below water surface. Net fish.
• Coat lure and 2' of leader with fish scent. (WD 40, smelly jelly. etc.)

BAIT LURE HOOK

3/4" Worm with white corn

MACKINAW RIG

Let out 2x the depth

15# to 25# Test

3 Part Swivel

12"-18" lead dropper line

4' to 5' leader 12-15 lb. test

LURE

DEPTH

TROLL

• Coat lure and leader with fish scent.
• Troll slowly or drift troll.
• Jig set-up same as kokanee rig.

8 oz. Drop Weight

SPINNING AND JIGGING

Spin fishing is a catch-all phrase for a variety of methods that can be performed with spinning tackle. Quite literally, a spinning reel spins when wound or cranked. Spinning reels are equally well-suited for casting, jigging, still-fishing, and even a modified form of fly fishing. Spinning reels are easy to learn with, affordable, and reliable, making them the single most popular type of fishing reel today.

To cast with a spinning reel, pin the line just above the reel against the rod or hold it in your hand. Open the bail. Swing the rod forward while simultaneously releasing the line. The combination of momentum, timing of release, and weight will pull the line off the reel. When the line stops flowing off the reel, turn the handle. This will automatically close the bail, readying the reel for the retrieve.

Your next action depends on the type of fishing you wish to perform. For instance, if you are casting with a lure, you will have to reel it back in order to give it action. By reeling quickly, you will cause the lure to run shallow. A slower retrieval allows the lure to sink. It's important to fish a lure at all depths until you find where the fish are holding. By fishing from top to bottom and casting to all the reachable water, you effectively cover an area. If you fail to catch a fish, move to another area.

Giving a little thought to each area before stomping or splashing through the shallows to get to deep water will bring rewards. Fish are frequently close to shore or hiding against undercut banks. Probe these shore areas first. If you are really patient, stay far back from the shore for a few minutes and see what you can see. If not disturbed, fish may reveal their location by feeding on the surface. Sometimes, when fish are really spooky, you may have to crawl on hands and knees through brush to get close enough to make a cast without scaring them away.

When river or stream fishing, always work upstream. Because fish swim against the current, their attention is focused upstream; therefore, you'll be approaching them from behind where they are least likely to see you. With a spinner, such as a Rooster Tail, cast upstream and work the lure back toward you. Reel just fast enough to keep the spinner blade turning but slow enough so that it runs near the bottom. It's okay for the lure to bounce occasionally along the bottom. The fish are looking for things drifting and tumbling in the current.

If you are fishing with bait, cast into a likely spot and let the offering – be it a worm, salmon egg, or other tempting goody – sink to the bottom. Once the bait has settled to the bottom, reel up just enough slack line so that when a fish bites, you will be able to see the rod bend or the line move. Bait fishing with a bobber means watching the bobber instead of the pole, and when it moves or goes underwater, you know the time has come to set the hook and reel in a fish.

Still-fishing is basically straight up and down fishing from a dock or boat. There's no casting involved; just open the bail and let the bait sink. Usually, it's best to fish just above the bottom then reel up in 5-foot increments until you find the depth the fish are holding. Once you catch a fish, put the bait back at the same level and chances are you'll catch some more.

Jigging involves raising and lowering your bait or lure. The technique works best with lures that flutter, such as Buzz Bombs, Crippled Herrings, and Nordics. Fish usually grab a jig while it's falling. Often, all the angler will detect is a slight bump or tap. That's the sign to set the hook. When fish are highly concentrated, such as often happens in the fall, jigging can be sensational.

To spin fish with a fly, use 4-pound test or lighter line and a clear, plastic bobber. Use whichever fly everyone says is working at the end of a 5- or 6-foot leader. Cast gently into an area where fish are feeding on flies and reel in very slowly. This is a good way to get hooked on fly fishing, which is covered on pages 223 through 225.

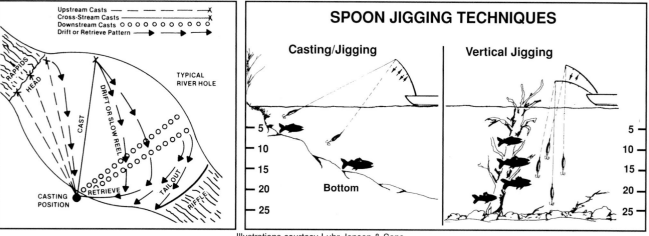

Illustrations courtesy Luhr Jensen & Sons

Angler's Code of Ethics

While enjoying the sport of fishing, please keep in mind this voluntary Angler's Code.

The Ethical Angler

1. Supports conservation efforts.
2. Practices catch and release where needed.
3. Doesn't pollute, and properly recycles and disposes of trash.
4. Practices safe angling and boating.
5. Obeys fishing and boating regulations.
6. Respects other anglers' rights.
7. Respects property owners' rights.
8. Shares fishing knowledge and skills.
9. Doesn't release bait into water.
10. Promotes ethical sport fishing.

READING WATER AND STALKING

For anglers to have much success at all, they must learn to read and fish the water effectively. Before stomping along the stream-side path, or wading and splashing water along the bank, anglers should stand back and analyze the situation before approaching.

Reading and stalking includes viewing the entire area, planning a cautious approach, and having a plan for the section of water to be fished. First, it is recommended to begin with water along the bank and then progressively work the water outwards, upstream, and downstream. While doing this, anglers should pay attention to structures that provide protection from the current, such as boulders, fallen trees, vegetation, or rock shelves, and study river flows that carry the fish's food supply near these structures. Back eddies and slower, deeper water where fish might be holding are promising areas. After the area is worked systematically and fished completely, anglers can move to another section and start the procedure over again.

Fish will often seek the shade and protection offered by undercut banks, and walking along a path close to (or above) the water will send vibrations to the fish, alerting them of the presence of danger, or spooking them out in a black, shadowy flash to deeper water. It is better to stay off the path, stay low, and sneak up to a point where a carefully presented offering will be drawn under the bank to the unsuspecting fish.

When undercut banks are not present, and shallow water leads to deeper, more interesting water, patience is necessary. Checking the shallow water for feeding fish, especially water just below riffles, is a good idea. The riffles provide oxygen and carry food. Fish face upstream, so anglers are smart to approach from behind and carefully present the fly, lure, or bait. Many nice fish have been caught in the shallows through which many anglers step to get to the deep water.

Sometimes, it is good to "take five" and relax under a tree, have a snack and drink, and watch the water. If feeding fish are located, it is best to figure out on what they are feeding. Fly fishers will "match the hatch." If fish are not surfacing, they are probably feeding under the surface on nymphs, emergers, or other aquatic delicacies, such as crawfish or minnows.

"Being sneaky" when stream — or lake-side fishing is a wise approach. Fish have very keen eyesight and can detect movement, especially against the sky and along high banks. Some helpful hints include staying low to the water; wearing clothing that blends with surroundings (as opposed to brightly colored clothing); staying as still as possible; hiding behind trees; crouching in bushes or high grass; limiting casting motion; moving slowly; and fishing upstream. It is the element of surprise that catches most stream fish, and it does not take much to spook them.

Larger streams, such as the lower Deschutes River, are a little more forgiving; the deep, wide expanse of water allows anglers to make long casts to undisturbed fish, but stealth is still important.

Stalking is not often done on lakes, but it can be very helpful, especially on back country lakes. Anglers should begin by hiking to a high vantage point (while carefully concealing movements) and observing any fish activity that might be taking place. Binoculars can be helpful in scouting from a distance. Fish may or may not be rising to bug hatches, but, even if they are not, the usually clear, shallow lakes will reveal where the fish are. Often circling an entire lake will only take a few minutes, but it is probably time well-spent. Many back country lakes do not have fish populations due to winterkill. Signs of winterkill might be detected by scouting.

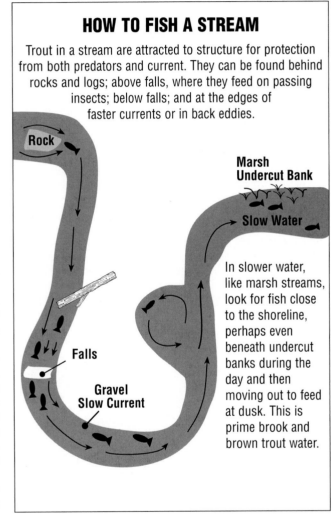

HOW TO FISH A STREAM

Trout in a stream are attracted to structure for protection from both predators and current. They can be found behind rocks and logs; above falls, where they feed on passing insects; below falls; and at the edges of faster currents or in back eddies.

Rock

Marsh Undercut Bank

Slow Water

Falls

Gravel Slow Current

In slower water, like marsh streams, look for fish close to the shoreline, perhaps even beneath undercut banks during the day and then moving out to feed at dusk. This is prime brook and brown trout water.

FISHING WITH BAIT

Although all kinds of bait work in Central Oregon's lakes and rivers, Velveeta cheese holds a special place in the tastebuds of trout throughout the region. The nearly indestructible cheese, which conveniently doesn't require refrigeration, milks an essence when submerged that trout love. The Kraft pasteurized product is so popular among bait fishermen that at least two good fishing holes on local lakes have been dubbed, "Velveeta Point."

You can make a cheeseball by rolling a chunk of Velveeta between your palms. Use just enough cheese to cover the hook points. Resist the urge to use more. The extra weight will cause the bait to tear off the hook during casting, not to mention the fact it will give the fish more bait to nibble on without getting near a hook. Trout tend to peck at cheese, so the smaller the cheeseball, the better.

Close behind is Berkley Power Bait. Quite simply, this is one of the most innovative products introduced in fishing in the past decade. Power Bait contains a "secret" fish-attracting formula. But unlike all other products that make such claims, it works. A majority of fish caught with Power Bait have swallowed it.

Power Bait is available in paste, allowing you to customize the size of your bait, in pre-formed nuggets that hold together longer, as salmon eggs, worms, and small grubs. To further spice the selection, all Power Bait products come in a variety of colors and flavors. At times, one color works better than another. In Central Oregon, green and yellow Power Bait seem to work best.

One advantage of Power Bait is that it floats, whereas cheese doesn't. Rig Power Bait on a treble hook and run the leader through a sliding or slip sinker. It's a simple matter of pinching on a split shot to control the amount of leader, and thus the height the bait floats above the bottom. In many fishing situations, the bait needs to float above the bottom vegetation in order to be visible. On the other hand, there are lakes and rivers with little or no weeds where the fish scour the bottom for food; thus, a bait that sinks is appropriate.

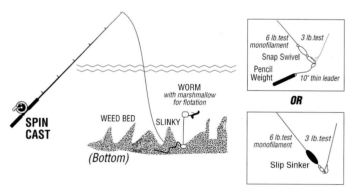

Worms and nightcrawlers catch their share of fish and will continue to do so long after the fish have learned to avoid other baits. Few things are more tempting to a trout than a wiggling, squiggling, juicy nightcrawler. For surefire action, drift worms in the eddies and pools of the Deschutes River for rainbow and brown trout.

Any bait can be floated with the addition of a marshmallow. Marshmallows, in and of themselves, are good bait. The fact that they're available in garlic and cheese flavors proves it. Marshmallows are often combined with other bait to make what local anglers euphemistically refer to as sandwiches. Such offerings might include marshmallows, salmon eggs, corn, and worms. Anglers often douse the entire works in anise oil, WD-40, or some secret sauce they've concocted.

Any conversation about bait fishing in Central Oregon wouldn't be complete without mentioning the myriad of natural baits available for free to those willing to spend a little time looking for them.

Crawdads, which, of course, can be bought at most bait stores, can also be caught in many waters. Crawdad traps, much like crab and lobster pots, baited with nearly anything and left overnight will usually be full of freshwater crustaceans come morning.

Another method of catching crawdads in a stream is to wade in shallow areas, turning rocks over until you locate one. With sleeves rolled up, you slip your arm in the water and slowly reach from behind the crawdad. When within three or four inches, you can make a quick grab for it, "pinching" its main body with your thumb and forefinger, just behind the crawdad's pincers. Their grasping claws cannot pinch you from that angle. Keep in mind that crawdads scoot backwards …very quickly. It may take a couple of tries to catch one, but your efforts won't be for naught: the tail, with the shell

Reach behind the crawdad's pincers. Photo by Brian O'Keefe

peeled off, or the entire body is an excellent bait. Furthermore, unlike most baits which aren't fit for human consumption, a hard boil in salted water and a dip in melted butter transform crawdads into a tasty treat.

Crawdads are good for duping large brown trout. Try drifting crawdad tails into deep holes of the upper Deschutes River for a shot at lunker browns. (Check current OSFR before fishing.) The best time is dusk and dawn. Just remember not to fish too early or late, as fishing is closed in Oregon until one hour before sunrise and one hour after sunset.

Periwinkles are easy to collect and make great bait. The larval form of caddisflies, periwinkles are essentially tiny grubs that build little cocoons around themselves of whatever material is most available. In some places, they'll look like little pin cushions, utilizing pine needles and sticks. In other waters, they may cover themselves with tiny pebbles. Simply peel the shell off to reveal the larva inside. Fish one or more of them on a small hook. Periwinkles are good for trout and kokanee.

Be sure to try fishing with the live damselfly and dragon fly nymphs when they make their annual appearance in late May, early June. These bugs will literally crawl onto your boat where you can grab them, skewer them on a hook beneath a bobber, and toss them back into the water to meet their fate in the jaws of a ravenous rainbow.

There's an abundance of bait to be found on dry land, as well. In the evening after any rainstorm, look for nightcrawlers above ground in landscaped areas. Approach quietly and grab firmly, otherwise, they'll zip back down their holes with astonishing speed. Usually, you can dig for worms anytime. Also look for grubs in the bark of decaying trees. Just peel back the bark of downed logs. Almost everything there, including ants, makes good bait. Late summer is a good time for grasshoppers. A grasshopper drifted along a grassy bank is too tempting for many trout to pass up.

Even though bait fishing is widely practiced, it has come under fire as being very harmful and, in some cases, fatal for fish. The rap on bait fishing is that too many anglers allow the fish to swallow the bait (hook) and, therefore, kill the fish while removing it. To avoid this malady, strike early when you first detect the nibble or bite, when chances are you'll hook the fish only in the lip. If the fish does swallow the hook, and you want to release it, just cut the line as close to the hook as possible, handling the fish with care. *(See Catch & Release on pages 234 and 235.)* The hook will rust apart in a short time, relieving the fish of it, and it will only take you a minute to tie another hook on your line.

When performed carefully, bait fishing is not bad. Instead, it can be safe for fish and a very relaxing way to spend a few hours enjoying the sights and sounds of the outdoors. Traditionally, bait fishing is how most anglers get started, especially small children.

BASS TECHNIQUES

Bass fishing is gaining popularity in Central Oregon as more and more anglers discover the pleasures of these mean, green fish. Opposed to the delicate takes of trout, bass literally mug their prey by swallowing whole in one vicious gulp, then charge back to their hideouts. Breathtaking jumps, vigorous headshakes and powerful runs follow explosive strikes after they feel the sting of a hook. With a basic understanding of their ambush style of feeding, a handful of simple lures and a willingness to fish near snags, anyone can catch bass.

There are two species of bass in Central Oregon: largemouth and smallmouth. The difference is the size of their mouth and habitat preferences. Largemouth have round, bucket-shaped mouths with a lower jaw that extends beyond their eyes. They thrive in shallow, warm, weedy water eating a variety of foods ranging from small fish, frogs and insect larvae to turtles, mice and even birds. Smallmouth, as the name implies, have smaller mouths, prefer cooler, deeper water and are more comfortable in current. Their diet is similar to largemouth, but they key on crawdads whenever the freshwater lobsters are available. Both species stay close to structure (rocks, stumps, weeds, etc.), grabbing things that stray too close, and then retreat to their lairs. Bass are homebodies, rarely venturing more than a few hundred yards from food and shelter. Where there's one, there's usually a bunch.

Plastic worms catch more bass than any other lure. Worm, lizard, grub or crawdad shapes, plastic's subtle movements and squishy feel closely imitate natural food items. Their primary advantage is they can be rigged weedless and fished in heavy cover where bass spend most of their time. Upon detecting a strike, which feels like a slight tug as a bass inhales the lure, point the rod tip directly at the fish, reel up the slack feeling for the weight of the fish, and set the hook. Use 10- to 20-lb. test line, stiff rod and a strong reel to horse bass out of structure before the line tangles or breaks on obstructions.

Crankbaits include a variety of diving and vibrating minnow-imitating lures that are effective when bass are actively feeding. Cast beyond a suspected bass lie then "crank" through the spot, pausing occasionally to imitate the struggles of an injured fish. Or troll the edge of weed lines and

Minnow-imitating crankbaits

underwater shelves. Strikes are obvious as bass attack from behind, pulling the rod down sharply. Commonly referred to as "Rapalas" (a popular brand) crankbaits come in a variety of shapes, colors and sizes that can be fished from the surface down to 25 feet.

Few things rival the thrill of seeing a big bass attack a top water bait. Hula Poppers, Jitter Bugs and buzz baits are the best known. Designed to splash and make noise as they move across the surface, top water baits get bit mostly in low light conditions, early morning before sunrise and late evening after sunset. Fly fishers get in on the fun with small popper style flies made of cork, balsa, and feather. In Central Oregon's clear waters, top water baits catch relatively few but larger bass compared to other methods.

Spinnerbait

Spinnerbaits don't resemble anything bass feed on. But their flashing blades and pulsing rubber skirts are an appealing combination. Cast and retrieve spinnerbaits like crankbaits, only slower through bulrushes, around trees and rocks, as they are relatively snag free. Because they sink slowly, spinnerbaits are particularly effective in shallow backwaters. Another good technique is to let them free fall down stumps and rock piles in water as deep as 20 feet, then hop them across the bottom.

Jig

Jigs are necessary when bass refuse to chase lures and the only way to get a bite is put a lure directly in front of them. Dressed with feathers, hair or rubber skirts, anglers frequently add live bait or pork attractors to create a "jig and pig" combination. The result is a heavy lure that sinks straight into a bass hideout then is bounced along the bottom. Detecting strikes is challenging, because bass normally strike a jigging lure as it sinks. Keep the line tight to feel the light tap then immediately set the hook.

Bass are fools for live bait. Large nightcrawlers, frogs, waterdogs (immature salamanders) crawdads, leeches and minnows are all very effective. Presentation can be as simple as a nightcrawler below a bobber fished near structure, to casting and retrieving the live bait as if it were a lure, albeit gently. The use of live minnows as bait is not legal in Central Oregon but fresh dead, dehydrated and frozen minnows are available.

HIRING A GUIDE

One's fishing trip begins not when one steps on the boat, casts a line, or brings in the first fish, but the day a call is made to reserve a trip. Reservations are a fact of life during the busy summer months. They can be had as little as 24 hours in advance, but it is safer to make a request a week or more ahead of the intended fishing day. Customers should note that guides listed under professional organizations are licensed and fully trained and are recommended for a safe and enjoyable trip. While arranging the guided trip, the customer should be told in detail exactly what to bring. Most likely, one will need a license, food, and a range of clothing suitable for cold to hot weather. A lot of people also bring along a camera, sunscreen, sunglasses, and hat. At the least, the guide will provide tackle, bait, boat and the expertise necessary to catch fish.

On many of Central Oregon's Cascade lakes trips, guides often will not pick up a customer until 8:00 a.m. the day of the trip. Trout keep bankers' hours in the cold waters of the high lakes. As most of the lakes are spring fed and very cold, the food chain needs to be energized by the sun for a couple of hours before the fishing really gets good. The stereotype of being on the water before dawn is soon dispelled. Fishers likely return home long before dark, as well.

Also, customers can expect a lot more comfort; the days of sitting on a wooden plank in a small dingy are over. Guides today use larger boats, featuring everything from swivel chairs to couches. Collapsible tops provide shade from blistering sun or a dry spot in the rain. Pontoon or deck boats are becoming increasingly popular,

Pontoon boats are spacious and comfortable.
Photo courtesy
Garrison's Guide Service

because of their large, stable surface area and wheelchair accessibility.

Lake fishing tactics in these parts include still fishing, trolling, casting, and fly fishing. Where the guide plans the trip and what expectations the client has dictate what techniques are employed. But whatever the method, anglers must be prepared to stick with it.

As mentioned before, the trout in the high Cascade lakes are mid-day biters. As for exactly when in the middle of the day they'll bite, no one can say for sure. Trusting one's guide to go to the right spot with the right fly, lure, or bait is the key, because when the fish bite, they're likely to be caught. While waiting, anglers can enjoy the scenery, ask questions, and let the clean mountain air and peaceful surroundings recharge the soul.

This unhurried approach lends itself to the low-key attitude fishers will want to take when it comes to minding one's line, lure, or bait. Most people, when they hire guides, assume the fish will come fast and furious. Likely at some point in the day that will happen, but probably not from the get-go. It's good to come prepared with an open mind and listen to the guide's instructions about what to do and when to do it.

In areas where fish are to be released, the guide will either remove the hook with a specialized tool or cut the line if the hook is deeply imbedded. The fish's digestive acids and rusting action of water will corrode the hook in a few days, giving the fish a very good chance of surviving.

On most of the high Cascade lakes, the limit is 5 trout per person, of which only one may be over 20 inches. A 20-inch trout weighs in the neighborhood of 4 pounds, enough to feed four or more adults. Ethical guides will quiz their customers extensively about how much one really needs to take home. While Central Oregon waters have a lot of trout, there is not an endless supply.

Planning a guided fishing trip on a river might require a little more preparation Most river guides are dedicated to fly fishing only and practice catch-and-release. Usually, fly fishers bring their own equipment: rod, reels, vest with tackle and hackle, waders, etc. Guides establish a meeting place, provide the river boat and a fishing guide, lunch, snacks, and the shuttle ride back to the meeting place.

Extended trips, up to three or four days, are available on the lower Deschutes and John Day rivers. Guides generally provide meals and utensils, snacks, beverages, and tents. Anglers will most likely be informed of what personal gear and clothing to bring along.

After a successful day on the water, anglers can be thinking about next year; guides accept reservations up to a year in advance. This way, fishers are assured of getting the guide they want for the trip they want during their next visit to Central Oregon.

Father and son enjoy a guided trip on the Lower Deschutes.
Photo courtesy The Riffle Fly Shop

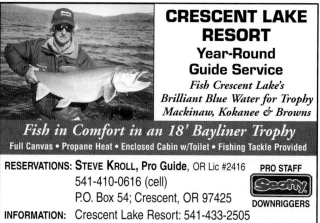

CARE OF FRESH-CAUGHT FISH

Unlike red meat, fish does not improve with age – the fresher the catch, the better the flavor. Fish flesh is extremely perishable; heat and humidity are its ruin. Keep your catch out of direct sunlight and heat. Fresh-caught fish have been known to spoil in the boat before the angler could get them home. The sooner the fish is cleaned and cooled, the better it will taste when cooked. This means that fresh-caught fish should be properly cared for within minutes of being caught.

When cleaning your catch, it is important to remove the guts, gills, and any blood, veins, or organs adhering to the backbone. To avoid improper disposal, boat anglers should carry a container for the storage of internal organs and blood. Wipe the fish dry inside and out and keep each fish dry in its own plastic bag. On cool days, some anglers allow large, cleaned fish to hang in the cool air until a pellicle, or sticky film, forms on the meat, sealing in flavor and moisture. However, the best method of preservation after cleaning, drying, and bagging is to keep the fish in an ice chest full of ice. It is important to prevent the meat's direct contact with ice by placing ice on the bottom of the cooler, followed by some sort of divider on which the fish is laid. This keeps the fish dry and cold, not wet and cold. Usually, one pound of ice for each two pounds of fish – with more ice used for longer trips home – will adequately cool the fish. Further, crushed ice, versus cubed, will not cut into the soft flesh, preventing tiny cuts in which spoilage bacteria can settle.

Keeping dead fish in the water to keep them cool is not effective. Unlike the cool water depths in which fish swim, surface water can reach temperatures of 70°F in the summer. Anything above 42°F (refrigerator temperature), will cause the fish to spoil. In fact, if warm enough, the surface water will start to cook the fish. Additionally, pollutants, such as oil and boat fuel, debris, and bacteria may be prevalent on the surface water, creating an undesirable place to store fish. A living fish kept tied to a boat's hull can thrash about, bruising itself. Finally, in the winter, wind can dry the flesh of the fish if not protected.

The finest flavor will come from fresh fish rather than from thawed frozen fish. But if your intention is to freeze your catch for later consumption, remember that air causes spoilage. Make sure you squeeze all the air possible out of packaging. Whole fish with gills and guts removed or fillets can be frozen. Anglers should be sure to wash the catch in fresh water before storing. The meat should be covered with several layers of protective wrap before freezing: a plastic wrap first, followed by heavy aluminum foil or heavy freezer paper. Fish should be good for 4 to 12 months in the freezer, where harmful bacteria will not grow. Fatter fish, such as salmonids, have the shortest freezer life. Thawing and refreezing will result in a tasteless offering when finally consumed. Thawed frozen fish should be cooked when still slightly frozen for the freshest flavor.

For refrigeration of fresh-caught fish, store the meat at 42°F for no longer than 3.5 days. Portable vacuum packers are becoming increasingly popular and allow the angler to seal fresh-caught fish immediately after cleaning, saving time and effort in storage preparation at home.

For more information on freezing, canning, drying, and pickling fish, anglers can contact Oregon Extension Service offices that offer descriptive pamphlets.

"Limit your kill, don't kill your limit."

FAVORITE RECIPES

GEOFF'S HI-HO FRIED TROUT

There's nothing like a good fish fry once in awhile, especially when you're camping out. I like pan-sized trout sprinkled inside and out with Hi-Ho® Cracker crumbs. Here's how to prepare:

Place a few Hi-Ho® (or Ritz®) crackers on a sheet of aluminum foil and crunch up with a rolling pin or, if out camping, with the base of a coffee mug. Mix 1 egg with a little milk in a bowl for an "egg wash," dip the fish in the egg wash, then roll it in the cracker crumbs on both sides, sprinkling some crackers in the cavity. You may add spices as you choose.

Place fish in a pre-heated, greased skillet and cook on each side until golden brown. The cracker-covered skin becomes my favorite part of the meal. I also believe in leaving the fish's head attached while cooking to retain flavor.

To go with a fish breakfast, I will usually bake a few potatoes the night before while sitting around the campfire. I wipe the spuds with butter (to keep from burning the skin), double wrap in foil, and place in hot coals for about 45 minutes, turning periodically with tongs. Store the cooked potatoes in a cooler overnight and, in the morning, slice them into a frying pan, add some chopped green peppers and/or onions, and fry them.

Fresh trout, fried potatoes, with a couple of eggs, make a delicious, hearty breakfast to start your day.

CAMPFIRE TROUT

1 large (2- to 3-lb) trout (or salmon or steelhead)
Apples
Sweet onions
Mayonnaise
Seasonings

Clean the fish well and coat the entire body, including inside the cavity, with mayonnaise. Stuff the body cavity with chunks of apple and sweet onion. Add preferred seasonings.

Double wrap the fish in heavy foil and seal. Place in the coal bed of a campfire for about 45 minutes (45 to 60 minutes in an oven at 350°F). Makes 4 servings.

—From Bob Penington, ODFW (retired), Bend

TROUT WITH ALMONDS

1 cup coarsely chopped blanched almonds
1/4 cup plus 2 tablespoons butter, melted
1 1/2 tablespoons fresh lemon juice
1 cup all-purpose flour
1 teaspoon salt
8 (8 to 10 oz each) trout fillets
3/4 cup butter, divided

Saute almonds in 1/4 cup plus 2 tablespoons butter in a large skillet over medium heat until golden brown. Stir in lemon juice. Remove from heat and set aside.

Combine flour and salt; dredge fillets in flour mixture. Melt 1/4 cup plus 2 tablespoons butter in a large skillet over medium-high heat. Add half of the fillets: cook 5 minutes on each side or until fish flakes easily when tested with fork.

Remove to a serving platter and keep warm. Repeat procedure with remaining 1/4 cup plus 2 tablespoons butter and fillets.

Sprinkle with reserved almond mixture. Garnish, if desired. Makes 8 servings.

—From "America's Best Recipes"

CATCH-AND-RELEASE

To release fish is to allow them to be enjoyed more than once and to produce more of their kind, especially important with wild fish. Unlike hatchery fish that are protected in a hatchery pond until adulthood, wild fish are faced from birth with the challenges of wild water and predators. Returning wild fish to their stream insures the maintenance of strong, wild fish populations, since the fish we catch are the survivors, the best of their species. When too many people take too many fish from a body of water, the quality of our angling declines. Since the largest fish are the ones usually killed first, over-harvesting leaves no large fish and eventually no spawning fish. Therefore, the fittest fish are unable to pass their survival skills on to offspring, stunting the growth of healthy and cunning populations of wild species. The phrase, "Limit your kill, don't kill your limit," is becoming more and more common. We can measure fishing pleasure by the angling difficulty involved in successfully hooking and landing the fish rather than in the heft of a stringer. Catch-and-release fishing can be practiced by anglers using all methods.

There are exceptions to the concept of catch-and-release. For instance, releasing your catch in a pond of stunted fish will not improve the angling. The ideal is to have healthy, self-sustaining fish populations with good age distribution in every body of water. Catch-and-release works only if fish recover after release to rejoin the fishery. Gentle handling and time out of the water are the most important factors in fish survival.

HANDLING YOUR CATCH

If you must handle a fish:

- Use a wet glove or rag to hold it; or, at least, wet your hands.
- Turn a fish on its back or cover eyes with a wet towel to calm it.
- Don't put your fingers in the eyes, mouth, or gills of your catch.
- Avoid removing mucous or scales.
- Get the fish back in the water as quickly as possible.

Information and illustrations courtesy ODFW

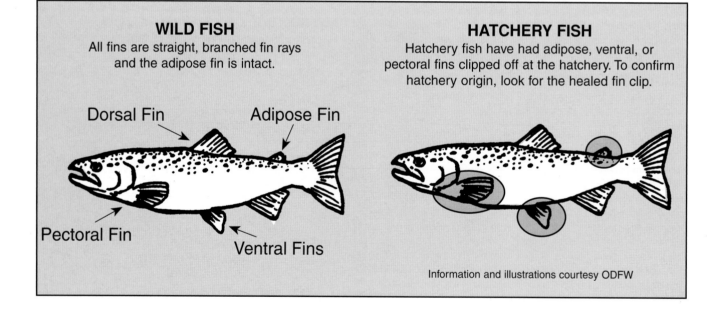

WILD FISH

All fins are straight, branched fin rays and the adipose fin is intact.

Dorsal Fin   Adipose Fin

Pectoral Fin   Ventral Fins

HATCHERY FISH

Hatchery fish have had adipose, ventral, or pectoral fins clipped off at the hatchery. To confirm hatchery origin, look for the healed fin clip.

Information and illustrations courtesy ODFW

TIPS FOR CATCH-AND-RELEASE:

- Use barbless hooks; it's the law on some waters.
- Use hooks that biodegrade quickly.
- Use hooks smaller than size 2 on lures fished for steelhead and salmon so that trout caught by accident will not be injured. Set the hook immediately and try to prevent a fish from swallowing the bait.
- Play fish briefly, land them quickly. Don't play the fish to exhaustion. This is especially important during spawning season and as water temperatures increase.
- Use appropriate size tackle. Gear that is too light can force you to play a fish long enough to kill it from exhaustion.
- Wet your hands before touching a fish and if possible try not to touch the fish at all. If you must handle a fish, wear a wet glove or rag to hold it.
- Keep release tools handy.
- Release a fish as soon as it is landed.
- Keep the fish in the water if at all possible. Every second out of the water decreases its chance for survival.
- Remove the hook gently.
- Avoid squeezing the fish.
- Turn a fish on its back or cover its eyes with a wet towel to calm it.
- Keep your fingers out of the fish's mouth, eyes, and gills.
- Do not remove mucous or scales (a fish's outer body protection).
- Don't let it thrash around on rocks.
- If the fish is hooked too deeply to safely remove the hook, cut your leader quickly. The hook will work its way out of the fish in a short time.
- If possible, don't use a net. Otherwise, use a cotton net and wet it before touching the fish. Do not use a nylon net.
- Revive the fish carefully before releasing. Grasp the fish in front of the tail, support it underneath, and point it into a slow moving current, holding it gently until it is strong enough to swim off under its own power. Make sure the gills are working before letting it go.
- To resuscitate an exhausted fish, move it back and forth in the water or tow it gently alongside the boat to force water into its gills.
- If the fish does not swim away, recover it and try again.
- Get the fish back in the water as soon as possible.
- A fish handled carefully and released properly has a great chance of survival.

THE BIOLOGY OF FISH

The fish's eye is much like our own, except that the pupils cannot adjust to the brightness of light. Fish cannot see surface food in bright sun as well as they can in the shade and may seek deeper, darker areas during bright daylight. Fish have a field of view of about 330°. The 30° directly behind the fish is its only blind spot. Consequently, stealth is required in the angler's approach.

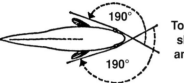

Top view of fish showing wide angle of vision

Objects above water and farther than 30 feet away are unclear to a fish, but at 15 feet, it can see any part of your body more than 2.5 feet above the surface of the water. At times you will need to stay lower and farther away than preferred in order not to be seen. Fish are seldom frightened by the sight of still, quiet objects in the water, such as your lower body. On the bank, keep vegetation between you and the fish or directly behind you as you approach the fish and move slowly. In rough water, the fish's "window" of vision comes and goes with the chop of the waves, and it is much easier to approach without being seen.

Normally, a fish can see insects on the surface quite clearly. A trout will follow what it thinks may be food downstream, whether on the surface or sub-surface, inspecting it before taking it. Bass lie in wait for prey to pass within reach. Recent research indicates that fish see mostly form and size but no detail, while contrast and perception of motion are heightened. They definitely see color. Fish are color blind at night but, nonetheless, can see well in the dark.

The fish's hearing is much more sensitive than ours, but they hear only low-frequency noises, such as the crunch of gravel under wading boots, the vibration of a lure hitting the water, or the sounds of noisy anglers in a boat. The sound of moving water in a riffle hides many of our noisy approaches, which are audible in calm water. The clump of boots along a bank carries into the water to alert the fish.

Equipped with nostrils and a very sensitive sense of smell, fish are able to distinguish between species and even recognize individual fish. A frightened fish releases an alarm odor that others can smell. Salmonids are repelled by the smell of human skin, so many anglers use masking scents on flies and lures.

Fish also have a good sense of taste. Taste buds on their "lips" allow them to investigate your offering without taking it into their mouth. They hate the taste of gas, oil, and insect repellent.

As wild species, fish have senses that are accordingly acute. Keeping this fact in mind is one key to angling success.

OFFICIAL OREGON COLD WATER GAME FISH RECORDS

Compiled By The Oregon Department of Fish and Wildlife. Revised February 2005.

Species	Weight Lbs./Ozs.	Caught Where	Date	Angler
Trout, Brook	9 6	Deschutes River (below Little Lava Lake)	6/21/80	Burt Westbrook
	6 12	Hosmer Lake	7/13/77	Tad Walker
Trout, Brown	35 8*	Paulina Lake *(See photo at bottom)*	7/3/65	Ike & Darrell Fox
	28 5	Paulina Lake	2002	Ronald Lane
	27 12	Paulina Lake	5/21/93	Guy Carl
Trout, Bull	23 2	Lake Billy Chinook (Metolius Arm)	3/25/89	Don Yow
	20 7	Lake Billy Chinook	3/19/88	William E. Reid
Trout, Coastal Cutthroat	6 4	Siltcoos Lake	8/20/84	Kay Schmidt
Trout, Lahontan Cutthroat	9 8	Malheur River	1986	Phillip Grove
Trout, Golden	7 10	Eagle Cap Wilderness	1987	Douglas White
Trout, Mackinaw or Lake	40 8	Odell Lake	6/11/84	Kenneth Erickson
	36 8	Odell Lake	6/76	H.V. Hannon
Trout, Rainbow	28 0	Rogue River	5/19/82	Mike McGonagle
	24 2.25	Lake Simtustus	6/74	Jerry Fifield
Trout, Steelhead	35 8	Columbia River	9/9/70	Berdell Todd
	31 4	Cascade Locks	9/63	Gus Hesgard
Salmon, Chinook	83 0	Umpqua River	1910	Ernie St. Claire
	71 8**	Rogue River	2002	Grant Martinsen
	62 (dressed)	Nestucca River	10/70	Craig Hansen
Salmon, Chum (species now catch & release only)	23 0	Kilchis River	1990	Roger Nelson
Salmon, Coho	25 5.25	Siltcoos Lake	11/5/66	Ed Martin
	23	Tillamook Bay	10/63	Chuck Walters
Salmon, Atlantic	No entries — catch-and-keep only legal at Davis Lake & East Lake			
Salmon, Kokanee	6 12	Wallowa Lake	2001	Pamella Fahey
	5 5	Wallowa Lake	5/00	Larry Campbell
	4 2	Paulina Lake	6/17/90	Howard Morgan
Shad	6 6	Willamette River	2004	Larry Arendt
	5 13	Columbia River	5/31/94	Patricia Ann Young
Whitefish	4 14 ***	Crane Prairie Reservoir	7/21/94	Roger A. Massey
	4 0	McKenzie River	1974	Todd Fisher

*Caught with net – not a legal catch   ** World record for fly rod   *** Not "officially" recorded*

See the information on the opposite page for entry instructions and how to obtain official entry forms for the Oregon State Record Fish.

The world's third largest brown trout
(35 lbs., 8 oz.) came from Paulina Lake.
The mounted fish is now back home at
Paulina Lodge restaurant.
Photo by Diane Kulpinski

STATE OF OREGON WARM WATER GAME FISH RECORDS

Compiled By The Oregon Bass And Panfish Club Inc. Revised August 2004.

Species	Weight Lbs./Ozs.	Length	Girth	Date	Caught Where	Angler
Bass, Hybrid White	18 8.32			2002	Ana Reservoir	Justin C. Marks
	18 8	29"	24.75"	2/21/96	Ana Reservoir	John Saunders
Bass, Largemouth	12 1.6			2002	Ballenger Pond, Springfield	B. Adam Hastings
	11 9.6	25.5"	21.25"	4/15/94	Farm pond near Butte Falls*	Randy T. Spaur
Bass, Smallmouth	7 14	—	—	10/8/00	Henry Hagg Lake	Kevin Silver
Bass, Striped	68 0**			1973	Umpqua River	Beryl Bliss
Bluegill	2 5.5	11.75"	14"	5/12/81	Farm pond near Prineville*	Wayne Elmore
Catfish, Bullhead	3 7			2001	Henry Hagg Lake	Bob Junkins
	3 6	20"	11.88"	6/10/86	Brownlee Reservoir	Loretta Fitzgerald
Catfish, Channel	36 8	38"	22"	9/17/80	McKay Reservoir	Boone Haddock
Catfish, Flathead	42 0	40.5"		6/27/94	Snake River near Farewell Bend	Joshua Kralicek
Catfish, White	15 0	30.25"	—	4/22/89	Tualatin River	Wayne Welch
Crappie, Black	4 6.1	18.5"	16.88"	6/29/95	Private pond, Corvallis*	John E. Doss
Crappie, White	4 12	18.5"	17.75"	5/22/67	Gerber Reservoir	Jim Duckett
Perch, Yellow	2 2	—	—	6/5/71	Brownsmead Slough	Ernie Affolter III
Perch, Sacramento	0 11.2	—	—	1998	Lost River	Jonathan Cogley
Sturgeon: There is no state record information for sturgeon in Oregon because the maximum size limit is 60". It is unlawful to remove an oversized sturgeon from the water because the bouyancy of water can cause internal organ damage and death.						
Sunfish, Green	0 11	10"	9.25"	4/25/91	Umpqua River near Tyee	John L. Baker
Sunfish, Redear	1 15.5	13"	12.75"	8/1/92	Reynolds Pond near Redmond	Terrence C. Bice
Sunfish, Pumpkinseed	0 7.68	—	—	1996	Lake Oswego	Linda Mar
Walleye	19 15.3	37"	21.5"	2/20/90	Columbia River up from John Day Dam	Arnold R. Berg
Warmouth	1 14.2	11"	12.75"	12/27/75	Columbia Slough	Jess Newell

*Effective January 1, 1996, fish from private waters will no longer be accepted for state records. Records will be from public waters only.

** World record for fly rod

Instructions for Entering Oregon State Record Fish*

1. Submit all entries within one month to:

   COLD WATER ENTRIES:
   Oregon Dept. of Fish and Wildlife, Information & Education
   2501 SW First Ave., P.O. Box 59; Portland, OR 97207

   WARM WATER ENTRIES:
   Oregon Bass & Panfish Club
   P.O. Box 1021; Portland, OR 97202

2. The fish must be caught with a hook and line, and the weight of the fish is what will qualify it as a record catch.

3. A photo showing a recognizable side view of the fish must accompany the application for positive identification.

4. Please fill out application completely along with having the signatures of two witnesses, one being the person weighing the fish.

5. All catches must be weighed on certified scales.

NOTE: Official entry forms may be obtained from the addresses above.

OREGON RECORD FISH ENTRY FORM

Kind of Fish _____
Location Caught _____ Date Caught _____

Additional Fish Entry Information:

Weight _____ lbs. _____ oz. Length _____ in. Girth _____ in.
(Must Be Weighed on a State Inspected Scale)
Location of Scale _____ Date Weighed _____

Angler Information:

Name _____
Address _____
City _____ State _____ Zip _____

Witness Information:

Signature _____ Date _____
Affiliation _____ Title _____
Address _____
City _____ State _____ Zip _____
Phone _____

Signature _____ Date _____
Affiliation _____ Title _____
Address _____
City _____ State _____ Zip _____
Phone number _____

Contestant's Signature _____ Date _____

SEE REVERSE SIDE FOR ENTRY INSTRUCTIONS AND MAILING ADDRESS.

OREGON
Fish & Wildlife

GLOSSARY OF FISHING TERMS

Adipose fin - The small fin behind the dorsal fin and in front of the tail fin, found only on salmonids.

Anadromous - Fish which migrate from salt water to spawn and rear in fresh water.

Atlantic salmon - An anadromous species of salmon native to the East Coast, which survives well in landlocked lakes in Central Oregon.

Bait - Any item used to attract fish which is not an artificial fly or lure (ODFW).

Baitfish - A small fish of any species resembling a minnow, regularly eaten by larger fish of numerous species.

Banana weights - Lake trolling weights with swivels attached at each end. Shaped similar to a banana.

Barbless hook - A hook manufactured without a barb or a hook with the barb removed or bent down flush with the shank.

BLM - Bureau of Land Management

Bobber - A floating device attached to the fishing line to float bait or flies at a chosen level beneath the surface of the water.

Brood trout - Fish that are used by ODFW for breeding purposes, either in hatcheries or in their natural environment.

Brook trout - A long-lived species of char native to the East Coast, which does very well in western streams and lakes. Prefers cold water.

Brown trout (German brown trout) - A species of trout native to Europe, now broadly distributed throughout the Western United States. These trout are known for their pisciverous, nocturnal habits, and ability to grow to trophy size.

Bucktail - The long hair of a deer's tail, used to tie streamer-style flies which imitate baitfish.

Bullhead, brown - The most common species of catfish in Central Oregon, not native to this area.

Bull trout - A native inland char known for its trophy size; a state-sensitive species in Oregon; it is now on the federal threatened list in most Oregon waters.

Caddis - A very abundant insect in Central Oregon savored by trout. Over 1,200 species in North America, caddis are recognized by their "periwinkle" cases on river bottoms and, as adults, by tent-shaped wings lying over their backs. A popular and effective fly pattern.

Caddis larva - The "worm" stage of the caddis' life during which most species form a case composed of small pebbles, twigs, or other vegetation. A popular trout food and fly imitation.

Char - A group of fish in the salmonid family which includes brook trout, bull trout, and mackinaw (lake trout). Char technically are not trout.

Chinook salmon - The largest of the native anadromous salmon species in Oregon.

Chub - A rough fish found all too often in Central Oregon reservoirs, prone to overpopulate and out-compete game fish.

Coho salmon - A native anadromous salmon species in Oregon, hatchery raised coho are sometimes stocked in Central Oregon lakes and adapt well to landlocked situations.

Coyote Camp - A primitive campsite created by use by the public.

Crappie - A species of sunfish not very common in Central Oregon but good eating and fun to catch.

Crayfish - Also known as crawdads and crawfish, these little crustaceans are abundant in healthy Central Oregon waters. Excellent eating and for bait, they can be found up to 4 inches long.

CTWS - Confederated Tribes of Warm Springs

Cutthroat trout - A native Oregon trout species identified by the orange "slashes" under the jaw.

Damselfly - An abundant insect on most Central Oregon lakes and reservoirs, the adults are blue, delicate dragonfly-like creatures.

Damselfly nymph - The aquatic, swimming stage of the damselfly, a very popular food item for resident fish.

Depth finder - A battery powered electronic device with many variations but usually showing the depth and location of fish.

Dodger - A large trolling attractor blade.

Downrigger - A fishing system involving a pulley in place of a rod, used to troll heavily weighted lines at great depths.

Dragonfly larva - A commonly used bait on Central Oregon lakes, these big, ugly insects can be found under and around rocks and logs at the edges of lakes.

Drifting (wind drifting) - Letting your boat and/or bait drift at the same speed of the water or wind.

Dry flies - Fly imitations which float on the surface of the water and usually imitate adult insects.

Emergers - The insect as it changes from larva to adult on or just under the surface of the water.

False cast - A cast in which the fly does not touch the water. Used to dry flies, lengthen line, and change direction of the cast.

Fin-clipped - Hatcheries mark their fish by clipping adipose fins or a combination of other fins.

Fingerlings - Fish between 2 and 5 inches in length and less than 1 year old.

Fish finder - See *Depth finder.*

Flashers - A string of blades attached to a steel leader in front of a lure or bait. Used to attract fish by imitating a school of small fish.

Floating fly line - A waterproof fly line that stays on top of the water, used with dry flies but also sometimes with wet flies.

Fly (artificial) - A weighted or unweighted hook dressed with conventional fly-tying materials.

Fly angling only - Angling with an artificial fly, fly line, and fly rod.

Game fish - All trout; steelhead; Atlantic salmon; whitefish; grayling; coho, chinook, chum, pink and sockeye salmon; largemouth and smallmouth bass; catfish; crappie; sunfish; yellow perch; mullet; shad; striped bass; sturgeon; walleye; and bullfrogs. Game species are determined by Oregon statute and are subject to state fishing regulations (ODFW).

Gang troll - A string of attractor blades on a trolling rig.

Green Drake - An unusually large mayfly up to a size 6 that lives in flowing water and hatches in late spring to early summer.

Hackles - The feathers and/or materials used in artificial flies.

Hatchery trout - Fish that are raised and released directly from hatcheries at fingerling size or "legal" size, often finclipped.

Ice-out - When the ice on lakes first begins to melt in the spring, usually pulling away from the edges first. This is a great time to fish.

Jig - A type of lure and an action imparted to a lure by pulling it up in the water and letting it fall back down repeatedly to attract fish.

Kokanee - A landlocked variety of sockeye salmon, native to Oregon.

Largemouth bass - A popular species of game fish known for powerful fights and excellent eating. Prefers warmer water.

Lead core line - A very heavy trolling line with a lead core used to troll at great depths, usually for mackinaw.

Leader - Fine monofilament at the terminal end of the line and the part the fish are going to see (or not see). A large variety of "tests" or diameters is available.

Leech - A common worm-like organism in Central Oregon lakes and streams, they come in a variety of colors and lengths. Leech imitations are popular and effective.

Lunker - A trophy fish of any species.

Lure - An artificial device with hooks used to attract fish but is without molded, soft plastic, rubber bait imitations, or artificial flies.

Mackinaw (lake trout) - A char of deep, cold lakes that can grow to trophy size and is excellent eating.

Marabou - A fly tying material with excellent action used to imitate long, slender insects, baitfish, and leeches.

March Brown - A size 14 to 16 mayfly that hatches in late winter to early spring on flowing water, a popular hatch with fly fishers.

Marshmallows - The small, colored variety is used to float bait off the bottom. Some fish will even take the marshmallow.

Match the hatch - A fly fishing method by which the fly on the line resembles the insects on which the fish are feeding. Also implies that the angler is watching trout taking insects off the surface.

Mayfly - A common insect that is a favorite fish food, identified by delicate, upright wings resembling sails on a slender body.

Midge - A tiny insect that makes up a substantial portion of any self-respecting trout's diet, in the same family as mosquitoes. They come in a variety of sizes and colors, and both the adult and the "worm" stage are consumed by fish.

Minnow - Technically a small fish of a specific species, but the term is often used for any very small baitfish.

Native - Fish that are indigenous to the region. Different from a "wild" fish.

Non-game fish - Includes the minnow family, chubs, suckers, and pikeminnow. These species are not subject to state fishing regulations, but some are protected by law under the threatened and endangered species list (ODFW).

Nymph - The aquatic stage of an insect and a major portion of a trout's diet.

ODFW - Oregon Department of Fish and Wildlife.

OSFR - Oregon Sports Fishing Regulations.

Periwinkle - A caddis nymph that builds a case of tiny pebbles or grains of sand.

Pisciverous - Something which habitually eats fish; fish-eating fish.

Pikeminnow *(formerly squawfish)* - A native non-game fish species and voracious, pisciverous predator present in both flowing and still water.

Planted fish - see *Hatchery.*

Plug - Deep-bodied plastic or wood lures often used to catch larger pisciverous fish.

Power Bait® (Berkley) - A popular, scented, and flavored manufactured floating bait.

Rainbow trout - A trout species native to Oregon and capable of growing to trophy size in Central Oregon.

Redd - A fish nest dug in the gravel of a stream.

Redside - A strain of rainbow trout for which the lower Deschutes River is renowned, identified by their broad, deep red stripes and gill covers.

Riffle - Shallower water in a river that flows rapidly over rocks or gravel.

Roach - A rough fish found in some Central Oregon lakes. They can become a big problem when overpopulation creates competition with game fish in the same water.

Rubber snubber - A length of surgical tubing with a swivel attached at both ends. Absorbs shock of initial strike. Necessary for soft-mouthed species such as kokanee.

Rudder - An essential piece of trolling equipment to keep lake troll blades tracking straight without line twist.

Salmonfly - A huge stonefly up to 3 inches in length, an insect for which the lower Deschutes River is well-known. It hatches in late May to early June.

Salmonids - A family of fish which includes salmon, trout, char, whitefish, and grayling.

Sculpin - A small, native, bottom-hugging fish of flowing water and a favorite snack of larger fish.

Setting the hook - The action of sweeping the rod up and back to cause the hook to penetrate the fish's mouth.

Sink-tip fly line - A floating fly line with a variable number of feet at the tip which sinks. Often used in trolling lakes; heavier ones sometimes used in fishing big rivers.

Slip sinker - A weight with a hole through the center allowing the main fishing line to slip through it to attach to a swivel. Allows fish to take line without feeling the weight.

Smallmouth bass - Not too common in Central Oregon but excellent fighters like their cousins, the largemouth bass.

Spawners - Fish in reproductive condition, often showing changes in color and jaw deformations. Salmon in this condition are not good eating. Trout in this condition can be lousy fighters and easily exhausted.

Spin fishing - Fishing with a spinning rod and spinning reel.

Spinnerbaits - A popular bass lure with a rubber skirt covering the hook and a spinner blade just above or below the hook.

Split shot - Small lead pieces of various sizes and weight that clamp onto the line above the hook.

Steelhead - Native and hatchery sea-run rainbow trout, sizes of adults vary according to the rivers to which they are native.

Stickleback, three-spine - A small, non-game species native to the Oregon coast, illegally introduced into the Deschutes River above the town of Bend.

Still-fishing - Fishing with bait in one spot usually with a marshmallow or bobber.

Strike indicator - A colorful material attached to fly line leader a few feet above the fly to help track it and detect strikes.

Stocked - see *Hatchery.*

Stonefly - A very common insect in Central Oregon. Many species are present from tiny flies that hatch in the winter to the huge salmonfly on the Deschutes. Fish eat both the nymphs and adults voraciously.

Structure, in-stream - Any item in a stream or lake that provides cover for fish and habitat for insects. Includes rocks, dead vegetation, and manmade objects.

Streamer - A long, flowing fly tied to imitate baitfish, leeches, and long slender insects.

Tailout - The increasingly shallow, downstream end of a calm section of a stream where the water begins to pick up speed as it enters a riffle or rapid.

Thermocline - A layer of water, usually in a lake, which is cooler than the layer above or below.

Tributary - A stream or river flowing into a larger stream or river.

Trolling - Dragging a lure or fly behind a moving boat or other floating device.

Turning over - When wind and/or large differences in water temperature cause the bottom layers of water in a lake to come to the surface. Important in nutrient cycling.

Whitefish - An abundant native species of the salmonid family, often good fighters and definitely good eating; however, they don't get much respect.

Wild fish - A wild fish has been spawned and reared in the wild, not in a hatchery. Not all wild fish are necessarily native fish; they can be natural reproduction of hatchery fish.

Wind drift - See *Drifting.*

Winterkill - An occurrence in the high lakes whereby deep snow levels deprive fish of the oxygen necessary to live.

INDEX OF ADVERTISERS

Please Patronize Our Advertisers
And Tell Them You Saw Their Ad In

FIFTH EDITION

FISHING
Central Oregon
and Beyond

They Like To Know Their Advertising
Investment Is Working For Them